Guerrilla Warfare
in Civil War Missouri,
Volume I, 1862

ALSO BY BRUCE NICHOLS

Guerrilla Warfare in Civil War Missouri, Volume II, 1863
(McFarland, 2007; paperback 2012)

Guerrilla Warfare in Civil War Missouri, Volume I, 1862

Bruce Nichols

McFarland & Company, Inc., Publishers
Jefferson, North Carolina, and London

The present work is a reprint of the illustrated case bound edition of Guerrilla Warfare in Civil War Missouri, 1862, *first published in 2004 by McFarland.*

LIBRARY OF CONGRESS CATALOGUING-IN-PUBLICATION DATA

Nichols, Bruce, 1951–
Guerrilla warfare in Civil War Missouri, [volume I] 1862 / Bruce Nichols.
p. cm.
Includes bibliographical references and index.

ISBN 978-0-7864-6927-7
softcover : acid free paper ∞

1. Missouri—History—Civil War, 1861–1865—Underground movements.
2. United States—History—Civil War, 1861–1865—Underground movements.
3. Guerrillas—Missouri—History—19th Century.
I. Title.
E470.45.N53   2012   973.7—dc22   2003026708

BRITISH LIBRARY CATALOGUING DATA ARE AVAILABLE

© 2004 Bruce Nichols. All rights reserved

No part of this book may be reproduced or transmitted in any form or by any means, electronic or mechanical, including photocopying or recording, or by any information storage and retrieval system, without permission in writing from the publisher.

Cover image © 2012 PicturesNow.com

Manufactured in the United States of America

*McFarland & Company, Inc., Publishers
Box 611, Jefferson, North Carolina 28640
www.mcfarlandpub.com*

To my wife of almost three decades, Pat, whose patient
support and constant encouragement
has made this work a reality

Contents

Preface 1

ONE
Winter 1862 in Northwest Missouri 7

TWO
Winter 1862 in Northeast Missouri 15

THREE
Winter 1862 in Southeast Missouri 23

FOUR
Winter 1862 in Southwest Missouri 32

FIVE
Why Guerrillas? 39

SIX
Operating Deep Behind Enemy Lines 46

SEVEN
Policy Evolves (March through May 1862) 60

EIGHT
Spring 1862 in Northeast Missouri 63

NINE
Spring 1862 in Southeast Missouri 69

TEN
Spring 1862 in Southwest Missouri 76

ELEVEN
Spring 1862 in Northwest Missouri 86

TWELVE
The Enrolled Missouri Militia: Guerrillas' Controversial New Enemy 103

THIRTEEN
Summer 1862 in Southwest Missouri   106

FOURTEEN
Summer 1862 in Southeast Missouri   116

FIFTEEN
Summer 1862 in Northeast Missouri   129

SIXTEEN
Summer 1862 in Northwest Missouri   143

SEVENTEEN
Fall 1862 in Southeast Missouri   164

EIGHTEEN
Fall 1862 in Southwest Missouri   175

NINETEEN
Fall 1862 in Northeast Missouri   186

TWENTY
Fall 1862 in Northwest Missouri   199

Afterword   211

Notes   215

Bibliography   235

Index   243

Preface

This work is an in-depth study of all or nearly all known guerrilla operations in Missouri during 1862, the year such warfare became the primary type of military action there. It was my original intention to follow this subject throughout the entire war in Missouri, but I found this scope too broad to cover the detail I think the subject requires. While working with students of this period and those seeking their ancestors' roles in it, I have noticed great confusion and uncertainty about these shadowy beginnings of this irregular war. My purpose is to relate-from well-known and obscure resources-which southern partisan leaders and groups operated in which areas of Missouri, how they operated and how their warfare evolved, and to relate seemingly isolated incidents to other incidents to show patterns and chains of events. My method is a chronological narrative of events of guerrilla warfare, divided into the four seasons of the year. The state is subdivided into quarters, or quadrants, for regional analysis.

I have set some boundaries for this work in order to include many things and exclude some others, to achieve some balance and still make this work useful for a variety of readers. I concentrate on all southern partisan leaders I could identify and many of the Rebel recruiters, and I detail their methods, tactics, and incentives to present the full spectrum of their contribution to irregular warfare. Conversely, I detail the Union counteractions to this southern threat, but I keep the focus deliberately on southern personalities and less so on northern leaders. I mostly keep the focus of the Union combatants at the local level where they actually encountered southern guerrillas or bushwhackers. Wherever possible, I identify both sides in actual skirmishes in the field, and, where this is supposition, I use such qualifiers as "probably," "allegedly," "perhaps," and so forth.

Speaking of terms, I use the words "guerrilla," "bushwhacker," "irregular," and "partisan" to mean the same thing. I qualify such combatants as "southern," "Rebel," or "Confederate" as there was no real need for northern guerrillas in Missouri during 1862 because the state was under occupation by Union forces. In some instances where I could identify guerrillas who seemed to have no allegiance except robbery and personal gain, I use the term "renegade." I have resisted the temptation to call southern guerrillas "bandits," "robbers," "outlaws," and other terms typically found in northern accounts since these words do not accurately portray these southerners' warrior status. Similarly, northern combatants who forsook their cause and uniform to plunder and murder I could also call "renegades" or even "jayhawkers," the term particularly applied to some northern Kansas troops who engaged in revenge and plunder raids into western Missouri. Where I could iden-

MISSOURI DIVIDED INTO REGIONS

In this book, Missouri has been divided into four sections for regional analysis.

tify a southern irregular leader who was commissioned specifically to recruit for the Rebel army, or whose actions showed he acted as such, I call such leaders "recruiters" to differentiate them from guerrilla leaders, even though they operated and fought the same way and often worked together. These are all distinctions most of the northern and Union sources did not or could not make. Likewise, I call northern soldiers "Yankees," "Union," or "federals," when I can determine that they were in federal service and not the service of local militia or home guards. My purpose in differentiating the bewildering array of Union troops fighting guerrillas in Missouri is to show how the different training, leadership, and experience levels of these different units affected their behavior while in the field.

Preface

I divided Missouri into four parts for this study, generally by major rivers. My division line between the eastern quarters and the western ones was along counties that had relatively little guerrilla warfare. For most location descriptions I use county designations, since most period records also did and since those county names and boundaries have changed little to the present-day. I contemplated mapping the sweep of guerrilla bands and southern recruiters across the landscape in the manner of other war studies, but the movement of such forces and their antagonists is not as significant as specific skirmishes, raids, and other events. The present-day U.S. military identifies such events as spots on a situation map, and I feel such portrayal would not add clarity for this study. Therefore, I have purposefully included only general maps showing county lines, towns, rivers, and railroads.

For sources, I relied mostly on period sources such as the U.S. War Department's *The Official Records of the Rebellion,* those surviving issues of Missouri daily and weekly Civil War newspapers, journals and letters, and specific military-unit records such as those compiled in Broadfoot Publishing Company's newly issued *Supplement to the "Official Records of the Rebellion."* I also used skirmish summaries and northern unit histories in Frederick Dyer's landmark *A Compendium of the War of the Rebellion*, as well as separately published specific unit histories of both sides. Another vital resource I used extensively, which is removed from period works, are those histories of many of the 116 Missouri counties that included local Civil War material, particularly the large number published between the 1880s and the First World War. These local accounts are not always accurate, since they were written some years after the events, and some are flavored by wishful thinking, cover-ups, self-vindication, and the like. Many Missouri county histories written during this period omitted the Civil War period almost entirely due to understandably strong war sentiment.

Among the secondary sources on this topic, some of the finest general works are Richard S. Brownlee's 1958 *Gray Ghosts of the Confederacy* and Michael Fellman's 1989 *Inside War: The Guerrilla Conflict in Missouri During the American Civil War*. These relatively recent works avoid a northern or southern bias and employ sound scholarship. I refer to Brownlee frequently in this book. Fellman's book contains excellent social history of that dark period, but I did not refer to it much in the specific events that I describe here, simply because my approach is from different perspectives.

Many of the other excellent secondary works about guerrilla warfare in Missouri's Civil War fall in two categories. There are those published postwar up through the 1920s, although some of these have a northern or southern bias. These secondary books give valuable insight into the meaning and context of particular events and lead the reader through cause and effect relationships of otherwise isolated incidents. Among these are Wiley Britton's 1891 *The Civil War on the Border*, and William Elsey Connelley's 1910 *Quantrill and the Border Wars*. The other group of secondary works are those written after World War II and includes the first two already cited. These employ a wider scope of sources not available to earlier historians, display less partiality, and are more diligent about citing their sources. In this category are Thomas Goodrich's 1995 *Black Flag: Guerrilla Warfare on the Western Border, 1861–1865*, Elmo Ingenthron's 1980 *Borderland Rebellion*, Edward E. Leslie's 1996 *The Devil Knows How to Ride: The True Story of William Clarke*

Quantrill and His Confederate Raiders, and Jay Monaghan's 1955 *Civil War on the Western Border 1854–1865*. I find it difficult to limit this overview to just a few, so my bibliography is a better guide to what is available.

My goal is not to refute but to complement both types of existing secondary works and add to the available body of knowledge. My method was to provide more depth on individual events by using more primary sources and at the same time relate this narrative of events to regional trends and patterns on a broader scale. This two-fold approach helps the reader to concentrate on particular events and then shows how events relate to each other on a broader regional approach. This way, someone researching his own ancestor's role in guerrilla warfare in a particular community can perhaps place that person in a certain skirmish in that county and understand how that action affected other military actions in neighboring counties in this fluid form of mounted warfare.

I brought a variety of formal training and life experiences together to accomplish these stated purposes. My formal academic education toward a teaching degree in social studies and a Master of Arts in American History degree, both from Central Missouri State University, combined with my formal military education as a U.S. Army military intelligence officer, gave me disciplined training to produce a scholarly work. This book is, in a way, an extension of my master's thesis, "The Civil War in Johnson County, Missouri," on which noted Missouri Civil War historian Dr. Leslie Anders was my advisor. My twenty years of experience as a reserve officer in the U.S. Army in the fields of counterintelligence and psychological warfare ably demonstrated to me the need for high levels of accuracy and research applied to delicate real-world situations. This has been complemented by my simultaneous twenty-one years of experience striving for technical accuracy, attention to detail, and timely production values as a cartographer for a government agency. My many years pursuing genealogy as an avocation has instilled in me a need to balance fairness with precise research in order to portray real individuals accurately in their environment without judging them. My own soldiers who had served in Vietnam, when they tried to answer my questions as a non-combat veteran, could not make me understand what they had experienced. They were fully respectful when they would shrug and tell me in their most serious tone, "Sir, you weren't there, and you wouldn't understand." Likewise, I did not live through the guerrilla warfare in Civil War Missouri, and I won't ever fully understand it. But, I think I can begin to comprehend, and I think I can relate it well enough to help others begin to comprehend, too.

Some words of warning, though. Those who glorify war will not find in these pages the glory of mighty armies in attractive uniforms. Missouri in 1862 was a "backwash" of the war to both sides, and the North and South found better use of their mighty armies and attractive uniforms than to send them to Missouri. Those who have chosen even this long after that tragic war to trumpet one cause and demonize the other will find great frustration here, for I strive to find a middle ground in my search for truth. Bias just gets in the way. Besides, both my wife's ancestors and mine fought as southern guerrillas in Missouri and some of our ancestors also served the northern side, so I must keep peace at home.

I owe thanks to several institutions and numerous people who rendered assistance in the production of this book. I am particularly indebted to the St. Louis

Public Library, the St. Louis County Library, the State Historical Society of Missouri at Columbia, the Western Historical Manuscripts Collections at both Columbia and St. Louis, and the Missouri Historical Society of St. Louis for the fine help they all provided on numerous occasions. Among the individuals I wish to acknowledge are Clark Kenyon of Camp Pope Bookshop of Iowa City, Iowa, who was helpful particularly with publishing and copyright issues; Bob and Mary Younger and Andy Turner of Morningside Books of Dayton, Ohio, were very generous with many illustrations; my friend and co-worker Terry Harmon provided numerous new and out-of-print source materials over a number of years. I wish also to thank Terry Henderson of Florissant, Missouri, for sharing information about his Civil War guerrilla chieftain ancestor, Francis G. Henderson of St. Charles County. Among the numerous Missouri Civil War historians who have given me encouragement and shared knowledge are Carolyn Bartels, John Bradbury, Jr., Dr. Leslie Anders, Jim Thoma, Tom Pearson, Jim McGhee, and Bob Owens. I am unable to list all the relatives, friends, coworkers, friends in the Army Reserves, and friends at church who not only encouraged me but helped to hold me accountable to finish this book over the last several years. My greatest debt of thanks is to my wife Pat and our son Andy and daughter Anna, not only for believing in me, but also for their longsuffering, their encouragement and their support of the long production of this book.

ONE

Winter 1862 in Northwest Missouri

Jayhawker Invasion

Snow came to northwest Missouri in the early days of the new year, as it commonly does, but something terrible came with the storms this January of 1862. Spearheaded by Lt. Colonel Daniel R. Anthony, brother of women's rights advocate Susan B. Anthony, and the undisciplined 7th Kansas Cavalry, a large force of Kansas Union troops, called "jayhawkers" by Missourians, swept into Cass County during a severe snow storm. Undeterred by several miles of the white stuff, the blue-clad Kansas troops struck Morristown and Dayton in Cass County before riding northeast to raid Rose Hill in southwest Johnson County. They burned homes and other buildings, both to settle old scores from the "Bleeding Kansas" fighting dating back to the 1850s and to deny shelter to rebel recruits the jayhawkers believed were forming across the region. The Kansas regiments contained many border Missourians of northern sympathy forced to flee by their southern neighbors, and they gleefully showed the way to burn about 45 buildings in Dayton and 42 in the Rose Hill area, including some belonging to northerners by mistake. They shot at least one irate homeowner to death. The unfortunate families were turned out on foot into the snow, sometimes just with the clothes on their backs, as the jayhawkers seized stock and wagons for their own use. Some Confederate recruits were nearby, answering Major General Sterling Price's call for volunteers from the previous November, but they wisely kept out of view of the overwhelming raiding force, except for some skirmishing.[1] One of the few northern units in the area, Baptist preacher and Colonel Andrew G. Nugent's Cass County Home Guard Cavalry, stationed at West Point in northwest Bates County, rode with the jayhawkers, using their protection to recruit northern men. In time, Nugent's men would also join Kansas ranks, becoming part of 9th Kansas Cavalry.[2]

The jayhawkers' initial quarry, including Captain John H. Britts, a doctor of Austin, south Cass County, along with one of the Scott family of Rose Hill, southwest Johnson County, had already escaped with their precious recruits for the rebel army, but northern sympathizers rode into Lt. Colonel Anthony's camp at Morristown, west Cass County, and enticed his raiders deeper into the wintry Missouri countryside with word that there were other recruits in Johnson County.[3] Two Confederate officers, Colonel Benjamin F. Elliott, a Virginia-born farmer who was given a commission from private to colonel leading Lafayette County troops in the battle

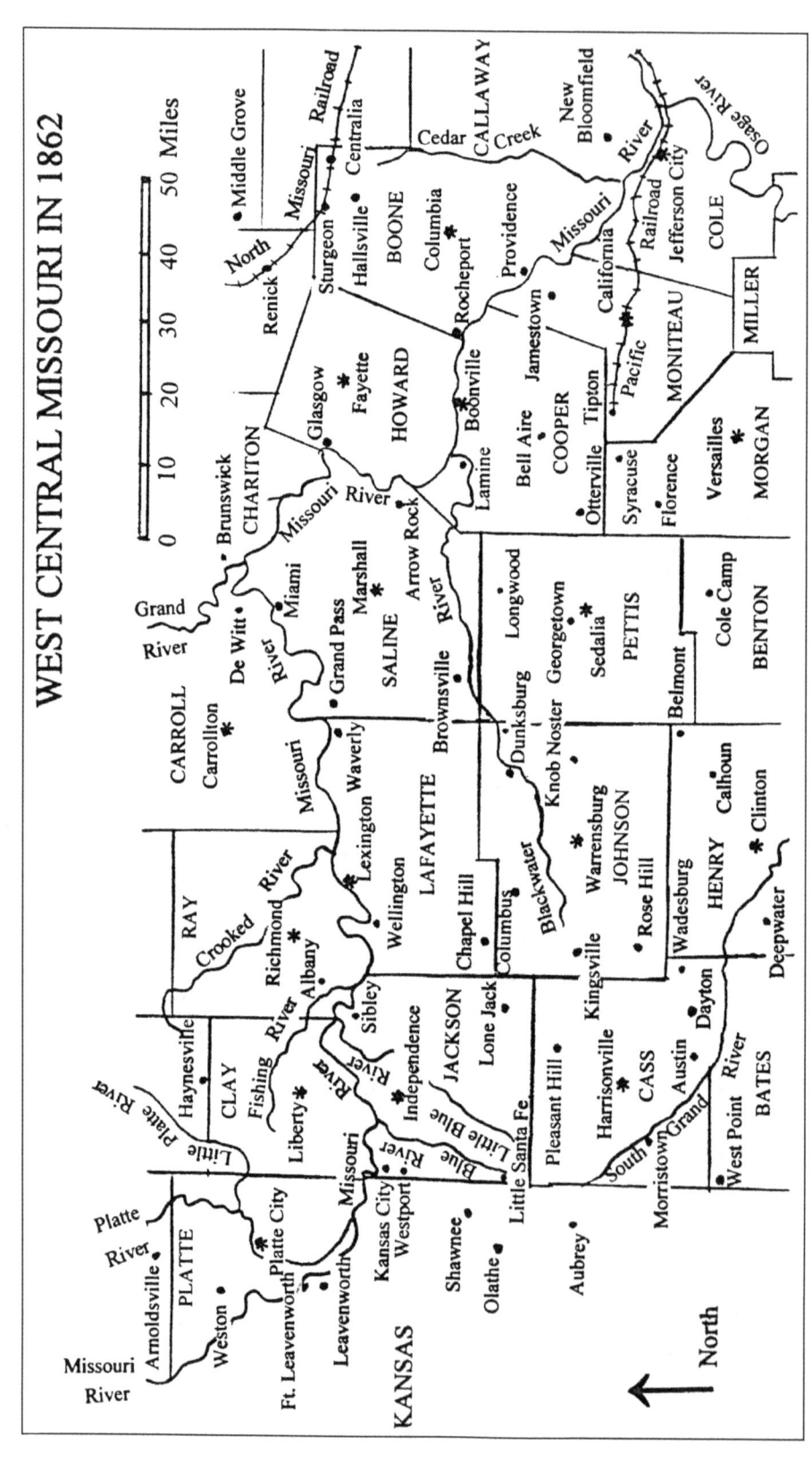

of Wilson's Creek, August 10, 1861, and Colonel Jeremiah Vardaman Cockrell, a Methodist minister from Warrensburg whose brother, Francis Marion Cockrell, would become a leading general of Confederate troops in the war's western theater, were reportedly gathering in southern men.[4] Therefore, Lt. Colonel Anthony dispatched Major John L. Messick, with 200 eager troopers of 7th Kansas Cavalry, deep into snow-covered Johnson County to punish the supporters of secession. Their own regimental commander, Dr. Charles R. Jennison, had warned these Missouri counties the previous November of their perfidy flirting with secession, saying "...playing war is played out...."[5] Between January 5 and 12, these arsonists fanned out in different columns and in Colonel Elliott's home neighborhood of northwest Johnson County burned about 150 homes and looted Kingsville, killing eight men of southern sympathy and cropping the ear of a ninth, as if marking a hog, with the remark, "We'll know you the next time you are caught." A woman of northern sympathy who suffered through this depredation with her southern neighbors later wrote, "...no age of barbarism or cruelty can show us such scenes of cruelty and plunder...." The Union general in charge of Missouri operations, Major General Henry W. Halleck, expressed his disgust for such unordered jayhawker incursions when he wrote to higher authorities that "...the conduct of the [jayhawker] forces ... has done more for the enemy in this state than could have been accomplished by 20,000 of his own army...." Meanwhile, the Rebel recruiting command pulled back but looked for a chance to strike back at this most hated enemy. Some townspeople of Columbus, north Johnson County, coyly assured Captain Clark S. Merriman's detachment of 50 troopers of 7th Kansas Cavalry that no Rebels were about, then Colonel Elliott's men ambushed them just outside town, January 8 or 9, killing five and capturing two of the Kansans. Their outraged comrades later burned most of Columbus to the ground. When Major Messick returned to his main camp in Cass County, January 12, he took with him only 50 families of northern sympathy, who chose to live in Kansas rather than face the enmity of their southern neighbors. Although Johnson County remained home to many northerners, for the rest of the war southern sympathy remained at fever pitch there, in large part due to eight days of havoc wreaked by 7th Cavalry and the seeming inability of the Union authorities to deter such atrocities.[6]

At about the same time as the Columbus skirmish, Colonel George W. Deitzler's 1st Kansas Infantry occupied Lexington, the seat of Lafayette County, bringing their own version of jayhawker depredations until January 25. Local southerners, perhaps of Colonel Elliott's command, fired on the Kansas foot soldiers near Garrison Creek five miles from town, mortally wounding one. The jayhawkers seemed to treat all residents as hostile after that. Colonel Deitzler's troops did not commit the same scale of atrocities as Jennison's 7th Cavalry, but they arrested a number of local southerners, freely robbed area farmers of foodstuffs and forage, and, when they marched away for Ft. Leavenworth on January 25 shot a man named D. Harris along their route of march, probably in west Lafayette County.[7] The Union general in charge of the Kansas department, Major General David Hunter, finally on January 30 published an order forbidding troops of Kansas from entering or operating in Missouri unless ordered by his office to do so.[8] Although Kansas jayhawker depredations in Missouri continued throughout the war, they never repeated the scale of those of 1861 and January 1862. Major General Halleck agreed and reciprocated with a like order, February 2. He wrote to Hunter, "...keep the Kansas troops out of Missouri and I will keep the Missourians out of Kansas. They can't agree and make infinite trouble. The only way is to keep them apart...."[9] Between January 20 and 24, Union authorities in Kansas employed parts of 1st Missouri Cavalry to track down and capture, around Atchison, Kansas, jayhawkers who had been raiding in Buchanan County, Missouri.[10]

Confederate Recruiting Continues in the Region

The operations of the Kansas interlopers in January did not stop Rebel recruiting in the western counties south of the Missouri River. Troops of the 1st Kansas Infantry captured two captains and a lieutenant of Colonel Elliott's recruiting force in Lafayette County on January 11, and unidentified Union troops captured another lieutenant in Sedalia, Pettis County, the same day and sent him off to prison in St. Louis.[11] Evidently, in mid-January, 1862, Major Emory S. Foster of Warrensburg and ten men of the local 27th Missouri Mounted Infantry captured twenty-seven-year-old Colonel Warner F. Lewis of Dayton, Cass County, at Holden, west Johnson County, along with his escort.[12] Another officer of Foster's home guard unit had to be rescued from his home northeast of Warrensburg January 15 by cavalrymen of 2nd Missouri Cavalry sent from Sedalia.[13] A Union captain nearby at Shanghai, south Johnson County, recruiting perhaps for the new 7th Cavalry Missouri State Militia (MSM), reported having captured and paroled 20 southerners.[14] On January 18, a Rebel leader identified only as "Hutchinson," with a small escort went to the home of Rebel Colonel Ebenezer Magoffin in west Pettis County to send Magoffin's belongings south, as the owner was in prison in St. Louis and could not attend to the matter himself. When one of the colonel's slaves refused to go, Hutchinson shot the man, as reported in a St. Louis newspaper later.[15] Meanwhile, the Union commander at Sedalia thought there was enough Rebel threat in Johnson County to the west to send Major George C. Marshall and a large patrol of 2nd Missouri Cavalry (Merrill's Horse). Marshall's men did capture several Rebel recruits between January 19 and 21, but the major himself was mortally wounded in a firefight with two southerners.[16] These Confederates probably were under Colonel Jeremiah Cockrell's command. Two more local men of southeast Johnson County, probably also under Cockrell's command, Captain Benjamin L. Snelling and a Doctor Warren, took as captive several local men of northern sympathy, until Major Marshall's command rode to their rescue.[17] At this same time, many miles east in Moniteau County, foot soldiers of 11th Iowa Infantry, guarding the vital Pacific Railroad, learned to listen to local black families. These black locals told them of Rebel recruits from Boone County who were traveling south to join the Confederate Army through Moniteau County. The Iowans acted on the tip and captured a number of men whom they sent to prison in St. Louis.[18]

Meanwhile, north of the Missouri River, elements of newly-formed 5th Cavalry Missouri State Militia (MSM), probably acting on an informant's tip, on January 23 recovered a number of kegs of Rebel gunpowder hidden in a north Platte County schoolhouse and a couple more kegs nearby in Buchanan County. This gunpowder was probably part of the southern Missouri State Guard reserve stock hurriedly hidden across western Missouri the previous summer when Union forces entered the state in force.[19]

Jackson County: A Man Named Quantrill

In the waning days of 1861, southern men of Jackson County had organized a posse of sorts to combat jayhawkers and other renegades who were preying on rural families. Andy Walker, the son of a wealthy plantation owner, had for a time led these vigilantes, but he was too well known and had too much to lose, so he stepped aside.[21] Many others, such as Westport freighting business owner Upton Hays, were capable leaders and had fought the Kansans before, but had ridden away to join Missouri regular Confederate forces to the south.[20] Into this vacuum stepped an opportunistic former school teacher, originally from Ohio, named William Clarke Quantrill. In late December 1861 Andy Walker and other Jackson Countians marveled how this returned Rebel soldier led the vigilantes in capturing and hanging an outlaw named Searcy, who had been stealing horses and mules from isolated farms.[22] Research later showed that, pre-war, Quantrill was an opportunist in east Kansas who flirted with pro-northern causes and had even stolen stock himself looking for fame or notoriety. In 1860 he had even betrayed several anti-slavery comrades to Andy Walker's father in a deadly ambush, in what seems to have been a bid to court admiration from Jackson Countians. Quantrill also fabricated stories about being born in Maryland and suffering atrocities at the hands of jayhawkers who murdered a brother he didn't even have, stories that would evoke sympathy from southerners.[23]

William Quantrill had dispersed his band of Jackson Countians in late December, to avert Union countermeasures. This became a standard Quantrill tactic. However, Kansas jayhawkers brutalized and killed some local men in late January, and Federal officials had a local man hold a dance to catch southerners, so Quantrill had his band reassemble.[24] Several compa-

Guerrilla Chief William C. Quantrill. (John N. Edwards, *Noted Guerrillas*, 1867; courtesy Bob and Mary Younger and Andy Turner)

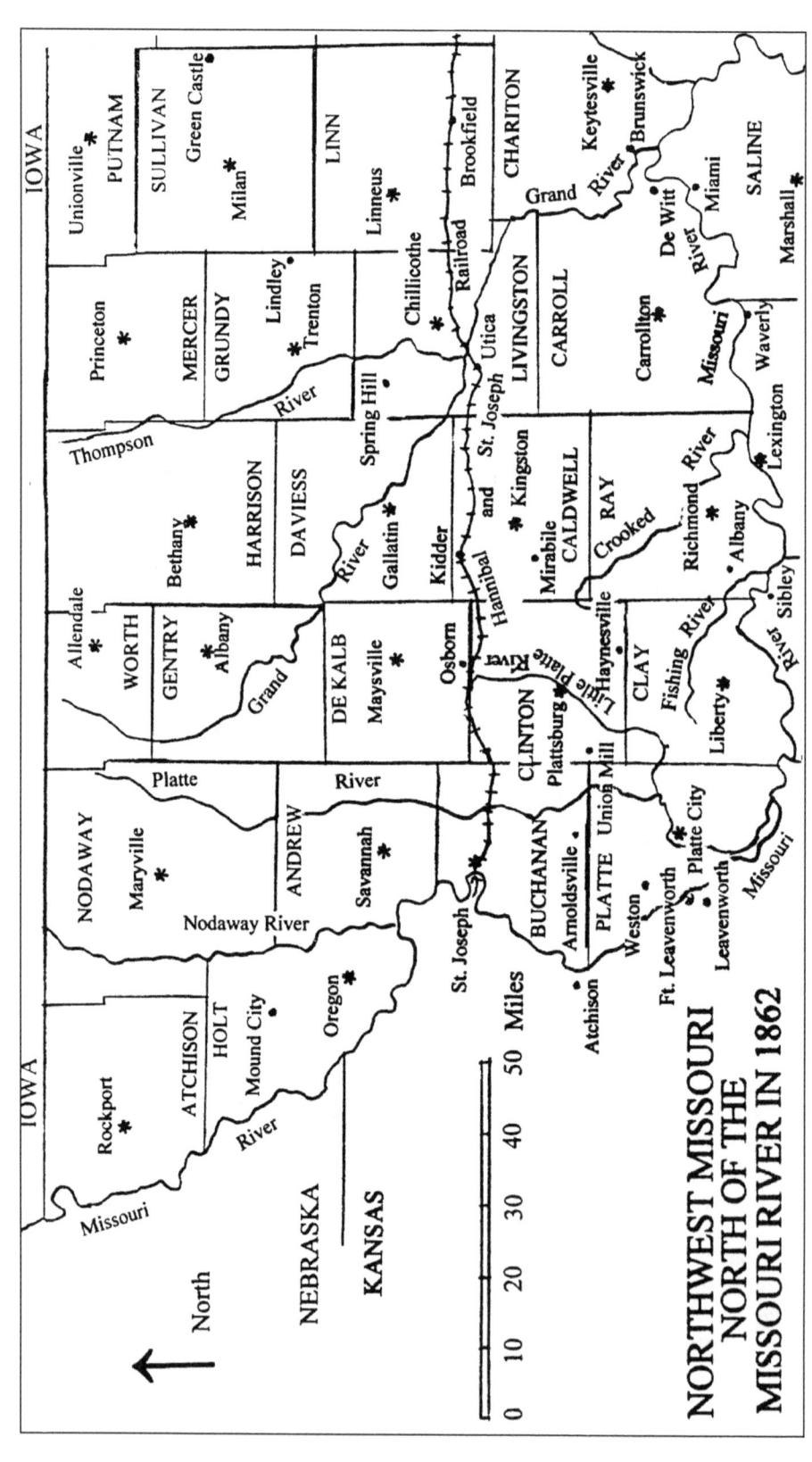

nies of 7th Missouri Infantry Regiment under Captain William S. Oliver had been garrisoned in Independence and seemed determined to squelch secession interest. Evidently, Captain Oliver had a part in arranging the dance trap and even years later, locals remembered that his troops committed "many oppressive and needless cruelties."[25] Therefore, it must have given Qunatrill some satisfaction when during the evening of January 29, with eighteen or twenty men, he ambushed Oliver and five of his men at Manasseth Gap near Little Blue on the Independence/Harrisonville Road—a site he used several times afterward. The results are debatable as Captain Oliver claimed his detail killed two Rebels, while postwar guerrilla accounts claimed they captured and paroled the Yankees. Captain Oliver's report of this incident also detailed other actions by Quantrill at this time in the area.[26]

Jo Shelby Quits the Guerrilla Cause

On February 3, the Confederate army of Missouri in the southeast corner of the state issued a call for 71,000 fellow southern men to come join their cause, and many groups of such men were carefully picking their way past Yankee patrols and pickets to do just that.[27] In Lafayette County a wealthy thirty-year-old rope manufacturer named Joseph Orville Shelby stepped out into the open. Shelby had gathered around him at Waverly a force of about 40 local men and all through 1861 had peppered away at Union troops that came by, sometimes even with homemade cannons. Shelby spurned several offers for a commission in Union service, only to conduct war as a guerrilla chief around home, taking pot shots at passing Federal columns and riverboats. Shelby had joined regular southern forces briefly to fight at Wilson's Creek in August and at Lexington in September, but each time he returned home.[28] Surprisingly, Union forces never considered Shelby's private homespun army a serious threat, even after November 18, 1861, when it robbed the side-wheeler, *Sunshine,* and hid stolen government goods on nearby farms, including a number of army wagons.[29]

On February 7, 1862, Shelby and his men came openly into Lexington, as no Union troops had come to garrison the river port after the 1st Kansas Infantry had left for Kansas, January 25. In fact, these Rebels had come to threaten northern sympathizers if three southern men taken away by the Kansans were harmed.[30] The fate of these three men is unrecorded, but Shelby's bold ultimatum signaled the end of his career as a guerrilla chief. Not long after, Shelby led his men south to join the regulars with wife Betsy and their two sons riding along in a wagon—perhaps one of those seized off the *Sunshine* the previous November.[31] Shelby would later distinguish himself as an outstanding cavalry general in the regular Rebel army.

Predictably, Union authorities hurriedly sent more Yankee troops to garrison Lexington and squelch any more talk of southern revenge. The soldiers this time were Colonel John D. Stevenson and a portion of his 7th Missouri Infantry Regiment, the same unit committing depredations in Jackson County to the west. On February 13 and 14, some of these soldiers raided rural families—threatening, stealing, breaking home furnishings and worse. According to a local diarist, some of these soldiers forced one woman to play the piano while they made lewd remarks, and at another home they groped a woman through her clothing. Colonel Stevenson took immediate steps to punish the perpetrators, but the Victorian sensibilities of locals were outraged, and more and more locals were wondering if the secessionists were right after all.[32]

Quantrill Starts Raiding Towns

The inability of either the Kansas troops or the 7th Missouri Infantry to apprehend Quantrill's growing band, or even to protect themselves, emboldened the guerrillas. In early February Captain Oliver and his three companies of 7th Missouri Infantry marched out of Jackson County to garrison with the rest of the regiment at Lexington, and only home guards were left to keep bushwhackers out of Independence.[33] This tempted Quantrill to lead his band in a quick raid on the town in about mid-February, according to guerrilla memoirs written later. Not much was accomplished except some quick riding and fast shooting, but the bushwhackers grabbed some supplies and perhaps some captives.[34] On February 22, 1862, Quantrill and 15 men joined forces with former Kansas City hotel clerk, Colonel Benjamin F. Parker, and his 60 guerrillas to raid Independence again. The Rebels believed Lieutenant A. Bayard Nettleton's large patrol of 2nd Ohio Cavalry had left town after searching the place at dawn. They rode in, gunning down either an Ohio straggler or a local northern sympathizer. Hearing gunshots, Nettleton led his patrol back into town, killing four guerrillas and capturing at least one, at the cost of one trooper killed in a madcap running fight through alleys and backyards of Independence. The guerrillas scattered into the fog. Quantrill himself was slightly injured when his mount was killed and dispersed his band for a few days to avoid Union countermeasures.[35] This also seemed to be Ben Parker's first fight with Yankees and would not be his last.

As February 1862 waned the warmer weather of spring was not far off. The several guerrilla bands mentioned so far were still operational and spring promised to be violent in northwest Missouri.

Two

Winter 1862 in Northeast Missouri

The new year did not come peaceably to northeast Missouri, particularly in that heavily-settled farm country, later called "Little Dixie," north of the Missouri River. Many if not most, of these residents had been born in the south—particularly in Virginia, Tennessee, Kentucky, and North Carolina.

During December 1861 many of these southern men organized into military units and rode south to join the Rebel army, then located in southwest Missouri, sabotaging the railroad lines as they went.

The railroad destruction especially irked the Yankee leadership, since professional military men, such as Department of the Missouri chief Major General Henry W. Halleck, had been taught to regard such irregular warfare as cowardly partisan fighting and apply the methods Napoleon employed with such severity years before. Therefore, Halleck had issued on December 22 a "shoot on sight" order for anyone caught in the act.[1] In hindsight, that order set a deadly precedent for Missouri's guerrilla war.

Those southerners torching bridges, depots, and rolling stock were from their perspective performing a last act of defiance against an occupying Yankee army as they rode to assemble with others. During the waning days of 1861, southern Colonel Caleb Dorsey of Pike County and about 900 of his men had been defeated by a Union force half that size near Hallsville, north Boone County, at the Battle of Mt. Zion Church. The Federals lost five killed and 63 wounded, but they stung Dorsey's command with 25 killed, perhaps over 100 wounded, and 30 captured. Dorsey dispersed the remainder of his battered force across the wild recesses of the Perche Hills of northwest Boone County, allowing locals to succor the hurt and discouraged. During the first days of January, he quietly led them south to join the Rebel army.[2]

A Cold Respite

The winter storm that struck in the first days of January, 1862, seemed to cool off southern activity, if not fervor, for few acts of guerrilla warfare took place the next few days in this part of the state. A guerrilla chief named Bill Dunn had been creating excitement with his band in Scotland County for some time. On Thursday, January 2, a force of 180 troopers of 3rd Missouri Cavalry tried in vain to come to grips with Bill Dunn's 100 or so Rebel recruits near Paris, Monroe County. Each side captured one of each other's men, and the Rebels got away.[3] On the following day, Yankees of 10th Missouri Infantry, guarding the North Missouri Railroad, skirmished with unidentified foes at Hunnewell, southwest Shelby County, with unspecified results. Hunnewell was close to the camp of guerrilla chief Tom Stacy and his band, known since the previous August for attacking passing Union troops, so this was probably Stacy's group again.[4]

Union Major General Henry W. Halleck. (*Battles and Leaders of the Civil War*, 1887–1888, vol. 1, p. 276)

The Silver Creek Fight at Roan's Tanyard

During this same time Rebel Colonel John A. Poindexter of east Randolph County had gathered about 800 men in a camp near Roan's Tanyard on Silver Creek, southwest Randolph County, near the village of Roanoke. Some of these men had destroyed nearby railroad installations, and Poindexter assured them that they would next drive Federal troops out of Howard County to the south. However, Major W.M.G. Torrence of 1st Iowa Cavalry, leading a combined force of his own troops as well as Ohio and Missouri cavalry—about 500 in all, attacked first on the cold morning of January 8. An alert Rebel picket heard the Yankees crashing through the brush and warned the camp, so that when the dismounted Federals first saw their quarry, the Rebels were drawn up in a battle line waiting. The antagonists traded two volleys, after which Poindexter's men fell back through the campground to the natural entrenchment of the creek bank and the tangled trees that lined it. Torrence ordered his men to attack and, as they came on, the defenders broke and ran off in all directions with the cavalrymen pursuing for a time. The Federals destroyed the camp and equipment, estimating Rebel dead at 40, with many more wounded and 28 shivering captives, compared to their own loss of six killed and 18 wounded. Many of Poindexter's escaping men returned home in disgust, and the colonel later led a much smaller force south to join the Rebel army.[5] Poindexter would return in a few months, but this defeat, coupled with Colonel Dorsey's December 28 loss in nearby Boone County, had a cooling effect on secessionist ardor throughout northeast Missouri.

Smaller-Scale Acts of Violence

Most guerrilla warfare was not stand-up fighting between large bodies of men like the Silver Creek fight, but was rather small hit-and-run affairs that hardly warranted attention in the press. Several such incidents took place in January, 1862. On January 8, the same day as Colonel Poindexter's fight, Union troops near Mexico, Audrain County, captured ten southern men in a skirmish, but no other details remain.[6] Troopers of 2nd Missouri Cavalry ("Merrill's Horse") on January 10 captured recruiter Captain James B. Watson and two of his men near Columbia, Boone County. Union authorities were pleased, since Watson was implicated as a leader in the railroad sabotage the previous month and the burning of the steamer *Magi*, but Watson would prove to be a good escaper in a few days and frustrate his enemy's plans.[7] On the night of January 10 guerrillas, probably of Tom Stacy's band, robbed a minister's home at West Ely, south-central Marion County, of the clothing and bedding his parishioners had made for the Union military hospital at nearby Palmyra. This act brought double satisfaction to the bushwhackers, obtaining for themselves items to keep warm, while denying their enemy the same. This same guerrilla band gunned down avowed northern sympathizer Robert Granville Carver in his own yard January 15 at Lick Creek, southwest Ralls County.[8] On January 26, miles to the north and east, 300 troopers of 3rd Missouri Cavalry discovered a few miles north of Hunnewell, southeast Shelby County, a camp of nearly the same number of Rebel recruits and attacked. The cavalry chased the startled campers south into Monroe County and captured eight.[9]

In northwest Callaway County a large patrol of 3rd Iowa Cavalry on January 18 captured accused bridgeburners Captain James P. Snedicor and Joseph Watkins hiding in an attic. The next day, the same patrol flushed 12 guerrillas from their hideaway cabin but not could catch any of them. One Iowan was wounded in the melee.[10]

Northeast Union authorities now turned to strike at Bill Dunn and his Scotland County band of 80 men. Union Colonel David Moore led 170 of his Missouri Volunteers on sleighs over the snow January 19 in Schuyler County to give Dunn a big surprise. Moore captured almost the entire Rebel company in a barnyard, then paroled and released most of them—a common practice in Missouri for both sides this early in the war. Bill Dunn himself escaped capture and would re-emerge the coming summer to enlarge his reputation.[11]

Some of the southern recruits forming in northeast Lincoln County on the evening of January 20 raided the homes of northern sympathizers and took firearms and ammunition. Evidently, the same group raided more homes of northerners the evening of January 24, this time in southeast Pike County, taking more firearms, as well as boots and a watch.[12] Just a few miles away in the Lick Creek neighborhood, along the Monroe/Ralls County line, unidentified guerrillas robbed a north-

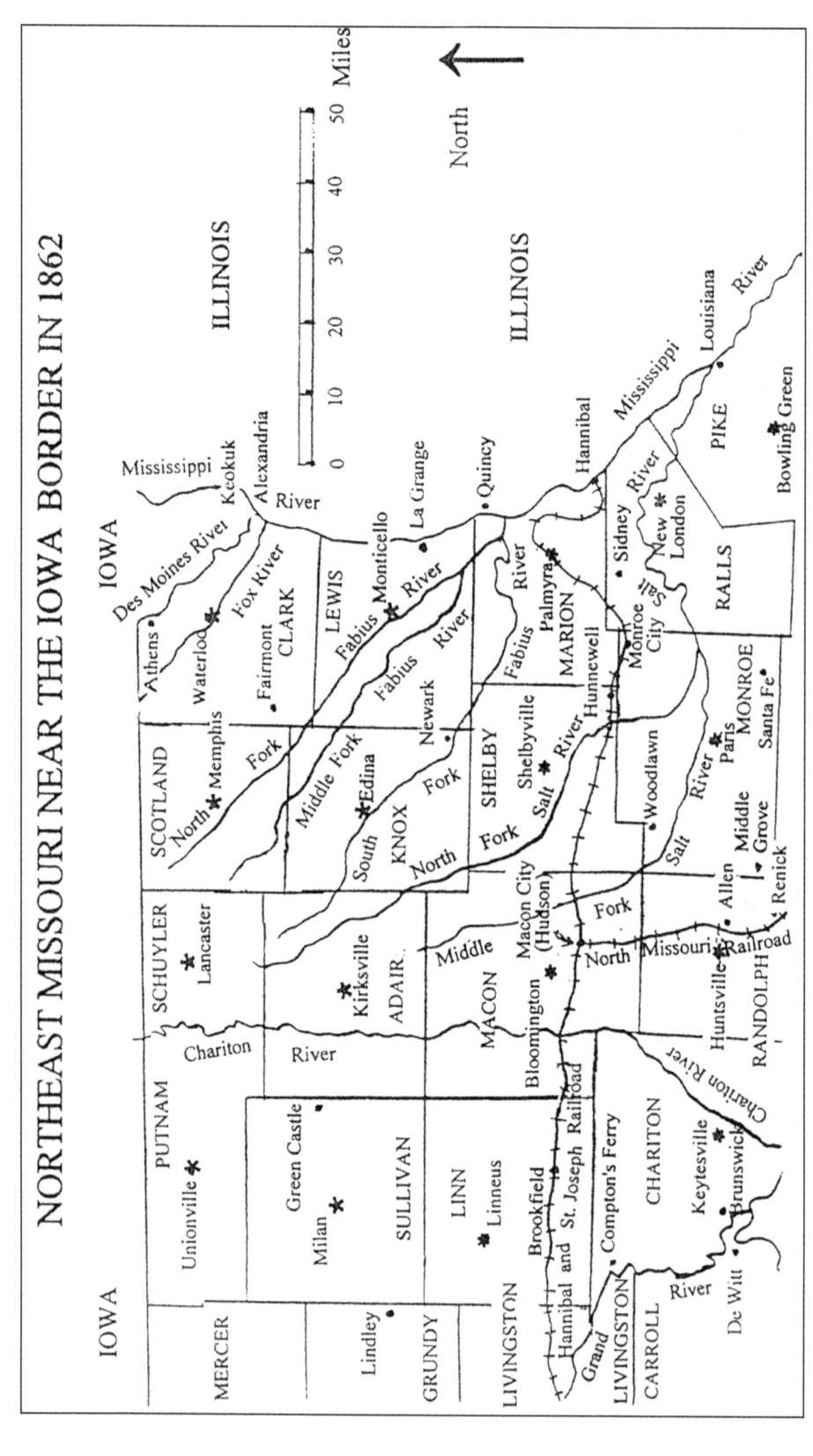

ern sympathizer's home and shot him dead in his yard, in front of his wife and children, because he "resisted."[13]

Another patrol of 3rd Iowa Cavalry, this time in south Callaway County, between January 23 and 27, captured about 100 Rebel recruits in the vicinity of Portland, St. Aubert, and New Bloomfield. These southerners were preparing to cross the frigid waters of the Missouri River and trek south to the Rebel army, but the Yankees were becoming more proficient in preventing that.[14]

On January 24, Union headquarters in St. Louis published in the newspaper orders that all river traffic henceforth would be under total Union military control, including requirements for all boat owners, officers, pilots, and crew to take an oath to the U.S. government.[15] Two days later Union cavalry at Novelty, southwest Knox County, captured notable Rebel leader Major Benjamin W. Shacklett of Scotland County, who was also attempting to lead some recruits south.[16] It would seem that this part of the "Show Me " state was becoming untenable for southern plans.

One bright spot for the South took place January 31, 1862, in Columbia, Boone County. Using tools secretly passed to them by female relatives, thirteen Rebel prisoners cut their way out of the Missouri University building that Federal soldiers had turned into a makeshift prison. Among the escapees was the same Captain

The Union military controlled Missouri River traffic during the war. (*Century Magazine*, March 1836, p. 761; courtesy Terry Harmon)

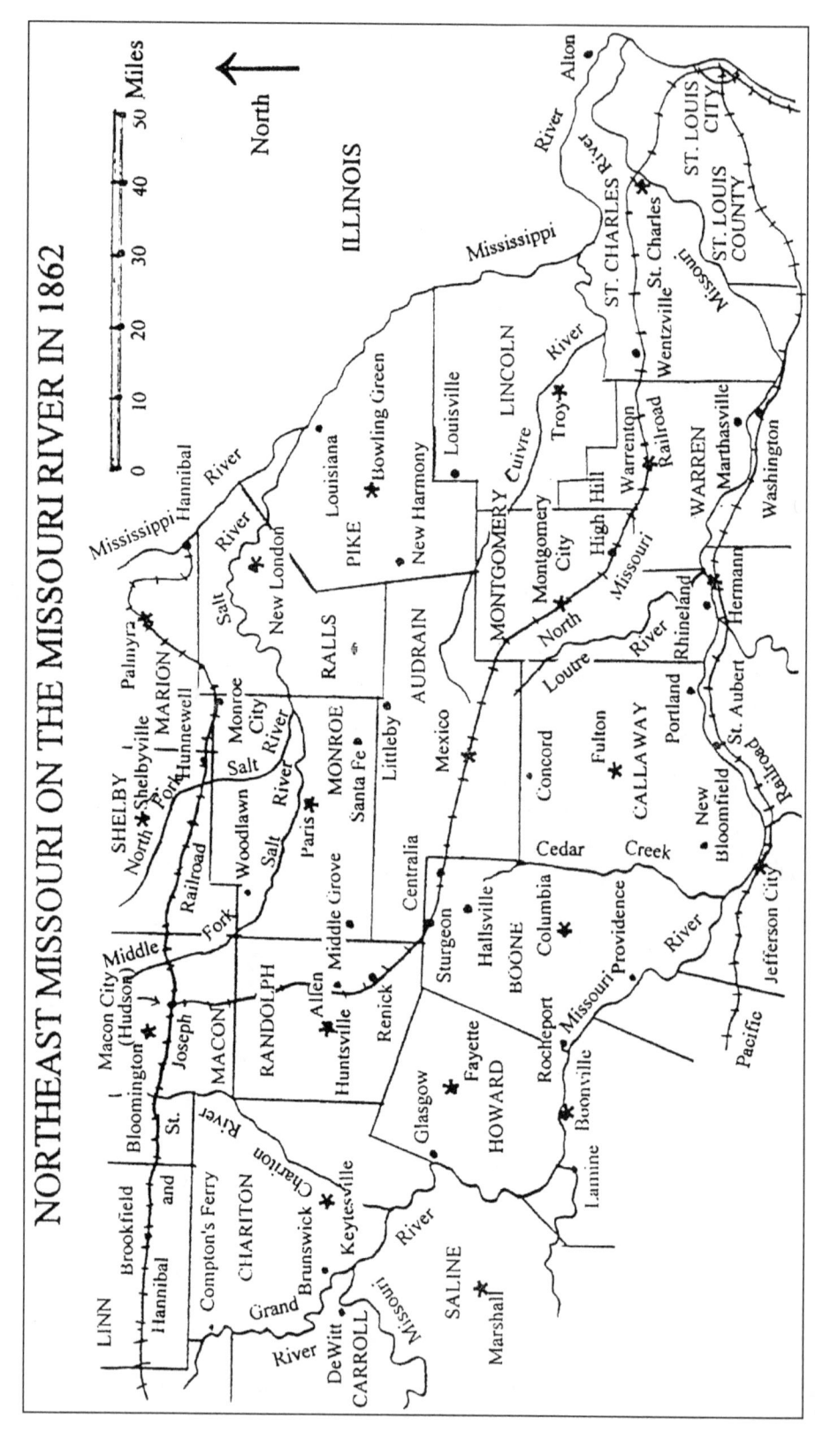

James B. Watson who had become a prisoner only a few days before. Troopers of 2nd Missouri Cavalry recaptured the captain, and perhaps others, soon after the escape, but some made good their getaway and eventually rejoined Confederate ranks.[17]

February 1862—The Pace of War Slows

The southern reverses of recent weeks, combined with a cold Missouri winter, had a stultifying effect on guerrilla activities in northeast Missouri. About February 11 Colonel John D. Foster's 22nd Missouri Infantry Regiment, scouting Chariton County, captured 19 Rebels, 18 horses, and 142 kegs of gunpowder. The previous June, before the southern Missouri State Guard hurriedly left the capitol at Jefferson City, some of them ferried hundreds of kegs of their gunpowder up and down the Missouri River to be hidden by friends. Union forces would keep turning up caches of the stuff throughout the war.[18] During the night of February 11 unidentified guerrillas, possibly under Bill Dunn, besieged the small Union garrison of Lancaster, Schuyler County. There is no record of casualties, but at dawn the southerners gave up on the project and moved on.[19] The next night, miles to the south near Fulton, Callaway County, a Union guard fired on eight unidentified guerrillas who approached his post outside town. The

Guerrillas made good use of the night for their type of warfare. (Charles C. Coffin, *The Boys of '61*, 1881; courtesy Terry Harmon)

guard could not tell if any of the intruders were hit.[20] If the slower pace of guerrilla activities in February seemed to indicate an acceptance of inevitable Union supremacy, in a matter of weeks events of guerrilla and Rebel recruiter resurgence in the region would challenge that thinking.

Three

Winter 1862 in Southeast Missouri

A vehement southern population in parts of southeast Missouri encouraged guerrilla warfare there this first winter of the war, in spite of large occupying forces of Union troops. The swamps of the "bootheel" and the heavily wooded hills of this portion of the Show Me state also provided havens for the hit-and-run warfare of the Rebel partisans. The aggressive tactics of secessionists, particularly of Colonel M. Jeff Thompson, formerly an attorney of St. Joseph across the state, and Colonel William O. Coleman, a Rolla businessman, would put area Yankee troops on notice that they would have to get out into the wintry countryside to hold the region.

Two Fights

The "Swamp Rats" led by Colonel Thompson, were watching the Yankee forces in the swampy "Bootheel" for a chance to strike. Seventy-five or 80 guerrillas, probably of Thompson's men, struck out January 7 at elements of 10th Iowa Infantry near Charleston, Mississippi County, killing five and wounding 17 other Iowans, two mortally. The infantrymen resisted and the ambushers withdrew, having done their damage.[1] This same month a Boone County, Missouri, newspaper printed this picturesque description of Colonel Thompson as he was seen around Columbus, Kentucky, just across the Mississippi River:

> Imagine a tall, lean, and wiry-looking customer, at least six feet high, and as slender as a pair of tongs ... what you would call a hatchet face; thick yellow hair, combed back behind his ears and bobbed off short ... without a vestige of beard or mustache, some thirty or thirty-five years of age; light blue eyes with friendly and benevolent expression ... with a half smile ... mild voiced and unassuming in a crowd.... He is perpetually full of fun, he never gets to talking without setting all around him to laughing; it is believed, indeed, that he fights chiefly for the fun of it. The camp is full of Jeff Thompson's jokes or rather the odd dialogues he has had with friends and enemies.[2]

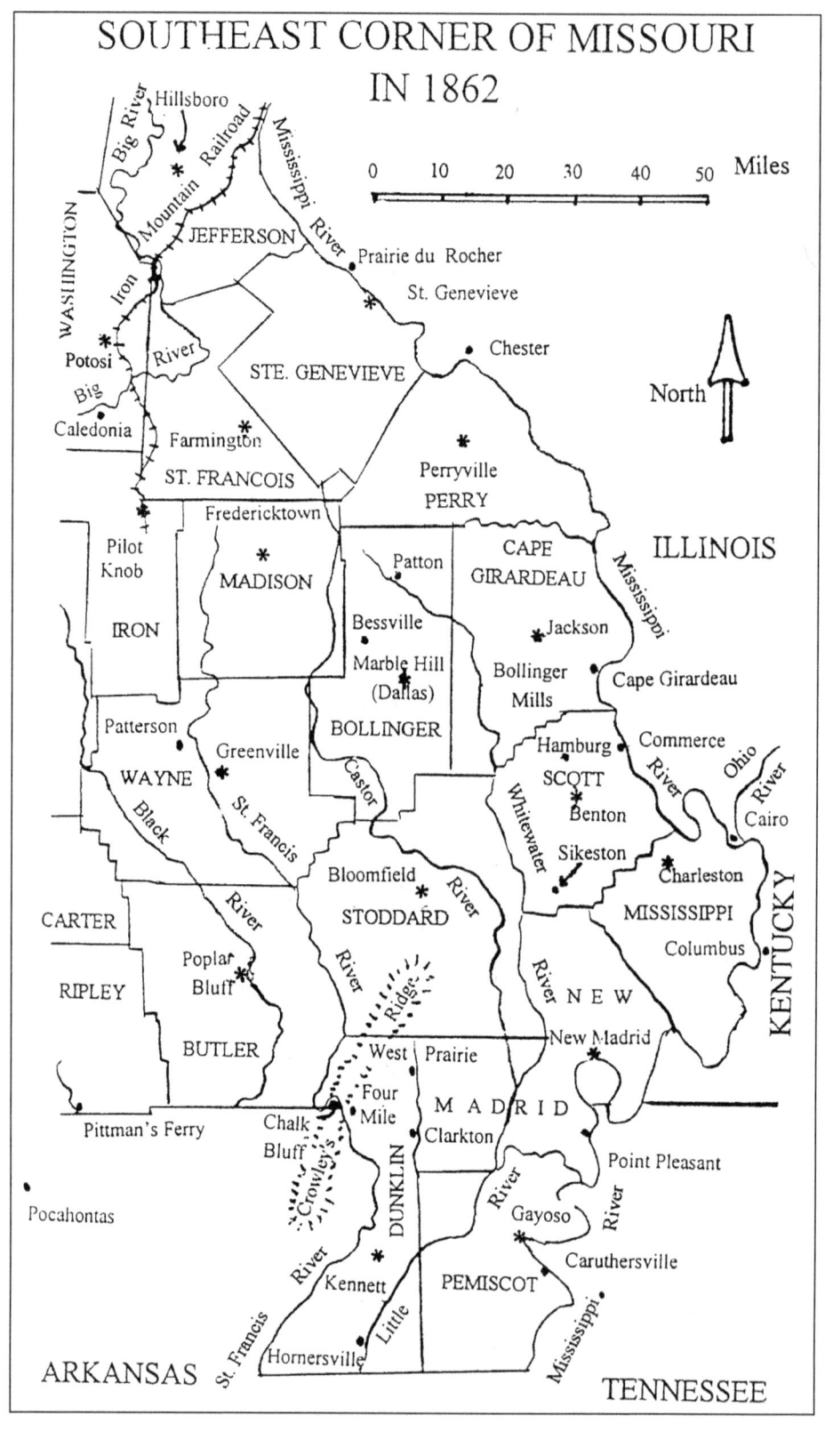

Five days later in the rugged hills of south Iron or north Wayne County unidentified Union cavalry tracked nine mounted Rebels all evening and eventually captured seven of them.[3] Federal units reported many disillusioned Rebel soldiers were filtering back through Union lines to return home, and perhaps this was the case here, too.

Counterguerrilla Expeditions

In mid–January, elements of 7th Illinois Cavalry, 17th Illinois Infantry, and 12th Cavalry MSM (Missouri State Militia) scoured portions of Scott, Stoddard, and Bollinger counties looking for guerrillas and returning Rebel soldiers. They bagged 19 prisoners at Dallas and at Bloomfield were delighted to capture 39 at a dance.[4] All through January and February, two companies of 1st Indiana Cavalry industriously patrolled St. Francois and Reynolds counties and captured several returning Rebel soldiers and guerrillas.[5]

The "Swamp Fox" of Missouri's bootheel: rebel Colonel M. Jeff Thompson. (*Battles and Leaders of the Civil War,* 1887–1888, vol. 1, p. 452)

St. Louis Prison Escapes

Most of the southerners captured in Missouri during the war were sent to several prisons in the St. Louis area. These military prisons were actually makeshift adaptations of pre-war establishments. One was formerly a medical college whose southern owner fled further south, and another, in an obvious touch of irony, had been a slave market. Since these were not originally designed for the incarceration of determined and imaginative soldiers, and since a large part of the city popula-

tion was willing to aid escapees, escapes were frequent throughout the war. In essence, these "make-do" prisons leaked inmates like a sieve!

During either December or January this winter, Captain Hampton L. Boone almost escaped disguised as a woman in a costume brought to him by a lady friend. Captain Boone was caught when a wind gust blew his skirt up, revealing his gray uniform pants underneath. His attempt was made from the former Lynch's Slave Market, renamed Myrtle Street Prison by Union officials.[6]

Another military prisoner, Giles McDaniel of Saline County, escaped from the former McDowell's Medical College, now known as Gratiot Street Prison, during January 1862 disguised as a black man. McDaniel was recaptured the following evening but slipped away for good after drinking with his guards.[7]

Obviously, part of the cause for prison escapes was poorly trained and motivated guards. Prison cadre were simply Union army units that rotated through the duty. Their lack of concern also led to poor health and unsanitary conditions in the often overcrowded facilities. For too many southern soldiers and civilians, their prison stay became a death warrant. These grim realities also spurred escape attempts.

Small Actions Along the St. Louis–Springfield Main Route

During 1861 some Rebels had already found tempting the Union military's reliance on the St. Louis-to-Springfield main route that threaded through the steep

Southern men held prisoner in Missouri. (*Harper's Weekly*, October 5, 1861; courtesy Bob and Mary Younger and Andy Turner)

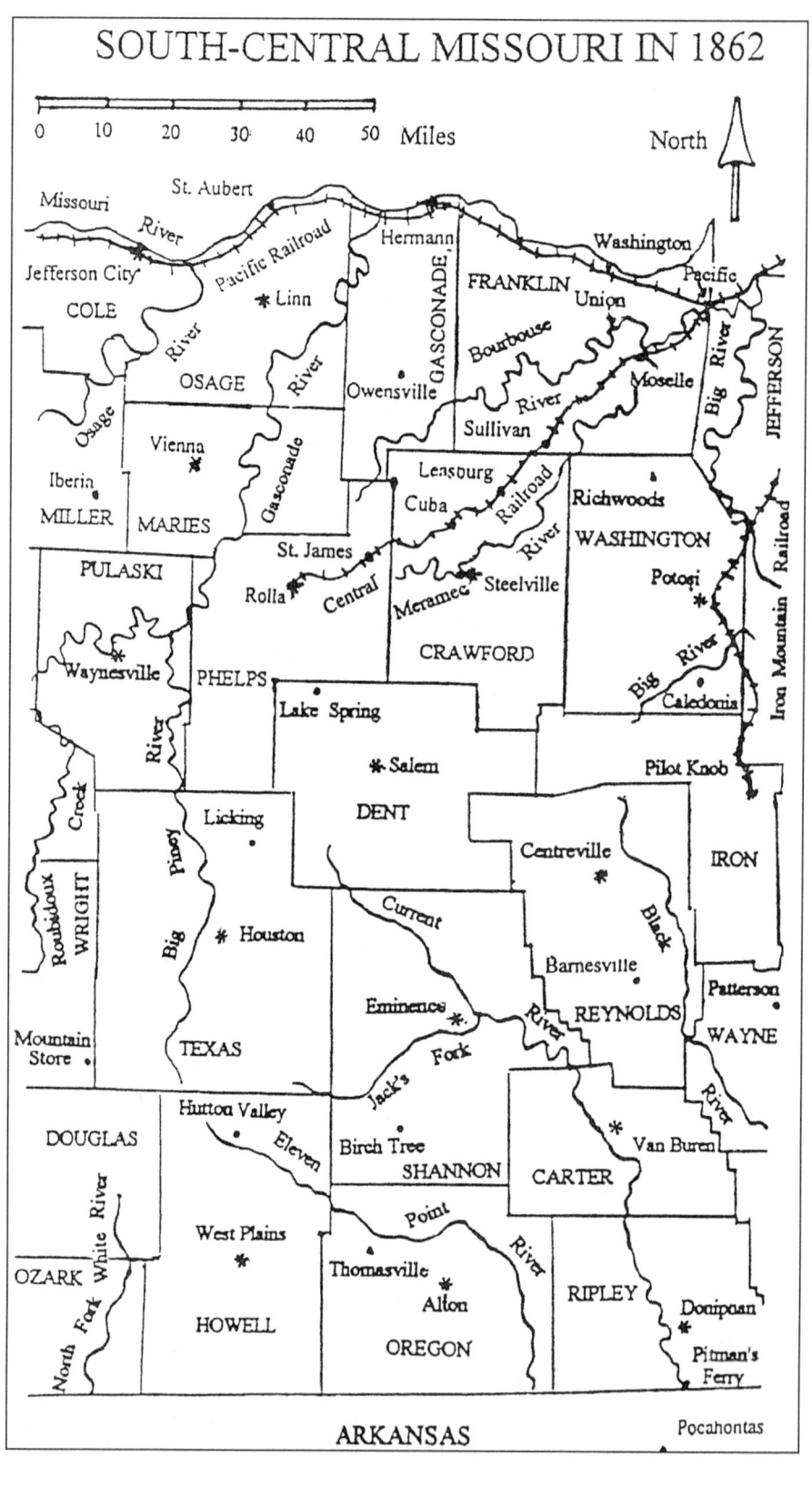

wooded hills of Franklin, Crawford, Phelps, and Pulaski counties, the same route modern-day interstate 44 follows. Then, the Missouri Central Railroad served as the major transportation artery from St. Louis at least as far as its terminus at Rolla in Phelps County. The Federal army transformed Rolla during summer 1861 into a major military base for this reason, and throughout the war guerrilla forces wisely avoided the bastion. A more tempting target was the traffic on the vulnerable wagon road between Rolla and the next major Yankee depot at Springfield, particularly as it was forced to travel through the craggy hills of west Phelps County and Pulaski County. Southern guerrillas flocked to this region throughout the war.

In the January 24 issue of the St. Louis *Daily Missouri Democrat*, a Rolla correspondent mentioned several small actions in Crawford, Phelps, and Pulaski counties involving either small numbers of guerrillas or returning Rebel soldiers.[8] On February 6, 1862, some partisans took horses from citizens around Moselle, east Franklin County. After Union forces captured one of them at the village of Union, they discovered that these were southern men from north of the Missouri River—Boone County, in fact—stealing horses in order to ride south to the Rebel army.[9]

Coleman in South Central Missouri

Colonel William O. Coleman, the former businessman of Rolla, and his force of irregulars doggedly refused to leave the region from Dent County south to the Arkansas border during January and February 1862. Union authorities, skittish about Coleman's intentions against their fragile supply line through the northern Ozark hills, sent what cavalry they had on hand to drive him away. Lt. Colonel Samuel N. Woods's 6th Missouri Cavalry had already fought Coleman during 1861, when they were known as Woods' Kansas Raiders. So, Colonel Coleman must have taken personal satisfaction when, with 25 of his men on January 25, he besieged two of Woods' troopers who had returned for a visit to their Texas County home. The guerrillas wounded one of the cavalrymen during an hour-long siege, and both were about to cave in to Coleman's ultimatum, when some of their comrades rode up and the frustrated southerners skulked away.[10] About February 12, Major William C. Drake's command of two 3rd Iowa Cavalry companies, riding south toward Salem in north Dent County surprised a lot of Rebels, probably Coleman's, at a dance. They captured sixteen.[11] On the night of February 12 near Houston, Texas County, Colonel Coleman's men, hidden in buildings along the road, shot up a Federal detail returning to Rolla from Houston, wounding one man. The Yankees returned to town for help, but their ambushers escaped.[12]

Lt. Colonel Woods's force, including Major Drake's Iowans, took the war to Coleman at his own bases in Texas and Howell counties through winter storms later in February. On the 19th this Union cavalry force rushed into West Plains, peppering the courthouse with howitzer fire, killing six and capturing 60 of William O. Coleman's men at no Federal loss. Woods sent part of his command crashing through the woodlands during February 24 and 25 in south Texas County, capturing 20 more and destroying a makeshift fortress. Woods and Drake reported that Coleman fled to Arkansas with some of his men.[13] He would return, however.

Fighting in the Bootheel

Miles to the east in the lowlands of Missouri's bootheel, other Union forces were striking out at unidentified guerrilla foes in and around Stoddard County. A combined force of 7th Illinois Cavalry and one company of 17th Illinois Infantry conducted a dragnet across Stoddard County about February 6 and 7, capturing 50 Rebels; then on February 8, in the south part of that county, they attacked and routed a large mounted partisan unit, killing seven and wounding many more. The Illinois troops were angered to discover the murdered remains of five local men of northern sympathy. An indignant Union officer at first published an order calling for hanging the same number of Confederate prisoners, but he was overruled by superiors.[14] The leader of the "swamp rats," the only guerrillas in this region the previous month, was Colonel Thompson, so the Rebels mentioned above were probably of his command.

Perhaps it was Colonel Thompson's guerrillas again that stampeded a combined patrol of 200 Federals under Major Robert M. Clendenning of 1st Indiana Cavalry near Mingo Swamp in northwest Stoddard County February 24. Clendenning's command, consisting of elements of his own unit, 12th Cavalry MSM, and 7th Missouri Infantry, had just mounted their horses when an irregular Rebel force estimated at 100–200, surprised and routed them. One of the Yankee officers, Captain William T. Leeper, a local man of the 12th Cavalry MSM, rallied some of his men and conducted a rear guard action while the rest of the Federals shamefully darted away in a panic. The Union loss was one killed, one wounded, and six captured.[15] The

Swampy ground was ideal for hiding guerrillas. (*Battles and Leaders of the Civil War*, 1887–1888, vol. 2, p. 385; courtesy Terry Harmon)

southerners would later regret missing the chance to eliminate Leeper, for he would be a scourge to them in this region for the rest of the war. Ironically, the 1st Indiana Cavalry served only a little bit in action against Missouri guerrillas but hereafter performed gallantly in Arkansas and Louisiana.

By the end of February, Federal authorities claimed to have cleared southeast Missouri of Rebel forces. What they had mostly accomplished was to move them around, a fact which would become obvious in the coming spring. Guerrillas and Rebel recruiters had many friends and places to hide in the region. Union forces were learning the value of cavalry to traverse quickly the wild, tangled countryside, and for the rest of the war what infantry remained was kept to man semi-permanent garrisons at such towns as Rolla, Pilot Knob, Waynesville, New Madrid, and Cape Girardeau.

Four

Winter 1862 in Southwest Missouri

Even winter weather during January and February 1862 seemed to little affect guerrilla warfare in southwest Missouri. The major reason for this was the continued presence of Major General Sterling Price's Missouri southern army which defied the strong Union grip on the state by remaining based in Springfield for a while. Detachments from this command perpetrated partisan warfare in the region while recruiting or scouring the countryside for scarce supplies, and southerners riding in to join the army created excitement in the communities they passed.

Vernon County Excitement During Early January

Miles to the north of the Rebel army Vernon County was rife with both southern recruiting and guerrilla activity. Early in 1862 brothers Brice and Crawford (Crack) Mayfield returned home to southeast Vernon County, ostersibly with a recruiting commission. Instead they began their own year-long private war against the Yankees. Both in their twenties and veterans of Wilson's Creek and Drywood Creek battles during 1861, these two preyed upon small details of Union troops out from Fort Scott, just beyond the Vernon County line in Kansas. Their specialty was capturing horses.[1]

The Mayfield's company commander during the previous year, Kentucky-born Captain James M. Gatewood, also returned from the southern army in early 1862 to recruit another company around home. The presence of the Federal garrison a few miles to the northwest at Fort Scott did not deter him, either.[2]

Another captain of the southern Missouri State Guard during 1861, Tennessee-born Bill Marchbanks of a large northwest–Vernon County farm family, also returned home in January and began raising another company of recruits. Marchbanks was only in his mid-twenties but was also a veteran of the 1861 campaigning. The leadership skills he had developed would enable him during 1863 and 1864 to become the leading guerrilla chief in the area.[3]

Marchbanks' superior during January 1862 was also destined to establish his

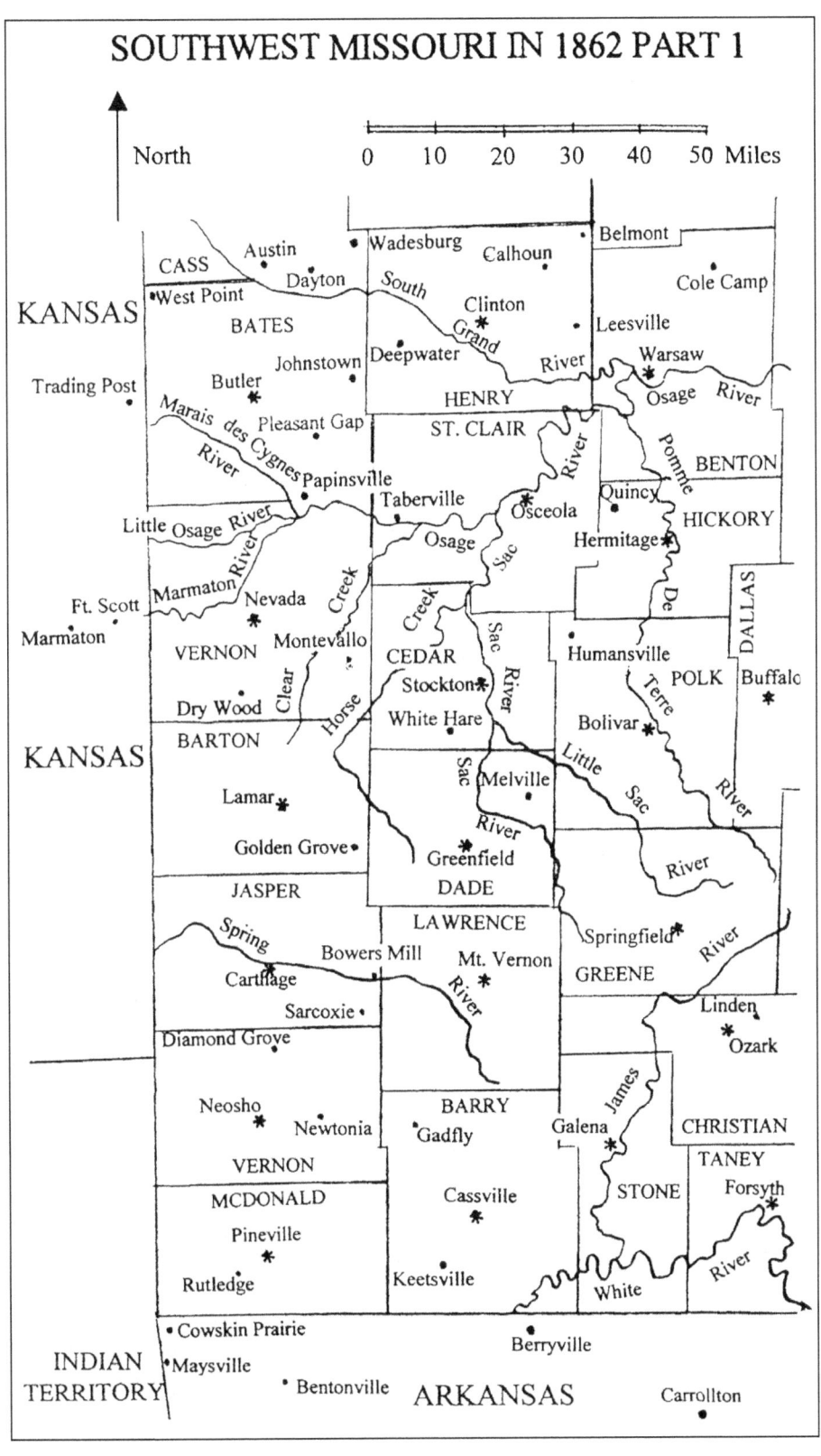

reputation later in the war as a master of partisan warfare. Born in Kentucky, Colonel Sidney Drake Jackman was raised in Howard County in central Missouri, but had moved to the Vernon County area before the war. He had been active in the southern side of the pre-war "bleeding Kansas" troubles, even guiding one of the expeditions. Now in his mid-thirties, Colonel Jackman oversaw Rebel recruiting across Vernon, Bates, and St. Clair counties over several weeks. A local account reports Jackman and Marchbanks defeated Union militia in Bates County during January of 1862.[4]

Another returned Rebel officer, former Vernon County Sheriff William Henry Taylor of Nevada, seemed to be ahead of most of the others. Henry Taylor, as he was called, assembled about 50 irregulars the evening of January 5 and went hunting Yankees. On the state line six miles east of Fort Scott, Taylor's band surprised a six-man guard post of 6th Kansas Cavalry trying to keep warm in a severe winter storm. This was still a civilized war because the guerrillas captured and paroled the Kansans. On the return trip, one of the gang accidentally wounded Captain Taylor in the foot. After all, guerrilla warfare was new in the region and some were still nervous about it and not adept in the handling of firearms.[5]

Guerrilla Actions in the Upper Ozarks

The hill regions of the Osage, Pomme de Terre, and Niangua Rivers, between Springfield and Jefferson City, were the scene for some irregular warfare in early 1862. About January 18, two newly-formed Rebel companies from the Stringtown neighborhood of west Cole County rode south to join the army as many others had before. To obtain their logistical needs, these unidentified southerners raided farms of northern sympathizers on their way, so Union authorities sent a large patrol of 1st Iowa Cavalry from Jefferson City in pursuit. The Iowans caught up to the travelers probably in north Miller County and, although few details remain of the encounter, records show the Yankees brought back seven prisoners and eight horses.[6]

The poorly-equipped southern army had to reach far out into the countryside to fill its supply needs. A commissary raiding party of 90, led by Rebel Captain George M. Swink, robbed the village of Linn Creek, Camden County, of "a few drugs, shawls, and flour sacks" on January 16 and then left.[7] As Union troops entered Lebanon, Laclede County, on January 22, they killed a local Rebel captain and captured a large cache of cut pork that the fleeing Confederates did not have time to transport.[8] On February 1 a patrol of 1st Missouri Cavalry in Dallas County captured 125 cattle that southern drovers were attempting to take to their hungry comrades.[9] At Marshfield in Webster County, blue-clad cavalry on February 9 shot up a small detail of Rebels operating a mill, killing two, wounding three, and capturing three.[10] During the next few days, Sterling Price's Missouri Rebel army retreated under pressure of advancing Union troops and left Missouri.[11] However, many remaining southerners would spend more than three years resisting Federal rule in the "Show Me" state.

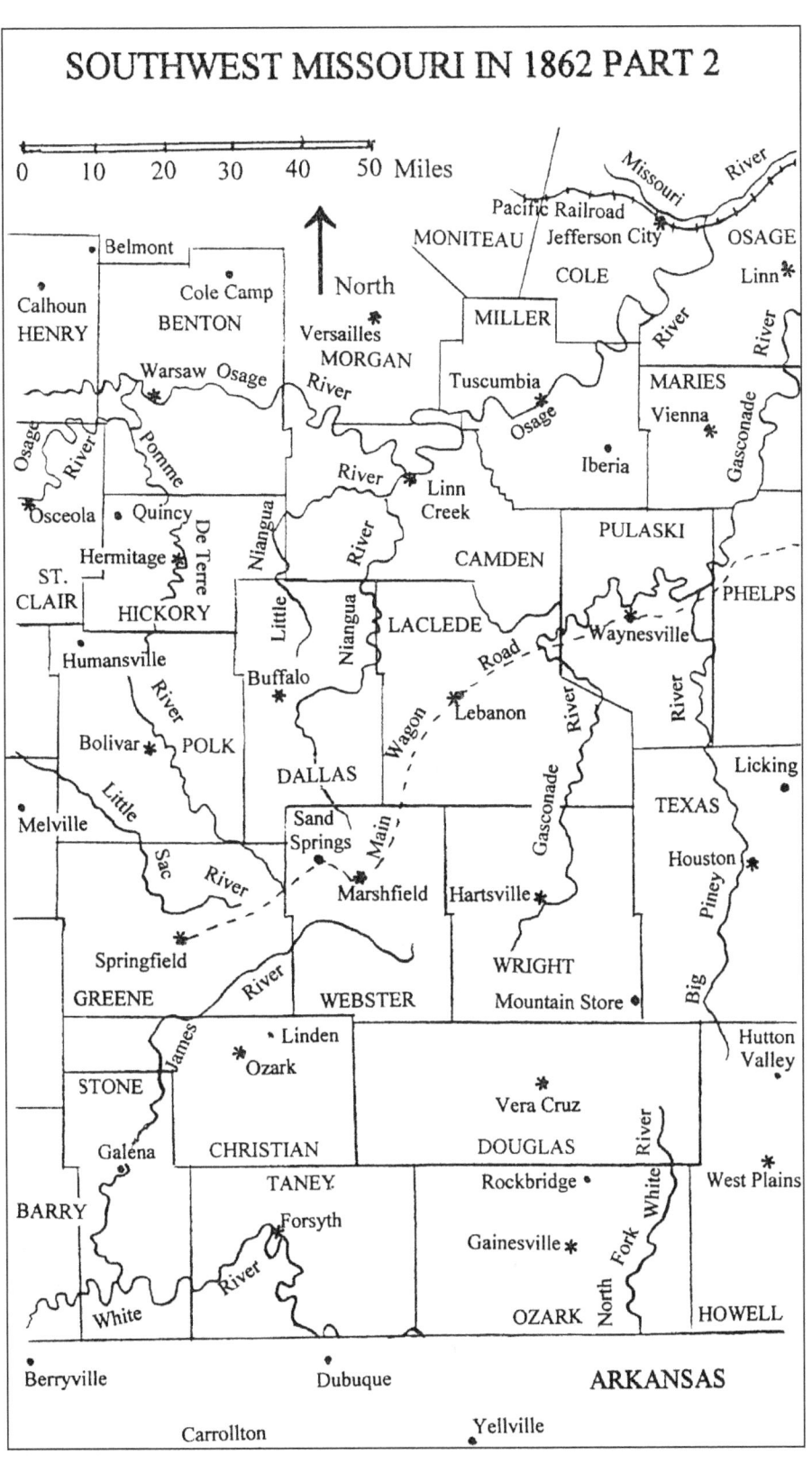

Guerrillas in the Southwest Corner of Missouri

While the Rebel army remained in Springfield, the counties in the far southwest corner of the state—McDonald, Barry, Newton, Jasper, and Lawrence counties—were mostly free of guerrilla actions for obvious reasons. However, local bushwhackers in south-central Jasper County killed a Union sympathizer, Brice Martin, near Jones Creek sometime during January. The frightened neighbors allowed Martin's body to lay until dark before they ventured out to bury it, thinking the guerrillas were lying in wait to claim more victims.[12] In early 1862 local guerrillas near Rutledge, north-central McDonald County, assassinated two of their neighbors. One, Mark Harmon, attempted to hold out behind a tree while shooting back, but the band of 19 picked him off with accurate rifle fire. Local lore states that family and friends of the slain northern sympathizer knew his killers' identities, and throughout the war exacted revenge on these men one by one.[13] Be that as it may, most northerners in this region eventually moved away under such pressure, leaving southern guerrillas few enemies to inform on them to the Union military.

Partisan activity increased after the regular Confederate troops were forced south in February 1862. On February 18 and 19, a patrol of 3rd Iowa Cavalry rode to Mount Vernon, Lawrence County, seeking Rebels bypassed by the Yankee advance. The patrol captured five.[14] Confederate cavalry from Texas, on February 25 or 26, surprised a portion of 6th Missouri Cavalry somewhere in Barry County, capturing over 60 horses and burning five sutler wagons while the chagrined Yankees

Confederate cavalry chasing Union wagons. (*Battles and Leaders of the Civil War*, 1887–1888, vol. 2, p. 501; courtesy Terry Harmon)

retreated to Cassville with losses of two dead, one wounded, and one captured. Evidently, in north Barry County the Texas raiders captured ten more Federals and burned three government wagons before turning back toward Arkansas—their own losses being three killed, several wounded, and one captured.[15]

Sometime in February, pre-war miner and noted brawler Thomas R. Livingston of the mine community in Newton and Jasper counties assembled a guerrilla band of other returned Rebel soldiers. Calling his band the "Cherokee Spikes," Livingston and his men would soon be the most feared and respected bushwhacker band of this region. Late in February they began a reign of terror that would last one-and-one-half years. This time the band abducted four men of northern sympathy in central Lawrence County, beat them, showed them around Mount Vernon to intimidate others, then made the captives kill hogs for the band before releasing them. These men were fortunate, as soon Livingston's band's trademark became the murder of most prisoners.[16]

Also in late February, a Union army report said the highly-respected, former state senator, Colonel John Trousdale Coffee of Dade County, was recruiting Rebels near Pineville, central McDonald County. Coffee was a regular officer of the southern Missouri State Guard, but throughout the war he would recruit and lead his men in partisan actions across southwest Missouri.[17]

Actions Further North During February

Many miles north in Vernon County, local guerrilla chief Henry Taylor was convalescing while his wounded foot healed, but Kansas troopers crossed over the border and killed one of his band—a brother-in-law of the Mayfield brothers mentioned earlier. At times, this was indeed a personal war.[18]

The war also became more personal to Missouri's stalwart Rebel General Sterling Price on February 16 when a combined force of 1st Iowa Cavalry, 8th Iowa Infantry, and 1st Missouri Light Artillery, raiding south from Pettis County, captured four rebel officers in Warsaw, Benton County. Among these was Price's son, Brigadier General Edwin "Stump" Price, caught resting at a Warsaw judge's home while leading a band of mid–Missouri recruits south to his dad's army. Ironically, Edwin Price's men managed to escape from this force.[19] A Yankee patrol from Hickory County captured eight more southerners the following day in the area, probably from Edwin Price's fleeing recruits.[20] The Iowans and Missourians who caught Price during February 25, 26, and 27 paid an unfriendly call on the village of Leesville, east Henry County, to stop southern men of that hamlet from marauding among their neighbors of northern sympathy. The Union force surrounded the village, arrested all men alleged to be disloyal, 16 in all, and took them back to Pettis County.[21]

Meanwhile, Captain Gatewood's guerrilla band was still active in Vernon County. At daybreak on February 27, near Little Drywood Creek, they attacked Lieutenant Reese J. Lewis's squad of 6th Kansas Cavalry sleeping inside Ewell Riggs's house. The Rebels blasted the groggy Kansans at close range wounding nine before the Yankees returned fire with their superior Sharps carbines and eventually drove off Gatewood's men. The following day, fifty of the Kansans' comrades

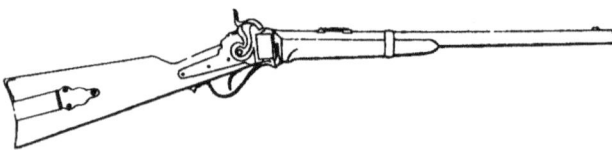

Sharps carbines were the favored shoulder weapon for cavalry on both sides of the conflict in Missouri. (*Atlas to Accompany the Official Records of the Union and Confederate Armies*, 1891–1895, plate 173)

tried in vain to find and punish Gatewood's band, while the Rebels themselves maneuvered without success to ambush the vengeful cavalry. This was Gatewood's last act of the war, as he mortally wounded himself by accident that very night. The Kansans vented their frustration by killing a man and his older son in the neighborhood, according to local records. Even though James Gatewood was now out of the war and Henry Taylor still recuperating, other guerrilla leaders and bands nearby promised an exciting spring to come.[22]

FIVE

Why Guerrillas?

Why did so many southern men take to the brush and fight as guerrillas? Why did so many rise up against an organized and equipped Federal occupying force, hundreds of miles away from the help of southern regular troops? What motivated many of these desperate men to fight for four and more years in a hopeless struggle hardly encouraged or even recognized by Confederate authorities? Many of these men and their contemporaries give answers that derive from five primary motivations—bitterness, anger, hope, desperation, and the seeking of excitement.

Bitterness

In May 1862 the Union Department of the Missouri chief, Major General John M. Schofield, wisely noted that much of Missouri's struggle resulted from "...the bitter feeling between the border people, which feeling is the result of old feuds, and involves very little, if at all, the question of Union or disunion...."[1] Indeed, during the previous August, future Army of the Potomac chief, Brigadier General John Pope wrote of northeast Missouri: "...the people in that region are merely fighting with each other in many cases to satisfy feelings of personal hostility of long standing...."[2] A railroad official of that same region also wrote: "...these men are exceedingly bitter in their feelings of hostility, and have been led on until many of them are fit for any deed...."[3]

Quite a few of the guerrillas faced some personal depredation or atrocity directed against themselves, their family, or community by neighbors of northern sympathy, marauding Kansas jayhawkers, or ill-disciplined Union troops. The most feared of all Missouri bushwhackers, "Bloody Bill" Anderson, wrote in 1864 to explain, "I have chosen guerrilla warfare to revenge myself for wrongs that I could not honorably avenge otherwise...," partially referring to his imprisoned sisters—victims of a Kansas City prison collapse that killed one and maimed another.[4]

One of Quantrill's men, Harrison Trow, addressed this motive directly: "Others came who had deadly wrongs to avenge, and these gave to all their combats that sanguinary hue which still remains a part of the Guerrilla's legacy. Almost from the first a large majority of Quantrill's original command had over them the shadow

Many southern men became guerrillas to avenge some wrong done to themselves, relatives, or friends. (*Autobiography of Samuel S. Hildebrand, the Renowned Missouri "Bushwacker,"* 1870; courtesy Bob and Mary Younger and Andy Turner)

of some terrible command. This one recalled a father murdered, this one a brother waylaid and shot, this one a house pillaged and burned, this one a relative assassinated, this one a grievous insult while at peace at home, this one a robbery of all his earthly possessions ... while all had more or less of wrath laid up against the day when they were to meet, face to face and hand to hand, those whom they had good cause to regard as the living embodiment of unnumbered wrongs. Honorable soldiers in the Confederate army—amenable to every generous impulse and exact in the performance of every manly duty—deserted even the ranks which they had adorned and became desperate Guerrillas because the home they had left had been given to the flames, or a gray-haired father shot upon his own hearthstone.... Every other passion became subsidiary to that of revenge. They sought personal encounters that their own handiwork might become unmistakably manifest.... As this class of Guerrilla increased, the warfare of the border became necessarily more cruel and unsparing...."[5]

Anger

Many southerners were compelled to join regular or guerrilla ranks not because of personal vendetta but due to general anger against tyranny real or imaginary. Some catalysts for this anger included the following:

- The suspension of civil rights;
- The occupation of Missouri by tens of thousands of Yankee troops in 1861 without an official mandate;
- The extremism of abolitionists and the emotional issue of freeing the slaves;

- The ruthless Kansas jayhawker raids on Missouri communities;
- Major General National Lyon's allegedly unprovoked seizure of the southern Missouri State Guard at Camp Jackson, St. Louis, in May 1861 and the street violence that followed;
- The use of thousands of recent German immigrants in St. Louis as Union troops and the depredations by some of them on duty in Missouri;
- Sensational southern press in Missouri and the squelching of it by Union authorities; and
- Harsh northern military measures such as the draft, impressing private property for military use, recruiting black men, control of all traffic on waterways, enrollment of all men of military age into the Enrolled Missouri Militia, foraging, enforcement of civil law by U.S. Army provost marshals, and the like.

Many of these measures and events, and others not listed, are regrettable and represent the acts of lawless or ill-disciplined men. Major General Henry W. Halleck in December 1861, complaining about the jayhawker incursions into Missouri, admitted "...the conduct of the forces under Lane [Kansas Senator James Lane] and Jennison has done more for the enemy in this State than could have been accomplished by 20,000 of his own army...."[6] Some can be defended as necessary by a government struggling to put down a civil insurrection. Some are bald-faced errors. Most were exaggerated by southern "fire-eaters" or extremists to a confused public. Calm, deliberate reason seemed to belong to a bygone era, but nothing is more unreasonable or emotional than a nation working against itself.

The call to oppose tyranny was strong to southern people and a large portion of Missouri people had been born in southern states. Many southern men in this state bore the name "Francis Marion" after the "Swamp Fox" of the Carolinas during the Revolution. Marion's brand of guerrilla warfare against the cruel British military was a popular part of southern tradition to people of the 1860s. Missouri's southern army commander and popular former governor, Sterling Price, brought this to mind in November 1861 and April 1862 in his proclamations to Missouri southern men. He referred to the following:

- "...struggling with the most causeless and cruel despotism known among civilized men...";
- "...a Federal hireling in the State to pollute our soil...";
- "...subjection to a despot...";
- "...to win our glorious inheritance from the cruel hand of the spoiler and the oppressor...";
- "...the insolent and barbarous hordes which have dared to invade our soil and to desecrate our homes..."[7]

These patriotic themes from such a respected notable appealed to many.

Hope

Akin to the southern call to fight oppression was the persistent hope that if southern men resisted the Yankee military in Missouri, they might open the door

Frequent foraging by Union troops did not endear them to victimized Missouri farm families. (*The Soldier in Our Civil War*, 1890, vol. 1, p. 163; courtesy Terry Harmon)

for some kind of Confederate victory if the Federals were careless. Sadly for the Union side, Yankee carelessness in Missouri seemed constant, and this served to encourage secessionists. With the passing of 1861, the tide of war moved away from the "Show Me" state and so did most troops, forcing Union authorities to create militias of various kinds and sometimes of dubious value. Most of the brightest Yankee leadership moved on, too, leaving behind many "hacks," narrow-minded, and prone to bickering. Northern thinking seemed to be that Missouri had been won and only "police" actions were necessary. Occasional guerrilla activity would be a nuisance but would provide some sport to drive away boredom. Another Union general moaned to one of his commanders during August of 1864, "...why should all the cunning and enterprise be on one side and that the wrong side?"[8]

A goodly proportion of the men and leaders of the Confederate Trans-Mississippi Department were Missourians and kept alive through most of the war the hope that they could some day liberate their home state. The Confederate military in Richmond had already sanctioned partisan rangers or guerrillas earlier, when Rebel Trans-Mississippi Department chief Major General Theophilus Holmes wrote to his enemy counterpart in the region October 11, 1862: "...we cannot be expected to allow our enemies to decide for us whether we shall fight them in masses or individually, in uniform, without uniform, openly or from ambush. Our forefathers and yours conceded no such right to the British in the first Revolution...."[9]

Accordingly, Holmes' antecedent, Major General Thomas C. Hindman, had ordered on June 17, 1862: "I. For the more effectual annoyance of the enemy upon our rivers and in our mountains and woods all citizens of this district who are not subject to conscription are called upon to organize themselves into independent companies...arming and equipping themselves, and to serve in that part of the district to which they belong.

"II. When as many as 10 men come together for this purpose they may organize by electing a captain...and will at once commence operations against the enemy without waiting for special instructions. Their duty will be to cut off Federal pickets, scouts, foraging parties, and trains, and to kill pilots and others on gunboats and transports, attacking them day and night, and using the greatest vigor in their movement....

"III. These companies will be governed in all respects by the same regulations as other troops. Captains will be held responsible for the good conduct and efficiency of their men, and will report to these headquarters from time to time."[10]

This approval of the guerrillas made them part of the overall effort and not mere outlaws or brigands, as many Union leaders considered them. In fact, as the partisan war progressed, actual Rebel recruiters sought and obtained assistance from many bushwhacker bands and noted Confederate commanders, such as Brigadier General Joseph Shelby, Colonel Meriwether Jeff Thompson, Colonel John T. Coffee, Colonel Joseph Porter, and others who had been guerrilla leaders themselves and operated in concert with partisans. One enlightened Federal colonel wrote his superiors in 1864 "...these guerrillas beyond all question are recognized by and are in constant communications with the trans-Mississippi rebel army...."[11] A newspaper correspondent to the St. Louis *Daily Missouri Democrat* scoffed in January 1862 that "some deluded rebels have faith in the 'second advent' of Price's victories...," but this was a constant source of hope to southerners and threat to northerners for most of the war, until Price brought his army back into Missouri in fall 1864.[12] When this came to pass, Missouri's Federal commander at the time received reports that southern women threatened their neighboring northern counterparts with statements like "...their time was now coming...."[13] This hope, bolstered by guerrilla daring, kept Missouri's ultimate fate a matter of speculation.

Desperation

Sadly, many men found themselves in guerrilla bands through desperation or the reality of having no real choice in the matter. In southeast Missouri, guerrilla chiefs like the Reverend Tim Reeves conscripted local able-bodied men into partisan service under actual threat of death. Many men left the southern Missouri State Guard in 1861 or after disillusionment with the secessionist cause, only to find they were marked at home by eager informants and beset upon by heavy-handed militia eager to call any suspect one of their elusive enemies, the guerrillas. These poor men sadly realized they were marked "Rebel" for good and if moving out was not an option (much of Missouri's population left during the horrors of war for greener pastures out west or elsewhere) at least found better treatment with the bushwhackers. Guerrillas had informants, too, and neutrals soon realized local partisans were a greater threat than often distant Union patrols. A Yankee district chief, Brigadier General Thomas Ewing Jr., confided to his boss during August 1862: "About one-half of the farmers in the border tier of counties of Missouri in my district, at different times since the war began, entered the rebel service. One half of them are dead or still in the service; the other half, quitting from time to time the rebel armies, have returned to those counties. Unable to live at their homes if they would, they have gone to bushwhacking, and have driven almost all avowed unionists out of the county or to the military stations...."[14] The draft also forced more men choose one side over the other, and during the summer of 1862 the well-organized effort to enroll all military age men into the Union militia fooled no one. It was really an effort to "separate the sheep from the goats." This clearly illustrated to all that neutrality was no longer a viable option.

Excitement

It seems ironic amid the bitterness, anger, and desperation of guerrilla war and the patriotism and hope of each side that some men became bushwhackers just for the thrill of it, but that is also true. There are always young men seeking adventure, and there were many in this border state on the frontier's edge who were already considered renegades against the law and against the niceties of civilized folks. The excitement of guerrilla fighting offered a great attraction to these, too. Quantrill's man, Harrison Trow, noted this in his postwar memoirs: "As strange as it may seem, the perilous fascination of fight under a black flag-where the wounded could have neither surgeon nor hospital, and where all that remained to the prisoners was the absolute certainty of speedy death—attracted a number of young men to the various Guerrilla bands, gently nurtured, born to higher destinies, capable of sustaining exertions in any scheme or enterprise, and fit for callings high up in the scale of science or philosophy...."[15] After all, even Missouri's southern military head, General Sterling Price, once referred to Quantrill's band as men of "that daring and dashing character...."[16]

Quantrill himself, from Ohio and not a southerner, was more of a soldier of fortune—playing both sides in the Missouri-Kansas border troubles pre-war. He seemed to be looking for a noble, daring cause to join. His able lieutenant, Canadian-born stone mason George Todd, hardly fits the profile of outraged southerner, either. Another lieutenant, the mysterious Andy Blunt, never revealed his true identity or name to fellow guerrillas and may have been a Kansas judge's son. Charles Harrison was a gambler and gunman in Colorado Territory and seems to have been a Yankee lieutenant in the Kansas cavalry before he was caught stealing horses and turned guerrilla in west central Missouri. Harrison later convinced someone to make him a Confederate colonel. Benjamin F. Parker was a Kansas City hotel clerk of northern birth, but turned bushwhacker, leading his own guerrilla band in west-central Missouri.[17] Clay County's Ferdinando Scott was a Liberty saddler born in Ohio, but he became a noted guerrilla chief, at one time leading future outlaw Frank James.[18] During 1861, New York-born Francis O. Gray wrote notes to the Union commander at Rolla, daring that officer to catch him. He later recruited rebels in Wayne County.[19] Rambunctious miner Thomas R. Livingston from the lead mines of Newton and Jasper counties, seemed to waiver in mid–1861 and even gave a pro-northern speech. Later, the Rebel cause seemed more to his liking and he became one of the most dreaded guerrilla chiefs of southwest Missouri.[20]

Six

Operating Deep Behind Enemy Lines

No Quarter

Southern partisans in Missouri had an advantage over their foes in that they readily knew what they must do to survive and also attack the Federal hold on the state. Nothing in their experience and training had prepared Union authorities to deal with a civil war. The main example remembered from their West Point studies was Napoleon's brutal treatment of the partisans he encountered. This may have been the background for Major General Henry W. Halleck's General Order Number Two on March 13, 1862, requiring Union leaders to shoot captured guerrillas on the spot as outlaws.[1]

Previously, southern irregulars had paroled and released captives, while their foes had sent theirs to prison where they were exchanged some weeks later like regular troops. Exchanging meant that, by mutual agreement, each side released prisoners, who would afterward be free to be combatants again. What Halleck's order meant was immediate death to those partisans caught in arms, while suspected partisans faced imprisonment and eventual military tribunal at the convenience of the Union command. This harsh move also tended to end chivalry in this portion of the war, for this "no prisoners" policy was of course reciprocated by guerrillas.

Every skirmish became a life-and-death struggle, and survivors became revenge-seekers. Colonel Fitz-Henry Warren of the 1st Iowa Cavalry referred to his regiment's experience fighting bushwhackers as "...a war of extermination..." with "...no half-way house and no neutral position...." "We are to be driven out and annihilated or they are...."[2] The "no quarter" practice applied between citizens and guerrillas, as well. To survive, bushwhackers could not tolerate informants in their operating areas, and so were ruthless driving them out or silencing them for good. Such savagery also convinced others not to cross local partisans. Any understanding of guerrilla warfare in Civil War Missouri must take into account this ruthless, desperate aspect of the fighting there.

All the Advantages

Missouri guerrillas gave themselves advantages that the Union military did not have. Guerrilla operations were by their very nature offensive, while the north's strategic objectives for Missouri had to be defensive. That is, Union strategy for Missouri was to defend it as a vital link to the West, while controlling the southern part of its population in order to prevent it from becoming a Rebel enclave. For example, the Yankees devoted much of their force to defending Missouri railroads, river ports, and shipment centers—especially St. Louis. Thus, the criticism arose "...that the guerrillas held the country and the troops the town...."[3] Partisan rangers also enjoyed the advantage of being able to concentrate offensive combat power at a time and place of their choosing. They even combined different bands for short periods of time for the maximum effect—as was done in the terrible Lawrence, Kansas, raid of August 1863. Federals often tried to concentrate troops to swoop in on guerrilla sanctuaries, only to find their foes had escaped the trap because of better mobility and a superior intelligence network. Speaking of mobility, Missouri's irregulars usually kept that advantage, too, as long as they stayed away from the Union-controlled railroads. As one of their enemies, Colonel John F. Williams of the 9th Cavalry MSM, aptly put it in 1864, the guerrillas "...ride the best horses in the country, and when pursued take to the brush and soon disappear...."[4] This was a often repeated truism, for Union forces were mounted on government-issued nags often worn down by constant patrolling over long distances. They simply could not keep up in a running fight.[5] The more successful and longest-lived guerrilla bands enjoyed the security of knowing more about their enemy and enemy operations than the Union troops knew about them. They used terror to drive out of their sanctuaries citizens who could be a threat to them as informers, and southern families there gladly kept watch for

Union Major General Henry W. Halleck seems to be the originator of the "no quarter" rule in Missouri guerrilla warfare. (*The Soldier in Our Civil War*, 1890, vol. 1, p. 243; courtesy Terry Harmon)

Yankee patrols. A small number of southern sympathizers easily watched over garrison towns and reported to partisans the comings and goings of the U.S. forces tied to such bases. Union army reports from Missouri repeatedly erred in identifying guerrilla chiefs and usually had no clue who led the enemy they faced in the field. Naturally, bushwhackers, holding the advantages of superior mobility and intelligence, could also enjoy the advantage of surprise over and over again. Generally speaking, guerrillas developed confidence over time, while Union troops developed frustration. These advantages enabled hundreds of Missouri irregulars to continue their operations against an enemy vastly superior in numbers and logistics for four long years.

Guerrilla Tactics

If the guerrilla strategy was to challenge Union control of the state and maybe even to seize it back, how did they fight to accomplish these aims? Just to say partisan rangers had to perfect hit-and-run tactics leaves much unsaid.

Missouri's southern guerrillas, almost from the start, operated exclusively as cavalry. The horse enabled bushwhackers to move toward or away from their enemies over Missouri's combination of rolling woodlands, farmlands, and prairie. The shock and speed of mounted operations was an advantage that guerrillas had to have to succeed as well as to survive. Indeed, after the first months of the war, Union military authorities concluded that their infantry was limited to roles of guarding installations, railroads, bridges, etc., and that only cavalry could beat cavalry.[6] Guerrilla and postwar train-robber Frank James even observed that in George Todd's guerrilla band—formerly Quantrill's—the preferred fighting stance was on horseback, so as to take advantage of sudden turns of events during a firefight to either pursue or flee.[7]

Since bushwhackers and Rebel recruiters operated hundreds of miles behind Union lines, often in the vicinity of hundreds of alert Federal soldiers, they had to pick their fights carefully. Yet, to attract recruits and keep morale high, these irregular commanders had to attack their enemy. Besides, capturing Yankee horses, armaments, uniforms, etc. was the best means to obtain such necessary items. By their very nature, then, southern irregulars relied on offensive tactics.

The favorite partisan tactic was the ambush. A properly prepared ambush tended to maximize victim casualties while minimizing attacker losses. Besides, once sufficient firepower drove away survivors, the guerrillas could quickly snatch up enemy horses, firearms, ammunition, clothing, bedding, and the like, before riding away from the inevitable pursuit. After all, men fleeing for their lives do tend to lose such things, as the bushwhackers knew full well from occasions when it was their turn to flee. Quantrill's men commonly used a few of their more daring members as decoys to draw gullible Union patrols to a prepared killing ground. Since the Union units were rotated every few weeks, especially in 1862, Quantrill's band even used the same ambush sites over again with impunity. Their preferred killing ground was a road cut, stream crossing, or ravine, where they could use their short-range but rapid-fire revolvers with maximum effect. For this reason, Federal cavalry learned to appreciate open country.

Battlefield acquisition. (*Battles and Leaders of the Civil War*, 1887–1888, vol 4. p. 195)

Another common guerrilla tactic was the raid on a town, garrison, or farmstead. If surprise was assured, raids served irregulars well both to assert their potency through intimidation and to obtain needed supplies. Successful town raiders like Clifton D. Holtzclaw, "Bloody Bill" Anderson, and George Todd developed the practice of gathering the men of the town to harangue them and look for known enemies while the rest of the band looted stores and residences. Astute guerrilla leaders would even forbid the robbing of southern sympathizers' property, to ensure continued goodwill and to convince by contrast other civilians of the fruitlessness of supporting a cause that could not protect them. The southerners in some raided towns like Versailles, Morgan County, and Keytesville, Chariton County, even celebrated the guerrillas' advent. Even the best pre-raid scouting could not predict how the local Union garrison would react to a bushwhacker raid. Some precipitously ran or meekly surrendered if promised quarter, giving the guerrilla band a great victory. Others would "fort up," making every shot count, and take a fearsome toll on the attacking raiders, frustrating southern hopes for the raid. Confederate recruiters, such as Colonel Joseph Porter, found town raids to be the most efficient method of supplying necessary material to large numbers of new recruits. Of course, local southerners supplied much of southern irregulars' needs, but taking food, bedding, horses, clothing, and the like from enemies or those sympathizing with enemies gave great personal satisfaction to partisan leaders. It also encouraged others to join. The Union command, though, unschooled in partisan warfare, could not always appreciate the psychological victory that taking supplies

Southern horsemen raiding a town. (*The Soldier in Our Civil War*, 1890, vol. 2, p. 301; courtesy Terry Harmon)

in this manner gave the irregulars, and referred to the opposition as brigands or bandits. They did not consider southern partisans in Missouri as fellow soldiers— even the recruiting commands led by commissioned Confederate colonels and their staffs—but as outlaws. Hence, they were less inclined to give clemency.

Many skirmishes were mere chance encounters where opposing sides exchanged quick shots and "skedaddled," but when one side had an advantage in numbers, firepower, or nerve, a running fight would ensue. Some of these went on for miles. Of course, having superior mounts gave guerrillas a decided advantage in such chases. The standard and logical tactic for the quarry, when it could not outrun the pursuer, was to disperse or scatter. Wise guerrilla chiefs always designated in advance a rendezvous point in case of a quick dispersal.[8] When a Union patrol had to scatter to save their lives, the troopers always knew to get back to their post or garrison as best they could. Guerrilla Harrison Trow quoted Quantrill as saying, "...scattered soldiers make a scattered trail. The regiment that has but one man to hunt can never find him...."[9] One Union general complained to another: "The guerrillas have no line of retreat to cut off. They scatter when attacked, each man taking a separate route, meeting at some agreed point 20 miles off in four hours. Our troops understand this warfare, are full of zeal, are brave, and energetic, but

A running fight. (*Century Magazine*, 1887, vol. 32, p. 137; courtesy Terry Harmon)

it is an intangible warfare."[10] One Yankee trooper had this to say: "...they've all scattered but one man and there's no use following him, for he'll scatter like the rest of 'em...."[11]

Weapons

In the early months of the war guerrilla operations were rather a "come as you are" affair. Partisans brought to the arena the weapons they had at home—shotguns, hunting pieces, granddad's flintlock, self-defense pistols, knives, etc. Not that the Yankees were blessed with fantastic firepower, either. From start to finish Missouri was a "backwater" region compared to the total war effort, so Union troops fighting guerrillas were only partially armed and often with "leavings," at that. Companies, even of state troops, were issued only sabers or pistols or muskets. It is a tribute to the dedication of the men of both sides that they persevered, armed as indifferently as they were. Some Union patrols picked up southern weapons after a firefight that were so inferior to even the junk they were carrying that they broke them up on the spot. This situation changed gradually.

Artillery saw little use in Missouri's guerrilla war. Both the fast-paced cavalry-dominated tactics and Missouri's isolation and status as an "occupied" state contributed to this fact. Many of the major Federal posts, such as Rolla, Ft. Scott, New Madrid, and Springfield, had cannon, but primarily for defense against raids by Confederate regulars. Much of this ordnance was ill-suited to being dragged around in the brush.

Some guerrilla actions featured artillery, though. Before Lafayette County's Jo Shelby rose in Confederate ranks to become a general, he operated as a guerrilla chief with his own artillery. On the evening of December 10, 1861, he fired his one mortar and one cannon at the night camp of a 2nd Missouri Cavalry patrol near Grand Pass, northwest Saline County. No one was harmed, but the perturbed troopers later captured the mortar and noted that Shelby's cannon had burst.[12] In late May of the next year, Cole's Battery E of 1st Missouri Light Artillery returned the favor near the same location by shelling a suspected guerrilla hideout on a Missouri River island.[13] On the morning of July 26, 1862, Battery L of the same regiment, as part of a larger force, sprayed Colonel William O. Coleman's camp of 300 partisans in or near Texas County with canister fire. This shelling contributed to Rebel losses of eight killed, 20 wounded, and 17 captured.[14] This is not to say that irregulars never triumphed over Federal artillery. During September of 1862, Colonel H. E. Clark and 20 of his new recruits, or guerrillas, masqueraded as Union militia to gain entrance to the Yankee post at Bloomfield, Stoddard County. Once inside, they killed six startled soldiers and took away a brass 24-pounder. Having such a trophy undoubtedly contributed to Clark's success as a recruiter.[15] Other examples exist of artillery being used in guerrilla warfare, but they are mostly one-sided affairs where combined Yankee forces fired small, portable cannon at distant guerrillas who always wisely fled.

Edged weapons, such as sabers, bayonets, knives, etc., did not play a large role in guerrilla actions, either. Although bushwhackers often preferred close-in fighting, they seemed to feel knife range was too close. They commonly carried knives, but primarily for self-defense or camp-craft. Both sides found swords, pikes, and sabers too cumbersome in Missouri's vast brush and woodlands, even though they were fearsome looking when among friends and admirers. Missouri's head of militia, Brigadier General John M. Schofield, confided to another officer in April 1862, "...our men have no more use for a saber than for a columbiad, and yet all clamorous to get them...."[16] Unfortunately for them, some units, such as parts of 1st and 3rd Iowa Cavalry and 9th Kansas Cavalry, were sent into Missouri operations for a time armed only with sabers or with sabers and pistols.[17] Of course, to officers of both sides swords were symbols of their authority. During early September 1863, Rebel recruiter Colonel Caleb Dorsey unabashedly wore his to church in Pike County in spite of several nearby Union units who had been trying to capture him for months. They didn't get him, and such "cheek" undoubtedly helped make Dorsey a very successful recruiter.

Both sides used shoulder weapons a great deal. Union militia was commonly armed with rifle muskets, and some partisans had them, too, but their cumbersome reloading and slow rate of fire was a decided disadvantage in fast-paced horseback actions. Some Union cavalry in Missouri were issued Colt's revolving rifle, which gave them more firepower, and some partisans had them, too. Shotguns were common, as they had been in peacetime, and many guerrillas and some local militia liked them in brush fighting. The Yankee issue shoulder weapon of choice was the carbine, which was easier to wield on horseback than rifles or muskets. Their range was shorter, but guerrillas seldom presented themselves as long-range targets for long, and on horseback long-range targets were wishful thinking anyway. The breechloaders were particularly popular when available, and Sharps breechloaders were plentiful in Missouri as a result of the "bleeding Kansas" border warfare of the 1850's.

The preferred guerrilla weapon in the woods and brush of Missouri was the handgun—particularly the revolver, and most Union cavalrymen were issued one,

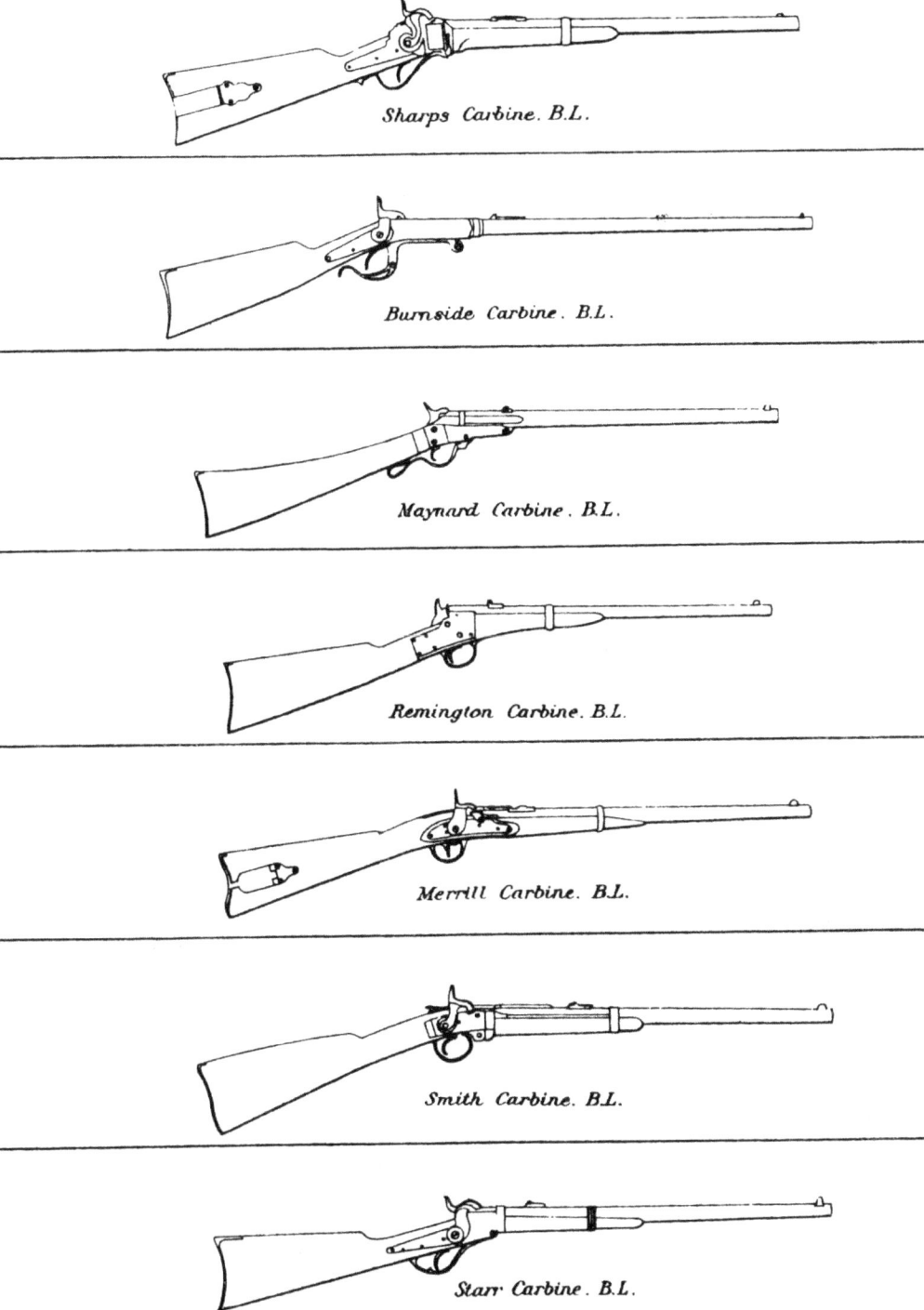

A selection of some Civil War carbines. (*Atlas to Accompany the Official Records of the Union and Confederate Armies*, 1891–1895, plate 173)

Colt Navy .36 caliber revolver. (Unidentified print; courtesy Terry Harmon)

too. The revolver's maneuverability and rapid rate of fire made it a staple for this kind of hit-and-run fighting. A practiced marksman could hit his target shooting a revolver from a moving horse and have the ability to keep shooting—something most shoulder arms could not do. Since Union cavalry had them, too, obtaining pistols by battlefield acquisition was common for partisans, as it was for many other things. Many varieties were used in Missouri either in the heavier .44 caliber, called the "Army" model by many manufacturers or the lighter .36 caliber, called the "Navy" model, but Colt seemed to be the favorite brand.

Experienced brush fighters of both sides carried the heavier pistols in holsters strapped to their horse and wore the lighter two-and-one-half-pound "Navy" models on their person. Some, like Quantrill's or "Bloody Bill" Anderson's bands, carried up to six or even eight fully-loaded revolvers on their person and horse, in order to issue forth a withering rate of fire in a sudden action. Some had so many they would discard one occasionally when empty, and some even carried pre-loaded cylinders in their pockets for fast reloading. In some instances guerrillas fleeing on foot would discard all but one of these to facilitate an escape. Union reports of skirmishes with these "human arsenals" would give astonishing reports of troopers recovering numerous pistols from the scene of a fight with only a few partisans, or finding the dead body of a bushwhacker festooned with revolvers. Such exploits in Missouri guerrilla warfare seems to have propelled the popularity of handguns in general and helped to lead to their proliferation in the settlement of the West that followed, as well as in American folklore.

Colt Army .44 caliber revolver. (Unidentified print, courtesy Terry Harmon)

Uniforms

The uniforms combatants wore in Missouri's guerrilla warfare were not the same as in other theaters of the war. Of course, the relaxed discipline of Yankee occupation troops in such a remote part of the war meant uniform regulations were not strictly observed. Some militiamen could only be identified as such by a badge or other symbol in their civilian hats, or by their government-issue firearms. Guerrillas or irregulars seemed to have three distinctive modes of dress.

Confederate recruiters, particularly, often wore Rebel uniforms, even way behind enemy lines in Missouri. Wearing a recognizable uniform and carrying papers authorizing them to recruit for southern forces kept many southerners from being shot as spies or guerrillas upon capture. Also, the bravado of wearing a Rebel uniform miles behind enemy lines won for recruiters the awe and respect of the southern men they sought.

Partisans mostly wore civilian attire, since this was mostly a come-as-you-are style of fighting. Some even fashioned a uniform of sorts from hunting shirts— already popular in the Missouri of the 1860's. The rakish hunting shirt, a collarless, decorated, casual shirt with several pockets, was already traditional in some parts of the South. Mothers, wives, and sweethearts embroidered such shirts for their men and also festooned them with beadwork and metal decorations, such as hearts, crescents, stars, particularly in the established bands, such as Quantrill's and "Bloody Bill" Anderson's. Along with a plumed hat, fancy saddle and bridle, long

There was little uniformity in the uniforms worn on both sides of the conflict in Missouri. (Drawing by Edwin Forbes, *The Soldier in Our Civil War*, 1890, vol. 2, pp. 302–3; courtesy Terry Harmon)

hair, and multiple revolvers, this attire contributed to the dashing, devil-may-care image so necessary for morale of men fighting a desperate war so far behind enemy lines.[19] On the other hand, some guerrillas wore civilian clothing so as to blend in with the peaceful civilian population.

Partisans occasionally used a third type of uniform for more diabolical reasons—the uniform of their enemy. When travelling outside their sanctuary regions, away from residents of known sympathy, guerrilla bands found passing themselves as Yankees tended to avoid suspicion. This was also an effective disguise to obtain information and to get close enough to attack unwary enemies.

Sanctuaries

Established bushwhacker bands learned that to survive they had to live and mostly operate in regions where they could be protected and succored by citizens sympathetic to their cause. Along Missouri's western edge, Kansas jayhawker raids preyed upon people of all sympathies early in the war and created a populace antagonistic toward the Federal government, which failed to stop the raids. This led to popular support enjoyed by such long-lived bands as Bill Quantrill's, Bill Marchbanks's, Benjamin Parker's, John Thrailkill's, and even the Kansas exiles that

"Bloody Bill" Anderson was to lead. Ironically, Anderson's small, violent band lost much of its public support in the Lafayette County area by terrorizing southern sympathizers as well as northern ones.[20]

Guerrillas had to have this citizen support for sustained operations. Not only did area people feed and harbor bushwhackers, willingly or not, but many actively spied for them and stood watch for them, too. This gave partisans the advantage of an intelligence network superior to their enemy's. By thus remaining among friends, guerrillas could maintain their elusiveness, that mysterious "will-of-the-wisp" quality that usually gave them the

Quantrill band member Woot Hill wears an embroidered hunting shirt. (John N. Edwards, *Noted Guerrillas*, 1867; courtesy Bob and Mary Younger and Andy Turner)

"last laugh." A shrewd Union commander compared this foe that refused to show himself to a flock of ducks that scatter "...when a boat goes through them, and settle down again as it passes on...."[21] These same willing residents in guerrilla sanctuary areas also tended wounded and sick partisans and hid them from capture. The notorious guerrilla hunter of Wayne County, southeast Missouri, Captain William T. Leeper, wrote to his superiors: "...many men and women who are at home do us more damage than the regular soldier; they feed, harbor, and conceal the guerrillas.... I fear we will never be able to destroy guerrillas while we permit their friends to remain amongst us...."[22] Another Yankee officer, district chief Brigadier General Clinton D. Fisk, wrote in frustration that "...nearly every house is a guerrilla picket station, and the men, women, and children spies in the bushwhacking service."[23] Indeed, Quantrill's lieutenant, Bill Gregg, wrote in his memoirs: "...heaven bless the women, they were friends in need and indeed no braver and truer woman lived than the southern ladies of Missouri, we often owed our lives to them...."[24] One militia commander bitterly summarized Union feelings about such large, rural Rebel sanctuaries when he wrote, "...our forces are, to all intents and purposes, in an enemy's country...."[25]

Guerrilla Seasons

Bushwhackers also made the best of Missouri's climate, leaving the state in fall to winter in Arkansas or Texas and returning in spring. This practice, begun in fall 1862, was not for convenience, but was a logistical and tactical necessity. The

Missouri's thick foliage concealed guerrillas from detection. (*The Soldier in Our Civil War*, 1890, vol. 1, p. 97; courtesy Terry Harmon)

guerrillas' total reliance on the horse left them vulnerable in winter, when Missouri's cold weather, November through March, debilitated both mount and rider and horse feed became scarce. Men could find or make shelter for themselves, but bushwhackers were helpless to get their horses out of the weather in large numbers for any length of time. Union militia methodically burned down churches and schoolhouses in guerrilla-prone areas to deny to them these "harbors" and frequently searched known caves for the same reason.

Winter also deprived bushwhackers of another of their advantages—the concealment of nature's foliage in the woods and brush. Federal army correspondence in Missouri made frequent references to the dreaded return of guerrillas in the spring with the return of the leaves: "…in a short time the foliage will place us at a great disadvantage…"; "…as soon as leaves come out they will give us great trouble…"; "…the warm days are upon us and greenleaf is the best general the whackers have…."[26]

Surprisingly, the southern cause in Missouri benefited from the guerrilla inactivity during the first two winters of the war. Union strategists noticed the lack of pressure in Missouri and sent scarce troops from there to hotter war regions. When the bushwhackers returned in the spring, they met reduced opposition, causing Federal leaders to scramble to re-deploy the few forces left in the region. This effect was noticeable to the civilian population and encouraged southerners, while northern sympathizers felt abandoned. All said, guerrilla warfare as practiced in Missouri was frightening, deadly, and frustrating to all participants.

Seven

Policy Evolves (March–May 1862)

The return of warm weather during spring of 1862 seemed to infuse new life into Missouri's guerrilla warfare, which had sputtered on throughout the first winter of the war. The number and intensity of incidents seemed stronger in the west part of the state than the east, but no part of Missouri was immune. Union authorities struggled to counter this growing surge of partisan conflict. The Union high command sent nearly all the infantry out of the state this spring, since they were needed elsewhere and were hardly able to keep up with the mounted combatants of guerrilla warfare.[1] To take their place, Yankee leaders turned to fifteen or so regiments of Missouri State Militia. These troops had been authorized the previous November and recruited across the state throughout the winter and early spring.[2] Many of these units had to fend off local guerrillas while performing recruiting duties, thereby learning their work "on the job," so to speak.

General Henry W. Halleck, chief of the Department of the Missouri, published on March 13 General Order Number 2 which deplored Confederate General Sterling Price's "licensing" of guerrillas "contrary to rules of civilized warfare" and declared that each man who enlisted in bushwhacker bands "forfeits his life, and becomes an outlaw."[3] This order directed northern troops that guerrillas they caught from then on "...will be hung as robbers and murderers...."

In contrast, the Confederacy's President Jefferson Davis, on April 21, 1862, legitimized this form of warfare by authorizing his military establishment to issue commissions to southern officers to form bands of "partisan rangers," as Davis called them. Partly, this declaration was to refute the Union claim that partisans were merely bandits or criminals not entitled to treatment as prisoners of war if captured. Of course, the U.S. government and the Union military were less than enthusiastic about accepting President Davis' proviso changing bushwhackers into legal combatants. But, particularly in Missouri, this legal step enabled formerly reluctant Confederate regular soldiers to embrace guerrilla warfare not only as legitimate, but noble reminiscent of that great Revolutionary War hero, General Francis Marion, the Swamp Fox, and the type of guerrilla warfare he conducted against invading forces.[4]

In apparent reaction to Davis' program, Missouri's Union state militia apparatus on May 29, 1862, issued its General Order Number 18, which stated "...the time is passed when insurrection and rebellion in Missouri can cloak itself under the guise of honorable warfare..." and declared that "these robbers and assassins," specifying both recruiters and guerrillas, "will be shot down upon the spot."[5] As a way out, this order offered to spare any partisans or Rebel recruiters who surrendered "...themselves and their arms at the nearest military post..." and took an oath not to bear arms against the U.S. government. Yankee military leaders had been encouraging Missouri men to take such oaths for many months already, and evidently many did. Quite a few devoutly southern Missourians took such oaths for convenience or to get out of a bad spot and later became combatants against the U.S. again. Such "oath violators" faced tragic fates when later caught in arms fighting against Union troops.

Missouri's Union military commander during most of 1862 was Major General John M. Schofield. (Private collection; courtesy Bob and Mary Yonger and Andy Turner)

The northern military also recognized this spring that guerrillas were not the only cause of the terror war in Missouri. General Halleck responded to Secretary of War Edwin M. Stanton's earlier inquiry on March 25 to admit that other contributors were the despised Kansas jayhawker incursions and depredations by Missouri's own northern troops.[6] Halleck alluded to poor leadership at troop unit level. Indeed, the District of Central Missouri commander, Brigadier General James Totten, sadly concluded on April 5 to his chief that many improprieties by his troops originated from "desire for personal revenge" for "past difficulties" and proposed a "constant system of inspections" to keep such problems in check.[7] Many of the new Missouri State Militia troops were stationed in their home areas for months at a time, often with such repugnant results.

General Halleck left Missouri's care and its problems on April 10 to Brigadier General John M. Schofield. Schofield had been teaching physics at Washington University in St. Louis on leave from the army when the war began, but he rose in esteem and rank through work on Major General Nathaniel Lyon's staff across Missouri in 1861 and in his work building Missouri's fledgling northern militia.[8] Schofield's approach to Missouri's issues differed little from Halleck's. Schofield, a native of New York, took the radical road on May 29 when he proclaimed guerrillas should be executed on the spot by local commanders, as mentioned earlier.

This policy set guerrilla war as a fight to the death in every skirmish, even to the war's end, and helped to portray the Federal cause as inhumane and uncaring to its many critics in Missouri. This spring, Schofield helped to restrict Kansas troops from operating in west Missouri due to "bitter feeling ... between the border people." He tried wherever possible to employ Union troops from other states or from east Missouri to lessen the vengeful nature of war in that part of the state.[9] However, Halleck's and Schofield's heavy-handed, tradition-bound policies to remedy Missouri's complex problems did little to slow the partisan warfare that seemed to grow as fast as the grass this spring.

Eight

Spring 1862 in Northeast Missouri

When guerrilla warfare blossomed across Missouri in March, April, and May of 1862, it came the least in the northeast quadrant of the state. The exodus during the winter of the large southern recruiting commands from this region perhaps took away the most fervent secessionists. Possibly the stern Federal prosecution of some of those who were caught sabotaging railroad facilities during December 1861 cooled the ardor of others. Whatever the reasons, spring 1862 in northeast Missouri was certainly less active in acts of irregular warfare than other parts.

Actions Near the Iowa Border

Even in the extreme northeast corner of this region near the Iowa line, guerrillas struck out this spring. Bill Dunn brought his Scotland and Schuyler County guerrillas to north Knox County in mid–March for a few days. While recruiting southern men and cajoling families of northern sympathy to give over their bedding to his men, Dunn's band also killed five militiamen and wounded two more. This action took place some time in March near Lancaster, Schuyler County, when the partisans ambushed Captain Perry D. McClanihan's small Union recruiting detail of 2nd Missouri Cavalry near a tobacco warehouse there.[1] On March 24 William Ewing's guerrilla band bushwhacked Lieutenant Joseph H. Call's patrol of 11th Cavalry MSM, which had been sent to arrest Ewing at his home near Sand Hill, south Scotland County. Ewing's ambush killed two and wounded several Yankees at no evident southern loss. The outraged militiamen then burned the guerrilla leader's house in his absence. Ewing, a 40-year-old farmer and father of four, showed no pity for his enemy. Two days later his band ambushed the funeral procession of the two dead Federals near Edina, central Knox County, killing two more. Such cycles of act and retribution were common in Missouri in this hateful warfare, but this one made William Ewing a marked man thereafter.[2] Union troops in the area desired to stop these ambushes by any means. Colonel John M. Glover of 3rd Missouri Cavalry declared on April 10 that area southern sympathizers would be levied to pay damages to local families of northern sympathy robbed by partisans. He sent his men out to bring in 65 known southerners to this end, but in their zeal, his cavalrymen killed seven men over the next several days.[3] Chivalry seemed to have no part in this corner of the Civil War.

Francis Henderson Strikes

Further south, along the counties lining the Mississippi River, a few guerrillas were still active this spring. Francis G. Henderson, a newspaper editor and devoted secessionist of Millville, west St. Charles County, brought his own brand of warfare to nearby Lincoln County. Henderson, a company commander in Colonel Caleb Dorsey's local regiment of southern Missouri State Guard, led his men on a raid to Troy on March 1. They took food, bedding, and other necessities and forced some northern sympathizers to take oaths not to bear arms on either side of the conflict.[4] This bold attack on a large town incensed area Union authorities, and they sent troops in to track down the raiders. On March 7 the 1st Battalion Cavalry MSM located and attacked Henderson's camp on Bob's Creek in southeast Lincoln County, but the guerrillas anticipated trouble and ambushed the advance guard. The balance of the Yankees took the offensive and drove the southerners through the encampment, killing at least ten, compared to Union casualties of three wounded cavalrymen. Henderson, son of one-time mayor of Baton Rouge, Louisiana, who had allegedly blamed the northern cause for his wife's earlier death in a steamboat explosion, escaped for the time being, and kept a few members of his company at hand. The searching Union cavalry found some members of his scattered band on March 9 at a house on Big Creek and killed two, including Henderson's lieutenant. Meanwhile, vengeful northern sympathizers of Lincoln County killed a returned Rebel soldier named Loving sometime in March.[5]

Meanwhile, further north in Marion County, prisoner Captain Robert E. Dunn of that county on March 14 overpowered his Yankee guard at Palmyra's town spring and dashed away to hide with friends.

Guerrilla chief Francis G. Henderson. (Private collection; courtesy Terry Henderson)

Later, he escaped the region by boating down the Mississippi River to Confederate lines in the south.[6] In nearby Emerson at about this same time, but probably unrelated to Dunn's escape, local guerrillas ransacked homes to obtain firearms to begin their own partisan warfare.[7]

Developments Along the Missouri River

Guerrilla war seemed to glow brighter this spring in the counties along the Missouri River to the south. One of the St. Louis newspapers related without details that on March 8 near Pendleton, west Warren County, a chance encounter between local partisans and unidentified Union troops produced shooting but evidently no casualties.[8] On March 19 at Bear Creek just outside Columbia, Boone County, hidden bushwhackers shot up a returning forage detail of 2nd Missouri Cavalry ("Merrill's Horse") wounding one teamster, and then made good their getaway.[9] Again in Warren County, but in the hills near Marthasville, on March 25 the embattled Francis Henderson fought his last battle, having moved south away from Union retribution in Lincoln County. Captain James W. McFadden's patrol of 3rd Cavalry MSM found and fought Henderson's band in a stone fort the rebels had made. Henderson had only twelve men with him this time, and they retreated to Dr. Warner Brisco's house nearby, which the exuberant Yankees riddled with bullets, confident that they had their quarry cornered for good. They allowed what they believed to be Dr. Brisco's wife and daughters to escape the maelstrom, only to discover later that the guerrillas had deceived them by wearing the ladies' clothing. After all, it is said, "All is fair in love and war." The disgruntled cavalrymen took some solace when they found a mortally wounded Francis Henderson left behind in the holed house. Henderson died of his wounds sometime later. This incident probably deeply affected Dr. Brisco's son, John, for later in the war he became a guerrilla leader in this neighborhood.[10]

Also on March 25, the Provost Marshal General for Missouri's Union troops issued an order forbidding the Reverend William Goff Caples in Howard County from preaching or other public speaking. Caples was already on parole for his role as chaplain to Missouri Rebel troops earlier in the war, and had recently given fiery anti–Federal lectures in Chariton, Saline, as well as Howard County. Of course, Federal authorities suspended Bill of Rights guarantees in insurgent-riddled Missouri during the war, and acted decisively when they felt public speech encouraged rebellion. Ironically, Caples, a Methodist Episcopal (South) pastor and head of a large family in Brunswick, Chariton County, had been born in Ohio—normally considered a home of northern supporters.[11]

Of course, many were taking stronger steps than giving speeches to oppose the U.S. government in this region. By early April Rebel recruiting returned to Boone County and unidentified southerners on April 9 fired from ambush on a patrol, probably of 2nd Missouri Cavalry near Sturgeon wounding two troopers at no Rebel loss.[12] Troopers of 2nd Missouri Cavalry captured 15 new Rebel recruits at a dance near Columbia, April 10 or 15, and also Rebel Captain Absolom Hicks, who had organized a southern company at Sturgeon the previous year. About this same time, Union troops also captured Captain Hicks's lieutenant in the Sturgeon company, Ambrose R. Tompkins.[13] Backed up by an escort of 9th Cavalry MSM, the Boone County sheriff on April 21 carried out a Cooper County writ to arrest two men wanted for bushwhacking in the previous fall. Such acts of civil law enforcement were quickly becoming rare by spring 1862 in rural Missouri, as escalating guerrilla war and violence in the countryside prevented civil officials from enforcing the laws. Those residents who remained in this virtual "war zone" learned to appeal to the nearest military force, Union or Rebel, to enforce their rights.[14] On May 3 near Columbia 1st Lieutenant James A. Adams and a private of 9th Cavalry MSM were riding to a nearby farm to invite the inhabitants to hear their regimental chaplain's upcoming sermon when hidden bushwhackers fired on the pair, wounding the private. The lieutenant suffered a broken leg when his horse took fright at the shooting and smashed him against a tree. Their assailants beat a hasty retreat.[15]

An example of civilians appealing to the military for law enforcement occurred May 6 in east Callaway County when a disgruntled Williamsburg-area farmer guided Captain Daniel M. Draper's patrol of 9th Cavalry MSM to a camp of six bushwhackers in order to retrieve his stolen horse. Draper's troopers killed one partisan and captured another, but records of the event fail to reveal if the farmer regained his property.[16] Early morning of May 23 Colonel Odon Guitar, with part of his 9th Cavalry MSM, discovered a large unidentified Rebel recruiting command crossing the Missouri River to the south–Boone County village of Stonesport. The two forces played "cat and mouse" in the woods and brush of Bonne Femme Creek for some time, but the Yankees were able to capture ten of the southerners, and the rest fled back to the south side of the river, where another part of the 9th Cavalry MSM from Jefferson City attacked them later. One of Colonel Guitar's captives was the Reverend David B. Cunningham. Cunningham, a wealthy, Virginia-born farmer with large land holdings and a large family in this neighborhood, would pay a severe price for his activity in the southern cause. With one of his sons, he would spend most of the rest of 1862 in St. Louis-area prisons, lose another teenage son to a Federal bullet on a Boone County road, then return to recruit for the Confederacy and lose his own life in 1864.[17]

Rebel Recruiting in the Central Counties

The central region of northeast Missouri witnessed the most guerrilla actions this spring. Daring behind-the-lines recruiting, as well as guerrilla skirmishing, kept southern hopes high here. On March 12 Lieutenant T.H. Barnes and 15 troopers of 1st Iowa Cavalry arrested Rebel recruiter Captain Silas Hickerson at his home 14 miles out from their base at Mexico, the county seat of Audrain County. Before the Iowans could get their captive back to town, they discovered they would have to fight their way through over 100 of Hickerson's mounted men blocking the road in battle line. The patrol gamely attacked, which dispersed Hickerson's men, evidently without casualties on either side, and they brought their man in, along with two other recruiters, Lt. Colonel John F. Murray and Lt. Colonel Joseph H. Daugherty, who they had come upon and arrested during their ride back to Mexico.[18] Also near Mexico on March 17, Colonel Arnold Krekel's 1st Battalion Cavalry

MSM caught and executed four young Rebel recruits of the county who had contracted measles and were returning home to recuperate.[19] It was these men's misfortune to have been captured by the hard-bitten, mostly German-born troopers of Krekel's command and not the more humane Iowa cavalry. Many of Krekel's men spoke no English, and the language barrier with rural Missourians, along with local distrust of these "foreigners," led many of these soldiers to regard all rural citizens as enemies and act accordingly. There are numerous local stories that survived the war of atrocities committed by men of this command and similar ones that contained large percentages of foreign-born Yankee troops.

About this time, hundreds of other Rebel recruits were concentrating at Florida in nearby Monroe County, attracting the notice of the worried Union military.[20] Accordingly, beginning March 27 for five days around east Monroe County, Major David McKee led a 280-man patrol of 7th Cavalry MSM. McKee's large force skirmished some and brought back 28 prisoners but missed the large concentrations of southern recruits.[21]

Union Colonel Odon Guitar, 9th Cavalry Missouri State Militia. (Private collection; courtesy Bob and Mary Younger and Andy Turner)

Tom Stacy's Guerrilla Band

On April 2 long-haired Tom Stacy, with about 15 bushwhackers, attacked a detachment of 11th Cavalry MSM at Walkersville, south Shelby County, killing two soldiers and one citizen. Later that day, the dead men's comrades tracked Stacy's band ten miles to Black Creek and killed about four guerrillas, capturing Stacy's horse, coat, hat, and shotgun. Tom Stacy continued the cycle of violence over the next several days, replacing his lost belongings by plundering rural families of northern sympathy near Emerson, north Marion County. His band also murdered two or three men who may have earlier informed on them to the Federals.[22]

More Recruiters and Guerrillas

In Randolph County this spring, Confederate Colonel James A. Poindexter successfully evaded Federal patrols and arrived home in disguise to begin recruiting southern men. In time, Poindexter's recruiting prowess would make his presence felt by Union authorities.[23] During the night of May 3, between Florida and Paris in Monroe County, unidentified guerrillas attempted unsuccessfully to steal the horses of a resting patrol of 9th Cavalry MSM. It was still a victory of sorts for the bushwhackers, as the excited troopers shot to death their own lieutenant by mistake.[24] Near Mexico two troopers of 3rd Iowa Cavalry, out looking for a lost horse about May 20, were set upon by Young A. Purcell's band of about 15 guerrillas. One Federal was killed and the other barely made his way back to his garrison in town through a fusillade of shots. Purcell, in his mid-thirties, was from Littleby, north Audrain County, but had previously run a livery business in Mexico. This event seems to mark the beginning of his long career as a guerrilla chief.[25] On May 22 elements of the same Iowa regiment skirmished with unidentified Rebels at Florida, but the results were not recorded.[26] On May 28 unidentified Union forces captured Rebel recruiter Captain John Calvin Whaley in Shelby County and sent him to prison in St. Louis.[27] Major Henry C. Caldwell's patrol of 3rd Iowa Cavalry on May 31 skirmished with about 20 partisans near Florida. Casualties were slight on both sides, but the Federals seemed to get the best of the fight as they captured seven horses and much of the Rebels' camp equipment. The expected outcome of such losses meant that these guerrillas would probably beg replacement horses and camp equipment from friendly farmers or plunder such things from farmers of other sympathies.[28] By the end of May the increasing tempo of guerrilla actions in northeast Missouri was clear warning that the summer of 1862 would be very violent here.

Nine

Spring 1862 in Southeast Missouri

The tempo of guerrilla warfare increased in southeast Missouri during March, April, and May of 1862, as it did in other parts of the state. Warmer weather and the new growth of forage and concealing vegetation encouraged guerrilla chiefs and recruiters who were already around. New units from the Confederate forces in Arkansas rode into the region to begin work, too. The length of their stay in Union-occupied southeast Missouri, as in other parts, was a combination of their own wiles and the ability of the Yankees to apprehend or destroy them.

Quiet in the Hills

The quietest part of this quadrant of the Show Me state was that composed of the hilly, forested counties of Wayne, Carter, Ripley, and Butler, northwest of the bootheel, although some actions took place there to break the tranquility. At Patterson, northwest Wayne County, on March 3, unidentified Rebels captured two Yankee officers of Hawkins' Independent Company, along with the company books.[1] On March 9, 1862, an obscure skirmish between unidentified foes took place on Big Creek in northwest Wayne County, during which three Federals were wounded. This may have involved local guerrillas and members of the 21st Illinois Infantry, known to be patrolling in this area at the time.[2] Sadly, the bravery of combatants of all sides this early in the war was lost due to poor record-keeping.

During early April, Colonel W. P. Carlin marched his Union brigade through this area on an expedition into suspected Rebel enclaves in northwest Arkansas. On April 1 his advance guard inflicted a few Rebel casualties at Pittman's Ferry on the Current River in south Ripley County. The Union troops also captured an empty Confederate camp there, including supplies and dispatches. Three days later elements of Carlin's own 5th Illinois Cavalry skirmished with irregulars at Doniphan in central Butler County, before the expedition moved on south into Arkansas.[3]

Action in the North—Sam Hildebrand Begins His Personal War

This spring there were more guerrilla actions far to the north near the Missouri River and in the St. Francois Mountains. Local northern sympathizers saw and reported Captain Joseph A. Spilman's Rebel recruiting band March 8 in east Maries County, but the Union cavalry patrol failed to find anything. Spilman, of Colonel William O. Coleman's regiment of irregulars, evidently lived in Texas County pre-war, but seemed to find his way around well enough in Maries County.[4] Just a few miles to the west local guerrillas robbed and abducted Miller County's Union deputy provost marshal, Tolbird Bass, on March 15 from Tuscumbia, the county seat. They took Bass to a remote Morgan County hideout, but released him unharmed a few days later.[5] Southerners particularly disliked provost marshals, which was a Missouri-peculiar adaptation of military police instituted by the Federal high command early in the war. The Union generals forced the system on the populace to replace the now-unenforceable civil laws. The provost marshals and their men were given power to spy on local southerners in order to detect and apprehend those they believed were a threat to the Union cause. In effect, even the most humane and fair of them became a dreaded "secret police," and some became drunk with the power of the office and even used it to rob southerners for their own gain.

Missouri Union provost marshals enforced oath-taking by citizens of southern sympathy. *The Soldier of Our Civil War*, 1890, vol. 2, p. 363; courtesy Terry Harmon)

Also in Miller County, part of McClurg's Battalion Cavalry MSM, later part of 8th Cavalry MSM, captured in late March a group of nine Confederate recruiters who were also carrying mail from comrades in Arkansas back to their Missouri families.[6] Ironically, about this same time, at least three Rebel prisoners, including two captains, escaped from the military prison at Alton, Illinois.[7] This typifies the "revolving door" aspect of the frequent prison escapes, particularly of the St. Louis–area prisons, which greatly irritated Union troops in Missouri. They were frustrated that they worked so hard to capture Rebel recruiters, only to have them escape from prison later and face them on the field of battle again.

During April a local Yankee militia unit unknowingly began a chain of events that throughout the rest of the war would grievously harm the Union cause in southeast Missouri. It began simply enough in north St. Francois County when these militiamen attempted to kill or capture farmer and southern sympathizer Sam Hildebrand at his home. Though wounded, Hildebrand escaped and made his way south to join Nathan Bolin's guerrilla band. Some of the local militia were conducting a campaign to drive known southerners out, even to the extreme of arson and murder; they had already marked others of Hildebrand's family. To Sam, this was atrocity, not war, and he later began a one-man war against the militia and their informants in his home area that lasted the rest of the long war and eventually snuffed out scores of lives.[8]

March in the Bootheel

The lowlands and swamps of Missouri's bootheel were alive with guerrillas during spring 1862. The "Swamp Rats" of Colonel M. Jeff Thompson inflicted

Sam Hildebrand is driven from his home. (*Autobiography of Samuel S. Hildebrand, the Renowned Missouri "Bushwacker,"* 1870, courtesy Bob and Mary Younger and Andy Turner)

casualties on unidentified Federals at Sikeston, south Scott County, on March 1.[9] Major Jonas Rawalt's large patrol of 7th Illinois Cavalry probably also faced Thompson's partisans on March 23 by the swamps of Little River in New Madrid County. The Illinois troopers could not come to grips with the Rebels, who maneuvered through the watery wastes on little boats.[10] At the end of March, Rebel recruiter Solomon Kitchens and guerrilla chief Dick Bowles combined their 120 men to raid briefly in Bollinger and Cape Girardeau counties. They abducted officials, destroyed the Bollinger County records, seized horses, and murdered two evidently unarmed men, and then "went to ground" and hid before Union forces could organize an effective pursuit.[11]

Bill Jeffers Strikes Back

Irregular Confederate forces in the bootheel had become a sizable threat to northern troops in the area by April 1862. On April 9 Captain William Flenty's patrol of 60 men of 3rd Cavalry MSM suddenly became the hunted instead of the hunter. They were looking for Rebels reported to be in south Cape Girardeau County when they rode into Colonel William Jeffers's ambush on Hubble Creek. After a brief, frantic firefight, Flenty's battered patrol retreated, partly because their firearms would not work properly. The problem of inferior arms was rife in the Missouri State Militia (MSM) early in 1862, and it occasionally got someone killed. In the Hubble Creek fight, both sides suffered one to four men killed and one or two captured. Jeffers's reputation was enhanced for further recruiting, and the Yankees were further away from driving their foes out of the region. Jeffers, a Mexican War veteran, was a persistent recruiter in this region and would return several times throughout the war.[12] After the Hubble Creek fight, this neighborhood seemed quiet for about a month.

Colonel William G. Phelan, Recruiter

Confederate recruiters, particularly Colonel William G. Phelan, a lawyer of Bloomfield, Stoddard County, before the war, continued surreptitiously to bring in southern men to their camps, willing or not. In spite of their secrecy, Union authorities found out and sent troops. Colonel Edward Daniels led a task force of 300 troopers of his 1st Wisconsin Cavalry with artillery support to the bootheel for ten action-filled days beginning May 10. On that day, Daniels's command stormed Phelan's camp in south Stoddard County capturing eleven men, lots of weapons, and Phelan's own chest of documents. The Yankees learned the main Rebel base was on Chalk Bluff on the Arkansas side of the treacherous St. Francis River in north Dunklin County. Daniels's force attacked this new base May 15 by seizing the Chalk Bluff ferry, crossing the river under Rebel fire (suppressed by the Union fieldpieces), and routing the southern force, employing the Wisconsin cavalry in a dismounted role. Daniels' scrappy task force killed 11 and captured 17, at a loss of two troopers killed and seven wounded.

Sometime between May 16 and 20, the Yankees assaulted another Rebel camp a few miles south in Dunklin County by creeping through the swamps and along cattle paths to surprise their foe. No other details remain of this skirmish. The last part of this expedition took place at Hornersville, south Dunklin County, on the Little River. The Federals surprised Rebels loading the 110-foot-long steamer, *Daniel E. Miller*. The boat attempted to pull away, but two well-placed cannon shots compelled the crew to surrender.[13] Thus, at spring's end, much of the southern recruiting had been swept out of the bootheel, leaving only some guerrillas.

Colonel Coleman's Brand of Warfare

Guerrilla warfare was most violent and frequent this spring in the central Ozark counties of Howell and Oregon on the Arkansas border and north to the Rolla area of Phelps and Pulaski counties. This was mostly due to the influence of Colonel William O. Coleman of Phelps County, who pushed his irregulars and recruiters into this area to challenge the Union hold on it. The Union was especially keen to protect the main line of supply and communications along the Rolla-Springfield road in west Phelps and Pulaski counties. This spring's first battle took place between March 8 and 13 when Lt. Colonel Samuel N. Wood led 250 troopers of his own 6th Missouri Cavalry and 3rd Iowa Cavalry in a major expedition. Wood's command swept Coleman's guerrillas before it, starting in Phelps and Dent counties March 8 and 9, then south through Texas and Oregon counties to a swamp near Salem, Arkansas, on March 13. A fierce battle rang out in the swamp, with Wood's cannons taking a fierce toll on the southerners, until the Yankees ran short of ammunition and retired across the Missouri state line. The Federals lost four killed and 18 wounded, but the Rebel casualties were greater.[14] These Union actions in early March kept the region mostly free from partisans for several weeks, although Yankee cavalry made several captures there in April, including some Rebel officers in or near Maries County. Late that month, unidentified southerners burned bridges in Reynolds County, and a patrol of 13th Illinois Cavalry captured nine men that may have been the culprits.[15]

May Heats Up and Coleman Returns

On May 4, 1862, MSM cavalry and elements of 24th Missouri Infantry skirmished with unidentified bushwhackers at Licking, north Texas County, losing one killed and two wounded, compared to unknown and unrecorded Rebel casualties.[16] Miles to the south the next day, local guerrillas under a commander named Highfill, at Mammoth Spring, Oregon County, on the Arkansas line, attacked Iowa soldiers guarding sick comrades in a house. The bushwhackers fired through the windows and doors of the dwelling at the small group of infantrymen. The frantic shooting eventually drove their tormentors away with no known casualties on either side.[17]

In mid–May William Coleman brought his regiment of guerrillas back to the region. On May 16 near Houston, Texas County, at least 200 of his command riding north from Arkansas captured a northern dispatch rider and four other soldiers, then paroled and released them the next day without their horses and weapons.[18] This Rebel force rode on north, bypassing the relatively large town of Waynesville in Pulaski County, before going into hiding a few miles north of town. It soon became obvious that Coleman had sent them to harass the main Yankee supply line between Lebanon and Rolla. They captured a Union wagon train containing 25 wagons of rations on May 20 near the Pulaski-Phelps line. Before the startled federal command could give effective pursuit, the raiders took the 86 mules, burned the wagons, and returned to their forest hiding place.[19] A couple of days later, elements of 13th Illinois Cavalry defeated Rebels, perhaps of this same command, in Reynolds and Carter counties, killing six and capturing eleven.[20] About this same time, some miles to the south near Thomasville, southwest Oregon County, some of Coleman's command attacked three furloughed troopers of 3rd Illinois Cavalry who were riding along the road in this guerrilla-infested region. One of the trio survived, though badly wounded, and made his way to a small Union outpost at West Plains, Howell County. His comrades were never heard from again.[21]

Colonel Coleman Fights On

Meanwhile, Federal authorities were frantically seeking ways to counter the large numbers of bushwhackers flooding the area. They put Colonel Coleman's wife and child, and other prominent southern sympathizers, into custody at Rolla as hostages and beefed up troop escorts for the army wagon trains that left the rail terminal there.[22] This did not prevent Coleman from attacking a large, well-armed wagon train near Licking on May 26. Coleman and Captain Henry Andrae, also

Southern horsemen attack Union wagon train and its infantry guards. (*The Soldier in Our Civil War*, 1890, vol. 2, p. 156; courtesy Terry Harmon)

of Rolla, with 170 yelling raiders, rushed the 102-wagon convoy escorted by Captain James T. Tallaifarro and his 80 men of 24th Missouri Infantry. The guerrillas got close enough to burn twelve wagons, kill two soldiers, and wound the captain, but the desperate infantrymen fought for their very lives, killing and wounding 13 of the raiders and driving the Rebels away.[23] It seemed that if Coleman knew the Yankees held his family and friends, he was going to demonstrate his indignation. It was probably also Coleman's men who skirmished with troopers of 10th Illinois Cavalry near Waynesville the last day of May 1862, but details are lacking.[24] On June 1, the 1st Indiana Cavalry sent a patrol from West Plains to Thomasville to investigate the ambush of the three Illinois cavalrymen mentioned earlier. They found no sign of the missing men but exchanged shots with six or seven southerners near the approximate ambush site. One Indiana trooper was severely wounded.[25] The approaching summer promised to be exciting here.

Ten

Spring 1862 in Southwest Missouri

The months of March, April, and May, 1862, were particularly violent in the southwest quarter of Missouri. This is hardly surprising given the high level of guerrilla activity here throughout the winter. After all, the southern army was not too distant in northwest Arkansas, so this region was easily accessible to Confederate recruiters and other returning Rebels.

A Large Rebel Force in the Hill Country

Naturally, the least activity took place in the least accessible part of this part of Missouri—the rugged, hilly upper–Ozark counties of Miller, Camden, Dallas, Laclede, Wright, Webster, Douglas, and Greene. This land is dissected by the Gasconade and Niangua Rivers and in 1862 was lightly populated. The main action here took place mostly between March 5 and 12, when an estimated 300 Confederate irregulars, led by undetermined leaders, surged out of the forests to attack Union outposts, then rode back to Arkansas. It seems strange that the Confederate army would spare such a force as they battled the northern army at Pea Ridge or Elkhorn Tavern just a few miles to the south, but that is exactly what happened. Yankee troopers took documents from the captured and dead to reveal Missouri's own General Sterling Price had detailed these men in early February to infiltrate back into Union-held Missouri to recruit and harass their enemies there.

These raiders first caught Union attention March 5 and 6 when some of them appropriated some cattle in south Laclede County and herded them south toward the always-hungry southern army.[1] At the same time, residents at Hartville, county seat of nearby Wright County, saw 25 guerrillas at or near town; and others were reported at Vera Cruz, seat of Douglas County to the south. At daybreak on March 7, a force of these raiders attacked a startled 42-man detachment of 4th Missouri Cavalry camped on Fox Creek seven miles from Vera Cruz. The Rebels wounded five of the troopers, but the blue-clad cavalrymen rallied and drove back their antagonists, then wisely retired north to Hartville, where they joined 50 of their comrades.[2]

Two days later these Yankees were reinforced by elements of 10th Missouri Cavalry and Phelps' Regiment Missouri Infantry and rode back south to strike back. It was the Rebels' turn for surprise on March 9. This combined Union force found and attacked 35 or 40 of them in the buildings of the Mountain Grove Seminary near Montreal, southwest Texas County. The Federals gunned down 11 southerners and badly wounded six more before the remaining 21 under the command of J.C. Campbell surrendered.[3] (Campbell was a former magistrate.) The rest of the Rebel raiders or recruiters infiltrated back to the southern forces in Arkansas as quietly as they had come.

Colonel Frazier's Brief Campaign

Guerrillas were more organized and active this spring further north in the prairie counties along the Sac River and west to the Kansas border. Fledgling patrols of the newly-formed 14th Cavalry MSM in Lawrence County had one or two shootouts with local guerrillas during March with one or two casualties on each side.[4] In north Cedar County on March 21, former Wright County-attorney Julian Frazier, with a Rebel recruiting force of about 100, routed a careless patrol of the newly-formed McClurg's Battalion Cavalry MSM—later 8th Cavalry MSM—which had neglected to post sentries during dinner at a farmstead. Frazier's southerners killed one and wounded another Yankee before the rest scrambled back across the Sac River to their base at Humansville, northwest Polk County. Their commander, Lieutenant Colonel Joseph W. McClurg, complained to his superiors that guerrillas in large numbers were swarming across the region.[5] Five days later, Colonel Frazier and his men came calling. On March 26, four companies of McClurg's men stared incredulously as Frazier slowly and deliberately paraded his consolidated force of about 400 Cedar and St. Clair County Rebel recruits past their garrison town of Humansville. The four Yankee captains accepted the lawyer's challenge and, with help from eager civilian volunteers, carefully deployed their troops, not in the open, but in a patch of brush near town. The confident Rebels surged forward on the attack, but their fire killed only two Federals and wounded two more before the northerners' Austrian carbines shot dead six and wounded others. The fight could still have gone either way, but Frazier himself was one of the dead, and the disillusioned Rebel recruits withdrew.[6] This may have been a grudge match among neighbors of both sides, for McClurg's men were known across the region for depredations against southern sympathizers—even eliciting a sharp rebuke from district headquarters on April 4. Perhaps Colonel Frazier had meant to put them in their place.[7]

The Montevallo Fights During April 1862

The partisans around Montevallo in southeast Vernon County had been organizing since winter and found an attractive target on which to sharpen their skills on April 14. The previous evening, Colonel Charles E. Moss had led a force consisting of 75 1st Iowa Cavalry and 100 of McClurg's Battalion to town during a sweep of the area. Most of the Yankees bedded down outside the village. At day-

Southerners attacking in a village. (*The Soldier in Our Civil War*, 1890, vol. 1, p. 100; courtesy Terry Harmon)

break local guerrillas attacked Moss and 25 men who slept in town, killing two and wounding six. The rest of the Federals rode to the rescue, killing two of the raiders and chasing the rest across the prairie landscape until they had captured 22. The indignant Yankees burned most of the village before moving on, taking their captives with them.[8] The records of the 6th Kansas Cavalry indicate that elements of that regiment skirmished with Thomas R. Livingston's guerrillas the following day somewhere in the region, but no other records of the fight survive.[9] However, sometime this spring the Mayfield brothers, Brice and Crawford, from this part of Vernon County, surprised and captured seven troopers of this unit on McCarty's Branch in southeast Vernon County. They may have been the ones, rather than Livingston, who fought 6th Cavalry. The Mayfields attempted unsuccessfully to trade their captives for guerrilla chief and former Vernon County sheriff, Henry Taylor, held at nearby Fort Scott. When their efforts proved fruitless, the Mayfields released their prisoners anyway.[10]

Prairie Fights in Early May

About May 1, guerrillas near Rock Prairie, southwest Dade County, attacked two foraging parties of 5th Kansas Cavalry, killing a trooper, then shot at a dispatch rider from the same regiment. Kansas regiments had little love for Missourians, nor respect for their property, and the infuriated men of the 5th set their minds on revenge. Their reaction force found and pursued these Rebels to near Greenfield, where they captured and hung one of the leaders—a man named McCullough—then burned 20 or 30 homes in the region to discourage future help for bushwhackers.[11] Such measures resulted in vast parts of southwest Missouri being uninhabited from 1862 until the war's end.

On May 7, 40 patrolling troopers of 2nd Ohio Cavalry out of Fort Scott happened onto Captain Sidney D. Jackman's southbound band of 60 rebel recruits on Horse Creek in northeast Barton County. Jackman, a local Baptist preacher before the war who had since sided with the Missouri "border ruffians" and would be a federal marshal in west Texas postwar, was always a tough, resourceful enemy of any Yankee force that had the misfortune to cross his path. This day was no different. The Ohio patrol quickly realized this was no ordinary guerrilla band, which usually ran or dispersed on contact, and the Federals had to flee for their lives with Jackman's men after them like a disturbed hive of bees. The Rebels captured three cavalrymen, one on each side was killed, and the patrol was fortunate to get off so well.[12]

Local records tell that sometime this spring an unidentified guerrilla band raided Greenfield, Dade County, abducting Union recruits, terrorizing a church service, and forcing residents to take oaths for the southern cause. The raiders then robbed a store and hurriedly left town before pursuit overtook them.[13] This was only one of several times Greenfield was raided by southerners during the war.

March Fights in the Southwest Corner

Another violent part of southwest Missouri this spring was the far southwest corner of the state bordering Arkansas and the Indian Territories, between the

Spring and White Rivers. On March 19 and 20, Lt. Colonel Powell Clayton led elements of 5th Kansas Cavalry on an expedition through Barton and Jasper counties and in Carthage arrested 15 or 20 southerners based on the testimony of northern sympathizers there. A patrol from this expedition had a firefight with guerrillas in which three Kansans were wounded and one captured.[14] Clayton's force skirmished again with bushwhackers on March 23 near Carthage. Rebel losses are unknown, but one Federal was wounded.[15]

Newton County in Early April

On April 8, 1862, Colonel Clark Wright led elements of 6th Missouri Cavalry on a similar expedition through Newton County to the north. His command skirmished three times with guerrillas, killing at least three for slight Union losses. They arrested 125 southerners, but then released all but 25 of them. Colonel Wright noted in his report that he used discretion in his captures and seizures so as not to further alienate the populace. Such a revelation marks Clark Wright as a thoughtful commander ahead of his contemporaries, for the concept that resident aggravation with Federal troops aided the guerrillas' cause was still a novel idea in spring of 1862. Colonel Wright also noted that he took his troops back to garrison when it appeared that the local guerrillas had fled to the Indian Nations.[16]

A few days later on April 14, parts of 1st Iowa Cavalry and 6th Kansas Cavalry at Diamond Grove, north-central Newton County, exchanged shots with bushwhackers but reported that no casualties seemed to result.[17] The next day in nearby Lawrence County guerrillas shot down a man of northern sympathy simply for flying the U.S. flag, and the militia garrisoned nearby was unable to catch them.[18] Rural Missouri during spring 1862 was not a safe place for residents to broadcast their affiliation.

First Missouri Cavalry Struggles in Barry and McDonald Counties

After mid–April, guerrillas in this corner of southwest Missouri seemed to have organized into larger bands in order to more effectively counter the various Union cavalry regiments roaming the prairie. Between April 20 and 23, hundreds of Confederate irregulars, allegedly including Stand Watie's Indian contingent up from the Indian Nations, battled repeatedly with Major James M. Hubbard's 146

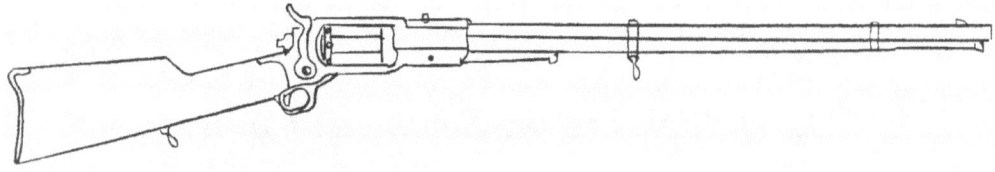

Colt revolving rifle. (Drawn by the author)

troopers of 1st Missouri Cavalry across the grasslands of west Barry and east McDonald counties. Yankees' superior firepower in the form of their Colt revolving rifles, helped to keep their casualties slight and was partly responsible for the capture of 30 or 40 of their foes in the three days of skirmishing.[19] About a day or two later, Hubbard's force was escorting families of northern sympathy away from their homes along Buffalo Creek in west McDonald County when the troopers noticed about 40 local guerrillas, under William Isbell of Neosho, shadowing the column looking for a chance to attack. The Federals fired two six-pounder cannon at the bushwhackers, which kept them at a distance. This was one of the few known instances of the use of mobile artillery in Missouri's guerrilla warfare.[20]

Coffee's Missourians and Cooper's Indians

Major Hubbard's scouts convinced him large numbers of Rebel forces were riding into McDonald County from the south, so his command withdrew north to Neosho, Newton County, on April 26. As they moved, about 200 irregulars under former Dade County attorney, Colonel John T. Coffee, and Indians under Colonel Douglas H. Cooper pursued the blue-clad column to the outskirts of Neosho. Once again the troopers' high volume of fire from their revolving rifles kept the Rebels away, while inflicting 30 casualties and capturing 62 prisoners, compared to only three Federals killed, three wounded, and three captured.[21] This same day, elements of 5th Kansas Cavalry skirmished inconclusively with unidentified bushwhackers along Turn Back Creek in south Dade and north Lawrence counties.[22]

Coffee's May Victory

In May Union authorities pushed their cavalry back into Missouri's southwest corner to drive Confederate irregulars out. This mostly prairie-covered land offered little terrain troops could fortify and defend. Horsemen could only roam the grasslands like ships at sea, looking for an enemy to strike. Therefore, offense or defense in such landscape had to be mobile.

A large expedition of 2nd Ohio Cavalry and 9th Wisconsin Infantry proved this point during their expedition from Carthage, Jasper County, across the prairies of Newton and McDonald counties from May 6 through May 10. Major George A. Purington led the 250 Ohio troopers throughout the trip, but the Wisconsin infantrymen had to turn back to Carthage after a day or two because they could not keep up. Meanwhile, Purington's cavalrymen tangled with three gangs of unidentified guerrillas in west McDonald County, near Cowskin Prairie in southwest McDonald County, and near Neosho, Newton County, on the return to Carthage. In a newspaper account of the expedition, the Ohioans claimed to have killed and wounded a number of southerners in these fights and even captured a few, all at no apparent loss to themselves. They seemed to attribute some of their success to using some of their more adventuresome troopers disguised as bushwhackers to draw out their enemy. Several of their captives warned them that Colonel Coffee's Missouri Rebels and Colonel Cooper's southern Indian force was nearby, but this expedition failed to see those units.[23]

Between May 7 and 11, Captain Martin Breeden led a patrol of newly-recruited 14th Cavalry MSM from Mount Vernon, Lawrence County, southwest through Newton County then back to Sarcoxie in southeast Jasper County. They had several firefights with as many as 100 guerrillas, but with only slight casualties on each side. Captain Breeden and his men were disgusted by citizens of northern sympathy along the way who refused to give information about their southern neighbors for fear of reprisals. Of course, these residents had more at stake than the success or failure of one Yankee patrol.[24] On May 22 guerrillas killed a trooper of this same regiment who had evidently strayed too far from the base at Sarcoxie. His comrades were incensed when they learned his body had 16 bullet wounds.[25]

The last day of May brought new terror to this fledgling regiment. They did not realize that Colonel John Trousdale Coffee, with 400 rebel irregulars, had targeted them for attack and had ridden without their notice to the outskirts of Neosho. During the evening of May 31, these mounted Confederates overwhelmed the ill-guarded camp of 14th Cavalry MSM near town, killing two and wounding three at the cost of about that many casualties themselves. Coffee's men ignored the Yankees fleeing for their lives and helped themselves to the firearms, horses, and camp equipment left behind. After the gleeful southerners made good their getaway, a Union military investigation discovered many of the regiment's leaders had been staying in comfortable quarters in the nearby town and had not been available to exercise leadership in a crisis. They were no doubt grateful the Union loss had not been greater in such a vulnerable state, but area southerners were certainly buoyed by this success, and these chagrined Yankees had a severe lesson in the harsh realities of guerrilla warfare.[26]

Iowa Cavalry Along the Osage River

Judging from the number of guerrilla incidents and the savagery of the fighting, the most violent portion of southwest Missouri this spring was along the Osage River, many miles to the north. About March 1, 1862, frantic Yankee recruiters reported bushwhackers gathering in large numbers across Johnson and Henry counties, creating "a reign of terror" to people of northern sympathy and making recruiting hazardous.[27] Consequently, Union authorities sent a large task force of 1st Iowa Cavalry, as well as Iowa, Indiana, and Missouri infantry riding in wagons, from their base at Sedalia, Pettis County, through Henry and Bates counties from March 3 through March 8. This polyglot expedition returned with one wounded trooper, but with 57 captives in tow, confirming the earlier report that lots of Rebels were in the area. Some of these prisoners, such as Captain Bill Marchbanks—later to be an important guerrilla chief in this region—were caught because they did not suspect Federal troops were in the area and had been staying inside buildings due to the cold weather.[28] Now fully convinced of the danger to this region, Union authorities sent several poorly-armed companies of 1st Iowa Cavalry to the Osage River country of Henry, Bates, and St. Clair counties with instructions to live off the country and break up the guerrilla concentrations and Rebel recruiting. Throughout the rest of spring, 1862, the woods and prairies of these three counties rang out almost daily with the crack of pistol shots, as most of these Iowans

Union cavalry marching Rebel captives. (*Frank Leslies's Illustrated Newspaper*, February 20, 1864)

were armed only with pistols or pistols and sabers.[29] Among their deadliest foes in this area were Colonel Sidney Drake Jackman, the wily, truculent Rebel recruiter introduced earlier, and Bill Rafter, a little-known but aggressive guerrilla chieftain who operated mostly in east Henry County around Leesville. However, many area southerners also made it their business to give these newcomers grief.

Morgan County Erupts During March 1862

A few miles east, along the Osage River in Morgan County several incidents of guerrilla warfare took place during the second half of March 1862. In mid–March, 15 to 20 local southerners, hiding their identity behind fake beards and slouch hats, made threatening visits to their neighbors of northern sympathy.[30] On March 22 they stopped two Federal soldiers, made them strip off their uniforms, then released them. Union authorities at the nearby Tipton base were already receiving complaints about altercations in Versailles, the county seat, but due to other pressing concerns they could only spare local militia. In late March these militiamen dealt with Morgan County's problems using a heavy hand—killing one man, beating confessions out of others, and forcing oaths. This created much ill will, which promised more problems in the future.[31]

An Action-Packed April in Benton, Polk, and Hickory Counties

During April 1862 guerrilla violence flared in Benton, Polk, and Hickory counties along the Osage and Pomme de Terre Rivers when a large, unidentified bushwhacker band felt bold enough to strike out at Yankee patrols. On April 8 or 9 near Quincy, northwest Hickory County, several guerrillas ambushed six of McClurg's Battalion Cavalry MSM, mortally wounding one of them. At about the same time a few miles away in northeast Hickory County, this same band or another caught and killed a corporal of the same unit, taking his weapons, horse, and equipment. On April 10, his comrades plus a detachment of 4th Missouri Cavalry found and destroyed the guerrilla camp along the little Niangua River, capturing several bushwhackers and reclaiming the dead corporal's gear.[32]

The next day Lt. Colonel Charles E. Moss, leading a task force of his own 26th Indiana Infantry and 1st Iowa cavalry, discovered and attacked a band of about 40 partisans who were waiting out a violent rainstorm in some houses. The Iowa cavalry killed twelve and captured eight before the sodden infantrymen even arrived on the scene. This action demonstrably illustrated the necessity of mounting antagonists on horseback in this style of warfare, for the Rebels were defeated because they dismounted to get out of the weather, and the Indiana infantry, gamely slogging through the wet brush, arrived too late to get into the fight.[33]

One of the Indiana infantrymen—evidently a straggler from this expedition—underwent a harrowing experience about this same time. Somehow six guerrillas captured him, but he escaped and accosted two farmers driving a wagon who, luckily for him, just happened to be men of northern sympathy. The two farmers agreed to drive him back to his base at Sedalia many miles to the north. The soldier's new found friends stuck to their plan, even though it eventually meant driving through various bands of Rebel recruiting groups and guerrillas across Benton County with the frightened infantryman hiding in the back of the wagon. This account even specifically mentions the trio bluffing their way past "Long" Henry Thurston of Morgan County—a prewar farmer who later traveled with the P.T. Barnum circus because of his over-seven-foot height—and his men at Warsaw. Once back safely at Sedalia, the soldier was greeted as one returning from the dead, and the farmers were hailed as heroes.[34]

In answer to reports of guerrillas robbing farmers in northwest Hickory County, a force of 85 cavalrymen of 4th Missouri Cavalry and McClurg's Battalion returned to the scene of the April 11 action on April 12. They captured one bushwhacker, burned the buildings that had sheltered the guerrillas the day before, but found nothing else of interest.[35] Two men of McClurg's Battalion were killed by ambush near Bolivar, Polk County, about April 14. The assailants escaped.[36] Part of this battalion skirmished with unidentified Rebels near Warsaw, Benton County, April 17, but details were not recorded.[37] Also in Benton County about April 24, troopers of this unit chased a band of southerners in vain, but took several men and women captive for aiding and harboring Rebels.[38] Yankees of McClurg's Battalion also exchanged shots with partisans again near Warsaw on April 28, but, as before, no details of the fight remain.[39] The large numbers of guerrillas and Rebel recruiting groups roaming the countryside probably kept these outnumbered Union units too busy for detailed record-keeping.

May in Henry and Bates Counties

In May much of the fighting shifted to Henry and Bates counties, with Colonel Fitz-Lee Warren's indefatigable 1st Iowa Cavalry representing the Union side of most contests. The Iowans skirmished May 11 at or near Deepwater and May 15 near Butler against unspecified foes, with light casualties reported.[40] A Henry Countian sent the fantastic story to a St. Louis newspaper of a Kansas man who, while traveling through northeast Henry County in mid–May, was set upon by five bushwhackers. The account claimed this gentleman from Lawrence, Kansas, aptly defended himself with a sword cane, dispatching some of the startled attackers and escaping through a fusillade of shots, if this story can be believed.[41] Bill Trueman's band of local guerrillas on May 17 or 18 ambushed a foraging detail of 1st Iowa Cavalry at Miami Creek near Butler. They killed three Federals and wounded the sergeant leading the detail before returning to their hideout on an island in the Marais des Cygnes River in south Bates County.[42] The Iowans also fought a skirmish at or near Butler on May 26, probably with the same band, but details are lacking.[43] The following day, bushwhackers killed three more troopers of the ubiquitous 1st Iowa Cavalry and wounded two more at Monegaw Springs, central St. Clair County, but Rebel casualties are not known.[44] Guerrilla activity slackened noticeably after May in this area, indicating perhaps that partisans either left or stayed hidden. With June and the advent of summer, Missouri's vegetation would be in full leaf, offering concealment to any who would take advantage of it. With warmer weather and the lush foliage, summer of 1862 promised to be even more violent in the southwest part of Missouri.

Eleven

Spring 1862 in Northwest Missouri

The most concentrated guerrilla war this spring of 1862 took place in northwest Missouri as the Southern bands here, particularly Quantrill's, became more organized and methodical. Conversely, the Union military here grappled awkwardly with that situation.

Sparse Action North of the Missouri River

The part of northwest Missouri north of the wide Missouri River bore few marks of the brush war this season, although it would later. One of the Jackson County bushwhacker bands crossed the river to raid Liberty, county seat of Clay County, on March 20, an episode to be detailed later. On April 8 guerrillas, probably of Kentucky-born northwest Livingston County farmer Charles Cooper's band, fired out of the night at Yankee militiamen at Medicine Creek near Chillicothe, killing one and wounding two.[1] In early May the matter of a stolen horse escalated into an interstate rivalry between Union chiefs in Kansas and Missouri. It began May 6 when a Kansas man and woman searching in Platte County, Missouri, for purloined stock seized a mare at gunpoint. When they attempted to return to Kansas with the animal, a citizens' posse arrested and jailed them in Platte City. Platte City authorities were startled the following day when 30 armed Kansas soldiers from Fort Leavenworth rode into town, rescued the pair, and returned them to Kansas soil with the horse in question and five Missourians as hostages to boot. After a flurry of communiqués between Yankee leaders in both states, the five hostages were allowed to return to the Show Me state, but the nag remained in Kansas. There would be many more such interstate "stock transfers" during the following three years.[2]

There was some violence in Clinton County that began near Plattsburg the morning of May 14 when some guerrillas, from ambush, shot a private of the 6th Cavalry MSM through the back as he rode by, killing him. The assailants then robbed the dead trooper's sole companion and escaped. 1st Lieutenant William

Newby and a patrol of the same regiment were probably looking for retribution for this bushwhacking the night of May 19 when they arrested returned Rebel soldier Asa Davis near Cameron, northeast Clinton County. It seems Davis admitted to the short-tempered patrol that he had been hiding in the brush and knew of some guerrilla activities, and they soon killed him, allegedly while he was attempting to escape. The following day the dead southerner's father, Ambrose Davis of near Plattsburg, happened upon 1st Lieutenant Newby's patrol. He, too, spoke too freely for his own good, and he, too, died suspiciously. The patrol did eventually return to garrison with ten living prisoners who must have been more careful with their speech.[3]

Later in May troops of 1st Cavalry MSM under Lt. Colonel Alexander M. Woolfolk rode out to stop the operations of a large troublesome guerrilla band in the Spring Hill area of northwest Livingston County. Charles Cooper's and Joe Kirk's 60 or 70 irregulars had been needling the northern cause in that area since the previous summer, with occasional sniping and other violence. Charles Cooper, in his late-thirties, was part of a large extended family that had moved from Kentucky some years earlier; while Kirk, of a Virginia family, was known for his tact and bravery and had served with the Missouri southern army the previous year. Their band represented just about the only organized Rebel resistance left in northwest Missouri north of the Missouri River at that particular time. During the evening of May 24, the Federals conducted a thorough sweep of the Spring Hill neighborhood and captured both chieftains and a couple of their men, effectively breaking up that band for the rest of the war, although Kirk would return for more guerrilla war later in 1862.[4]

More Fighting in the Center of the State

The central Missouri counties along the south bank of the Missouri River echoed with gunfire and the frequent movement of Union patrols and guerrilla bands throughout the spring of 1862. Much of the Rebel movement through these counties—Pettis, Saline, Cooper, Moniteau, and Cole—consisted of southern recruiters making their way north for recruits and back south with their new enlistees. About March 7, a man's corpse was found shot and mutilated in the road in east Saline County, but the reason for the killing is not recorded.[5] Perhaps his death was in some way related to five days of patrolling by the Boonville Battalion Cavalry MSM in Saline County. These German-Americans under Captain John B. Kaiser skirmished several times with guerrillas during this long patrol. Near Marshall they captured local Rebel recruiter Captain Joseph Englehart and his recruits but were confounded by the disappearance of a sergeant and 11 Yankees sent toward Miami. Captain Kaiser could not know that a band of Rebel recruits riding south from Livingston County came upon the sergeant's scouts killing one and capturing the rest. The southerners had to be amazed at their good fortune, not even part of the army yet and already conquering their enemies, but they thought it best to turn their prisoners over to local southerners to guard, and they continued to ride south. A few days later on March 15, a patrol of the newly-organized 7th Cavalry MSM near Cow Creek surprised a Rebel camp and inadvertently rescued these captives, who had been well-kept in a church all this time.[6] Other patrols of 1st Iowa Cavalry and 7th Cavalry MSM in and near Saline County between March 15 and 19, also captured a few Rebels they came across.[7]

Sometime this spring two local militiamen took paroled Rebel officer Captain Ed Brown a short distance from his home in north-central Saline County and shot him dead. Also during this season a local militiaman murdered the pro-southern chairman of trustees for the village of Arrow Rock, southeast Saline County, on the town wharf. Men of Eppstein's Boonville Battalion Cavalry MSM liberated the soldier before his trial could begin.[8] Clearly, some of the local northern militia were establishing their own ruthless, unprincipled version of warfare in the region.

Moving Bands of Southerners Attract Union Attention

On March 23 elements of 6th Missouri Infantry Regiment guarding the Pacific Railroad between Syracuse and Jefferson City fought a skirmish somewhere along that line at a place identified only as "Sink Hole Woods." Their antagonists were probably Rebel recruits heading south, and the scanty record does not state the outcome.[9] Several southern recruit companies from Boone and Shelby counties north of the Missouri River were riding through this region hoping to avoid Union patrols. A large combined task force of 6th Missouri Infantry, local militia, and even artillery searched the countryside of northeast Cooper and north Moniteau County in late March to intercept these passing Rebels. The Yankees found nine Confederate recruits on March 26 in north Moniteau County, incredibly, marching along in twos at shoulder arms. The Federals shot up the marching men killing seven and capturing two. Those two captives warned the northerners of other groups that had already moved through the area.[10] That same day across the county line near Pisgah, east Cooper County, 25 of Eppstein's Boonville Battalion exchanged shots with 40 or 50 Rebels, killing one. The smaller patrol seemed content not to bring on another firefight with the larger body.[11] About March 27 the Union commander at Sedalia voiced to his superiors his alarm that Tom Woodson and his band could endanger Sedalia. Despite the alarm, youthful, Kentucky-born Woodson, of a large, extended farm family from north of town, evidently did not conduct guerrilla operations for long in 1862. He would return later in the war.[12]

Newspaper Censorship

April was quiet in this region, but Federal officials arrested the editor of the *California Weekly News*, C.P. Anderson, on April 19, then released him on May 7. Anderson had attended the state secession convention months before, and his vitriolic editorials blasting the Lincoln government had helped galvanize southern thought in the region. Union troops had earlier ransacked Anderson's office, and this imprisonment served as a reminder of the Union intolerance. In the face of determined opposition Anderson gradually moderated his stand and continued publishing his paper, unlike many other newspapers of southern views which ceased to exist.[13]

Violent May Episodes in Central Missouri

Near Jefferson City on May 15 Union troops captured two Confederate colonels, originally from St. Joseph, who were attempting to cross to the north bank of the Missouri River, evidently to recruit.[14] This region had lots of such secretive travelers. In late May or early June, Union militia arrested then shot a man from northwest Saline County whom they accused of taking part in a skirmish there in early March.[15] At about this time in south Cole County, a slave tipped off passing troopers of 2nd Wisconsin Cavalry that his master had hidden a large cache of Rebel gunpowder nearby. This regiment was passing through on its way to a distant post, but it took the time to investigate. The curious cavalrymen convinced the master, a local judge, to take them to his hideaway, which turned out to be a secret chamber beneath the pulpit of a nearby church. The slave was correct, for inside were seven kegs and 48 cans of gunpowder, probably part of the Missouri State Guard stocks hidden across this region in June 1861 when Union troops first marched in. The fate of the judge and slave is not recorded, but it is probable that the first lost his freedom and the second gained it.[16] Union troops discovered more hidden powder in the Tipton area about this same time in at least three more hideaways.[17]

About May 23, a force of 9th Cavalry MSM out of Jefferson City in north Cole County attacked an unidentified body of about 50 Confederate recruiters who had earlier attempted to cross to the north side of the Missouri River into Boone County. Colonel Odon Guitar and part of the 9th Cavalry MSM attacked them that morning near Stonesport in Boone County and drove them back across the river, while communicating to the Jefferson City garrison their whereabouts. The patrol from Jefferson City found the Rebels and killed one and captured eleven before the rest could disperse into the woods and hills of north Cole County.[18]

Grim Struggle in Johnson County

Guerrilla warfare took on a personal flavor further west in Johnson County this spring. Johnson County's crossroads location—midway between the shipping terminals and Union headquarters of Kansas City and Sedalia and the river ports of Lexington and Warsaw—made it the frequent scene of roving units of armed horsemen looking to attack each other. Add to this Johnson County's mix of vocal leaders from both sides, and any observer in spring 1862 could sense the tension in the air. Here, northern home guards of the former 27th Missouri Mounted Infantry, along with the newly-recruited members of 7th Cavalry MSM, seemed to carry on a private war with local guerrillas, returned Rebel soldiers, and southern sympathizers.

Southern recruiting in the countryside, and the zealous local Yankee troops, set the match to this volatile mix and noticeably increased the level of activity in and around Johnson County, beginning in the second half of March 1862. The northern troops had grown fearful by this time for their own safety and that of their homes and families. The main concern was not so much the Confederate recruiters, but aggressive local partisan bands led by Matthias Houx of west county, John

Brinker from south of Warrensburg, a Dr. Warren, and others. Desperate soldiers do desperate things.

About this time 11 of these guerrillas raided the village of Calhoun just over Johnson County's southeast border in Henry County, robbing houses and mortally wounding a woman when her husband fought back.[19] Nearby, a passing column of 1st Iowa Cavalry acted on a tip and arrested a Rebel recruiter, identified only as Burris, the evening of March 19. Perhaps Burris' men had conducted the Calhoun raid in order to get supplies for their expected trek south to join the southern army in Arkansas.[20] At any event, the shooting of a woman, even accidentally, was rare, even in the violence of these times.

Also on March 19, in or near Warrensburg, the government seat of Johnson County, the local Yankee troops discovered 125 kegs of Rebel gunpowder near guerrilla leader John Brinker's home. This discovery may have been the spark that set off an orgy of depredations by these men. Over the next several days soldiers, mostly of Captain Thomas W. Houts' Johnson County MSM, assassinated at least six local men known for their southern sympathy and burned the homes of prominent southerners, even in Warrensburg itself, including the Brinker home. This terror wave prompted nearby Union authorities to investigate, but witnesses were understandably reluctant to testify, and little came of it except the recommendation that, henceforth, Union troops should not be stationed in their home district.[21]

The northern terrorism did bear fruit of a sort. Local bushwhacker chieftain and wealthy farmer Matthias Houx sent word on March 25 to the Yankee commander at Warrensburg that he wished to discuss surrender terms. Regional Union authorities would not grant much largesse, at least this early in the war, so the deal fell through, but a short time later the middle-aged family man left the area and bushwhacking, to return postwar and resume a peaceful life on his war-ravished farm a few miles northwest of Warrensburg.[22]

Before Houx retired from the scene, probably angry at the northern rebuff, he led 85 local guerrillas in one last attack on the Warrensburg garrison on March 26. Somehow forewarned, Major Emory S. Foster led his newly recruited 7th Cavalry MSM to intercept the Rebel force three miles south of town. Although initially outnumbered, Foster gamely attacked, driving Houx' horsemen four miles to the west to the brush of Post Oak Creek. There, the guerrillas stood their ground briefly in some corrals until Foster attacked them again and they fled. Foster's losses were two killed and seven wounded, including himself and one of his brothers, while Houx lost five dead and many wounded.[23]

Other guerrillas, like Warrensburg merchant's son, John Brinker, took over command from the war-weary Houx at the same time the area northern command sent in elements of 1st Iowa Cavalry to bolster the bloodied and apprehensive Warrensburg garrison. The local bushwhackers got reinforcements, too, when Jackson Countian Ben Parker brought his band into west Johnson County. On March 29, the bandaged but still truculent Major Emory S. Foster, leading 50 of his own men, 130 of the 1st Iowa Cavalry, and mounted members of 1st Missouri Light Artillery, caught up to Parker with his band of 60 or 70 men 14 miles northwest of Warrensburg. Major Foster was relieved to see that the Rebel horsemen did not number 300, as he had been led to believe, so he energetically attacked. Parker and his men took one look across the prairie at the onrushing blue-clad horsemen and wisely fled, precipitating a four-mile running fight in which the troopers unhorsed any bushwhacker they could catch. The Rebel retreat quickly degenerated into a rout as the wide-eyed southerners even tried galloping through brush and woods to throw off their pursuers. Parker's band, veterans of weeks of guerrilla fighting to the west, was dealt a severe blow, losing at least ten dead, several wounded, and 15 captured. Among the captives was Parker himself, captured lying behind a log feigning death. Federal losses were one killed and two wounded in this lopsided victory.[24]

Some may think that two costly defeats in three days for the Rebel cause in the Johnson County area would be enough to call for a rest and refit, but they would not understand the determination of the southern cause here. Thirty-five of Matt Houx's or John Brinker's guerrilla band on April 1 attempted to ambush 40 of the 7th Cavalry MSM in either east Johnson County or west Pettis County. Although they mortally wounded three Yankees and injured six others, the northern troops gamely attacked the ambushers, killing four and wounding several as they scrambled to get away.[25]

Finally, these defeats of Houx, Brinker, and Parker during the end of March and early April seemed to turn the tide of war temporarily to the Union side, as is reflected in a slower pace of actions in the Johnson County area the rest of April. Unit records of 7th Cavalry MSM record some kind of skirmish with unidentified foes April 8 near Warrensburg, but no other details were kept.[26] On April 16 a patrol of 1st Iowa Cavalry shot into a party of mounted bushwhackers near Blackwater River somewhere in north Johnson County, wounding two before they scattered.[27] A peace of sorts had come to Johnson County, but it would not stay long.

Quantrill Invades Kansas

William C. Quantrill's band attracted the most regional attention this spring during its operations in and near Jackson, Cass, and Lafayette counties, where residents were still bitter from Kansas jayhawker raids in recent months. Partly to avenge these raids, Quantrill led 40 men into Kansas at daybreak on March 7 and raided the border village of Aubrey, just west of Cass County, Missouri. The guerrillas shot to death three or four civilians who fired at them and wounded a former state representative, Abraham Ellis, whose only provocation was peering out a second-story window. Quantrill was apologetic when he recognized Ellis, who had employed the guerrilla leader briefly as a schoolteacher before the war. While Quantrill was chatting with the slightly-wounded Ellis, his men robbed the stores and dwellings and threatened to burn the town. They left hurriedly, however, after torching only one house, when they heard some Kansas troops were stationed nearby. They took with them as captive 2nd Lieutenant Reuben A. Randlett of 5th Kansas Infantry, with the intention to hold him as hostage for the release of a partisan held by Federals. When the inevitable pursuit proved to be ineffectual, the bushwhackers remained in the neighborhood several days, probably looking for a fight with the hated Kansas Yankee soldiers. Finally, on March 12 or 13, a 42-man patrol of 8th Kansas Infantry obliged the adventure-seekers with a firefight near Aubrey, killing two and wounding several of the raiders, at little cost to the Kansans.

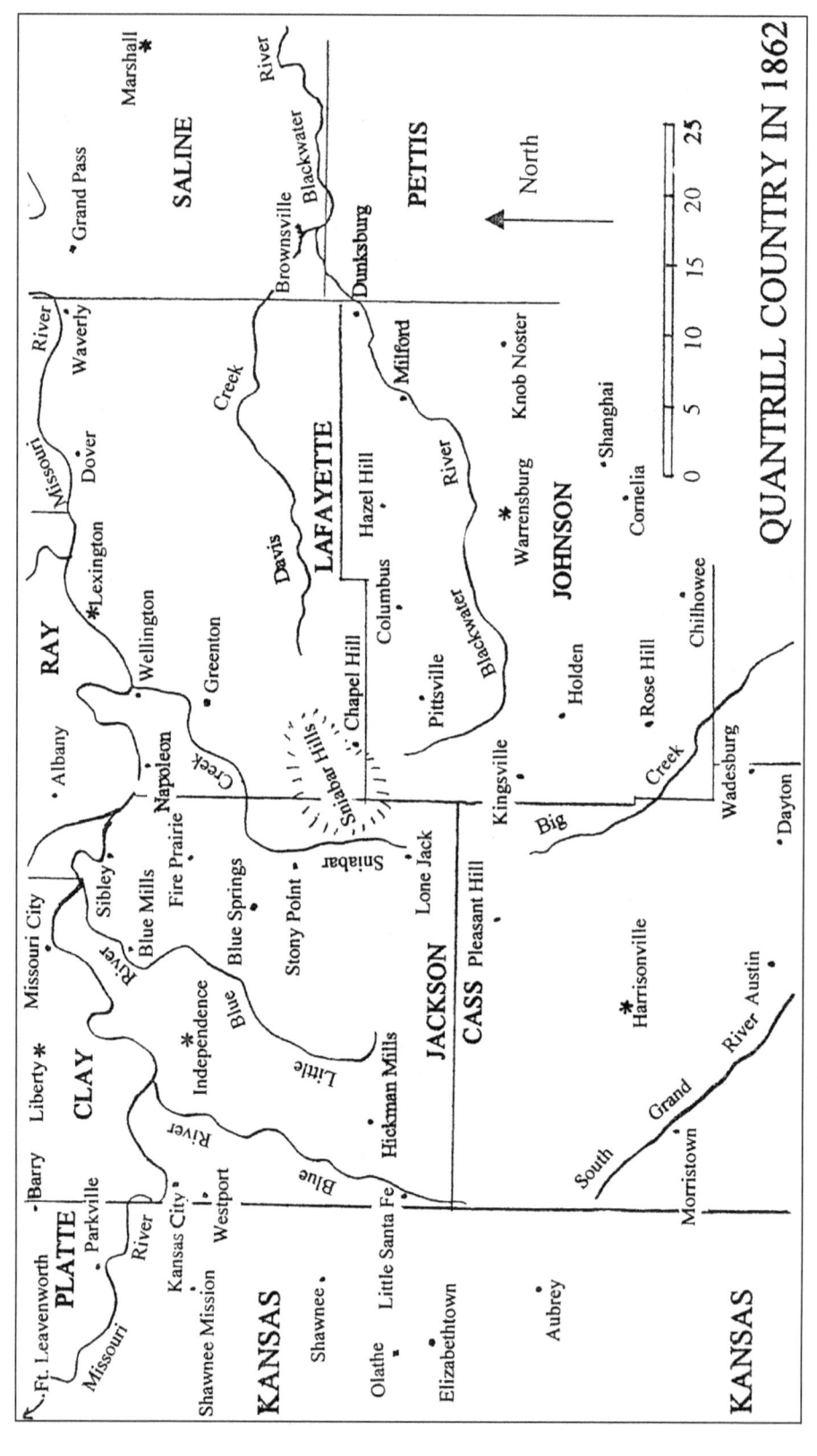

Quantrill's band scampered back across the border to their Missouri haunts in Jackson County, having enlarged both their reputation and their confidence. While St. Louis and Chicago newspapers printed stories about Quantrill and his mode of warfare, his men discussed what easy targets Kansas towns were and vowed they would cross the border again.[28] Perhaps it was some of these same men who ambushed and wounded two local militiamen on March 16 near Austin, south-central Cass County, then escaped unscathed.[29]

Two Other Area Guerrilla Bands

Quantrill's was not the only active guerrilla band in this area. Benjamin F. Parker had between 20 and 40 men beginning operations this spring in and around Jackson County. Sadly, history apparently has not left a record of how Parker came into this role. Also, a band of exiled Kansas southerners of about the same size made its base near Sibley, northeast Jackson County. This motley bunch had a colorful makeup. Its members included several from the Council Grove area of Kansas, namely Bill Reed, who would later lead the group, and brothers Bill and Jim Anderson—the former destined to take over from Reed in 1863 and later become known throughout Missouri as "Bloody Bill" Anderson. One of the more flamboyant members was notorious Denver gambler and gunfighter Charles Harrison, who chose to join the guerrillas when, as a lieutenant of Kansas Yankee troops, he had evidently been caught stealing horses. Some southerners who had formerly been officers in the Missouri State Guard in 1861 were also part of this band. One of them, Bill Haller, would later join Quantrill's group and be named one of his officers. Parker's band shunned Quantrill's for reasons that were not well recorded, and both of these groups disliked the Kansas exiles, who would rob both southern and northern families for their subsistence. As a rule the three bands shared roughly the same operations area but did not operate together.

One of these bands, containing 30 or 40 men, was robbing farm families in central and south Lafayette County while Quantrill's men were busy in the Aubrey raid. Thirty troopers of 1st Iowa Cavalry, armed only with sabers and pistols, rode out from Lexington to investigate and surrounded the unidentified bushwhackers at William Greer's farmstead near the Johnson County line March 11. After a ten-minute firefight, the unidentified Rebels feigned surrender, but then pulled their firearms out of hiding, and the battle raged on anew for 30 minutes more with no quarter asked or given. During the firestorm, farmer Greer ran from the house holding his small child in a successful gamble to save both their lives, although he suffered an arm wound. The fight ended when the buildings burned down and the remaining bushwhackers escaped to the brush, leaving behind nine dead and three wounded. The Iowans lost one dead and three wounded.[30]

Kansans Invade Missouri

After March 12, six companies of 6th Kansas Cavalry crossed into Missouri, set up temporary bases at Independence and Westport and perhaps Harrisonville,

The Kansas incursions into Missouri were usually accompanied by looting and destruction. (*Frank Leslie's Illustrated Newspaper*, December 12, 1863)

and swept through the countryside for a few days looking for guerrillas in reaction to Quantrill's Aubrey raid. Some accounts state that Quantrill and his men skirmished with some of these troops in Cass County. The Kansans' own records describe a sweep of the Sni Hills of southwest Lafayette County, where they claim to have broken up eight guerrilla camps and killed 37 bushwhackers. Some of this may be exaggeration, but bushes and trees would not be in leaf by mid–March, and it would be possible for wary soldiers to detect hideouts in the Sni Hills that would be all but invisible during the summer. The remaining question is, who were the 37 or so partisans the 6th Kansas Cavalry claims to have dispatched? Memoirs of Quantrills men preclude such a heavy loss at this time and, as will shortly be seen, Ben Parker's band could still muster 40 or so men. Unless the Kansans' victims were neophyte Rebel recruits moving through the area, these dead men could have been part of the colorful band of Kansas exiles known to base in this very area. After all, little was heard from this mysterious band for months after this time. The sad truth is that war had grown so grim and desperate in Missouri that nearly 40 men could be killed over a few days and not be noticed in the records of the time.[31]

The Robbing of the Rowena

The latest Kansas incursion may have convinced Ben Parker to lead his band in adventures outside Jackson County for a while. About March 16 or 18, his band captured the side wheel steamer, *Rowena*, on the Missouri River near Jackson or Lafayette County. No one was harmed, and the guerrillas contented themselves with taking only six dozen pairs of new boots and a few other things from the cargo before they allowed the boat to proceed undamaged on its way.³² As the guerrilla war in Missouri grew more desperate, encounters between boats and bushwhackers would not end so peaceably.

Quantrill's Band Reaches a Turning Point

Guerrilla memoirs tell us that in one of their Jackson County hideaways on March 18 or 19, Quantrill's men happened on a recent edition of a St. Louis newspaper in which Missouri's Union commander, Major General Henry W. Halleck, ordered on March 13 that "...captured guerrillas will not be treated as prisoners of war...." This sobering discovery unnerved many of the band who had heretofore considered themselves southern military. Indeed, several of the men had already served in Missouri's southern Missouri State Guard, which had mostly been incorporated into the Confederate army only a few weeks before. Quantrill allowed 15 to 20 of the disillusioned men to go home. About this same time, he released 2nd Lieutenant Randlett, who they had kept captive since the Aubrey raid. From this point on the remainder of the guerrillas faced the prospect of "no quarter given or taken" in their operations. Indeed, guerrilla warfare across Missouri became increasingly grim after Halleck's pronouncement.³³

Parker Raids Liberty

Quantrill's recent raid may have inspired Ben Parker to go town-raiding, too. Since the Kansas military was watchful on the border, Parker and his 40-

Union Major General Henry W. Halleck. (*Harper's Weekly*, November 30, 1861; courtesy of Bob and Mary Younger and Andy Turner)

or-so men, including sometime guerrilla chief Kit Chiles—full name, Christopher Lillard Chiles Sr.—turned north. Since the Union military had seized all known Missouri River boats to control guerrilla movement, Parker's men rounded up small skiffs and used them to ferry men and horses to the Clay County side. They raided Liberty, the county seat, on March 20. Perhaps they knew that Liberty's entire Yankee garrison at the time was only Captain Henry Hubbard and eight men recruiting for the 6th Cavalry MSM. At any rate, the raiders galloped down the dusty streets and angrily shot down the first of Hubbard's men they encountered when he stubbornly refused to tell them where the rest of the soldiers could be found. This shooting precipitated a siege, perhaps as long as three hours, before the remaining Federals surrendered. The townspeople were mostly southerners, who eagerly made the bushwhackers welcome, so Parker forbade looting, and the gang left the town intact when they departed with the captives in tow. Parker later paroled the prisoners. Area Union authorities were incensed by the citizens' cooperation with the guerrillas and arrested several prominent southerners. They hung one man for feeding Parker's raiders. Officials were probably still distrustful of the townspeople's role in the Rebel seizure of the U.S. arsenal nearby almost a year before. Oddly enough, although period historians from nearby Platte County credit Parker with leading this raid, the Union military and other notable historians claim the ubiquitous Quantrill and his boys did the deed, even though Quantrill-band memoirs claim nothing of the sort.[34]

Quantrill's Tate House Fight

Meanwhile, back in Jackson County on the evening of March 22, Quantrill, with about 100 men, demonstrated "no quarter" to a sergeant and private of 1st Missouri Cavalry guarding the Little Blue bridge near Little Santa Fe, in the southwest corner of the county. Quantrill himself shot the sergeant and others dispatched the private, sadly in front of his young son, who was inexplicably keeping company with his soldier father at the bridge. The guerrillas then fired the bridge, and Quantrill dispersed his band into four parts to seek shelter for the cool night in neighborhood homes and barns. His callous disdain for the inevitable Union counterstroke demonstrates Quantrill's low opinion of local northern troops, especially after their inept reactions to his Aubrey, Kansas, raid. This was nearly his undoing. The Ohio-born leader, with about 23 men, settled for the night in the David Tate house, but at ten that evening Major James Pomeroy and two companies of 2nd Kansas Cavalry that had been stationed nearby came calling. The Kansans surrounded the little frame house and demanded the surrender of the Rebels inside. Three guerrillas—said to be brothers—did give up, then a gun battle ensued, and the Yankees fired the house to force the issue. The troopers were dumfounded, however, when the remaining bushwhackers kicked down a burning wall and ran for safety with revolvers blazing. The Kansans listed only Major Pomeroy and one trooper severely wounded, but they counted seven corpses in the ruins of the house and grounds. One wonders if any of the dead included Pennsylvania-born David Tate and some of his five children, who were 13 and older and who probably had little choice about bedding down twenty-some heavily armed guerrillas who came without invitation in the night. The Kansas cavalry had to be content with their three prisoners, several other suspects, and burning several other neighborhood buildings before they rode back to base, leading 25 guerrilla horses.

This was a defeat for Quantrill, but it could have been a disaster with his own lack of caution to blame. Ironically, the memoirs of his men show they regarded the "Tate House Fight" as a trial by fire that demonstrated Quantrill's coolness in a crisis and their ability to survive any calamity using sudden offensive action and a high volume of gunfire.[35]

Parker in Cass and Johnson Counties

Still flush from his victories over the *Rowena* and in Liberty, Ben Parker now led his band south to operate in Cass and Johnson counties. About March 27, he determined that the Kansas cavalry was no longer in Harrisonville, so his men rode into town while unarmed home guards scuttled for cover. There was no mention of casualties, so the home guards probably hid. Parker's aim in this raid is not known; looting or burning is not mentioned, so perhaps he was seeking to attract new recruits among the locals.[36]

Parker's good fortune abruptly changed when he led his men into western Johnson County shortly afterward probably to recruit. His severe drubbing at the hands of Major Emory S. Foster's command out from Warrensburg has been described in detail earlier. The partisan leader's own fate as a captive was in jeopardy for a time because of the standing Missouri-wide order to execute those captured in arms bushwhacking. An anonymous southerner even wrote a plea for clemency for Parker in the April 3 Kansas City newspaper. Perhaps this helped convince Union authorities to spare his life by classifying Parker as a captured Confederate officer. They sent him to prison instead of the gallows. Like many other Rebel officers in Yankee prisons, he was exchanged after some months and returned to Missouri the following year to pick up guerrilla warfare again.

Meanwhile, the remnants of Parker's band remained in the Jackson County area but refrained from most active operations with their leader gone. A patrol of local northerners of 2nd Battalion Cavalry MSM from Pleasant Hill on April 7 killed two Rebels and captured one along Big Creek in east Cass County. A patrol of 1st Missouri Cavalry that night claimed to have slain pickets of Kit Chiles's guerrilla band on the Little Blue in Jackson County. These actions could have involved Parker's band, especially since native-Jackson Countian Chiles was featured in Parker's gang earlier in the spring.[37] The fate of the remnants of this band is unknown, except that memoirs of Quantrill members indicate that Parker men met near Quantrill's band in Cass County in the fall of 1862 and accompanied them south to Arkansas for the winter.[38]

Quantrill's Clark House and Balls Ford Fights

On March 31, 1862, Quantrill and about 60 of his bushwhackers were camped at Samuel Clark's log house near Stony Point, east Jackson County, when Captain

Albert P. Peabody and 65 troopers of 1st Missouri Cavalry found them. Once again, the Federals surprised the band and this could easily have ended in disaster for the guerrillas. Peabody's troopers quickly laid siege to the house. They kept the partisans from getting to their horses for about 90 minutes, in spite of sniping to their rear by some of the pro-southern neighbors. Quantrill's men disdained carbines and other long-range shoulder firearms in favor of pistols and shotguns, and this preference put them at a disadvantage here. However, the trapped Rebels noticed that their antagonists' single-shot carbines provided a slow rate of fire. Some of the boldest guerrillas exposed themselves to draw fire, then, while the cavalry was reloading, the band dashed on foot into the nearby woods. Quantrill's losses at the "Clark House Fight" were six killed, several wounded, and all their horses captured, compared to three wounded Yankees.

The escape from the "Clark House Fight" did not mean the bushwhackers were out of danger, for they were on foot, and area Union forces were closing in. The following day, the footsore Rebels came to the bluffs of Sni-A-Bar Creek, overlooking Balls Ford, just as 50 troopers of Eppstein's Boonville Battalion Cavalry MSM rode into pistol range below. Quantrill and his men quickly took cover on the boulder-strewn height and gamely fired on these new antagonists as they surged up the slope after them. After a gun battle of only a few minutes, Quantrill wisely broke off the engagement before other pursuing Yankees came up on his rear toward the sound of the shooting. The Boonville Battalion reported a loss of only two wounded, but reported Quantrill's losses at five dead, several wounded, and one captured. This last part was probably exaggerated. The Rebels readily obtained remounts and medical care from their many friends in the area over the next few days and dispersed to different hideouts to await a rendezvous a few days later. Once again Quantrill's band came close to disaster through faulty security and once again they escaped little hurt and with an enhanced reputation and confidence through the effective use of the offensive. Federal troops had engaged them in open combat twice in the field, and still could not effectively eliminate Quantrill's band as a threat.[39]

Quantrill's Lowe House Fight

Lieutenant George W. Nash's patrol of 1st Missouri Cavalry thought it had come upon a solution to the Quantrill problem when at two in the morning of April 16, it captured two of the guerrilla band seeking shelter from the rain in a house. The troopers forced the pair to disclose part of the band's location, so at daybreak Nash's patrol rushed Quantrill and 23 men attempting to dry out at an isolated log house known as "the Lowe place" in south-central Jackson County. Again the Rebels were caught by surprise, and they ran for their lives to the nearby woods, leaving behind not only their horses, but weapons, hats, etc., and two rearguards who were overpowered and captured before offering much of a fight. Some of the troopers, tired of chasing the "will-of-the-wisp" partisans, placed the captives on a stump and shot them before Lieutenant Nash could prevent it. One of them, Andy Blunt, survived and later escaped from an Independence hospital and carried on an aggressive war of his own for about two more years before being killed in the field. Blunt seems to have used an alias to hide his real name and protect his family from northern countermeasures, and his real identity has never been proven.

Meanwhile, this latest shameful defeat—the third surprise for the band in two months—was not viewed as such by the guerrillas themselves. Their own accounts indicate that they regarded these close scrapes more as trial-by-fire and proof of their survivability than tactical setbacks. Early Union elation at these small tactical wins quickly faded when they realized they had lost another opportunity to destroy the notorious band. The guerrillas' ability to endure and even continue in operations despite such defeats in the field frustrated the northerners and seemed to indicate bush war would remain in at least this part of Missouri for a long time.[40]

Through the crucible of these setbacks and such hard-learned lessons, Quantrill was slowly developing tactics of his own to ensure his band's survivability. He was learning to disperse his men in small groups after every fight or raid, anticipating the unimaginative Yankee countermeasures. Small groups could obtain remounts and medical care from locals and nimbly evade the clumsy Federal dragnets. In his memoirs, Harrison Trow quoted Quantrill as saying, "...scattered soldiers make a scattered trail. The regiment that has but one man to hunt can never find him."[41] In his postwar account, Bill Gregg wrote that after the "Lowe House Fight" the group of four he was with lost their horses to a northern patrol near Stony Point. He sadly noted that the Federals killed one of the guerrillas who could not run due to a previous wound. It was truly an exciting but deadly war these men fought.[42]

Union Countermeasures

Meanwhile, Union authorities groped for methods to counter the growing bushwhacker menace. On April 19 Colonel Egbert B. Brown, a rising star in the new Missouri State Militia, held a town meeting in Independence where (1) he shared the citizens' abhorrence of Kansas jayhawker raids; (2) he discouraged support for the guerrillas; and (3) he encouraged residents to support the law and not interfere with U.S. military operations.[43]

The district commander, Brigadier General James Totten, on April 21 declared Quantrill's band—ignoring the other bands—to be outlaws. They were to be shot on sight, just in case any Union soldier was still unsure.[44] The effect of this attention directed specifically against Quantrill's band was to elevate the band to legendary status forevermore and relegate many of the others to obscurity. This notoriety also galvanized southern support of Bill Quantrill's band in the region and tended to dissipate the notion that his men were mere renegades or outlaws—just the opposite of the Federal intent!

Small Actions in Late April and Early May

Eppstein's Battalion Cavalry MSM, led by Captain John B. Kaiser, were the main guerrilla-hunters in this region in late April and were veterans of several months of this kind of fighting. Confederate Captain Louis Lloyd from Holt County was leading his small company of recruits along the long trek to join the rest of the southern army in Arkansas when they ran into Eppstein's efficient guerrilla-hunters. It happened April 22 in Lafayette County, and details do not survive, but the bluecoats easily captured Lloyd's whole command, severely wounding one man in the process.[45] Also in Lafayette County near Lexington, according to a local citizen's diary entry, on May 3 either Eppstein's men or some from the 7th Missouri Infantry shot into a party of unarmed farmers camping in the countryside. These men had evidently been to the Lexington market and couldn't make their way home before dark. One farmer was wounded before the Federals realized the yeomen were not bushwhackers. This is a good example of how partisan warfare was interrupting normal rural life.[46] The local diarist recorded that the next day these same Union soldiers skirmished again somewhere in the area, giving no details except to say that men were killed and wounded. Evidently, they ran into someone more lethal than sleepy farmers.[47]

In south Cass County, many miles south of Lafayette County, four of Ben Parker's guerrilla band were attempting to steal some farmers' horses on May 19 when the owners saw them and shot up the marauders. Three of the Rebels were killed and one got away, and the farmers discovered nearby some horses stolen from the northern home guard at Harrisonville in March.[48] Elements of Eppstein's battalion and 7th Missouri Cavalry skirmished, evidently with part of Quantrill's band, May 11 at Pink Hill, northeast Jackson County, resulting in the deaths of two Yankees and the wounding of three. Bushwhacker and future sheriff's deputy Bill Gregg may have referred to this fight years later in his memoirs, writing that at Pink Hill about this time Eppstein's Battalion captured his comrade James Tucker, but that Tucker managed to escape three nights later.[49] About this same time, men of Eppstein's command killed two probable guerrillas camping in southwest Lafayette County because they ran when challenged.[50]

By mid–May, 1862, guerrilla actions increased in Jackson County. About May 15, Lieutenant George W. Nash's patrol of 1st Missouri Cavalry killed two partisans in a firefight near the Little Blue.[51] Approximately one day later, another patrol of this regiment received an unexpected welcome when they rode out to a local man's home to ask him to guide for them. When the man shot at them, wounding a bugler, they took it as a firm refusal and shot him dead.[52] On May 16, Quantrill and band ambushed the 13-man mail escort detail of Captain William A. Long, also of the 1st Missouri Cavalry. It was easy for the bushwhackers. They hid in the brush at one of their favorite ambush sites, the road cut near where the Independence-Harrisonville Road crossed the Little Blue River in central Jackson County. The rebels held their fire until their victims were well into the road cut, and then shot the Yankees to pieces with accurate revolver fire. All of Captain Long's detail were hit except two; one was killed outright, and six were badly wounded. Needless to say, Captain Long led a hasty retreat, or they would all have died. Evidently, Quantrill had used this same site for ambushes before, and if Union authorities had left any of the various units they rotated through Jackson County there long enough, they would not have allowed themselves to be slaughtered at the same location time after time. As it happened, each succeeding northern unit sent to squelch Quantrill in Jackson County had to learn the same painful lessons over again. As indicated in such battle reports, all they seemed to pass along to each other was an ignorance of who they were fighting and how to do it. The 1st Missouri Cavalry pursued Quantrill back to his campsite near an old log house. The cavalry patrol shot it out with the few guerrillas at the camp, killing one, wounding several who escaped, and capturing two others. The troopers also recovered the mailbags taken at the ambush earlier that day and discovered 2,000 pounds of bacon the bushwhackers may have hidden in the old log house for future use. The newspaper account of this part of the long day's actions fails to address whether the cavalry captured the bacon to take back to eat, burned the house down around it, or a little of both.[53]

An Unexpected Respite from the Fighting

Postwar guerrilla accounts tell the surprising story that after Quantrill's ambush of Captain Long's mail escort at the road cut near the Blue River, an acute shortage of revolver percussion caps forced Quantrill to leave the area to and get more. He ordered his men not only to disperse but to "lay low" in small groups while he and Lieutenant George Todd, the former Kansas City stone mason, took an extended trip in disguise to Hannibal in east Missouri to buy an ample supply of caps for the pistols. Evidently, all other efforts to obtain this one item in sufficient numbers had failed, but why Quantrill felt the need to rectify the situation personally is not addressed in the guerrilla accounts that describe the three- or four-week excursion. After the hectic pattern of almost daily guerrilla actions, Union authorities had to be perplexed at the sudden peace that came over Jackson, Cass, and west Lafayette counties between May 16 and June 11. As if to underscore this fantastic story, a man claiming to be Quantrill robbed a bank in Bloomington, Macon County, sometime in 1862. This would have been along the route Quantrill and Todd took to Hannibal on the train, and this bank robbery may very well have provided them the funds they used to purchase the percussion caps.[54]

Although Quantrill's guerrillas "laid low" during this strange quiet period, the Union military was still actively trying to find them in their hiding places. A large patrol of 6th Kansas Cavalry discovered one of these lairs south of Lone Jack in southeast Jackson County on the morning of May 31. Near another one of those isolated cabins so common in this area, they found one of the many bushwhacker camps and engaged the few guerrillas there in a gunfight, killing one and wounding another. The Kansans were surprised to find a large quantity of gunpowder hidden in the house and were disgusted to find a large variety of freshly prepared food, obviously provided to the guerrillas by nearby residents. The cavalry burned the cabin, enjoying the great explosion it made, and probably burned some of the neighboring houses, too, to discourage any further catering to the bushwhackers.[55]

Violence Along Lafayette-Saline County Line

Meanwhile, guerrillas other than Quantrill's were active around east Lafayette County in late May. About this time troopers of Eppstein's Battalion fired into another party of farmers they mistook for guerrillas on a country road near Lexington and evidently killed one this time.[56] The mostly German-speaking members of this unit from Boonville were getting a reputation for shooting first and asking questions later. Along the Lafayette-Saline County line, local guerrilla leader Captain William B. Edwards was attracting the attention of northern troops. About May 25 Edwards, with eight men, ambushed Captain Foster R. Hawk's patrol of 7th Missouri Cavalry near Waverly, killing a lieutenant and mortally wounding Captain Hawk. Edwards lost two of his own men and all his horses in this fight. Major Eliphalet Bredett and 131 troopers of Hawk's regiment, with some artillery from Lexington, returned to the ambush area May 28 to settle with Edwards. The guerrilla leader and his remaining men wisely kept hidden, and Bredett had to content himself with shelling a cabin on an island in the Missouri River that looked suspicious. The next day near Dover, this Union force killed three men they believed to be guerrillas. Edwards survived this experience and later joined the Rebel army to the south. It is not surprising, in the light of this heavy-handed treatment of area residents that hundreds of men from the Waverly and Dover areas eagerly joined a Rebel recruiting command that made its way into this neighborhood later this same year.[57]

Summary of Spring 1862 Actions in Northwest Missouri

On the whole, guerrilla operations in this quadrant of Missouri this spring brought frustration to the northern side and some satisfaction to southern hopes, particularly in west-central Missouri. Bushwhackers seemed to adapt more quickly to the mode of warfare they chose than did their blue-clad antagonists. However, even the clumsy Federals scattered several of the local bands, such as Coopers' in Livingston County, and occasionally scooped up Rebel recruits, such as those in Moniteau and Lafayette counties. Yankees also affected guerrilla leadership by capturing Ben Parker and convincing Matt Houx to retire from Johnson County. The "no quarter" rule set by Union leadership forced the remaining guerrillas to learn fast or forfeit their lives, so beginners seasoned quickly. Bill Quantrill's carelessness nearly brought his growing band to disaster several times this spring, yet his reliance on nothing but offensive tactics and pistol firepower carried his men through this tenuous testing period. Although other bands continued the fight aggressively in Johnson, Jackson, and other counties, Quantrill's band eclipsed all others in notoriety. The endurance of these partisans in the countryside also encouraged those southern residents who harbored, fed, and spied for them in large numbers. Although the southern army remained far to the south, this hit-and-run fighting style was keeping southern hopes bright in Union-occupied Missouri. The onset of summer promised only more fighting and killing in northwest Missouri.

Twelve

The Enrolled Missouri Militia: Guerrillas' Controversial New Enemy

One of Missouri's most controversial innovations, initiated by the northern side during summer of 1862, actually helped to encourage the guerrillas. On July 22 Missouri's northern governor, Hamilton R. Gamble, in General Order Number 19, ordered all able-bodied Missouri men to report in six days to enroll in a new local militia organization called the Enrolled Missouri Militia. This drastic measure was to provide for the state's defense against large numbers of guerrillas while replacing the troops that Federal authorities were ordering out of this lackluster, "backwater" military area to more strategic fronts elsewhere. After all, to the Union high command, Missouri was not an occupied enemy territory, but a legitimate Union state already contributing much to the U.S. war effort. The state could handle a few pesky bushwhackers out of its own resources and not tie up thousands of trained and armed veteran troops needed more on the "real" war fronts. Facing this removal of most of the troops in Missouri, the state Union command and governor knew they had to raise an army of Missourians to protect Missouri.

In practice, the Enrolled Missouri Militia (EMM) was a form of home guard. Now, Federal authorities had outlawed home guards in Missouri some months earlier, on the grounds that they were disorganized, unprofessional and ineffective, unable or unwilling to answer to Federal military command, and hindered the recruiting of Union soldiers in the same neighborhoods. Earlier in the spring the state Union command had recruited, organized, and fielded over a dozen regiments of Missouri State Militia (MSM), which gradually proved themselves in combat as active state troops. The EMM, on the other hand, would serve as inactive state troops. That is, the members would remain at their civilian employment and at home until needed by a threat in their home region, at which time they would report to their local rallying point as sort of a "minuteman" quick reaction force. In theory, this would save the strained state coffers much money by paying the EMM only for those occasions they were called to active duty, but in reality little pay was available. Missouri's Union military head, Major General John M. Schofield, and the governor originated and implemented this emergency army evidently without the consent or permission of the Federal war authorities, who had, after all, outlawed a similar practice in Missouri some months before. One unhappy and unforeseen result of this haste, years later, would be that EMM soldiers and their families would be mostly ineligible for Federal pensions for this service, since it was not in accredited Federal military units.

The sticking point for southern and neutral men was the way the EMM would "separate the sheep from the goats," that is, divide all local able-bodied men into those who could be counted on to serve loyally in an emergency and southern men who could be a threat or a hindrance if armed in a home guard type of unit. General Order Number 19 provided that ALL able-bodied men would report to local Union military authorities and enroll. Those local authorities would, in turn, decide who was loyal to the U.S. and who was not. Southern and neutral men correctly saw this enrollment procedure as a convenient way for local bullies and hacks wearing Union blue to stigmatize southern sympathizers for later targeting and assessment. Under earlier legislation pronounced, or "notorious," southern sympathizers were already assessed to pay for Missouri's northern war needs. To dishonest local leaders, this had become a legal way to steal a man's real and personal property, and some found ways to divert such confiscated money into their own pockets. This new law would allow officials to designate thousands more as loyalty threats, for possible property seizure or imprisonment. Furthermore, many viewed enrollment into the EMM as a precursor to being moved into active military service, as a form of pre-draft. After all, the announcement of the first national U.S. draft would not occur until the following month, and that proclamation would result in dismay and rioting in other parts of the country. With General Order Number 19, Missouri faced that same anxiety a few weeks before the rest of the nation.

Meanwhile, the state's entire adult male population was made to enroll at local military stations into scores of these EMM units. Over 52,000 men were eventually sorted into more than 70 separate regiments. After an initial organization, arming (with weapons that most often would be left at the meeting place and not go home with the enrollees), and training, Missouri had a more-or-less inactive militia that in theory could counter both guerrillas and local Confederate regular incursions. In action, each EMM local unit was organized to serve for brief periods of active duty to augment Missouri State Militia (MSM) and other Union troops in the field around the home area. The EMM could, from time to time, guard vital transportation and other facilities and perform other, less-threatening military duty, freeing MSM and other federal troops to concentrate on combat with southern forces. The sad reality is that the EMM was not always led or trained in a professional military manner, and EMM blunders and depredations became an embarrassment. After all, those with military experience or ability and real fervor for the Union cause had plenty of opportunity to enlist in regular units during the first year and a half of the war. Some may have said those who were left were not well motivated. This said, various EMM units became professional in their demeanor and execution, defended their home areas with distinction, even won acclaim for occasional combat, and often performed these feats with their own private weapons, clothing, and horses. Those 70-or-so regiments of enrolled Missouri men ran the gamut from laughable to laudable.

The widespread dissatisfaction with being commanded to enroll in a Yankee unit led literally thousands of southern and formerly neutral Missouri men to "take to the hills" rather than submit to General Order Number 19. The scores of guerrilla chieftains and Confederate recruiters already operating in many parts of the state suddenly experienced a great influx of able-bodied adult men who chose to "enroll" with them rather than with the Yankees. True, many of these new recruits were not the most motivated fighters, but hundreds of these "sudden Confederates" served the South faithfully and well through the rest of the war. Large numbers of men, disaffected with General Order Number 19, simply left the state, for the duration of the war or permanently, generally going into the western territories. There were also large numbers of men who chose neither to serve one side or to leave Missouri. These men simply hid out in the wilds of rural Missouri hoping for the time when General Order Number 19 would fade way. Many of this last group hid near home in some brush pile or cave or dugout, and their family would carry food and other needs to their lair when they thought nobody would see. Few of these stalwarts could endure this new hermit life more than a few days, and nearly all who chose this course either sheepishly returned home to enlist in the EMM, joined the southern forces, or left the state, too.

The sum total of this very upsetting Enrolled Missouri Militia business was to force all Missourians to decide which side they would support. General Order Number 19 forced many, if not most of the neutrals, to pick a side. The war was no longer some distant thing to read about in the newspapers, but now took on the character of a general war in which the whole populace took part in some way.[1]

Thirteen

Summer 1862 in Southwest Missouri

Summer 1862 found both sides in a grim contest across southwest Missouri. The "no quarter" rule, begun across the state in the spring, was acknowledged everywhere by this summer. Southern interests in this corner of Missouri were determined to make their presence felt and to recruit men to man the southern army in Arkansas. The Union military was no less determined to squelch such southern aims in this quarter of the state, but war demands elsewhere had caused the northern leaders to strip away most troops. They left only enough cavalry to hold this region against light opposition, because that was all they had faced here since the spring. They seemed to anticipate only will-of-the-wisp hit-and-run tactics from the few remaining small guerrilla bands.

Evidently, the Yankee leadership failed to grasp the southern intention to use southwest Missouri as a conduit to funnel recruiting commands into the state and fresh recruits back out. Union troops concentrated at the railroads, large towns, and strategic river ports of southeast Missouri. This dissuaded thoughtful southern leaders from sending recruiters through there. But southwest Missouri had no railroads and few large towns—especially on navigable rivers. Moreover, the southwest quadrant was lightly populated, which meant fewer people to inform against passing Confederates or guerrillas, and those few that lived there were, perhaps, easier to intimidate, as things progressed. In fact, both sides had already been pushing the locals to leave with terror, house burning, and forceful recruiting. Then there was the pressure of feeding strange soldiers and their hungry horses. Many locals had already left their farmsteads and hamlets for refuge in less warlike climates, and by summer of 1862, much of the landscape was deserted.

Another factor which made southwest Missouri a natural Confederate conduit was the ease of horseback travel through the vast prairies of this section. Although there were enough hilly and forested parts to allow large bodies of men to hide when necessary, southern mounted forces could move fast enough here so that even the Yankees' telegraph could not send pursuers fast enough to catch up to them. In military parlance, these vast natural grasslands provided the southerners with a high-speed avenue of approach to the large pools of potential southern recruits further to the north. As a result, much of the fighting here took the form of meeting engagements, running fights, pursuits, and the like—very little standing still. Whether the antagonist here lived or died depended sometimes solely on whether his horse was less tired than the mount of the man shooting at him. In the grand scheme of this prairie fighting, the southerners learned to ride better horses than the Union cavalry's regular issue nags. That way, a northern patrol could only effect casualties during the opening seconds of any fight. After that, it was just a horse race, and the southern side seemed to win most of those.

June and July Actions in the Southwest Corner

Indeed, the prairie counties of the far southwest corner of this region were the scene for the earliest violence of June 1862. The Federals smarted from the humiliating defeat of the 14th Cavalry MSM by Colonel John T. Coffee's irregular Rebels May 31 at Neosho, Newton County. Colonel Charles Doubleday, of the 2nd Ohio Cavalry, led one thousand Yankees south to McDonald County to settle the score and drive the Dade County lawyer out of the area. Doubleday's force caught up to Coffee's just at the southwest corner of McDonald County—and Missouri—June 4 or 6 at a popular Rebel rendezvous known as Cowskin Prairie. The action was not conclusive, for Coffee's rear guard held the Federals at bay until the Confederates could cross the Grand River at dusk and slip away in the dark. Confederate recruiter Colonel Sidney Jackman was with Colonel Coffee's command at the time and recorded in his memoirs that Doubleday captured several of Coffee's men. Surprisingly, Colonel Doubleday released these captives and sent them to Jackman with a note that Jackman could return the favor sometime. Such largesse was unusual in this type of warfare.[1]

On June 11 five soldiers of 37th Illinois Infantry set out across the prairie from Cassville, Barry County, with two regimental wagons but without waiting for proper armed escort. An eager, unidentified guerrilla band made short work of the incautious little detail—taking the wagons, four horses, and one Yankee as captive. They left behind one dead infantryman, and the rest were wounded.[2]

Tom Livingston's guerrillas skirmished with Colonel William F. Cloud and his 10th Kansas Cavalry at Pilot Grove in north Jasper County on June 17. Few details of this fight remain, but it must have been a tough one for Livingston, as this was the last heard of his band in this region until August.[3]

By June 20 Union leaders reported a new innovation they hoped would improve their ability to prevent southern bands from roaming this region at will. They established a chain of cavalry posts across the prairie to both retard Rebel movement and react against it. This move would also serve to wean the troops away from the seductive comforts of the larger towns where they had established their garrisons heretofore. Of course, the leadership would incur the wrath of northern sympathizers in those towns, who would clamor to have troops closer at hand to protect them. The conflicting demands of providing troops for protection versus active offensive against rebel irregulars would haunt Union high command in Missouri throughout the war.[4]

At daybreak on June 23 a battalion of 2nd Wisconsin Cavalry defeated Major Frank Russell's Rebel force at Pineville, McDonald County, capturing several. Since

The intensity of guerrilla warfare depopulated large parts of southwest Missouri. Many of these refugees fled to St. Louis. (*Harper's Weekly*, December 28, 1861; courtesy Bob and Mary Younger and Andy Turner)

Pineville is located in a wooded, hilly terrain, this victory probably had little to do with the new chain of Union posts across the nearby prairie.[5]

In late June or early July, elements of 2nd Ohio Cavalry ventured out from their Neosho base into northwest McDonald County, evidently to ferret out bushwhackers disguised as peaceable farmers. The inability to tell the difference between ordinary country folk and guerrillas, who would raid at times and pretend to be innocent farmers when the pursuit would ride by, haunted all Union troops who served in Missouri during the war. Different units acquired reputations based upon how they approached this constant problem. Some just treated everybody in the country as enemies, and the Union cause suffered accordingly. The 2nd Ohio Cavalry had no such reputation, yet one of its patrols in this sweep faced a true test and acted as most Yankees did. Two local men panicked and ran when approached, and the Ohioans gunned one of them down. Northern cavalrymen regarded flight as a sign of guilt, not simply fear, and it was a case of "shoot first and ask questions later."[6] Also during this sweep, local partisans under a man named Yocum skirmished with some of the Ohioans, but few details remain.[7]

About July 4 or 5, unidentified Union cavalry in east Newton County killed three of five guerrillas near Gadfly and ten of 18 close to the nearby hamlet of Jollification in prairie chases. Either these northerners had good horses or had learned how to cope with grassland fighting.[8] In mid–July a Union patrol on Buffalo Creek, west McDonald County, came upon eighteen Rebels stealing horses and shot them up, killing and wounding nine or ten.[9] During the rainy night of July 19 a large patrol of 14th Cavalry MSM scoured neighborhoods in Dallas and Polk counties and took into custody 37 suspected guerrillas found at their homes. This was another attempt to take the war home to the partisans. The patrol record does not say, but if this effort was predicated by the finger-pointing of a local informant, it was probably very effective from the Union viewpoint. With their bread-winners away in a Yankee military jail for weeks or worse, many of these families undoubtedly left their homes and became refugees, further depopulating this sparse region.[10]

June and July Actions in the Osage River Basin

In early June, Colonel Upton Hays of Jackson County led his recruiting detail of 130 men north through southwest Missouri to recruit near home. His command avoided contact with northern patrols until they got to St. Clair County. There, elements of 1st Iowa Cavalry picked up Hays' trail and dogged his steps, skirmishing repeatedly with his rear guard, particularly as he crossed the Osage River at Taberville about June 11. In that last fight the Rebels lost three killed and four wounded, including Hays, who dislocated his shoulder. Being unable to lead, Hays was forced to disperse his command in the woods of west Henry County. Later, the reassembled recruiting command continued north to Jackson County.[11]

On June 17 unidentified guerrillas attacked the Yankee military mail escort somewhere between the posts of Independence and Fort Scott, probably in Bates or Vernon counties. No other details remain of this action.[12]

A patrol of 1st Iowa Cavalry in or near Henry County on June 25 captured three Rebels, one of whom was Colonel Michael C. Goodlett of nearby Johnson County, former aide to Governor Claiborne Fox Jackson, Missouri's Rebel governor in exile. Apparently, Colonel Goodlett had lately been a member of Colonel Hays' long-riding recruiting command.[13] The rest of June and July was strangely quiet in the Osage River basin, as the remaining recruiters went about their behind-enemy-lines business, perhaps with assistance from local guerrillas.

Action resumed July 20, for on that day a patrol of 6th Kansas Cavalry exchanged shots with unidentified bushwhackers near Taberville, west St. Clair County. Other details of this fight have not survived.[14] A patrol of 7th Cavalry MSM from Syracuse, Morgan County, on July 25 killed one partisan and wounded another in the southwest corner of Morgan County.[15] Likewise, part of the 8th Cavalry MSM had a firefight with unknown bushwhackers at Cross Timbers in north Hickory County on July 28.[16] On July 30 or 31, a small guerrilla band near Calhoun, northeast Henry County, killed a farmer, looted a doctor's home, then fired on a patrol of 1st Iowa Cavalry sent out from Clinton to stop them. The partisan band then made good their escape.[17]

July and August Actions in the Niangua-Gasconade River Basins

East of the prairie, the wooded, hilly part of southwest Missouri along the Niangua and Gasconade Rivers was spared the large volume of guerrilla warfare taking place just to the west, but some actions took place here. Sometime in July a citizens' posse in east Christian County captured eight guerrillas and gave them to a Union patrol already in the area looking for them. Residents of northern sympathy actively assisting the Union military were not uncommon in this area, possibly due to particularly callous local southern actions here earlier in the war, and to the vicious Alf Bolen band to the south.[18] These eight Rebels could have been a part of Rebel Colonel Charles H. Clifford's command of 150 who two days later approached the Union garrison town of Ozark a few miles west. Clifford's body maneuvered to assault the place, then unexpectedly turned south. The Union commander sent 60 cavalrymen, who pursued Clifford to near Forsyth, Taney County, in a long running fight in which five Rebels were killed, several wounded, and six more captured.[19]

Dallas County was on the western edge of this quiet, wooded region, but it was the scene of some actions this summer. Captain Thomas Lofton's band of Rebel recruits ran into a small patrol of 14th Cavalry MSM in west Dallas County about July 23, and the result was one Confederate killed and two captured. Lofton, who escaped, was a local farmer, about 40 years of age, originally from North Carolina and Tennessee, with a large family, and he had served as a captain in the southern Missouri State Guard earlier in the war.[20]

Captain Milton Burch of this same Yankee regiment began to acquire his reputation as a guerrilla hunter this year. On August 1 he was commanding a camp of 80 troopers near Ozark in north Christian County when his scouts and friendly locals warned him that a large Rebel recruiting command, led by Colonel Robert Lawther of Jefferson City, was maneuvering through the steep hills nearby to attack his camp. Forewarned is forearmed, so when Lawther's men rushed the Union encampment, they found only empty tents. Burch's command counterattacked from a ravine. Burch's smaller command drove the startled Confederates south to Taney County, resulting in a total of about ten southern casualties.[21] Just to be sure Lawther's men kept going all the way back to Arkansas, Burch's troopers tracked them to Snapp's Mill on the White River where they attacked them in their camp on August 4, this time killing four and wounding many, before the northern force returned to their own camp in Christian County.[22] Meanwhile, Major John C. Wilber took 100 men of the 14th Cavalry MSM out from their Christian County garrison along the White River in Taney County. Between August 7 and 9 his men traded shots with several small bands of Rebel irregulars, driving them south of the White River.[23] The Federals at Ozark sent a third expedition to White River between August 14 and 17. This combined force of 37th Illinois Infantry, 14th Cavalry MSM, and some artillery found the White River Valley peaceful. Just to be certain, though, these northerners fired their cannon at suspected guerrilla hideouts in the river bluffs before returning to base.[24] This Union thoroughness makes it is easy to see why this small portion of Missouri remained mostly quiet for the rest of the war.

August Invasion of Confederate Recruiters

The tenuous hold Federals had on the prairies of southwest Missouri faced a severe test during August 1862. The numerous Rebel recruiting details that rode quickly through the region before this seemed like a trickle compared to the flood tide of Confederate regulars who galloped over the prairies now in large numbers. Some of these were Missouri's most capable, cunning military men, sent home by Confederate commanders in the Trans-Mississippi region to bring back fresh troops to fill the gaps in the ranks. The Yankee cavalry regiments were now veterans of local guerrilla warfare, consisting mostly of tedious patrols which wore down men and horses. How would they fare now against battle-tested Confederate regulars? As earlier detailed, Upton Hays had slipped through almost unnoticed in June with over 100 riders, while Robert Lawther's command was blunted and ejected in early August from forest-covered Christian and Taney counties. That was just the beginning.

The capable barrister, Colonel John T. Coffee, with several hundred mounted men, raided Greenfield near his Dade County home the afternoon of August 2, both to obtain supplies and to assert his return to Missouri. Coffee skillfully timed the raid with simultaneous rushes from different parts of town and easily overwhelmed the Union garrison. He enforced respect for life and most property during his command's overnight stay in town, forced many to swear oaths supporting the southern cause, then took his men galloping away to evade pursuit.[25]

On August 5 part of 1st Missouri Light Artillery skirmished with unidentified Confederates or guerrillas near Newtonia, Newton County, but no other details remain of the fight.[26] By August 5 or 6, Coffee camped on Horse Creek not far from the notorious southern village of Montevallo, southeast Vernon County, and sent word throughout the area for southern men to come enlist. Colonel Hiram E. Barstow, with 115 troopers of his 3rd Wisconsin Cavalry, rode into the ruins of Montevallo on August 5, but certainly not to enlist with Coffee. They drove 20 of his new recruits out of the battered hamlet, capturing horses, weapons, and some of Coffee's own records, including a unit roster. A day or two later it was Coffee's turn, with 200 of his own horsemen, who drove the Wisconsin cavalrymen back toward their Fort Scott base, capturing their surgeon, two supply wagons, and a large supply of ammunition.[27]

The dreaded guerrilla chieftain Tom Livingston and the able Confederate recruiter Colonel Sidney D. Jackman announced their re-entry into Missouri's war on August 6 when their combined bands were feted in a joyous celebration by the southern sympathizers of Neosho, Newton County. They were all enjoying the temporary absence of the town's Yankee garrison, busy elsewhere chasing Rebel recruiting commands. Livingston's and Jackman's partnership was brief, however, for Jackman was only passing through on his way to the Kansas City area, miles to the north, while Livingston would remain.[28]

Most of the other southern recruiting commands did not take time out to exchange pleasantries with local sympathizers, as they were grimly aware that the Yankee cavalry was riding out to catch them, and they had a long, harrowing ride to their assigned recruiting areas of Lafayette, Johnson, Ray, and Clay counties far to the north. Meanwhile, the area northern military command was trying to figure out what was happening to this normally quiet sector. They knew Coffee was in or near Montevallo, so on August 7 Major Samuel Montgomery led his own 6th Missouri Cavalry with newly-formed, local Enrolled Missouri Militia, toward Montevallo. Near town, they came upon 13 Vernon County men on their way to join Coffee. The Yankees killed five men outright, then conducted a "drumhead court martial" after which they shot seven more, in accordance with directives to shoot guerrillas captured with weapons.[29]

If these southerners had been wearing uniforms or carrying papers identifying them as regular military, they would have been captured and sent off to military prison at Fort Scott, Fort Leavenworth, or Springfield. Of course, Confederate uniforms were hard to come by this far behind Union lines, and puzzled Union troops were always indignant about peaceable farmers who might be deadly partisans in

Union troops in the field were authorized to execute guerrillas captured with firearms, and many did just that. (*Autobiography of Sam S. Hildebrand, the Renowned "Bushwhacker,"* 1870, courtesy Bob and Mary Younger and Andy Turner)

disguise. Throughout the war, northern soldiers in Missouri were often uncertain whether they faced legitimate southern soldiers or "murdering, thieving" bushwhackers. From the northern perspective, both looked and acted the same when encountered in the field. In Union-held Missouri both kinds had to take needed weapons, horses, clothing, bedding, food, and forage from the nearby populace—preferably northern sympathizers, so as not to deprive friends. To the Federal military leadership, such taking from citizens was theft, and therefore the acts of partisans, not protected by military law. For these reasons, the Union leadership was often confused about the identity of their enemies in the field, and the common cavalryman was no less confused.

The Yankee leaders were certainly confused about these large bodies of southern horsemen riding "pell-mell" through southwest Missouri. They were slowly starting to discover some of them were regulars, not mere local bushwhackers. Major J. M. Hubbard and his large patrol of 1st Missouri Cavalry, with artillery from their Newtonia base, discovered this to their amazement while out hunting what they thought were Colonel Coffee and 500 guerrillas. On August 8 Hubbard was nonplussed (as he reported later) to discover a regular Rebel force of one thousand horsemen on the prairie of east Newton County, demonstrating to entice him to attack them. Major Hubbard wisely held his outnumbered force back, lobbed about 30 artillery shells at the large Rebel command—which the veteran Rebels seemed to ignore with indifference—then almost seemed relieved when the Confederates moved off. Hubbard's experience was with guerrillas, who were always intimidated by artillery.[30] Such reports made Union leadership fear that their isolated garrisons were now in grave danger from such roving bands of professional soldiers.

Actually, these southerners were not in Missouri to seize towns and defeat the Yankees in the field. As these bands rode north, some of the recruiters would peel off in small numbers to quietly ride to their home neighborhoods and recruit their friends and neighbors. The timetable agreed to was only days long, not weeks, so these recruiters had to act fast. Some worked well under the pressure, but others failed. When Colonel Jo Orville Shelby returned to his home area near Waverly, northeast Lafayette County, he gathered about one thousand recruits in only four days, then quickly took them toward Arkansas to evade the Yankee dragnet sure to follow. More common was the story of a Confederate lieutenant captured at his home in Bolivar, Polk County, on August 11 by Union forces. Fortunately for him, he was able to establish himself as regular military and was sent to military prison, not the firing squad.[31] At daybreak on August 12 a large body of 4th Cavalry MSM actually caught up to the rear guard of one of the large northbound recruiting commands in northeast Cedar County, but the vanguard was already reported riding quickly north through St. Clair County, and the Yankees were unable to maintain contact with their quarry.[32]

These same bodies of southern recruiters also created chaos further north among the startled northern troops near the Osage River basin. Even though forewarned, these were not the kind of Rebels the guerrilla-hunters were accustomed to facing. On August 2, 135 troopers of 1st Iowa Cavalry, still only armed with revolvers, were fired upon from cover by Colonel Sidney D. Jackman's command of 200 recruits near Taberville, St. Clair County. The Rebel fire emptied some Federal saddles, but after one Iowa counterattack the southerners retreated from their rail fence position, losing eleven killed and several wounded compared to five Iowa dead and 14 wounded. The Federals followed the southbound Confederates the following day into Vernon County, killing a couple more. This was the same Jackman's command that celebrated at Neosho on August 6, obviously grateful to survive their baptism of fire.[33]

Meanwhile, on August 7 in east Morgan County, elements of 7th Cavalry MSM captured noted local southern men along with three wagon loads of gunpowder—2,500 pounds, an unusual capture for such a normally quiet neighborhood. In hindsight, this powder was probably a portion of the large amount secreted by the southern Missouri State Guard during the summer of 1861 when the Union forces rapidly took control of the state. Perhaps its caretakers were bringing it out of hiding now to help arm the thousands of new recruits being mustered into duty by the quick-acting recruiters.[34]

Also on August 7, the 1st Iowa Cavalry commander, Colonel Fitz-Henry Warren, was ordered to pull his men, garrisoned at Butler, Bates County, back to Clinton, Henry County, to consolidate in the face of the large, organized Rebel threat. As the Butler garrison complied during the night of August 7, local guerrillas near Johnstown fired on the column, killing one horse, and then escaped into the darkness.[35]

The large Rebel recruiting bodies rode quickly through the Osage and Grand River basins between August 12 and 14, heading north. Their numbers were continually thinned as small details peeled off to go to their respective homes along the way with instructions to recruit quickly and meet their commands in a few days as the whole lot rode back south toward the southern army in Arkansas. The Federal pursuit flagged through this region and did not produce casualties except in their own exhausted horseflesh, but the tired blue-clad cavalry realized those Rebels would have to return through this same region on their way back south, and they rested and prepared.

The Rebel recruiting bodies reached their apex in west-central Missouri during mid-August and, while gathering in recruits by the hundreds, defeated a smaller Yankee force at Lone Jack, southeast Jackson County, in a desperate pitched battle to be detailed elsewhere. The main body, led by Coffee of Dade County and Colonel Vard Cockrell of Johnson County, and now swollen to about 3,500 men, headed south to face a grim gauntlet. They crossed the Osage River near Taberville, west St. Clair County, the morning of August 19. Once across that natural obstacle, this Rebel force was chased off and on over the next several days along their southern trek by Union cavalry waiting along their expected line of march.[36] In St. Clair County, Federal cavalry also captured some Confederates and a few new recruits returning to meet the column from their brief visits home.[37] Colonel Jo Shelby, with his 1,000 recruits from Lafayette and Saline counties, came along two days later behind the main body and saw little action. The Federals did not know they were coming and were still recovering from the pursuit of the main body. These men became the kernel of Shelby's famed "Iron Brigade" later, but many remembered that fast-paced, grueling ride south out of Missouri during August 1862.[38]

The main Rebel body met its greatest threat from Colonel Clark Wright and his own 6th Missouri Cavalry starting in north Jasper County. Colonel Wright followed them south through Newton and McDonald counties into Arkansas. Wright's cavalry chopped away at Coffee's and Cockrell's rear guard every few miles, now and again killing a few and taking prisoners, for a total of about two dozen slain and about fifty captives at almost no Union loss. The Yankee command structure was elated at reports that regional guerrillas bands were leaving with the regulars, which would have eliminated all their enemies from the region in one swipe, but this was not totally true.[39]

On August 24 Colonel William F. Cloud, leading 300 troopers of his own 6th and the 2nd Kansas Cavalry and 3rd Wisconsin Cavalry back to their Fort Scott base after the long pursuit, discovered a large Rebel body resting at Coon Creek, southwest Barton County. After a short skirmish Cloud mistakenly figured he had stumbled onto his old nemesis Tom Livingston and his band of bushwhackers, and maneuvered to attack. Colonel Cloud expected the miscreant partisans would scamper away from a real fight as was their custom, but he was in for the surprise of his life. The Rebel body was not rag-tag, lightly armed local guerrillas eager to run away, but Colonel Jo Shelby's one thousand recruits desperate to leave Missouri in one piece and anxious to prove themselves to their adored new commander. As the over-confident cavalrymen climbed a fence Shelby's men cut them down in a withering fire, then chased the startled Federals for several hours, killing four or five, wounding about 22, and capturing six, at no known Rebel loss. These northerners did not come back at Shelby's force again, but allowed the belligerent Rebels to continue their ride south unopposed.[40] Thus, Yankees still held tenuous control over southwest Missouri at the close of August 1862, but with the unsettling knowledge that a large Rebel force of cavalry had come and gone through their assigned area at will. They could only deal with the guerrilla menace and the occasional Rebel recruiter, and that not always effectively. Far from asserting their mastery over southern intentions to use this region as a conduit to reach other parts of Missouri, Union authorities and southern ones alike now realized how vulnerable southwest Missouri was in the coming autumn of 1862.

Union Colonel Fitz-Henry Warren, 1st Iowa Cavalry. (Dr. Charles H. Lothrop, *A History of the First Regiment Iowa Cavalry Veteran Volunteers*, 1890; courtesy Bob and Mary Younger and Andy Turner)

Fourteen

Summer 1862 in Southeast Missouri

The rising tempo of guerrilla warfare in southeast Missouri during the spring of 1862 resulted in a continual high level of violence during the long summer of that same year. The spring fighting left the area Union troops in a high state of readiness by the start of June, 1862. They seemed to be in firm control of this quadrant of the state, with garrisons at Rolla, Ironton, Cape Girardeau, New Madrid, and several villages—but many of these troops would soon be sent to more troubled parts of the war. Southern leaders were still determined to assert their challenge to the Federal hold on this region, and the large swampy areas of the far southeast corner and the vast wooded hills that covered the rest of this part of Missouri provided myriad avenues of approach for large Rebel recruiting bands and guerrilla forces to move undetected. Northern troops had come to rely on resident informants, especially slaves, to keep them aware of southern irregulars in the area, but the light population density across the northern Ozarks made this form of "early warning system" unreliable. This meant the Union military had to patrol frequently to detect the presence of southern intruders. Movement, even by horseback, in the vast wooded parts of southeast Missouri was slow, and the opportunity for ambush was ever present. There were enough citizens of southern sympathy still living in this region to warrant the solicitation of Confederate recruiters and to provide "aid and comfort" to bushwhackers. All these factors combined to make a climate of continuous violence throughout the summer of 1862.

Colonel Coleman in the North-Central Ozarks

Just as had happened in the spring, Colonel William O. Coleman and his Rebel irregulars were responsible for much of the summer fighting in the south-central area, running from the Arkansas line north to Rolla, his pre-war home. They struggled during June and July to hang on, despite the persistent efforts of the Union cavalry patrols searching for them through the woods.

It was probably Coleman's men involved in several skirmishes in Texas, Shannon, Dent, and Crawford counties during June and early July. The first of these took place June 7 on Little Piney Creek near Licking in north Texas County, according to local records. No other details remain of this fight.[1] It may also have been some of Coleman's irregulars involved in a short murder spree in Crawford County during the third week of June, 1862. They shot to death an aged northern sympathizer riding home from church and a furloughed Union soldier standing in his yard. These assassinations seem like the work of a southern neighbor returning to settle old scores, but little record remains to make it clear. Crawford County and the counties north and east to the Missouri River—Maries, Osage, Gasconade, and Franklin—seemed mostly inhabited by northern sympathizers, so guerrilla acts were scarce in this area throughout the war, as there was little help for partisans here.[2] On June 17, as most of 5th Kansas Cavalry was riding through Eminence in remote central Shannon County on their way south to Arkansas, troopers skirmished with some of Coleman's guerrillas, but no particulars remain.[3] About a week later, somewhere near Reynolds or Shannon County, a Yankee cavalry patrol captured a Rebel flag that carried the motto "Equal Rights." Ironically, this banner had been captured from Union troops in Washington County earlier in the war, and southern seamstresses had replaced the northern motto with one more to their liking. This was another example of the "make-do" kind of warfare fought in Missouri.[4] Another patrol of the 5th Kansas Cavalry fought bushwhackers on July 6 near Salem, Dent County, but again the results were not recorded.[5] Also not recorded is the effect these various skirmishes were having on the rather large, scattered command of Colonel William O. Coleman. It seemed the determination of his men to challenge the Federal hold on this portion of the northern Ozarks was impervious to all Yankee counter efforts.

Starting with a fight July 7, Union cavalry began a series of actions that one month later would eject Coleman's bothersome command from the region for a while. This first action began when veteran guerrilla fighter Lt. Colonel Joseph A. Eppstein, originally from Boonville, and his 30-man patrol of 13th Cavalry MSM out from Waynesville, captured a deserter from one of Coleman's companies. Somehow, the dispirited southerner agreed to lead the Yankees back to the camp of his former comrades on Big Piney River in north Texas County. The Federals crept along a dry creek bed in the dark in order to surprise the Rebel camp, estimated at 100 men. The southerners must have heard the patrol approach on the rocks, as they were waiting in battle formation. The defenders fired first, but their shots went high. Eppstein's troopers, veterans of irregular warfare against Quantrill in west-central Missouri, conducted a bayonet charge on foot which routed the Confederates, killing at least four, wounding several, and capturing three more at the cost of one trooper slightly wounded and the deserter guide bayoneted to death allegedly when he tried to escape. Lt. Colonel Eppstein withdrew his force due to darkness and his uncertainty if other of Coleman's camps might have been nearby.[6]

His suspicions must have been correct, for on that same day, aptly-named Major Henry A. Gallup with over 200 troopers of 3rd Missouri Cavalry, attacked a like number of Rebels just a few miles away in the southwest corner of Dent County. Gallup's force also failed to surprise their quarry at Inman's Hollow of Spring Creek, because Rebel pickets three miles from camp carried the alarm. These Federals had to settle for chasing scattered groups of bushwhackers as they fled, killing eleven, wounding several, and capturing one at no Union loss.[7] If these large Rebel camps had not been detected and scattered, Colonel Coleman could have used them to overrun an isolated Union post or patrol, or to sever the Rolla-Springfield main supply line.

The Yankee search for more of these guerrilla groups continued. In north Texas County on July 17, Lt. Colonel Eppstein and a large patrol of 13th Cavalry MSM caught another of Coleman's bands literally with their pants down. This band of 55 led by Joe Heall Mooney, evidently of Texas County, and Captain George H. Hume, probably of Dent County, had been drenched in a summer rainstorm and that night were drying their wet clothes by a big fire high on a bluff when the Yankees saw the blaze from some distance. The patrol rode to the fire and into the shivering knot of Rebels. Eppstein did not want to lose the element of surprise, so he had his men ride right into the camp shooting from horseback, killing four, wounding several, and capturing three, including the embarrassed Captain Hume.[8]

About July 22 another 13th Cavalry MSM patrol in west Phelps County or

On rare occasions when Union forces could use artillery against guerrillas in the field, the effect on the southerners was demoralizing. (*The Soldier in Our Civil War*, 1890, vol. 1, p. 174; courtesy Terry Harmon)

east Pulaski County captured two guerrillas, evidently of Coleman's command, attempting to sever Federal communications. When captured, the pair was trying to break the telegraph line with their bare hands.[9]

One of the pesky Yankee patrols discovered Colonel Coleman himself, although only briefly. Coleman and 60 of his men were attacked in a clearing July 25 or 26 near Mountain Store, southwest Texas County, by Captain James Call's patrol of over 100 troopers of 3rd Missouri Cavalry. The initial Union charge killed two, captured seven, and scattered the rest. The eager troopers pursued the fleeing rebels into the woods, killing one more and capturing six, who revealed the location of Coleman's main force of 300 not far away. At 6:30 the next morning, Captain Call's force attacked this camp with cavalry and artillery, killing eight, wounding many, and capturing 17, but Coleman escaped. The total Union loss in this series of fights was one horse killed.[10]

Federal forces kept up the pressure on Coleman in the form of a task force of 10th Illinois Cavalry and 6th Missouri Cavalry led by Brigadier General Egbert B. Brown. This body chased the southern colonel and the remnants of his command through Texas, Wright, Howell, and Douglas counties back into Arkansas between July 27 and August 7, killing 38 more Rebels at the loss of one Federal killed.[11] Obviously, the northern military considered Coleman a major threat to their presence and operations in this region, and had finally accelerated their response to his force until they were pursuing his command with a general officer and a major task force. If every Confederate irregular regimental commander could have created that much havoc in Missouri, the Federal command would have been hard pressed to hold the state. Meanwhile, although Coleman's fast exit from the Missouri war in early August signaled the end of his expedition, many of his surviving warriors, native to south-central Missouri, would look for an opportunity to bring the war back to their home ground.

Bitter Developments in the Black-St. Francis River Highlands

The Civil War became personal and bitter to the people living in the hills of southeast Missouri, which run from Butler and Ripley counties on the Arkansas border north through the St. Francois Mountains almost to St. Louis. The desperate, hateful, melancholy nature of this conflict seemed to come about particularly during the events that transpired in the summer of 1862.

In mid–June a one-man war began that would last throughout the conflict and foment legends that long outlived the participants. During spring 1862 either Union militia or vigilantes had wounded farmer Sam Hildebrand and driven him out of Saint Francois County, killed some of his relatives, and vandalized his property, all because he was believed to be a southern sympathizer. About June 14 Hildebrand returned alone to his neighborhood and tracked down and assassinated two of the ringleaders. The local Union military command condemned Hildebrand's acts and sought ways to repress area southerners in order to prevent a recurrence of such southern backlash. They refused to acknowledge that northern atrocities were responsible for bringing on the desperate actions of this man. They also failed to appreciate Hildebrand's determination to bring punishment to the Union cause.[12] Few events of note took place in this region over the next three weeks, lulling Yankee authorities into a belief that these hills were in solid Union control, but violence returned in July.

Local Yankee countermeasures against Sam Hildebrand continued clumsily, for on July 10 militia, allegedly from the Ironton base, rode to Saint Francois County and murdered Sam's uncle at home.[13] According to Hildebrand's own memoirs, written just after the war, Sam and two companions rode out from their sanctuary in Greene County, Arkansas, about this time on a second guerrilla punitive expedition to southeast Missouri. On their way north, they sought out and assassinated a northern informant near Bloomfield, Stoddard County, who had been telling the Union military about his southern neighbors. Thus, Sam Hildebrand became kind of a southern hit man, who would bring retribution to particularly odious northerners throughout southeast Missouri. The three-man expedition continued north performing similar errands along the way, back to Hildebrand's home neighborhood. Indeed, a St. Louis newspaper related how guerrillas attacked and severely wounded three northern sympathizers in south Iron County about this time. Hildebrand's memoir relates how when they arrived at his mother's house in west-central Jefferson County, they could only watch helplessly from the brush as local Yankee militia evicted the old woman from her dwelling and burned the place down. With such a small band, Hildebrand was impotent to strike back, but on the way back to Arkansas contented himself with robbing a store, probably in Washington County.[14] He would come back.

Another fixture in the bitter hill fighting was the Reverend Tim Reeves—before the war and after known in the region as a preacher and organizer of several Baptist

Sam Hildebrand assassinated a northern leader who had previously driven him from his home. (*Autobiography of Samuel S. Hildebrand, the Renowned Missouri "Bushwacker,"* courtesy Bob and Mary Younger and Andy Turner)

churches. Throughout the long war here, the reverend recruited and fearlessly led partisan Rebels, looking for any opportunity to challenge Union military hold in this rough country. One of Colonel Reeves's many victories took place on July 20 with another leader named Dees and about 150 men. They crept up to Greenville, Wayne County, under cover of a rainstorm and routed Captain William T. Leeper and 100 troopers of 12th Cavalry MSM who were garrisoned there. The jubilant guerrillas captured all the Yankee horses and most of their rifles and Savage revolvers at a cost of four killed and five or six wounded on each side. Thereafter, Captain Leeper and his men had a score to settle with Reeves' men and spent the rest of the war doing it. Leeper became an aggressive, relentless, and, some say, ruthless, enemy to area guerrillas—particularly Colonel Reeves.[15]

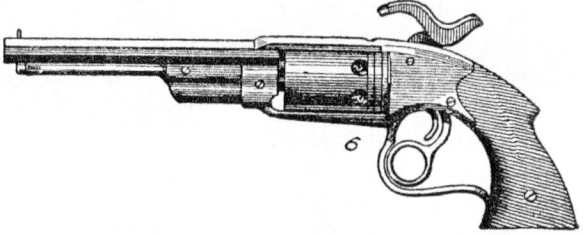

Savage revolver. (Francis Brannerman sons', *Military Goods Catalogue*, 1919)

The hill region was particularly violent during the last several days of July, 1862. Local accounts state that on July 23 Captain Bernard Essroger led a patrol of 1st Regiment United States Reserve Corps—a rather fanciful name for Missouri militia—from Ironton into St. Francois County. Essroger's patrol killed Sam Hildebrand's younger brother Henry, but the details are hazy.[16] The results are also hazy regarding a skirmish that parts of 3rd and 12th Cavalry MSM fought at or near Greenville again on July 26. Perhaps they fought Reeves and Dees here again, but all the record shows is that two Federals were slain and five wounded, with no mention of Rebel losses.[17] About this same date, a company of 12th Cavalry MSM chased about 200 guerrillas or Rebel recruits in north Bollinger County, capturing two, including a Captain Patterson, at a cost of three troopers wounded.[18] These Rebels were probably part of a recruiting command led by Colonel William L. Jeffers, evidently an Ohio-born saddler from Bollinger County before the war. The 130 Yankees of 12th Cavalry MSM again pursued this same band in west Cape Girardeau County, and later in Madison County on July 28, killing ten to 15 and capturing two before the Confederates dispersed near Fredericktown.[19] Jeffers' command remained in the area still recruiting, and on August 7 a company of 12th Cavalry MSM from Wayne County attacked and routed 108 of them in west Cape Girardeau County, killing ten, wounding several, and capturing two.[20]

Sam Hildebrand returned to the hill region in August of 1862, and so did other Rebel groups. Hildebrand told later how with two other companions he killed yet another Union informant—this time in Wayne County—then remained in Madison and St. Francois counties for a few days without attracting much notice. At about this same time, Yankee authorities reported some guerrillas in south Washington County, August 6, who allegedly killed three northern sympathizers and abducted several others (whose eventual fate is not mentioned). Whether this was Hildebrand's doing or the actions of others is not clear, but another report said that during August some Rebel recruiting took place not only in Washington County, but also in Iron, St. Francois, and Reynolds counties.[21] Sometime in August,

Union officials seized the press and type of the *Ste. Genevieve Plaindealer* for publicizing "matters against the Government."[22]

Late in August, Major Bazel F. Lazear was sent out with a force of 270 men of 12th Cavalry MSM, from Patterson and Greenville in Wayne County, to east Bollinger County to stop what they were told was a large guerrilla band stealing horses there. Actually, the Rebels were Mexican War veteran Colonel William L. Jeffers and his recruiting command of about 200, taking mounts for his new men from farmers of northern sympathy. The two forces collided on August 24 on Crooked Creek near Dallas, and Jeffers seemed to take the best of it. Jeffers' men startled the Federal advance company, which started a retreat. Major Lazear, of Pike County, Missouri, threw together a skirmish line behind a picket fence and stopped the advancing Confederates, but he realized his force was not strong enough to best Jeffers and withdrew. Jeffers was left to lead his recruits out of the area at his own chosen time and speed, and with the enhanced recruiting advantage of having just beaten a strong Federal force. The casualties at Crooked Creek were three Union and six Rebel deaths, two Federals captured, and several wounded on both sides. Jeffers, mistakenly called "Jeffries" in Yankee reports throughout the war, operated a hotel in Dexter, Stoddard County, after the war.[23]

Sam Hildebrand's account says that in late August, with three other guerrillas, he was attacked by about 50 Federals eight miles from Fredericktown, Madison County, and barely escaped. His account is not corroborated by any other source, however; even in this remote corner of Missouri, in this poorly documented period, a fight like that should have been mentioned.[24]

By the end of August, 1862, Confederate Colonel James White was recruiting noticeably in the Ripley County area, so a large Union task force was sent out from Greenville, Wayne County, to stop him. The northern force, led by Major Lothar Lippert, consisted of parts of his own 13th Illinois Cavalry, 24th Missouri Infantry riding in wagons, and one section of 2nd Missouri Light Artillery. Lippert's expedition pursued Colonel White's men well into Arkansas, but along the way on August 31 skirmished with small parties of guerrillas, probably of White's Rebels, near Ponder's Mill, southwest Ripley County.[25]

Some Actions in the Bootheel

The swampy bootheel of southeast Missouri, scene of so much violence during the previous winter and early spring, seemed peaceful and free from guerrilla warfare this summer, at least until late July. Some bushwhackers or Rebel recruiters operated there for a few weeks, but left incomplete records, both of their identity and their operations.

On July 23, elements of 1st Wisconsin Cavalry out from their Cape Girardeau garrison exchanged shots with unidentified foes near West Prairie in western New Madrid County, but no other details remain.[26] Part of the same regiment also fought with unspecified Rebels near Bloomfield, Stoddard County, July 29, but the record is incomplete.[27] Some records state that a firefight took place August 4 at Gayoso on the Mississippi River in Pemiscot County, but fail to identify either antagonist or other specifics.[28] During the afternoon of August 7, guerrillas wounded two of

Capturing a guerrilla in the swamp. (*Harper's Weekly*, August 19, 1862; courtesy Bob and Mary Younger and Andy Turner)

a party of 1st Wisconsin Cavalrymen and citizens riding along a road near Jackson, Cape Girardeau County. The troopers' commander at Cape Girardeau seized ten prominent southern sympathizers as hostages and no further attacks took place.[29] Even though accounts of these seemingly scattered incidents are sketchy, they do reveal that starting in late July there was guerrilla activity of some kind in the area. Indeed, local accounts state that Rebel recruiters identified only as Ice, Judge Taylor, and Hayes were covertly signing up southern men in early August. These Confederate leaders had previously served in this region under bombastic Swamp Rats commander Colonel M. Jeff Thompson.[30]

During the night of August 15 a bushwhacker band led by a man named Fowler raided Charleston, Mississippi County, and captured a Yankee captain who happened to be in town. Fowler paroled and released the hapless captain. The captain's unit, 2nd Illinois Cavalry, sent out a patrol, which tracked the partisan band of 18 men to south Mississippi County on August 19, where they killed one or two of the Rebels and captured several, including Fowler, all at the cost of one Federal wounded.[31] The area Union command then sent Major Lothar Lippert of the 13th Illinois Cavalry, leading a combined task force of cavalry, infantry, and artillery from Greenville, Wayne County, to the swampy bootheel for a week to clean out any remaining Rebels. Between August 20 and 23 Lippert's force of over 100 Federals fought three skirmishes across Stoddard County and at Four Miles in north Dunklin County. They suffered negligible losses but killed 25 Rebels and captured 24 prisoners.[32] Guerrillas refused to give up the area, though, even as summer drew to a close. Fowler's bushwhacker band, now led by a man named Pottenger, ran afoul of a 2nd Illinois Cavalry patrol on Hogskin Ridge in south Mississippi County on September 4, losing one killed, one wounded, and five guerrillas captured.[33]

Guerrillas in South-Central Missouri During August

Even with the departure from the south-central Missouri region of Colonel Coleman and most of his southern command during early August of 1862, other guerrilla bands were active. Also during early August near Waynesville, Pulaski County, local bushwhackers robbed a family of northern sympathy, despite the proximity to the Union garrison in the nearby town.[34] Charles Barnes was a subordinate of Colonel Coleman in this region during 1862 and 1864 and was leading recruits south in early August. During the morning of August 4 Captain Thomas C. Black's patrol of 3rd Missouri Cavalry found and attacked Barnes' camp near Sinking Creek, north Shannon County, killing four Rebels and capturing Barnes' private papers. Captain Black concluded that Barnes and company would continue riding south to join Coleman in Arkansas.[35] An experienced recruiter from south Cole County and north Miller County, known only as "General " Crabtree, along with Colonel Abraham Castleman of Iberia, south Miller County, were moving another band of Rebel recruits through this region about this same time. Union troops from Rolla were too late to intercept them in Maries County, and the band rode on south, probably also looking to rendezvous with Colonel Coleman in Arkansas.[36] On August 9, elements of 3rd Missouri Cavalry skirmished with unidentified guerrillas near Salem, Dent County—perhaps Crabtree's men. The surviving record of the action gives no other details.[37]

Colonel Sempronius H. Boyd led portions of his 24th Missouri Infantry west from their Greenville base to raid a guerrilla camp at Van Buren, Carter County, on August 12. The foot soldiers killed two bushwhackers, captured three more, and captured mail from some of Coleman's irregulars based in nearby Oregon County addressed to their families in Washington County. Some guerrillas sniped at Colonel Boyd himself from a hilltop, barely missing the regimental commander, and later the Union force returned to their base in Wayne County.[38] Just after mid–August, Henry Smith, a guerrilla reputedly of Colonel Coleman's command, robbed a south-Reynolds County store twice and murdered a man near there.[39] Guerrilla war was still a personal war, after all.

Indeed, partisan warfare in this part of southeast Missouri took on a personal but savage twist over the next few days because of revenge-taking. About August 21 the southern Cole County recruiter known only as "General" Crabtree, with Colonel Castleman and about 200 Rebels, rode through western Phelps County on his way south to Arkansas, evidently his second such trip in August. On Little Piney Creek in southwest Phelps County, they collided with Lieutenant John Heusack's supply wagon train escort of 50 troopers of 4th Missouri Cavalry. In the instant both sides saw each other they halted, each trying to decide whether to fight or flee. Lieutenant Heusack, however, needed no time to decide. He single-handedly charged the large body of Rebels. Crabtree and company shot the impulsive lieutenant dead from his saddle, but suffered six dead themselves before they could break contact. Crabtree had hoped to avoid contact with Federal patrols on this trip—which was his custom—so he promptly dispersed his newly-recruited command, anticipating Yankee countermeasures.[40] Indeed, on August 23 Captain

George S. Avery, with 200 men of 3rd Missouri Cavalry from Rolla, caught up to 60 of Crabtree's scattered command at Wayman's Mill, Big Piney River, in southwest Phelps County, killed six and captured nine in a one-sided fight. The following day at Rolla, Avery's returning patrol turned over the prisoners to members of the late Lieutenant Heusack's unit for them to march the prisoners to the lockup at the nearby fort. Undoubtedly, harsh words were exchanged between these new guards and the prisoners, and the Yankees later claimed that their prisoners bolted for freedom. In the melee the 4th Missouri Cavalry troopers killed three and wounded two of the Cole County rebels in a hail of gunfire. The Union military investigated the regrettable incident, but could not refute the guards' version, even though their actions appeared to be mere revenge for their dead lieutenant.[41]

There would be more. A patrol of 3rd Missouri Cavalry from Salem also went hunting for Crabtree's scattered recruits. Their five-day patrol through Shannon County beginning August 24 was very eventful. They escorted some families of northern sympathy to safety, seized stolen U.S. government property, gunned down three southern men who ran when approached, and arrested six suspected guerrillas. Three of these prisoners were of the prominent Chilton family of Shannon County, strong supporters of the Confederacy since war's start. Evidently, the patrol failed to encounter any of Crabtree's rebels in their adventures. Back at garrison in Salem, this patrol turned their Shannon County prisoners over to Lieutenant Alexander H. Lacy's patrol, also of the 3rd Missouri Cavalry, which set out August 30 to take the six prisoners north to Rolla. Only three miles down the road and behind Lieutenant Lacy's back, some troopers gunned down the captives, except one, who escaped into the brush during the shooting. The troopers later claimed the southern men were trying to make a break. One of the dead was Missouri State Senator Joshua Chilton, called the "King of Shannon County." Of course, the cavalrymen may have told the truth, but the possibility looms that the death some days before of Lieutenant Heusack had set off a series of vigilante actions by frustrated individuals in the Union ranks.[42]

It is indeed ironic that while Crabtree was leading his men south through this area in late August, 1862, Rebel Colonel Robert R. Lawther of Jefferson City and Major Myscall Johnson—a lawyer and Methodist Episcopal minister of this region—were leading a party of Confederate recruiters through the same region on their way north to recruit in Cole and Maries counties where Crabtree had just recruited. Lawther's command had already been roughly handled further west in Christian and Taney counties during early August by the 14th Cavalry MSM as described earlier in this narrative. Now they were attempting to continue their interrupted journey using a route further to the east. During the night of August 29, Lawther's and Johnson's command, estimated to be about 300 men, rode onto a cavalry screen of 13th Cavalry MSM astride the Union's coveted Rolla-Springfield transport route near California House inn in west Pulaski County. The Yankee shooting punctuated the darkness and confused the Rebel force, causing part, under Major Johnson, to veer south and the rest, under Lawther, to continue north into Miller County. The 13th Cavalry MSM pursued Lawther's men and, joined by elements of Miller, Maries, and Pulaski County's' newly-formed Enrolled Missouri Militia, soundly defeated the Rebels along the Miller-Maries County line, until the remnant scattered into southwest Osage County. Union losses were small, but

Lawther lost about ten killed and forty captured, among the latter Lawther and some of his staff.[43] A sad end befell two men of this force at the Yankee garrison at Waynesville. Evidence seems to say that Colonel Albert Sigel, commander of 13th Cavalry MSM, during the night of August 30, had two of these prisoners removed from the guardhouse, executed, and buried in the woods.[44] If true, this would be the third incident in a few days involving suspicious deaths of captured guerrillas or Rebels by Federals in this region. Perhaps the strain of this relentless type of warfare, the frustration of trying to come to grips with the "will-of-the-wisp" Confederate irregulars, and the death of Lieutenant Heusack a few days earlier triggered these depredations.

A Different Type of War in St. Louis

A tense guerrilla warfare continued in and around the large city of Saint Louis during the summer of 1862, but it took different forms from that fought in the countryside. Daring Rebel recruiters boldly solicited new soldiers under the very noses of the strong Union military presence in and around the city, but the large numbers of Rebel captives in military prisons here showed a marked tendency to dispute the assertion that "for them the war was over."

Chronic "escape artist" Captain Hampton L. Boone of central Missouri and Colonel Walter Scott of St. Joseph successfully escaped from the Myrtle Street Prison in St. Louis, May 29, by wrenching bars out of a window and creeping across the roof past the guard while a violent thunderstorm covered the noise. Captain Boone had escaped from the same prison five months earlier disguised as a woman, but had been recaptured.[45] This second escape seemed to inspire others, for on June 3 a Confederate private originally from west Missouri somehow escaped from the Alton prison.[46] Two inmates of the Gratiot Street Prison in downtown St. Louis escaped June 10 by wrenching out window bars and avoiding the guards. One of these escapees was a man named Carlin, reputedly the son of a former Illinois governor, and the other was Captain Robert W. Swinney, former sheriff of Monroe County, who had lost an arm fighting under William Walker in Nicaragua in 1855. Swinney had given Union authorities fits in northeast Missouri the previous fall with his aggressive southern recruiting, and he was not the sort of man they wanted on the loose again.[47]

One of the more notable St. Louis prison escapes took place some time between June 20 and 25. It was poorly documented, possibly due to the embarrassment it caused Union officials. In the middle of the day at least six and perhaps more P.O.W.'s, nearly all from the Howard-Boone County area, somehow walked out through the busy kitchen of the Gratiot Street Prison. Among the escapees were railroad saboteurs Captain W. F. Petty, George Pulliam, and Matthew Thompson (at least two already facing death sentences), Calvin Sartain, who had attacked steamboats carrying Federal troops at Howard County in August of 1861, and Captain John Hanson McNeill. The latter acquired fame after this escape by traveling to Virginia and conducting his own guerrilla operations there for the rest of the war. Some of the others continued to bedevil Yankees in Missouri afterwards.[48]

The greatest escape, as far as numbers of escapees is concerned took place

July 25 or 26. Several prisoners of war at the former condemned state penitentiary at Alton dug with tableware through six or seven feet of dirt under a shed by the wall. The diggers were shielded by comrades, who hung clothes around the building and hid the dirt in the latrine and around the oven. One of the more frequent diggers was amazed to discover that he wore the hair off the back of his head by digging lying on his back, but the poor nutrition in the prisoners' diet was probably partly to blame. The escapees even obtained the cooperation of a sympathetic guard to effect this "great escape." The first prison officials knew of the feat was when their count came up 35 short. The frantic Union military in the area only brought back a few—including one man who had been hiding in the top of a tree—and another they found in St. Charles County, Missouri. Many of the escapees had been captured mid–December, 1861, at Milford in Johnson County, west Missouri. Others had been captured at the Battle of Pea Ridge or Elkhorn Tavern in northwest Arkansas in March. Some were high-ranking Rebel recruiters and organizers of west-central Missouri, men that Union officials were understandably upset to learn were loose again. Among the escapees were Colonel Ebenezer Magoffin and his son Major Beriah (the latter was recaptured), Lieutenant Colonel R. K. Murrell, Major J. C. Wood, and the same Captain Swinney who escaped June 10 and had only been recaptured and placed in Alton prison a few days before. That so many could deliberately escape and evade recapture indicates that they found help readily and that the Federal military was not yet proficient in these matters. Nevertheless, prison escapes from the St. Louis area continued throughout the war, despite all countermeasures.[49]

There were other less spectacular prison breaks and attempts this summer. In late July several prisoners of war escaped from the Gratiot Street Prison disguised as black men, but the details of this feat do not survive.[50] One prisoner, Charles E. Woodward, who had been part of the July mass escape from Alton prison, was recaptured,

Civil War prisoners languishing in military prison. (Charles C. Coffin, *The Boys of '61*, 1881; courtesy Terry Harmon)

attempted another break August 2, and was recaptured again. Union authorities later executed Woodward, but the record gives little clue why this was done.[51]

One of the most daring plots to recruit for the Confederacy in the outskirts of Saint Louis was thwarted in mid–August. Colonel John C. Boone had gathered about 60 southern men in south St. Louis County by August 12, when Federal forces heard of it. Over the next seven days Colonel John B. Gray's 1st Infantry MSM scoured south St. Louis County and north Jefferson County, engaging Boone's recruits in two battles before finally capturing 49 of them, including two lieutenants. At one point during this period, Boone captured the Yankee's assistant surgeon and two soldiers, but they were rescued during the final fight, after which Boone himself escaped.[52] Later in August, Federal detectives discovered Colonel Boone was frequenting the home of the prominent Sappington family in west St. Louis County. The St. Louis provost marshal's office raided the house on August 29. There, they arrested several people they accused of selling pistols to Rebels, but, once again, Colonel Boone evaded them.[53] Missouri's Union commander, Brigadier General John M. Schofield, headquartered in St. Louis, alarmed over this spy ring and the conspiratorial attitude of Missouri southerners, wrote to his superiors on August 30 complaining and requesting more leeway to thwart such threats to Union control of Missouri.[54] As if to highlight the tenuous Union control, at least four prisoners escaped from the Gratiot Street Prison the day after Schofield's communiqué, but details of the break do not survive.[55] Thus ended a summer of embarrassment for the northern cause in the St. Louis area, and a long summer of bitter irregular warfare across southeastern Missouri.

FIFTEEN

Summer 1862 in Northeast Missouri

The summer of 1862 in northeast Missouri marked the heyday of the behind-the-lines Confederate recruiters, particularly in the work of Colonel John Chrisman Porter of Lewis County and Colonel James A. Poindexter of Randolph County. Especially in the vast multi-county region of southern sympathy there (later known as "Little Dixie"), these shooting stars, plus the mandatory enrollment of all men in the Union militia, sent southern or previously-neutral men flocking to enlist in Confederate service. So widespread was the effect and so complete were the Union military's often harsh countermeasures that northeast Missouri flashed hot as a threat to the Federal cause for weeks but then burned out never to recur at this scale for the rest of the war. In other words, what transpired here this summer so shook this region that bearing arms against the Union military never approached this level again. Southern hopes burned bright for two more years, but southern men never again responded to the call of arms in the numbers they did this violent season.

Scattered Incidents in Early June

As June 1862 began guerrilla war seemed to continue little changed from the spring, with little hint at the firestorm to come. On June 8 a detachment of 11th Cavalry MSM seized and shot to death returned Rebel Major John L. Owen at his home in southwest Marion County. Southern guerrillas had been active in the area, and Major Owen had not surrendered and taken the oath of allegiance when he returned from the southern army. Actually, there seemed to be no evidence Owen was doing anything other than peaceful activities.[1] On June 16 six or eight guerrillas called on Joseph Wiseman's home in south-central Lewis County, announcing that they came to arrest the man because of his northern sympathy. Mr. Wiseman wisely escaped to the woods, but his wife unnerved the guerrillas by screaming for help out of an upstairs window. In a rare example of violence toward women, one or more of the unnerved guerrillas shot at the hysterical woman, but the bullets went wide of the mark, whereupon they searched the house, took a horse, and left.²

Porter's Long Campaign Begins

By mid-June Kentucky-born Colonel Joseph Chrisman Porter had returned from the Rebel army in the south with a recruiting detail to the neighborhood near his Lewis County home. Perhaps the men at the Wiseman house June 16 were part of his growing command. Porter began to mount and arm his recruits from the ample stocks of the enemy, civilian and military. On June 17, with 43 men, Porter captured and paroled four Federals of 11th Cavalry MSM in west Marion County. Of course, Porter's men kept the Yankee's weapons and equipment.³ Such daring acquisitions not only fulfilled the logistical needs of his men, but boosted the recruits' morale, encouraged others to join, and thoroughly aggravated the enemy. During the next few days it was probably Porter's band again that shot up Union troops in Lewis County. A Boone County newspaper reported that eight Federals were killed, but other details are sketchy.⁴

Porter on the Iowa Border

By the end of June Colonel Porter moved his band to north Schuyler County and united with Bill Dunn's guerrilla band, bringing his total strength to between 130 and 200 men. On July 1, Colonel H. L. Lipscomb led a combined force of his own 11th Cavalry MSM and 2nd Cavalry MSM to stop Porter at a place called Cherry Grove near the Iowa line in northeast Schuyler County. Porter led his motley force away from the better-armed Federals in a long running fight until darkness brought an end to the fighting. The results of the fighting on the Rebel side were 12 killed and about 20 wounded. A Yankee captain was mortally wounded, two Union soldiers were also wounded, and Colonel Lipscomb was relieved by higher authorities for his lackluster pursuit of the Rebels.⁵ In other regional events, that same evening in nearby northeast Sullivan County, Tice Cain's guerrilla band harassed men of northern sympathy, but details are lacking.⁶

Jim Porter Raids Newark

There was plenty of excitement in Knox County to the north a few days later. Joseph Porter sent his brother Jim, with about 75 irregulars, raiding in southeast Knox County on July 7. Just outside the village of Newark that day, Jim Porter's men attacked a passing column of 175 troopers of 2nd Cavalry MSM riding along the road from their Palmyra base. In spite of their smaller numbers Jim Porter's raiders initially overwhelmed the cavalrymen, using the element of surprise, by attacking from the woods, and pushed the startled Federals a half mile down the road to a brick house. The guerrillas besieged the cavalrymen in the house most of the day while some of Porter's men took what they pleased from the nearby town.

Perhaps the northern troopers never realized they were not facing Joseph Porter's whole force or that they outnumbered their antagonists two to one, but the Rebels finally rode away to end the siege, and the Yankees returned to base with only two wounded to show for their day of struggle.[7]

Raphael Smith

Meanwhile, guerrilla chief and recruiter Raphael Smith conducted a five-day reign of terror, July 8 through 12, in northern Lewis County. Before the war Raphael, or Ralph, Smith was a Kentucky-born tanner of central Lewis County with a large family. The night of July 8, Willis Baker, with five or six of Smith's bushwhackers near Williamstown, murdered Ezekial Pratt over the protests of his family and then took what they wanted from the house.[8] The next day Smith, with 80 men, raided Monticello, the county seat, and compelled a prominent Union sympathizer there to take an oath to the Confederacy. In fact,

Rebel Captain James W. Porter. (Joseph A. Mudd, *With Porter in North Missouri*, 1909; courtesy Bob and Mary Younger and Andy Turner)

Smith was meticulous to victimize only people of northern sympathy and encouraged southern families when he could.[9] On July 12 he raided Williamstown and farms nearby, mainly looking for horses for his men. While doing this, his men abducted a northern man. It was probably also Smith's band that raided Fairmont in southwest Clark County that same day and carried away two more leading citizens of Union sympathy. The surviving records are mute about the fate of these captives.[10]

Joseph Porter's Memphis Raid

Colonel Joseph Porter, with his full force, including the men under Raphael Smith, Bill Dunn, and Tom Stacy—about 250 in all—raided Memphis, central Scotland County, July 13. The guerrillas rounded up all townsmen of northern sympathy and kept them in the courthouse for several hours while they took what they needed from the town. Porter's men were delighted to find and take 82 U.S. muskets and clothe themselves in a number of Yankee uniforms. When the Rebel command left town, they took with them a Yankee militia captain who they released a few days later, but they hung another captive—prominent northern sympathizer, Dr. William Aylward.[11]

Porter's Vasser Hill Fight and Shooting Incident in Shelby County

Joe Porter next resurfaced July 18 in southwest Scotland County in the Vasser Hill fight on the Middle Fabius River. Now with only 125 men, Porter clobbered the advance guard of Major John Y. Clopper's combined force of his own 2nd Missouri Cavalry (Merrill's Horse) and 11th Cavalry MSM and then fought the remainder of the Union force in the brush for about two hours before retiring. The Rebels had stung the Federals hard this time, killing 24 and wounding 59, compared to their own loss of six killed, three mortally wounded, and ten other wounded. Porter managed to withdraw from contact, leaving only one of the mortally wounded behind—guerrilla chief Tom Stacy, long a pest to the Union cause in northeast Missouri.[12] The Vasser Hill fight is typical of Colonel Porter's basic tactic while recruiting so far behind enemy lines. He aggressively attacked isolated Union commands and garrisons in order to attract more recruits and weld them into a cohesive and somewhat disciplined force. Porter realized that if he remained hidden and inactive, the pressure of the Union efforts to find his men would wear down their resolve, and they would leave him. He had to give them victories to keep their morale high. Further, he had to strike out to meet his recruits' needs of horses, clothing, weapons, forage, food, and even camp equipment. Of course, this whole tactic was a gamble that the Union command would not be able to pin down his fledgling command with sufficient force to defeat him in open battle. How long could Colonel Porter hold off that eventuality?

Meanwhile, miles to the south near Hunnewell, southeast Shelby County, on July 20 a detachment of 11th Cavalry MSM, perhaps guarding the nearby railroad bridge over the Salt River, conducted their own version of guerrilla war. They arrested three local men, then claimed guerrillas fired on the whole party from the brush. When the smoke cleared, the three captives lay dead, and the troopers claimed they were forced to shoot when the southern men attempted to escape in the confusion. Whether or not this was the truth, such events did little to ease war tensions across the region.[13]

Union Major John Y. Clopper of Merrill's Horse. (Joseph A. Mudd, *With Porter in North Missouri*, 1909; courtesy Bob and Mary Younger and Andy Turner)

June and July Incidents Near the Missouri River

Far to the south along the counties just north of the Missouri River, some guerrillas were making their presence known. Unidentified guerrillas in southeast Callaway County on June 17 assassinated an aged farmer, allegedly for informing to the Yankees.[14] Unidentified bushwhackers perhaps of the same gang, robbed a man near St. Aubert in southeast Callaway County the evening of July 3.[15]

To the west in late July there was a brief surge of guerrilla activity in and near the Missouri River village of Rocheport at the border between Boone and Howard counties. During the week of July 20 through 26, an unidentified guerrilla band of about forty men raided Rocheport, taking firearms from several residents and 15,000 percussion caps from one of the stores. Of course, it seems suspicious that a private store would have in stock such armaments in the first place.[16] The Perche Hills near Rocheport was a natural place for bushwhackers to hide, and off and on during the remainder of the war many took advantage of these brushy, wooded hills and the accommodating southern families that lived in the neighborhood.

Sometime during the following week James Rucker, of the notorious southern family of Ruckers in that neighborhood, somehow stopped the two-year-old side-wheel steamer *H. D. Bacon,* intent on seizing any U.S. Army cargo onboard. To Rucker's disappointment the vessel carried only private cargo and passengers, and he permitted the vessel and all aboard to proceed on their journey. Throughout the rest of the war, guerrillas would stop or fire on a number of river steamers near Rocheport, and many would not come away from the encounter as well as did the *H. D. Bacon.* Sadly, this particular vessel was destroyed by an accidental fire at St. Louis in October of 1862, but various members of the Rucker family would make an impact on guerrilla war in this region for the rest of the war.[17]

Porter Moves South

After the Vasser Hill fight Joseph Porter took his force south, evading the Union pursuit. These Rebels on July 22 collided with Major Henry Clay Caldwell and two companies of 3rd Iowa Cavalry at Florida, Monroe County, and skirmished with the Iowans for a couple of days before pushing on through them to the south. Caldwell's men suffered less than four

Union Major Henry Clay Caldwell of 3rd Iowa Cavalry, post-war. (Dr. Charles H. Lothrop, *A History of the first Regiment Iowa Cavalry Veteran Volunteers,* 1890; courtesy Bob and Mary Younger and Andy Turner)

killed, but about thirty wounded, while the guerrillas evidently had even fewer casualties.[18]

Colonel Joseph Porter's embattled band rode on south, evidently with the intent of continuing all the way to the southern army in Arkansas. On July 25 they were joined by Alvin Cobb and 75 Montgomery County guerrillas and other area recruiting companies on Auxvasse Creek in north Callaway County.[19] Porter kept his now larger command at Auxvasse Creek for a couple of days to reorganize, while his pickets skirmished several times with Yankees attempting to pinpoint the location of the main body. Now that area Union troops knew Porter's approximate location, Colonel Odon Guitar, a former state legislator from Columbia and now commander of the 9th Cavalry MSM, quickly gathered together all forces within reach and rode to stop Porter's southern trek. At Moore's Mill on Auxvasse Creek, ten miles northeast of Fulton, July 28, Guitar, with about 550 Yankees from various units and artillery, grappled in stifling heat with Porter's smaller band, estimated between 260 and 350 rebels.

Union Colonel Odon Guitar, 9th Cavalry Missouri State Militia, as a brigadier general later in the war. (Private collection, courtesy Bob and Mary Younger and Andy Turner)

Porter held his own against the larger force for about four hours, until his Confederates ran low on cartridges and he disengaged. Guitar considered his command unfit to pursue until the following morning, because of fatigue and thirst, and Porter escaped, riding back toward the north. Casualties from the slugfest appeared to be about 20 Federals killed and 55 wounded, compared to about 60 rebels killed, including recruiter Captain Sylvester Penny, and more than 120 wounded. Disgusted new additions to Porter's force, such as Alvin Cobb of Montgomery County and Young A. Purcell of Audrain County, soon left their new commander and took their battered bands with them. The Union side claimed a victory, since the battle curtailed Porter's southward ride and claimed greater southern casualty numbers than northern ones. Guitar became a Union hero.[20]

Porter Turns North and Rebuilds

Porter, however, was a resilient commander, and set about to rebuild his shattered force and prepare it to ride south in the future. He received unexpected assistance from the much-despised General Order Number 19 at about this time, for southern men flocked to Porter's command to avoid the mandatory enrollment in Yankee militia mandated by the pro–Union Governor Gamble. Porter moved his command back into neighborhoods known for strong southern sympathy in order to take full advantage of this windfall.

To further encourage local men to enlist with his force and obtain needed supplies, Porter sent Joe Thompson ahead of the main body to raid Paris, Monroe County, July 30. Once in town Thompson arrested county officials and other residents of known northern sympathy, and then his raiders took what they wished from stores and townspeople and turned loose a murder suspect from the jail. Porter brought the rest of the command, about 400 altogether, into town later for about an hour and then resumed his march.[21] Federal leaders lost track of Porter for a day, but Captain Wesley Lair, with 73 men of 11th Cavalry MSM found out where they were on August 1 when the Rebels attacked Lair's camp outside Newark, southeast Knox County, at five in the morning. Captain Lair had his men retire to a brick church and Masonic hall in town, where they withstood a Rebel siege for one and one-half hours before surrendering. The Federal loss was four killed and eleven wounded and all the command captured, although Porter later paroled and released them. Porter's loss was eight killed and 13 wounded, several mortally.[22] Porter next sent a large raiding party, August 2, to Canton, in east Lewis County, to get arms and recruits. These raiders killed one man, abducted another, and robbed the community of weapons, ammunition, and medicines.[23] Thus, Porter's force, combat-hardened and battered, although growing in numbers, returned again to the colonel's home county, where he had begun hostilities weeks before in mid–June.

Actions Involving Other Rebel Recruiters

Although by early August many Confederate recruiters operating in northeast Missouri had joined their recruits to Porter's command, some still operated on their own. Some 60–80 recruits had gathered at dusk, July 29 or 30, at the Chariton River near Keytesville in Chariton County, hoping to go to Rebel Colonel James Poindexter's command from nearby Randolph County, when a large Federal force found them instead. Their attackers were Lt. Colonel Alexander M. Woolfolk and over 200 troopers of his own 1st Cavalry MSM and newly-formed Enrolled Missouri Militia (EMM). The Rebels fired on the approaching column before retreating into the woods, but the eager troopers pursued the fleeing men into the gloomy forest, firing pistols at the backs of their enemies until darkness made further pursuit impossible. There were no Union losses but the Yankees counted eight dead southerners and calculated several were wounded in the one-sided fight.[24] On August 1, while Porter was raiding Newark in Knox County, guerrilla chief William Ousley with 30 bushwhackers raided Alexandria, in east Clark County near the Iowa line. They took mostly firearms and blankets before riding back out of town.[25] Far to the south in eastern Boone County Rebel recruiting captains Allen, Charles Selby, and Julius McGuire concentrated their three bands near Cedar Creek during the first three days of August, then dispersed again to make detection more difficult.[26] On August 2 three guerrillas accosted a corporal of 9th Cavalry MSM on the road near New Bloomfield, southwest Callaway County. When the corporal explained he was returning to his post after attending his wife's funeral in Fulton, the partisans spared his life but made him swear an oath to the Confederacy.[27] Meanwhile, in normally-quiet Howard County on August 5, Captain T.W. Houts' patrol of 7th Cavalry MSM from across the Missouri River at Boonville scattered a guerrilla band, killing several. Perhaps these were southerners on their way to join Colonel Poindexter's Rebel recruiting command, active then in neighboring Randolph County.[28]

Porter's Battle at Kirksville

Meanwhile, in Adair County Colonel Joseph Porter and his growing command were approaching a decisive confrontation. Emboldened by the large number of southern men coming to join his ranks because of the hated enrollment order—about 1,000 men by this time—Porter felt it was time to discipline his new men in battle and give them a victory. At Kirksville, Adair County, August 6, he turned on Colonel John McNeil's Yankee force, which was steadily trailing his, but the Federal superior armaments and training, plus artillery, produced a Rebel rout. McNeill's Federals blasted the under-gunned Rebels out of the town and harassed them across the countryside for a considerable distance. That the fight was one-sided is shown in the casualty figures of six Union dead and 33 wounded, compared to over 100 Rebels dead and perhaps as many as 200 wounded.[29]

After the Kirksville debacle, Porter abandoned any thought of striking at the Federals and concentrated primarily on the preservation of what remained of his stricken force. From this point on Porter was only a threat to small parties of Yankees or the careless. He turned his attention once again to the eventual objective of readying what was left of his command for the long, dangerous horseback trek south to the Rebel army in Arkansas.

The day after the battle, some of the new EMM captured one of Porter's fellow recruiters and co-leader, Colonel Frisby H. McCullough, in Knox County. McCullough was quickly court-martialed at Kirksville for being a guerrilla and just as quickly executed by shooting. Such acts, ordered by the radical Colonel McNeil, earned him the hatred of a large portion of the northeast Missouri populace, even though current Union military orders authorized such an act. McNeil's executions in a way reflected the desperation of the Union military across all of Missouri after the first week of August. The Federals found themselves awash in a sea of guerrillas and Confederate recruiting commands in a part of the United States supposedly safely in Federal control. Certainly in northeast Missouri, these deliberate killings marked a departure from the formerly gentlemanly, even chivalrous, conduct of the war. This action also underscored the distinction between Confederate recruiters and bushwhackers—a difference that southerners could see, but which northerners could not. To many Union soldiers and their commanders, these southern irregulars were all bandits, thieves, murderers, and not fellow soldiers, because they were hundreds of miles behind Union lines, not in uniform, and were bearing arms against northerners keeping peace in a northern state—no matter what the Confederacy's "Partisan Ranger Act" stated.[30]

Meanwhile, after regrouping from the Kirksville fight, the Federal pursuit of Porter continued. Porter now had hopes of uniting with Colonel James Poindexter's recruiting command in Randolph County, but the Union pursuit was too strong and too swift. On August 8 Lt. Colonel Alexander Woolfolk, with 100 troopers of his 1st Cavalry MSM and artillery, riding from the west, struck the Rebels near Stockton, west Macon County. Later that same day the Federals attacked Porter again at Panther Creek in southwest Macon County. Only the advent of darkness and a summer storm saved the Confederate force from further destruction. Union losses from six hours of fighting were two killed and ten wounded, but Porter lost 20 killed and 50 wounded, and his band faced the distinct danger of annihilation. Apparently, Colonel McNeil's Federals discovered that some of the southern captives carried papers given them earlier in the war after taking oaths not to bear arms against the U.S. Several were summarily shot.[31]

Rebel Lt. Colonel Frisby H. McCullough, who was captured and executed after the Kirksville battle. (Joseph A. Mudd, *With Porter in North Missouri*, 1909; courtesy Bob and Mary Younger and Andy Turner)

Seeing that converging Yankee forces made any hope of continuing south fruitless, Porter changed the direction of his battered command back north toward Adair County on August 9. At Walnut Creek in the southwest corner of that county, he deployed a rear guard to buy time, but the large combined northern force, moving up fast, merely blasted them with canister rounds from their cannon. Seeing his rear guard rendered ineffective, Porter had no choice but to disband to save his command and his men's lives, and his haggard warriors dispersed through the woods and brush to escape the large Union force.[32]

Colonel Poindexter's Campaign

The Yankee military was grateful for the dissipation of Porter's command as they turned to counter a new threat—the recruiting command of Kentucky-born Colonel James A. Poindexter of east Randolph County. Poindexter had recruited successfully in his home region the previous winter, but a decisive defeat January

8 on Silver Creek, as described earlier, taught him to be more cautious. Since his clandestine arrival back in Randolph County in June, he had scrupulously avoided the more visible raiding techniques Porter used to recruit, arm, and equip his force. By early August, Poindexter had secretly amassed between 700 and 1,100 men, when the Federals somehow discovered what he was doing. Colonel Odon Guitar, veteran commander of the Callaway County fight with Porter in late July, gathered area Yankees under his command once again and went hunting this new Rebel recruiting command.

On August 9 Guitar's veterans discovered Poindexter's recruits on Silver Creek, not far from the scene of the January fight, and attacked them during dinner, beginning a six-day pursuit. Guitar had only 550 men, but these men were detachments of 2nd Missouri Cavalry (Merrill's Horse), 7th Cavalry MSM, and 13th Cavalry MSM, as well as an entire battery of light artillery, all veterans of months of guerrilla fighting. Poindexter's hundreds were mostly untried, raw recruits, well-mounted but under-gunned and poorly equipped for what they would now face.[33]

The following day, troopers of 2nd Missouri Cavalry captured Poindexter's rear guard, and again drove the rest from their dinner at Switzler's Mills, on the east branch of the Chariton River in east Chariton County. Poindexter continued west to distance his command from their pursuers, and at sunset on August 11 barely got his men and horses across the Grand River at Compton's Ferry into the southwest corner of Livingston County when Colonel Guitar's task force galloped into view on the Chariton County side of the river. If the inexperienced Confederates thought they were now safe behind a natural obstacle, they failed to reckon with Yankee artillery, and eight projectiles fired into their midst caused the rookie Rebels to abandon many of their weapons and flee in panic into the dusk. Federal cavalry pursued some of the Rebel horsemen for over 20 miles and then returned to the temporary base at Compton's Ferry. Some estimates of southern losses from these actions included about 100 killed and wounded and about 200 prisoners. Poindexter dispersed what was left of his command after Compton's Ferry, and the Union pursuit thereafter was directed only at fragments.[34]

On the morning of August 12 Colonel Poindexter led part of his battered force across the railroad at Utica, western Livingston County, but Yankee Brigadier General Benjamin F. Loan unexpectedly confronted him with another Union task force coming from the west, and the startled Rebels turned back to the south.[35] Federal troops in Missouri had been frustrated for months, swatting away ineffectively at "will-of-the-wisp" guerrillas and Rebel recruiters, who seldom presented themselves in the open for combat, but for these few days in late July and early August, the tables were suddenly turned. All Union troops in Missouri were truly alarmed with the large volume of bushwhacker and Confederate recruiting bands that seemed to swarm over the countryside, but at least now there were bodies of mounted Rebels they could confront in battle.

On August 13 Colonel Guitar's Federals caught up to Poindexter with his remnant force, this time near Yellow Creek in northwest Chariton County, and further scattered the exhausted Rebel horsemen.[36]

Alvin Cobb, Young Purcell, and Others Near the Missouri River

Guerrilla activity continued throughout northeast Missouri even while Federal task forces grappled with Porter and Poindexter. On August 8 Union troops apprehended a lone guerrilla when he allegedly tried to derail a passenger train somewhere in the region.[37] The guerrilla or Rebel recruiting commands of captains Young Purcell, Julius McGuire, Charles Selby, and man named Allen rendezvoused August 8 in Boone County. They remained united and avoided Union attack for several days only by moving camp every night and sleeping during the day.[38]

Meanwhile, guerrilla chief Alvin Cobb had earlier left Joseph Porter's command after the costly battle at Moore's Mill in Callaway County, July 28. He had taken his band back to their lair in northern Montgomery County and was attracting new recruits himself in early August. Kentucky-born Cobb was truly a colorful character, and even his appearance was notable. An area newspaper described the notorious chieftain for posterity later in August:

> He is about forty-five years old, six feet tall... His right arm has been cut off about the wrist [a pre-war shooting accident]. He has an iron hook fastened to his arm by which he holds his bridle. He dresses awkwardly and oddly—He has a savage looking countenance, (what can be seen of it) his hair hangs down to his shoulders, and his face is covered with beard, which is long reaching to his waist. His eyes are grey and piercing. He looks but little like a military man. To say the least of him, he is a "hard looking customer."[39]

Perhaps it was some of Cobb's men who sniped at a Union captain riding on August 12 in northwest Montgomery County. The shaken officer later displayed a bullet imbedded in the saddle and three new holes in his coat.[40]

That same day the U.S. military commander of northeast Missouri, Brigadier General Lewis Merrill, gleefully reported that rebel Colonel Joseph Porter, now with only twenty men, had gone to ground somewhere in the Fabius River hills, probably in Lewis County. He added that Federal cavalry chased a remnant of Porter's former force across Monroe County.[41]

Meanwhile in Boone County the guerrilla bands of Young Purcell and John Brown raided Columbia, the county seat, on August 12 during the absence of the Union troops normally stationed there, and broke several comrades out of the jail. The raiders did not molest the few Federals who ran to the courthouse as they rode in, but took a U.S. flag from a pole and about 100 government horses before riding away. This was only one of several Columbia raids during the long war.[42]

Joseph Porter Rides Again

Joseph Porter displayed his remarkable resilience just days after General Merrill had all but dismissed him as a threat. Porter had remained in the Emerson area of north-central Marion County a few days trying to collect his scattered men and any recruits who would still come to him. By about August 15 some credited him with gathering 150 Rebels back to his banner.[43] However, Union troops in the region, agitated by the recent southern uprisings, remained alert and active, and continued to track down remnants of both Porter's and Poindexter's scattered forces throughout this period. Porter struck back at some of these Yankee patrols in order to restore southern confidence and re-equip his men, as was his custom. His men shot up a ten-man EMM patrol in south-central Lewis County, August 22, but moved off before the inevitable pursuit materialized.[44]

The situation was reversed when Lieutenant A. A. Piper, with 60 veteran troopers of 2nd Missouri Cavalry (Merrill's Horse), attacked Porter and about 200 Rebels near Paris, Monroe County, about August 25. Piper's men attacked the Confederates as they prepared dinner, killing and wounding several before they scattered. Then the troopers returned from the pursuit to the captured Rebel camp and ate their enemy's meal.[45] This reverse caused Porter to "lay low" for several days thereafter and to avoid contact with the Federals. Even then, at the end of August, two companies of 11th Cavalry MSM rode from Shelby County through Monroe and Ralls counties, killing several southern irregulars they found along the way, probably members of Porter's force.[46]

Guerrilla Bands of Cobb and Ewing

There were other actions of guerrilla warfare during this same period in the region. At Laclede, in south Linn County, Union authorities on August 15 killed by firing squad one of Colonel Poindexter's captured lieutenants—identified only as "Sartain." It seems this same Sartain had been convicted earlier in the war for his part in Rebel Captain James Cason's August 17, 1861, attack on the steamers *White Cloud* and *McDowell* as they passed down the Missouri River laden with Yankee troops, and this is the Calvin Sartain who broke out of the St. Louis military prison in June. The local newspaper account of this execution added that Sartain had escaped from northern custody before the earlier sentence of the military tribunal could be imposed, and the Federals at Laclede did not wish him to escape justice again.[47]

Also on August 15 Montgomery County's irrepressible guerrilla chieftain Alvin Cobb and his band, accompanied by two Rebel recruit companies, raided Portland in southeast Callaway County. It seems that Cobb was helping equip the recruits, in the manner of Joseph Porter, by town raiding. The Rebels took clothing, boots, hats, liquor, and a small amount of money, but, unlike Porter, they paid little attention to the rightful owners' loyalty. Nobody was harmed, but they made some prominent residents of northern sympathy, along with a Yankee soldier who happened to be in town, take oaths to the Confederacy. Then Cobb made the cowed residents prepare supper for all the raiders and left after eating.[48]

It was Fulton's turn to be raided the next day while the Union troops normally stationed there were out in the field. This time, the raiders were a Rebel Captain Fowler and sixteen guerrillas. They took some clothing and other things and demanded unsuccessfully that a wounded Rebel held at the nearby asylum be turned over to them. Evidently, they were not strong enough to force this issue, and they left town in disgust without the wounded comrade.[49]

About August 18 or 19, elements of 3rd Cavalry MSM caught up to Cobb's guerrillas and recruits near Reedsville in east-central Callaway County and killed three of them, including a Captain McConnell, before the rest scattered into the brush.[50] On August 19, unidentified guerrillas shot at Union guards just outside Columbia in Boone County. Nobody was hit, and the Federal pursuit failed to find the shooters.[51] So many guerrillas and Confederate recruits were wearing captured Union uniforms in the region that General Merrill, the regional Yankee commander, issued an order on August 19 that all the newly-formed Enrolled Missouri Militia while on active duty wear broad white hat bands to simplify recognition by other northern troops.[52]

Recognition was not a problem when Alvin Cobb, with 180 Rebel irregulars, raided Fulton on August 20 flying a large Confederate flag and singing "Dixie" as they galloped into town. Unlike their Portland raid on August 15, the raiders took goods and horses only from northern sympathizers and harmed no one. The hairy chieftain lectured the awestruck townspeople, who recognized him by the hook protruding from his arm. He warned them of the dire consequences of interfering with the southern cause or helping the Yankees, then took his force off to the east.[53]

A patrol of 2nd Missouri Cavalry (Merrill's Horse) in north Boone County skirmished with unidentified guerrillas on August 23 and 24, killing four at the cost of one government horse killed.[54] Also on August 24, near the forks of the Chariton River in east Chariton County, Union troops discovered 14 kegs of hidden Rebel gunpowder and some lead. Possibly these munitions were among those hidden by the southern Missouri State Guard during the summer of 1861 when Yankee troops first marched into the state.[55]

Guerrillas, led by Kentucky-born William Ewing of south Scotland County, were active in Knox and Adair counties during the last days of August. Perhaps it was Ewing's band who fought a skirmish with elements of 3rd Iowa Cavalry in or near Adair County, August 26. Unfortunately, no other details of this fight remain.[56] Little had been heard of Ewing in northeast Missouri since his violent guerrilla actions in March and April. He was definitely back in the area by August 28, for on that day Yankee soldiers of the newly-formed Knox and Adair County Enrolled Missouri Militia fought him and his gang of 28 near Millport in north-central Knox County. These EMM rode onto the farm of northern sympathizer Robert Cunningham just as the older farmer was trying to fight off the partisan band. Between the shooting of the Cunningham family and the militiamen, Ewing was killed and one of his lieutenants wounded. The EMM captured the wounded lieutenant, fifteen horses, and papers listing each gang member. The northern loss was one militiaman killed and Cunningham's son shot to death. This was one of the rare instances in northeast Missouri where a guerrilla chieftain was killed.[57]

August 28, 1862, was notable for fighting in other parts of northeast Missouri, too. Elements of 4th Cavalry MSM skirmished with guerrillas in Howard County that day, but no other details seem to survive.[58] Also on that day, the Federal commander at Hermann, northern Gasconade County, just south of the Missouri River, reported that Alvin Cobb with hundreds of guerrillas or Rebel recruits were attempting to cross to the south side of the great river at nearby Portland. Joseph Porter had tried to take his men south one month before, but perhaps Cobb was more successful on August 28, for there is no further mention of him in northeast Missouri this season.[59]

Over in south Pike County on this same date, a savage battle raged in the village of Ashley. There, Clinton Burbridge and Moses Beck, leading 150 guerrillas or Rebel recruits from the area, attacked Captain William H. Purse and 30 of the newly-formed EMM just at daylight. The southerners knew that many of the local militiamen of this garrison had been sent away on other duties days before, and they calculated on being able to overwhelm the remainder to obtain the EMM weapons cached there. Burbridge was a local man whose more famous brother, Jack, served during 1861 in southeast Missouri under Colonel M. Jeff Thompson, the colorful Swamp Rats commander. There was another brother, William, who also served the Confederate cause in Missouri, even though their family came to the state from Ohio in about the 1820s. Moses Beck, on the other hand, was a Kentucky-born farmer and family man from neighboring northern Montgomery County, who evidently came from Alvin Cobb's neighborhood.

The morning battle at Ashley got underway when Captain Purse and his outnumbered EMM, plus some civilians, fortified themselves into four buildings of the hamlet and refused Burbridge's and Beck's ultimatum for their surrender. The southerners then opened fire on the Yankees in the buildings, and both sides kept up a lively firefight for about an hour. Moses Beck was killed, along with two other rebels and several wounded, compared to northern losses of one killed and five wounded. Perhaps the loss of Beck and the fear that nearby Yankee troops would come to Purse's aid weighed heavily on Clint Burbridge's mind, for the Rebels retired from the embattled hamlet after one hour and then successfully evaded Yankee pursuit.[60]

Final Actions of Summer in Northeast Missouri

There were other incidents in this quadrant of Missouri as August and summer drew to a close. During the last days of August or first days of September, unidentified Union troops south of Columbia, Boone County, shot and killed a man who ran away from a house as they rode up.[61] Elements of 1st Cavalry MSM evidently skirmished with unidentified guerrillas in Putnam County near the Iowa border on September 1, but left few details of the encounter.[62] About this same date, Raphael Smith and his guerrillas raided Monticello, Lewis County, but left after only a few minutes in town, upon learning of the approach of a large force of the 11th Cavalry MSM.[63] Down in Randolph County a small body of EMM captured a dejected Colonel James A. Poindexter who had been wandering alone in the woods for several days pondering the failure of his recent campaign. It is ironic that members of the Enrolled Missouri Militia captured Poindexter, as their formation under the General Order Number 19 had been responsible for motivating so many southern men to join his ranks rather than be forced into Yankee militia.[64]

Even though William Ewing, Moses Beck, and several other rebel leaders were dead, and Poindexter and many others captured as September began, Joseph Porter and other recruiters still attracted new members to their hidden locations across northeast Missouri. With several weeks of good campaigning weather ahead, fall of 1862 promised a continuation of the violent summer. Somehow, the several Confederate recruiters and guerrilla bands still operating across the region would need to bypass Yankee patrols and make their way south to join the Confederate army in Arkansas before the advent of winter.

Sixteen

Summer 1862 in Northwest Missouri

Guerrilla War in Full Bloom

Guerrilla warfare reached a noisy crescendo in the northwest parts of Missouri during the summer of 1862, due to the determined partisan bands there and the large, well-organized bands of Confederate recruiters sent into interior Missouri by their army hundreds of miles to the south in Arkansas. In many cases the bushwhackers worked alongside the Rebel recruiters for mutual benefit and survival. In late July and August, as the much-despised General Order Number 19 requiring universal militia enrollment sent southerners to the recruiters and guerrillas in droves, these behind-the-lines southern forces acquired sufficient strength to be a real threat to Union forces.

Early June in Saline and Pettis Counties

Portions of the 7th Missouri Cavalry were frustrated by the large numbers of bushwhackers that they had encountered beginning in late May roaming through Saline County. Throughout early June of 1862 these troopers set out to clear their enemies from the area. They arrested several men returning home from the Rebel army, searched villages like Miami in north Saline County, and scoured the countryside to catch elusive southern horsemen. The 7th Missouri Cavalrymen never managed to kill or capture more than a few Rebels at a time for all their efforts.[1]

Their comrades to the south in Pettis County met similar frustration. On June 5 a detail sent out from Sedalia to bring back forage for the mounts was attacked north of town by guerrillas who captured the Federals' wagon. Lieutenant G. W. Nash's patrol of 78 troopers of 1st Missouri Cavalry followed the tracks of the lost wagon and the information of local blacks to the lair of twelve bushwhackers. In the ensuing firefight Nash's patrol killed two Rebels and its own reluctant guide when he ran, and they recovered the wagon and captured many horses and mules. The guide was a Colonel Fields, who formerly was a Louisville, Kentucky, attorney of note, and his violent death created quite a stir in the Kansas City newspaper.[2]

Union troops searched homes for firearms, which were forbidden to Missouri citizens under martial law. (*Harper's Weekly*, November 16, 1861; courtesy Bob and Mary Younger and Andy Turner)

Early June in Quantrill Country

Bill Quantrill's celebrated band remained mostly inactive into early June because Quantrill was away buying percussion caps. Nevertheless, there was some action in the Jackson-Johnson-Lafayette-Cass County area. In fact, this region would soon arguably become the hottest part of Missouri. The Union side in nearly all these early June actions involved exclusively parts of the 7th Missouri Cavalry. Evidently, a patrol of 7th Missouri Cavalry fought somebody on the Little Blue River in Jackson County, June 2, but in the excitement of the times failed to record the specifics.[3] Unidentified bushwhackers on June 9 easily killed two sergeants, probably of the 7th Missouri Cavalry, at the Big Blue River ferry between Independence and Kansas City. In spite of the large number of guerrillas about, these two sergeants were foolishly traveling without escort while returning to their Independence duty station after a visit from their wives, who had been staying in Kansas City.[4] This incident seemed to incite the 7th Missouri Cavalry to increase its activity, for their patrols in the area on June 9 and 12 slew five guerrillas without loss to themselves. During June this regiment's patrols also brought in numerous prisoners, mostly men who had returned from the Rebel army and had failed to report themselves to the nearest Federal post.[5]

Meanwhile, in Johnson County, murder and vendetta seemed to be the order of the day. An anonymous correspondent there wrote to a St. Louis newspaper on June 6 to describe several killings, including men killed at home feeding horses and milking cows. The article also referred to large numbers of rural refugees moving into Warrensburg, the county seat, to find safety.[6]

In neighboring Cass County to the west, near Pleasant Hill, bushwhackers called a man to his door and shot him repeatedly until he was dead. The only reason his neighbors could find to explain the murder was that the victim had shot at some guerrillas attempting to steal his horses a day or two before.[7]

Near Lexington in Lafayette County to the north, a patrol of 7th Missouri Cavalry captured eight armed guerrillas or Rebel recruits on June 7 and immediately executed them. Their commander, Colonel Daniel Huston Jr., had given standing orders for his men to do so to any "...guerrillas taken during lurking or ambuscading, with arms in their hands...."[8]

A Memorable Quantrill Ambush

Quantrill must have returned from his trip to east Missouri with George Todd by June 11, for on that day, with only ten or twelve men, he conducted an ambush on Union troops that would be used as a standard for future bushwhacking. The relative quiet in Jackson County during late May and early June may have caused local Yankees to grow careless. This small number of guerrillas easily shot up the six advance riders of Captain J. Franklin Cochran's 24-man mail escort of the 2nd Battalion Cavalry MSM at a road cut on the Independence-Harrisonville Road. Captain Cochran and the rest of the detail galloped the 50 yards to the ambush site to find two comrades dead and two wounded, but Quantrill and the small part of his band with him had vanished into the brush. The local Union commander, Lt. Colonel James T. Buel of the 7th Missouri Cavalry at Independence, angrily ordered known southern sympathizers to carry the mail thereafter between the two towns.[9]

Stagecoach Robberies and a Skirmish

Stopping a stagecoach is not usually viewed as a Civil War action, but many guerrillas viewed passing coaches as a convenient way to obtain horses, firearms, valuables and perhaps torment a northern sympathizer. Evidently, some men, perhaps of Quantrill's band felt that way when they stopped a stagecoach near Lexington on June 13 or 14. The report from the scene said these bushwhackers were armed with about seven pistols apiece. They required each of the startled passengers to identify themselves, then released the people but took the horses.[10]

About June 15 a patrol of 7th Missouri Cavalry near Pink Hill in east Jackson County fought with Quantrill and about 30 of his men. The Yankees reported killing two partisans, wounding two, and capturing three at no Federal loss. This battle report is missing the usual exaggeration of Rebel losses, which is surprising in light of the recent June 11 ambush, and therefore seems plausible compared to many others of this period.[11]

Six bushwhackers conducted another stage robbery on the Kansas side of the state border, eight miles from Westport, June 17, when they waylaid a stagecoach packed with 15 passengers, including four children. The robbers took watches, money, firearms, overcoats, and blankets, and repeatedly threatened to kill a discharged soldier aboard, although it appears other passengers finally dissuaded them.[12]

Some Union Successes in Saline County

The expansive rolling terrain of Saline County, forming the south bank of the Missouri River for so many miles and yet not heavily populated in 1862, was a frequent crossing place for Rebel recruiting bands throughout the war. Like most of the other Missouri River counties, Saline County had a predominant southern population, so Union authorities found it prudent to station and patrol it with troops. Elements of the same 7th Missouri Cavalry regiment, which were searching for guerrillas to the west in Jackson and Lafayette counties, found some here as well. About mid–June and led by Major David McKee, they captured a passing Rebel recruiter from Shelby County identified only as "...the notorious Captain Johnson." During the war more than one "Captain Johnson" recruited Rebels in and around Shelby County, and unless this report refers to the capture of Captain Henry or Harry Johnson, from nearby Moniteau County, it is difficult to identify this prisoner. Major McKee's troopers also found 20 more kegs of Rebel gunpowder, probably more of that hidden one year before by the southern Missouri State Guard upon the sudden movement of Union troops into the region.[13] These were not glorious battlefield victories, but such successes were eagerly sought by the hard-pressed northern troops in mid–June.

Colonel Upton Hays Revitalizes Johnson County Guerrillas

The beleaguered guerrillas in Johnson County, stunned by recent defeats by Union cavalry, received welcome encouragement around June 15 when former Jackson County businessman, Colonel Upton S. Hays, rode up from the Rebel army in Arkansas into this area with a body of over 100 southern recruiters. Although his command was battered from skirmishes on the way north, Hays himself suffering from a dislocated shoulder, his arrival was a needed "shot in the arm" to the southern hopes of Johnson County and the area. Not only had Hays been a respected businessman of neighboring Jackson County before the war, but during the previous November he had led Jackson County southerners in a brief guerrilla campaign against marauding Kansas troops.

Before Hays's arrival in the area, Johnson County's once-powerful guerrilla force had dwindled under Federal battering to about 80 active members, led now by Warrensburg resident John Brinker and Benjamin Snelling from the southwest corner of the county. Perhaps buoyed by the presence of the nearby recruiters, Brinker and Snelling launched a new offensive against northern interests in mid–June. In just three violent days they gunned down a northern sympathizer plowing in his field, killed another standing in the doorway of his home in the presence of his family, seriously wounded another man, and accidentally wounded his 13-year-old daughter who happened to get in the way. They also robbed four homes and burned one or two, causing another rush of rural northerners to take refuge in Warrensburg.[14]

The Fight at Mrs. Davenport's

On June 17, Lieutenant Sandy Lowe, with a patrol of 18 men of 7th Cavalry MSM out from Warrensburg, rode west hoping to find some of the bushwhackers who had been making all the trouble. As they rode up to Mrs. Davenport's farm, nine miles west of town, they encountered a small number of partisans sitting down to eat. Lowe's excited patrol chased the diners into the brush for about a half mile and suddenly found themselves surrounded by an estimated 80–90 guerrillas—Brinker and Snelling's whole force. Now the tide of battle turned against the Yankees. Lieutenant Lowe quickly sent a rider back toward town to summon help and began to fall back, fighting the larger force for the next thirty minutes. When Lowe's embattled men had fought their way back to within three miles of town, Major Emory Foster came up with reinforcements, and the bushwhackers fled. Federal losses were two dead and two wounded, compared to perhaps as many as 11 dead southerners. The Union force then fired the Davenport home for harboring partisans and arrested guerrilla chief John Brinker's sister and younger brother, whom they accused of riding through the countryside carrying messages for the bushwhackers. Southerners latter claimed that Major Foster arrested Mattie Brinker and made her ride at the head of his column as protection against her brother's men shooting at the cavalry.[15]

Some sources indicate that about this time Quantrill brought his band into northwest Johnson County to meet Upton Hays and recruited John Brinker and some of his Johnson countians into the celebrated band. It appears that Colonel Hays tasked Quantrill with providing security for his Rebel recruiting in the region, and Quantrill probably thought it best to bring in local men who knew the country.[16]

Another Guerrilla Band in Jackson County

Another guerrilla band, led by Christopher Lillard "Kit" Chiles Jr. of Jackson County, was active in the northern part of that county in mid–June. This was probably the remnant of Benjamin Parker's former band that Kit Chiles had helped lead during the spring. A patrol of 7th Missouri Cavalry failed to find Chiles, but local blacks pointed out some of his men hiding in a haystack. The troopers opened fire, killed two of the guerrillas, and wounded another. Acting on specific orders, the patrol then burned the nearby grocery of a southern man who informants evidently reported had been aiding Chiles's men.[17]

Some Violence North of the Missouri River

A war of intimidation and terror was also underway north of the Missouri River during the last half of June, 1862. About mid–June unidentified soldiers arrested

Columbus Spencer, evidently for being a southern sympathizer, at his home near DeKalb in southwest Buchanan County. The arrest was merely a pretense, however, for the soldiers shot Spencer half a mile from the house.[18] In the Missouri River bottoms of south Carroll County, local guerrillas on June 20 shot and killed a local man who had joined the Union 7th Cavalry MSM.[19]

During the evening of that same day, two partisans shot an elderly man while searching for firearms in his home on Shoal Creek, in south-central Livingston County to the north.[20] About this same time local guerrillas in the strongly southern Spring Hill neighborhood of northwest Livingston County began a short campaign of terror. They shot into the home of a northern sympathizer and wounded a soldier. In reaction, Captain John Ballinger led 30 of his troopers of 1st Cavalry MSM to the area at the end of June or early July and split them into small search teams. This did not seem to intimidate the partisans, who shot up one of the search parties, although details of the fight do not survive.[21] The guerrillas may have left soon after, for the neighborhood grew quiet again after this.

Further to the west in the large town of St. Joseph, several military prisoners in the jail attempted to force their way out of the building while the guard was outside. Hearing the ruckus, the guard bounded back inside and stopped the attempt with rapid shooting, killing a "noted jayhawker" named Melville Bond.[22]

Renewed Fighting in Jackson County

Late June also brought another surge of guerrilla fighting in embattled Jackson County. Major Wyllis C. Ransom crowed to his superiors that his command of 6th Kansas Cavalry, based at Little Santa Fe, southwest Jackson County, routed Upton Hays' recruiting band in a June 21 action, capturing some southern weapons without suffering one Union casualty. Ransom's report showed that Colonel Hays had moved his operations west to Jackson County, closer to Hays's Westport home. A local newspaper account added that the Kansans caught the Rebels at supper, killed one and badly wounded another, and captured numerous weapons, apparently including Hays's personal rifle. Just to show they were not beaten, some of Hays's men later that night crept up to the Yankee camp and shot at the guards.[23]

Either Quantrill's or, more likely, Chiles's, band raided the Missouri River steamer *Little Blue* near Sibley, northeast Jackson County, on June 22. The guerrillas bullied but did not harm 40 sick and wounded Union soldiers on board and carried away a large quantity of military supplies, but did not otherwise harm the boat itself. This raid on a river steamer is reminiscent of Ben Parker's late March robbery onboard the *Rowena*, another indication that the raiders were Parker's former bushwhackers, now led by Chiles.[24]

The following day Captain James Breckinridge's 30-man patrol of 7th Missouri Cavalry, near the Jordan Lowe farm east of Independence, discovered a recently-occupied guerrilla camp. While the troopers were examining the camp, they were suddenly confronted by large numbers of bushwhackers shooting from cover and had to beat a hasty retreat. In the hurried gunfight each side lost one man killed. Captain Breckinridge was wounded but could not identify the guerrilla band that confronted him.[25]

As a result of the *Little Blue* robbery and the skirmish near the Lowe farm, Major Eliphalet Breditt led 188 men of the 7th Missouri Cavalry on an intense dragnet of northeast and east Jackson County between June 23 and July 1. Major Breditt was particularly anxious to find the culprits from the steamer robbery and a guerrilla band he thought was led by a "Ducates," but he found few bushwhackers to fight and no stolen government property. The patrol did arrest 107 civilians whom the Federals considered suspect. Breditt's expedition fit the pattern of expected Union countermeasures, and the wily partisans of Jackson County would have known to "lay low" for a few days until the troopers returned to base. A Frank Ducates was convicted the following year by a military tribunal in St. Louis for guerrilla activity, and there had been a Kentucky-born young man of that name living across the Missouri River in Platte County in 1860, but, again, it appears that the Yankees had no real idea of the identity of the guerrilla chieftains in their area.[26] Indeed, in early July area Federals raided a dance near Lone Jack in southeast Jackson County and took into custody several men of military age, but later released them for lack of evidence. One of the men they released was Harrison Trow, a member of Quantrill's band.[27]

A New Yankee Tactic in Johnson County

Union patrols of the 1st Missouri Cavalry kept busy in nearby Johnson County in late June and early July. On June 28, one such patrol near the Blackwater River chased and killed three bushwhackers, and the next day another killed two and captured two guerrillas.[28] About this time the local commander of the 1st Missouri Cavalry stationed at Warrensburg, European-born Major Charles Banzhaf, devised a method to beat the partisans at their own game. He sent patrols out to northwest Johnson County between July 6 and July 9 with instructions to hide in the brush three or four days in order to ambush the guerrillas for a change. This time three bushwhackers were killed, but this method, used hereafter, enjoyed only marginal success in such strong southern neighborhoods, where citizens operated "early warning" networks to help guerrillas. In such regions the hunters could easily become the hunted.[29]

Quantrill's Big Creek Fight

One of Quantrill's most famous battles had its origins in a series of skirmishes during the time Quantrill's band was helping Colonel Upton Hays recruit near Wadesburg at the southeast corner of Cass County and the northwest corner of Henry County. First, a patrol of 6th Kansas Cavalry encountered some of Hays's recruits in that vicinity on July 6 and killed one Rebel and captured a quantity of firearms. This was the second time in about two weeks that the despised Kansas military attacked the recruiting command, and Hays had lost some of his precious weapons each time. Perhaps this prompted Hays to seek the protection of Quantrill's band, if he hadn't already. At any rate, Quantrill's guerrillas were camped near Hays's command in this same area in the early morning of July 9 when a patrol of

1st Iowa Cavalry rode onto the camp on Sugar Creek. As the Iowa troopers attacked, they suddenly found themselves greatly outnumbered. After losing one man killed and having two men wounded, compared to like casualties in the Rebel ranks, the Federals withdrew and sent for reinforcements.[30]

While Union reinforcements galloped in from several directions, Quantrill convinced Hays to take his inexperienced recruits toward the northwest, away from the Iowans and out of harm's way with an escort of George Todd and 30 seasoned bushwhackers. To draw his enemy away from Hays and Todd, Quantrill took the rest of his band slowly north to Big Creek in northeast Cass County. Meanwhile, Yankees of 1st and 7th Missouri Cavalry and 1st Iowa Cavalry—from garrisons at Butler, Warrensburg, Clinton, and Harrisonville—converged at the western border of Johnson County during the night of July 10, eager to finally confront their guerrilla enemies in open combat.

Very early the next morning, Captain Miles Kehoe quietly led his contingent of 63 troopers of 1st Missouri Cavalry away from the Union camp without notifying the others and rode west into the woods along Big Creek to four miles west of Pleasant Hill, where he found and attacked Quantrill's band of about 70 bushwhackers. The seasoned guerrillas easily repulsed Kehoe's impulsive assault, emptying a number of Yankee saddles, but then fell back to rugged, wooded ravines when the remainder of the Federal force rode up and began to inflict casualties with long range carbine fire. For once Quantrill abandoned his customary "withdraw in the face of superior numbers" tactic and enticed the eager Yankees to attack his men in the brushy ravines, where the guerrillas' pistols produced more concentrated fire than the cavalry's single-shot carbines. This fight in the woods remained intense for a while, sometimes becoming hand-to-hand, until finally Quantrill dispersed his battered band, leaving each man to fend for himself. The total Union loss was ten killed, 19 wounded; Quantrill lost fewer killed but about the same number wounded. From the Federal perspective, lack of cooperation and the underestimation of the guerrillas' fighting ability helped to rob the Yankee force of another chance to conquer Quantrill in regular combat. Quantrill's men, however, thereafter cited this fight as evidence that they could hold their own in combat with seasoned opponents.[31]

Actions in the Center of the State

In mid–July and August there were also guerrilla actions to the east in the counties of Livingston, north of the Missouri River and Saline and Cooper to the south. On July 14 a patrol of 1st Cavalry MSM, tracking two guerrillas who had stolen a horse near Chillicothe, county seat of Livingston County, captured them hiding in a hayloft with firearms. The bushwhackers were wearing parts of captured Union uniforms, and the captain commanding the patrol had difficulty preventing his men from shooting the captives on the spot.[32]

In mid–July an unidentified band of guerrillas, probably Captain Bob Austin's Rebel recruiting command, raided the largely northern town of Frankfort in northeast Saline County. To the citizens' discomfort, the raiders seemed in no hurry, seemed to enjoy terrorizing the residents, and took whatever supplies they wished from stores and homes before leaving. The area newspaper account of this event did not mention if these southerners harmed anyone.[33]

Nearby, outside the village of Miami, a patrol of 7th Missouri Cavalry rode out to Judge Robert G. Smart's house on July 20. Someone had misinformed these troopers about the former Jackson County judge's sympathy toward the war, so when he ran out of the back of his house upon their approach they drew their own conclusions and shot him dead. Word of this regrettable shooting spread beyond the immediate area, was reviled by citizens of all affiliations, and was cited long afterward as an example of senseless violence in war-torn Missouri.[34]

On July 28 a large patrol of 7th Cavalry MSM at Pilot Grove, west Cooper County, attacked an unidentified Rebel recruiting body of about 150 men camped there. The southerners fled in all directions and the cavalry chased some of them several miles into Saline County, capturing several. These southerners may have been all local men, but there were so many Confederate recruiting commands then at work across central Missouri, that the identity of the leaders of this one remain a mystery.[35]

Just a few miles away outside the Cooper County seat of Boonville, unidentified Union militia on the evening of August 14 arrested alleged southern sympathizer and citizen of Scotland, Dr. George W. Main, at his home. Dr. Main's murdered corpse was later found near the Missouri River, and local lore relates that the militia threatened the same fate to anyone who dared to report the incident to higher authority.[36]

Daily Violence During July in Quantrill Country

By mid–July in the Jackson-Johnson-Lafayette County area frequented by Quantrill's guerrillas, violence seemed a daily occurrence. During the evening of July 15, guerrillas murdered elderly Samuel Gaston near Greenton, west Lafayette County. The following day a 7th Missouri Cavalry patrol sent from Lexington shot down one man allegedly involved, arrested several local southern men, and returned to base with the prisoners.[37] Gaston's murder was later attributed to the Bill Reed gang of exiled Kansas southerners, whose members included William "Bloody Bill" Anderson and his brother Jim. This small guerrilla band, known to forcibly take their sustenance from residents of all sympathies, made Lafayette County their base for many months.[38]

Over the next several days Union authorities in Lexington conducted tribunals for suspects that had been jailed there over a period of time. Evidently, the northern military was attempting to determine who among the largely southern population of this area was dangerous to the Federal cause and to punish them accordingly, although such measures did not seem to directly affect the bushwhackers.[39]

On July 21, unidentified guerrillas robbed the Warrensburg-to-Pleasant Hill mail coach near Holden, according to a Kansas City newspaper. The account stated that the bushwhackers took from the baggage two uniforms belonging to members of the 2nd Battalion Cavalry MSM stationed nearby and were later seen wearing them. In fact, from about this point forward, Missouri guerrillas readily took to wearing Yankee uniforms both to fool enemies and to travel freely in neighborhoods of mixed loyalty.[40]

Federal patrols were active throughout this area during late July. Near Columbus on July 23, a 12-man patrol of 7th Missouri Cavalry fought an estimated 25 bushwhackers, killing one, wounding about five, and capturing 15 horses at the cost of one trooper wounded.[41] That same day on the west edge of Lafayette County a 2nd Battalion Cavalry MSM patrol captured a former Jackson County congressman, John W. Reid, who seems to have been hiding in the countryside to avoid the governor's mandatory universal militia enrollment, as many other Missouri men were also doing in late July.[42]

Based on a tip from the Independence town marshal that guerrillas frequently used a certain crossing of the Little Blue River, elements of 7th Missouri Cavalry ambushed there in late July Quantrill's lieutenant, George Todd, and two other experienced members of the band. Canadian-born Todd, a Kansas City stone mason before the war, was the sole survivor of the ambush, and henceforth engaged in an almost maniacal personal warfare against Yankees for the loss of these two comrades. At least, this is the account given by other members of the band after the war. Quantrill's men learned about the Independence marshal's assistance to the northern cavalry and looked to a time when they could repay him personally for the harm he had caused them.[43]

A local newspaper reported that Confederate Colonel Upton Hays came out of hiding temporarily and entered the village of Westport near his home on the evening of July 30, accompanied by noted bushwhacker Dick Yeager and a few others. Allegedly, they were looking to kill two or three northern informants but instead killed a Yankee soldier and left promptly.[44]

Carroll County Erupts in Violence

Carroll County to the east and on the north side of the Missouri River seemed free of the partisan warfare that troubled other neighboring counties, although Carroll County's population was divided as to northern and southern sympathy. Three Rebel recruiters came to the area in late July, 1862, and that situation changed. Virginia-born Captain Robert Austin evidently had a family, including several small children and had lived in south Carroll County near the Missouri River. Captain John L. Merrick, also of Carroll County, served during 1861

Guerrilla George Todd wearing a captured Union coat. (John N. Edwards, *Noted Guerrillas*, 1867; courtesy Bob and Mary Younger and Andy Turner)

in the southern Missouri State Guard. Kentucky-born Captain Logan H. Ballew was a middle-aged family man of east Carroll County near DeWitt who had the previous fall been active in the area recruiting southern troops and fighting against passing Union troops. Captain Ballew would continue to be a thorn in the side of the northern cause for months to come, eclipsing the efforts of the other two.[45] All three had the good fortune to begin recruiting southern men in Carroll County at the very time the despised General Order Number 19, requiring universal enrollment in the Yankee militia, was announced and took effect. As a result, previously reluctant area men came to them in droves.

The first blow was struck July 27, when one of these three recruiting bands attacked a small detail of 5th Cavalry MSM sent to west Carroll County from nearby Richmond to distribute copies of the enrollment order in the countryside. When the Rebels ambushed the unsuspecting Federals they killed one and captured three others.[46]

This was probably not the work of Captain Robert Austin's band, for they were recruiting along the Missouri River bottoms in northwest Saline County across the river and beginning to attract the notice of Yankee troops there. On about July 29 or 30, Austin was looking for a way to get his men to the Carroll County side of the river to be closer to his home and leave behind the Federal patrols when he happened onto the four-year-old St. Louis-based side-wheeler *War Eagle* near the south bank. Austin had his Rebels fire on the vessel, compelling it to stop, then they boarded the 223-foot long ship and made the crew take his band to the Carroll County bank on the north side. Then the southerners took foodstuffs and other supplies and released the vessel to continue its interrupted voyage.[47]

These two events during the closing days of July certainly alerted Union authorities that there was considerable Rebel activity in Carroll County and they sent Captain Daniel H. David with two companies of 5th Cavalry MSM from Richmond to deal with them. Near the scene of the July 27 attack, David's Federals on July 29 or 30 fought with Austin's men, who had just arrived in the area from their boat ride across the Missouri River. The cavalry killed six and captured eight of Captain Austin's men, so the remainder quickly rode east and united with the companies of Merrick and Ballew in eastern Carroll County.[48] The combined Rebel force of about 300 men on August 1 briefly raided the county seat of Carrollton. They wrecked the office of the pro–Union newspaper, the Carrollton *Democrat*, but refrained from harming residents or other property. This raid now alerted Captain David of the whereabouts of the Confederate force, and that evening the two sides fought near town, resulting in ten dead Rebels and three as prisoners of the Yankees. Despite his victory, David wisely called for reinforcements.[49]

Soon, Major Thomas B. Biggers of the 5th Cavalry MSM brought help and took command of the combined force of about 350, consisting of troops from his own regiment from 1st Cavalry MSM, and from the newly-formed Enrolled Missouri Militia. On August 3, Biggers caught up to the still-combined Rebel force of Austin's, Merrick's, and Ballew's recruit companies at Compton's Ferry in southwest Livingston County. The southerners were attempting to cross the Grand River there, in order to join the larger recruiting command of Colonel James A. Poindexter to the east, but the Federals came onto them too rapidly. Major Biggers's cavalry overwhelmed the ill-equipped and poorly-trained Rebels and as many as 15 drowned attempting to escape the Union troops. The Yankees spent the next two days riding down much of the remainder across Livingston and Linn counties. The Federals reported no losses of their own but tallied 36 Rebel dead, many prisoners, and even recovered some of the goods taken off the *War Eagle*, which had been scattered at the Compton's Ferry battle site. Whether many of Austin's, Merrick's, or Ballew's men successfully joined Poindexter's command or found another way to eventually join the Rebel army south in Arkansas is not well recorded.[50]

No Mercy in Lafayette County

While a little war raged in Carroll County, on the south side of the Missouri River other Federals claimed they had found some of the *War Eagle* robbers. On August 1, Union troops in northeast Lafayette County captured two or three guerrillas, perhaps of William B. "Squirrel Tail" Edwards's band. These unfortunates had ridden up to the Yankees thinking they were other southerners. Union troops in Missouri were not always strict about proper uniform wear, after all. These southern captives evidently admitted taking part in the *War Eagle* robbery a few days before and were persuaded to guide a patrol of the 7th Missouri Cavalry to the lair of nine more of their comrades near the village of Waverly. Details did not survive, but the cavalrymen killed all nine of the comrades and shot down the guides as well.[51]

Effects of the Militia Enrollment Deadline

Throughout the last days of July and the first days of August, 1862, the countryside was teeming with southern men who were resisting the governor's deadline to enroll in their local Enrolled Missouri Militia (EMM) units. Some of these men were joining Rebel recruiters, but others were living in hiding. Captain George Murphy's patrol of 6th Cavalry MSM at this time reported encountering numerous bands of such men throughout Saline County.[52] Another patrol from Sedalia of the same regiment also reported many men hiding in the brush in south Pettis County.[53] On August 1, 140 southern men banded together in southwest Johnson County to form a Confederate company that later found its way south and joined the Rebel army.[54] A Union patrol from Harrisonville learned that this company was near Pleasant Hill three days later, but could not find it. Several men formerly belonging to Matt Houx's guerrilla band seemed to give up bushwhacking and joined this company to later serve as regular soldiers in the Confederate army.[55]

Sometimes it wasn't enough for reluctant men to enroll in the militia as ordered. On August 11, after five known southern sympathizers had dutifully enrolled at LaMine Bridge, west Cooper County, they were followed on their way home by cavalrymen of 7th Cavalry MSM, who shot into them near Syracuse, killing three.[56]

Early August Actions North of the Missouri River

Even as the fighting in Carroll County was ending, there were other actions north of the Missouri River in early August 1862. In Grundy County, 150 guerrillas or Rebel recruits took horses from citizens, August 2, and even forced some of their victims to swear not to take up arms against the Confederacy.[57] In nearby eastern Daviess and northwest Livingston counties, a man identified only as "Doctor" Davis and middle-aged Joe Kirk had assembled a band of 85 guerrillas or southern recruits. On August 5 their gang ambushed a patrol of 1st Cavalry MSM and newly-formed Enrolled Missouri Militia near Cravensville, north Daviess County. The Yankees fought back in a 90-minute firefight before Davis' and Kirk's men retreated with losses of six killed and about ten wounded, compared to Union losses of three severely wounded and two slightly wounded. Over the next several days, northern cavalry hunted down known southern sympathizers in the area in order to ferret out members of Davis' and Kirk's band, but only found a few.[58]

Confederate recruiters were busy also in Platte County to the west by the time Federal leaders discovered their activities. G. Byron Jones of Rushville, southwest Buchanan County, and perhaps Jefferson Patton had put together a group of southern recruits at a camp on Rocky Bluff on the Platte River, five miles north of Platte City, during early August. Lt. Colonel John T. Burris at Fort Leavenworth, across the Missouri River from Platte County, heard about the camp and on August 7 led a large combined task force of cavalry, infantry, and artillery to attack the base. Lt. Colonel Burris must have surprised the Rebels, for his sudden attack routed them, and his Yankees killed three, wounded several, and captured six at the loss of only two Federals wounded.[59]

Local resident, Captain James Gibson of the brushy area east of the Platte River in north Platte County, called the "Hackle," had amassed his own recruiting company of over 100 local southerners when Union authorities at St. Joseph heard about his camp. Using railroad transportation as far as the track would allow in the direction of the Rebel camp, they sent Lieutenant John S. Mirick with over 100 troopers of 5th Cavalry MSM on August 10. The southerners detected Lieutenant Mirick's approach and quickly scattered, with many swimming the river, and the Federals killed only two.[60]

Confederate Captain Henry Woodsmall had another small company of Rebel recruits near Parkville in south Platte County, just a few miles north of Kansas City. Area Yankees heard about this one, too, for on August 14 Colonel William R. Penick led his 5th Cavalry MSM against the camp scattering the recruits and killing three of them.[61]

Another southern recruit camp was established near Union Mills in the northeast corner of Platte County, possibly from the remnants involved in the fighting earlier in the month. An unidentified Federal cavalry force attacked this one, too, on August 20, but alert pickets spread the alarm and the Yankees had to settle for only two captives.[62] On the whole, August was an exciting month in Platte County.

Joe Kirk's Guerrillas from Livingston County

Joe Kirk's bushwhacker band in northwest Livingston County was still defying large numbers of Union militia in mid–August, despite its setbacks earlier in the month. About August 17, Kirk's men abducted five militiamen in nearby Daviess County, partly to counter the local militia's killing of two southern men a few days before. The two southerners evidently had taken part in the earlier fighting and were found in hiding by the angry northerners, who brutalized and killed them on the spot. Joe Kirk was hoping to use the five captives to force the release of some of his men held prisoner by the Yankees and to stop the killing of southern men. Meanwhile, part of Kirk's band under a subordinate, David Martin, on August 19 attacked 20 of the newly-formed Enrolled Missouri Militia on Hicklin's Branch near Spring Hill, killing one outright and mortally wounding another. That evening Lt. Colonel John H. Shanklin, leading parts of 3rd Cavalry MSM, determined to stop these pesky bushwhackers and swept the area around Spring Hill, causing Kirk to release his captives and leave the region.[63] Joe Kirk's last action north of the Missouri River occurred on August 22, when Grundy and Livingston County EMM companies found and surprised Kirk's band in a bend of the Grand River near Chillicothe. The militia drove the guerrillas across the river, causing one to drown and capturing a large number of horses. This was too much for Kirk, who led the remainder of his men south.[64]

Kansas Raiders in Clay County

Occasionally, Civil War violence in Missouri came from unexpected sources. On August 23, about 15 Kansas jayhawkers under a man named Swain rode into southwest Clay County and forcibly liberated about 25 black men, took about 40 horses, and headed back toward Kansas. There was a large Federal military expedition from Kansas operating just south of the Missouri River at this time, and perhaps these freebooters felt it offered protection for their raid. If so, this was a false hope, for Union cavalry stationed in Clay County chased the raiders to the Missouri River bottoms between Liberty and Kansas City, killed three and captured eight, and secured the stolen slaves and horses. Kansas military officials threatened retaliation if the captured raiders were not released, but Missouri Union officials held firm, kept their jayhawker prisoners, and nothing more came of the incident. The Federals probably returned the slaves to their owners, for slavery was not ended in Missouri until January 1865.[65]

Harsh Union Measures North of the Missouri River

The summer of 1862 drew to a close in the region of northwest Missouri north of the Missouri River, often with the heavy-handed acts of the available Union troops stationed there. Unidentified Union troops near Spring Hill, northwest Livingston County arrested Jesse P. Clark, who seemed to be setting out to join the Confederate army. They took him down the road, ostensibly to jail, but murdered him and left the body to be found later.[66] In late August the Union provost marshal in Chillicothe, Livingston County, conducted hearings against captured guerrillas and rebel recruits, and handed down harsh sentences to those who seemed to have violated earlier oaths not to bear arms against the U.S. Government.[67] There were similar tribunals across Missouri against the Rebels captured during the many uprisings this summer, and there was ample evidence that the Bill of Rights and the customary rights of American citizens were not honored during this "time of national emergency." Some of this was the reaction of these state and local troops and officials to the frantic fighting across Missouri between their comrades-in-arms and the legions of Confederate recruiters and southern bushwhackers who where challenging the Federal hold on the state. Except for similar actions in Platte and Livingston counties, little of that spilled over the Missouri River to this normally-quiet part of northwest Missouri. This was a reflection of the Union desperation at this time. Lastly, in late August Colonel William Penick, regimental commander of the 3rd Cavalry MSM, had two southern ladies of Hainesville, south Clinton County, arrested for refusing to take an oath supporting the U.S.[68] Perhaps this was an indication of a "general war," in which all members of a population were viewed as potential combatants. Perhaps this was merely excess by an over zealous official.

The Battle of Independence

Most of the guerrilla war of northwest Missouri in August 1862 occurred in the west-central counties of Jackson, Johnson, and Lafayette. On August 7 a patrol of 6th Cavalry MSM in Johnson County fought guerrillas in the brush, killing four and capturing two of the wounded. One of the prisoners astounded his captives by telling of 500 other Rebels in the area and plans to attack the Federal garrison at Sedalia, Pettis County.[69] No such Confederate attack on Sedalia materialized, but there could well have been 500 recruits assembling in the country, due to several Rebel recruiting officials in the area and the despised General Order Number 19 then in effect. Area Union commanders knew there was now a substantial threat of Rebel attack and moved troops around to meet it.

They did not foresee, however, that a sizable Confederate-guerrilla force would target the Union garrison of about 300 men at Independence, Jackson County, at daybreak the morning of August 11. There Lt. Colonel James T. Buel commanded elements of his own 7th Missouri Cavalry and the 2nd Battalion Cavalry MSM, which were hard-pressed in those days to counter Quantrill's band, Chiles's band, and Colonel Upton Hays's recruiting efforts nearby. The attacking force of about 400 to 600 was mostly composed of the recruiting commands of Colonel John T. Hughes of Jackson County and Colonel Gideon W. Thompson of Kansas City, having ridden up recently all the way from Arkansas, dogged by Federal cavalry, as far north as the Osage River. The commanding Confederates also added to their force the command of Colonel Upton Hays and the guerrilla band of Quantrill. The southerners had used one or more of their own men in disguise to scout the Federal defenses in town, whereas Lt. Colonel Buel had been lulled into a lack of caution and less-than-adequate defenses by the reassuring reports of his own patrols, which were avoided by the large Rebel forces. Some accounts even say Buel and his officers scoffed at anxious reports by citizen informants about large Confederate forces in the area.

Nevertheless, at four in the morning of August 11, Quantrill's men neutralized most of the Federal pickets, and the Rebel assault came into town from two directions, nearly taking the whole place by surprise. Most of the Federals did spring to the defense as they comprehended the situation, although they had been poorly placed in two separate locations in the town. Some of the garrison held out until after nine o'clock and then surrendered to overwhelming numbers of Rebels after gaining assurance that they would not be murdered by Quantrill's men. Earlier, the bushwhackers had killed a Union captain they had captured in a hotel, and George Todd gleefully murdered the unarmed former town marshal, who had caused the death of Todd's two comrades some days before.

The losses showed how desperate the fighting was. Of 312 Union troops, 26 were dead and 74 wounded, 11 mortally, and about 150 were captured and paroled. The remainder escaped to Kansas City when the assault began, or went into hiding while the Confederates were in town. The Rebel losses were 23 dead, including Colonel Hughes and a number of other officers, and a number of wounded, including 11 mortally, Colonel Thompson and several other officers. Christopher "Kit" Chiles, formerly a guerrilla chieftain himself who had by now joined Quantrill's band, was also among the dead. The loss of Hughes and several other officers, as well as the wounding of several others, did tend to limit the effectiveness of the southern force, and probably prevented it from engaging in other offensive actions planned before the attack. Henceforth, this force limited its activities to recruiting and getting its recruits safely back to the Rebel army in the south. They did benefit, however, from the large amount of weapons, ammunition, equipment, and supplies captured at Independence, which were used to arm and equip the new soldiers.[70]

Quantrill and his men, meanwhile, benefited from the help they had given to the southern recruiters. The day after the fight, August 12, one of the surviving colonels swore the band into Confederate service, evidently under the Confederate Partisan Ranger Act, and commissioned Quantrill as a captain—the only known rank given to him officially—and gave lesser rank to his chief subordinates: William Haller, a Pennsylvania-born local farmer and returned Rebel soldier; George Todd, who would take command from Quantrill in 1864; and William H. Gregg, a local farmer who would become a deputy sheriff, and the only one of these who would survive the war.

Officially, Quantrill now had 130 men in his band, and Quantrill gave to each the following general orders:

1. Any man wishing to escape mandatory enrollment into Federal forces can join the guerrillas and be given means to resist Union troops.
2. All men found going to enroll in Union forces or who inform against their southern neighbors shall forfeit their lives to the guerrillas.
3. "...anyone known to have paid money to the Federal government to exempt him from military duty, is liable to have his chattel property taken for the use of the Southern army."

Union troops later found a paper containing these orders in Lafayette County and allowed it to be published in area newspapers.[71]

Impotent Federal Reactions

The sudden and successful Rebel attack at Independence brought the customary Union reactions. Lt. Colonel John T. Burris and his combined cavalry, infantry, and artillery task force from Ft. Leavenworth, Kansas, seemed to play the part of a Federal guard dog, brought out to counter any danger to Union control of west-central Missouri and then taken back to the kennel when no enemy could be quickly found. In spite of the enormity of the Federal defeat on August 11, Burris' Kansas force accomplished less than usual, probably because there were so many reports of Rebel forces in the region that Burris was reluctant to deal in detail with any one of them, lest one of the others sneak by him and cause more harm somewhere else. The Fort Leavenworth task force arrived at the scene of the disaster in the early evening of August 13 and the next day sent out stout patrols which brought back a herd of cattle, eight prisoners, and the information that 800 nearby Rebels were awaiting reinforcements from the south with which to attack Lexington. Since Burris's orders this time were to protect the Kansas border, he quickly withdrew his force to Kansas City to counter any Confederate thrust there and left Lexington's protection to the Missouri troops. The late discoveries of Rebel recruiting companies north of Kansas City in Platte County, probably made this move a wise one in light of the need to protect Kansas City. Of course, the several Confederate recruiting commands already working or arriving in the area were more than content to allow the Kansas force to retire unmolested while they went about their business.[72]

The Battle of Lone Jack

The Union reports of hundreds of Confederates swarming across west-central Missouri, and more riding hard through southwest Missouri to join them, were

The Kansas expedition sent out several large patrols which found no guerrillas. (*The Soldier in Our Civil War*, 1890, vol. 1, p. 191; courtesy Bob and Mary Younger and Andy Turner)

correct. Colonel Joseph O. Shelby, formerly a hemp manufacturer from Waverly in northeast Lafayette County, returned to his home area with a staff of recruiters about August 14 and recruited nearly 1,000 new Confederates in four days. He had been a guerrilla chieftain earlier in the war in this same neighborhood, but he had served in the Battle of Elkhorn Tavern during early March, 1862, and he was definitely a regular soldier now.[73]

At the same time colonels Jeremiah Vardaman Cockrell (a minister from Warrensburg and brother to the more famous Francis Marion Cockrell, a general in the Rebel army), John Trousdale Coffee (a former lawyer of Dade County in southwest Missouri and a Mexican War veteran), DeWitt Clinton Hunter (an Illinois-born attorney of Vernon County, also in southwest Missouri), John Charles Tracy (a Kentucky-born farmer of near Columbus in south Lafayette County), and Sidney Drake Jackman (a Kentucky-born man with ties in both Howard County in northeast Missouri and Bates County in southwest Missouri), had arrived in west-central Missouri with their recruiting commands, joining those who had fought at Independence on August 11. Immediately, hundreds of southern men streamed in from the surrounding counties to sign up for the Confederate army. Numerous southern friends stood watch over their endeavors and provided a sort of ad-hoc security force to warn them if Yankees should ride into the neighborhood. Others watched the progress of Federal troops in the countryside and brought current intelligence to the recruiting commands.

The Union counter strike came early the morning of August 16, not from Kansas, but from a combined force of available units stationed in nearby Missouri garrisons, a total of about 1,000 troops led by Major Emory S. Foster of the 7th Cavalry MSM from Warrensburg. Foster's amalgamation of cavalry units and two pieces of Indiana artillery was greatly outnumbered and should have waited for proper reinforcements. His little force was duly reported by area citizens to the southern commanders as it rode west from Johnson County toward the little hamlet of Lone Jack in the southeast corner of Jackson County. Major Foster, however, strongly believed in the forceful use of the offensive to defeat Rebel irregulars. He had proved this tactic successful in and around Johnson County earlier that year, and doubtless he wished to offset the stain of the recent Independence defeat to Union forces. Foster's own intelligence served him well, and his force rode gamely into the midst of the assembly area of several of the Confederate recruiters and took over the hamlet of Lone Jack the night of August 15, setting up defenses for an expected battle in the morning.

Except for the Independence fight, the southern commanders had avoided contact with Union forces to protect their ill-armed, neophyte troops, yet Foster had ridden his force into the middle of their superior numbers, and they dared not allow the Yankees to remain so close unchallenged. Only Colonel Shelby, off in northeast Lafayette County, was too far removed to join in the strike at Foster's bold force. Also, southern scouts knew better than Major Foster that his backup was too far away to do him any good.

Therefore, the combined commands of colonels Coffee, Hunter, and Tracy, along with the Independence battle veterans, all commanded by Colonel "Vard" Cockrell, struck the Yankee force at Lone Jack at daybreak the hot day of August 16, 1862. Quantrill had left much of his band also in this area, with orders to remain inactive while he returned with a few to Independence to see what Yankee supplies still remained there to be taken. In his absence, some part of his band disobeyed his directive and joined in the fight. Although Foster's Yankees were outnumbered about two to one, they slugged Cockrell's Rebels almost to a standstill for several hours, wrecking the town in the process. However, the overwhelming odds eventually won the day for the southern force, and they defeated Foster, killing 43, wounding 154, including Foster, and capturing 75 Yankees and the two cannons. Over 500 Federals were still able to ride away, leaving the wounded and dead behind to the clemency of the enemy. Part of the reason the Federals had fought so hard was that they understood some of Quantrill's men were part of the attacking force, and feared they would be murdered if captured. Indeed, that happened to a few. Confederate losses were perhaps as many as 80 killed and many, many wounded, and the countryside around Lone Jack became a vast convalescent center for days thereafter. This slugfest convinced Cockrell and his leaders to return to their "avoid contact" policy and to gallop quickly away to the rest of their army with their numerous recruits before the Union military could throw any more Major Fosters at them to wreck their plans.[74]

Lafayette County Actions During Mid–August

As those able-bodied veterans of the Lone Jack fight rode away to the south, the scene of the action in west-central Missouri switched to Lafayette County. Jo Shelby was finishing his four furious days of recruiting in northeast Lafayette County while the Lone Jack battle raged, but by about August 17, he, too, had a force of about 1000 heading south. As these new Rebels passed through the decidedly pro–Union German-American community in Freedom Township in southeast Lafayette County, they helped themselves to horses, burned some homes, and evidently took into captivity some free blacks living near the Germans.[75]

At ten in the morning of August 18, Colonel Daniel Huston Jr.'s garrison at Lexington, fearing Confederate attack after Lone Jack, panicked upon some provocation and fired cannons at imaginary foes. Unfortunately, the fires these projectiles ignited were real enough, and a rope factory, two mills, a hemp warehouse, and other buildings were destroyed.[76]

Six or eight bushwhackers, on August 21 in central Lafayette County, murdered an aged War of 1812 veteran, Elias Barker, even after the man had given up his horses and arms to them, according to a Lexington newspaper account. The culprits were probably from the band of southerners exiled from Kansas and led by Bill Reed of Morris County, Kansas, known to be based in Lafayette County at this time.[77]

Tardy Union Counterstrike in Jackson County

Of course, the Yankee garrison up the Missouri River at Ft. Leavenworth had to make the expected show of force in Jackson County after Lone Jack battle. Lt. Colonel John T. Burris brought his task force back to the Jackson County area between August 21 and 26. His troops wrecked the newspaper office of the *Border Star* at battle-scarred Independence and burned homes of known guerrillas in the area, August 21 and 22.[78]

Lt. Colonel Burris then marched his force of about 350 south toward Cass County on August 22, encountering Rebel pickets and capturing one. Acting on a tip from a black man, the Yankee troops—consisting mostly of parts of 6th Kansas Cavalry, 8th Kansas Infantry, 3rd Wisconsin Cavalry, 1st U.S. Infantry and a light artillery battery—deployed toward the Cowherd or Cowert farm on the Blue River early the morning of August 23, hoping to find Quantrill's guerrillas there. For once the information was accurate, and Quantrill's men deployed in battle line about 1,000 yards from the Federal force, gamely looking to exert themselves as a newly-commissioned Confederate command. Burris cooled their ardor somewhat by having his artillery lob some shells at their line, and Quantrill wisely had his men ride south toward Pleasant Hill without offering a fight. The Union task force chased Quantrill's men around Cass County and west Johnson County for two days, accomplishing little, then rode back to Ft. Leavenworth through Independence and Kansas City, having made a show of force in a decidedly southern region.[79]

Remnants of Southern Recruiters Move Through

Burris' showy expedition was the last major Yankee effort in northwest Missouri for the waning days of August and the end of summer, but some late southern recruiting commands continued to ride south through the region. One unidentified group of about 50 quietly camped not far from Warrensburg the night of August 22, but left the next morning, giving the town a wide berth on their way south without attracting the attention of the normally alert garrison. Since all other known area recruiting commands had already left, this bunch may have come from north of the Missouri River.[80]

Captain Henry Woodsmall's Platte County recruit company camped in the secure company of Quantrill's band for a time in Jackson County in late August before riding on south. Based on the memoirs of Quantrill's men, Woodsmall's new Confederates got a taste of the harshness of Missouri guerrilla war during their stay in the brushy hideout. It seems that William Quantrill came by a copy of one of the St. Louis newspapers, from which he learned about the July 28 execution at Ft. Leavenworth of his band member Perry Hoy, captured back on March 22 at the time of the "Tate House Fight." Woodsmall had in his care two Yankee prisoners, perhaps taken in recent operations, and Quantrill held one more. In his memoir, Quantrill subordinate Bill Gregg wrote that the bushwhackers' prisoner, 1st Lieutenant Levi S. Copeland of the 2nd Battalion Cavalry MSM, was still being held and had not been paroled like the other Lone Jack captives because he was accused of killing elderly southern men, including two by the name of Longacre in west Johnson County. At any rate, Quantrill flew into a rage upon learning of the execution of his gang member, made Woodsmall give up his prisoners, and had all three shot immediately. Captain Woodsmall's command continued their trek to the south, but they probably contemplated the inhumanity of war as they rode.[81]

With the last of the southern recruiting commands riding toward Arkansas, northwest Missouri was left in the hands of the remaining guerrilla bands and the battered Union troops. Several weeks of favorable fighting weather remained ahead, and these partisans were determined to make the most of it to shake the Yankee grip on this part of Missouri. Rebel recruiting would not again approach the scale and intensity of the summer of 1862, although in two years several recruiters would try again. The newly-created Union Enrolled Missouri Militia (EMM) had undergone a frightful baptism of fire, just as had the Missouri State Militia (MSM) back in the spring. All remaining Missourians, particularly the guerrillas, watched to see how the EMM would conduct themselves as autumn approached.

Seventeen

Fall 1862 in Southeast Missouri

After August the remaining months of 1862 brought few new developments in Missouri's guerrilla war, now almost a year old. The forces on both sides that had been enrolled or recruited weeks and months before still had several weeks of good fighting weather before the grass and grain that fed the horses would be hard to find and the leaves that hid one side from the other would fall away. Many southern bushwhackers and recruits still had business at hand before they would infiltrate south through Yankee lines to the southern army and warmer climates. Although not among the most active regions of the state, guerrilla warfare in southeast Missouri abated slowly in the fall of 1862. Most of the threat to the Union grip on this region came from Rebel forces in Arkansas.

Actions in the Hill Country

The hilly regions of southeast Missouri were the scene of some actions this fall, but to a lesser extent than the fighting of summer. It seems that most of the southern recruiters had already left the region with their newly-acquired men.

Elements of 5th Cavalry MSM skirmished with guerrillas on September 11 in Iron County, but few other details remain of the encounter.[1] A mixed force of MSM and Washington County EMM attacked an unidentified guerrilla camp on the Black River in Iron County two days later, scattering the rebels after killing five and wounding seven and taking 35 horses, at the cost of two Yankees wounded. The blue-clad cavalry actually charged into the middle of the camp and rescued three men of Union sympathy held by the Confederates.[2]

Bushwhacker Sam Hildebrand claimed in his postwar memoirs to have conducted his fifth guerrilla expedition in southeast Missouri in late September, 1862. In Madison, St. Francois, and Wayne counties, with three companions, Hildebrand wrote that he assassinated two civilian informers, skirmished twice with Federals, and robbed a store in St. Francois County.[3] One contemporary account that tends to corroborate his story occurred the night of September 26 when a Union army report said unidentified guerrillas fired on their pickets, killing one Yankee and wounding two others near Greenville, Wayne County.[4]

In late September the southern recruiter known only as "Captain Crabtree"—but who called himself "General" Crabtree—was back in Cole County, just a few miles south of the state capitol. As was his custom, Crabtree forcibly took supplies from rural families of northern sympathy as he began to recruit another company of Confederates to take south to Arkansas. One particular farmer, who happened to also be a member of the local Yankee EMM unit, was particularly irked when Crabtree seized his wedding suit. Crabtree had now made one enemy too many, for the irate militiaman, with some of his comrades, tracked Crabtree and his small band to a barn, where they shot into the startled Confederates, mortally wounding the captain. The northerners were not content they were finally rid of Crabtree until they uncovered his dead body in a Cole County cave days later. To the disgust of that particular farmer, Crabtree's corpse was dressed in the stolen wedding suit. This may be seen as one example that the controversial Enrolled Missouri Militia, begun only weeks before, could actually function in local situations provided they were "suitably" motivated. Ironically, area Union officials either refused to believe Crabtree was dead or were never given the report, for they attributed guerrilla actions of Crabtree's former subordinates as his for the next two years in this region. This is a notable example of how poor was Yankee intelligence in Missouri.[5]

Some violence occurred in the hills in the northern part of this quarter of the state during this autumn. Accounts vary from early August to middle September as to the date, but in that period, secret Rebel mail carrier and former riverboat pilot Absolom Grimes of Ralls County was arrested in St. Louis with a quantity of such forbidden mail in his possession. Grimes made repeated trips carrying hidden mail between Missouri Confederates in Mississippi, Tennessee, and Arkansas, and their families back at home in Missouri. Union authorities even allowed newspapers to publish one or two of the seized letters, perhaps to discourage the practice and alert the loyal public to be on the lookout for more secret mail carriers. Grimes was fortunate to escape from custody on October 4, because it appears Union authorities were contemplating a severe punishment to discourage others in the network that Grimes had helped establish.[6] An unusual wartime incident occurred November 19 at Hermann, in northern Gasconade County, just south of the Missouri River. Southern "slave-catchers" from Montgomery County had tracked their particular quarry across the river to this quiet German-American town, but the justice-of-the-peace denied the pursuers a warrant and refused to help them reclaim their runaway property, whom the townspeople had evidently sheltered.[7] During the night of November 25 Charles Barnes and his band of five guerrillas seemed to go on a hunt for Union EMM members along Huzza Creek in southeast Crawford County. They shot down an EMM first sergeant at his home and nearby besieged an Enrolled Missouri Militia captain and his family at their house until the local EMM unit mobilized and rode to their captain's rescue. Barnes and company rode away to Iron County, where the Yankees caught up to them the next day, killing two and wounding one. Crawford County seems far afield for Charles Barnes, who throughout the war operated from Shannon County south to the Arkansas border.[8]

Colonel Clark in the Bootheel

A bold guerrilla campaign by Colonel Henry E. Clark in the bootheel stunned the Union command in southeast Missouri and signaled that fall would not be tranquil in that lowland region. The 1860 census seems to reveal that Ohio-born Henry E. Clark was a businessman in his mid-thirties with a young family in New Madrid County. Only the fact that he was active in the southern Missouri State Guard during the early part of the war would give any warning that, beginning in fall of 1862, Clark's Confederate recruiting would plague the Federals in this region for much of the rest of the war.

On September 11, Rebels of Clark's recruiting command, 20 in number, passed themselves off as local EMM in order to shoot down the gun crew of a Yankee 24-pound brass howitzer and steal the cannon from the startled garrison at Bloomfield, Stoddard County. The flabbergasted Federal commander, Captain Henry Hyde of 1st Wisconsin Cavalry, overestimated Clark's strength and led the remainder of the garrison of 250 in a panicky retreat to the Union post at Greenville to the west. Now it was Colonel Clark's turn to be astonished at his good fortune as he rode unopposed into Bloomfield and acquired a second cannon, 800 rifle muskets, and enough supplies and materiel to nicely equip his growing regiment of rag-tag Rebel recruits from what the Yankees had abandoned. The Union loss in manpower in this fiasco was three killed and five wounded, but a quick counterstroke by the Greenville garrison quickly put Clark, with his new found plunder, to flight. Nevertheless, the area Union command was very perturbed that one of their garrisons had armed and equipped a Confederate regiment.[9] Elements of the more intimidating 24th Missouri Infantry manned Bloomfield hereafter, and reported a skirmish with unidentified Rebels—probably Clark again, or Sam Hildebrand—on September 20, but gave no details.[10]

The cool weather of October did nothing to slow down the pace of action as Clark's neophyte Confederate force continued operations in the bootheel. About October 6 a local EMM company broke up a Rebel camp near Little River in east Stoddard County, killing two guerrillas or recruits and capturing all the camp equipment and bedding.[11] In Pemiscot County near the Arkansas line on October 16, Rebels with cannons—probably the Bloomfield ordnance captured September 11—fired on passing steamers *John H. Dickey* and *Continental* in the Mississippi River. Afterwards, Federal forces punished southern civilians living nearby, allegedly for harboring the guerrillas, and even banished 20 families from the Memphis, Tennessee, area to discourage future attacks on their vital river traffic. Looking at Yankee reactions to Rebel threats overall in Missouri this year, the Federals seemed most protective of their water and rail transport, and this is a good case in point.[12]

On October 19 Colonel Henry Clark, with an estimated 500 men, raided the river town of Commerce in Scott County. The Confederates captured 20 of the local militia, confiscated 20 to 30 militia horses, and took goods from two merchants. Crewmen on a passing steamer, the *Platte Valley*, knew something was amiss when they noticed the U.S. flag flying upside down over the village, but the Rebels left before pursuit could be organized.[13]

The frustrated Federals finally caught up to the wily Colonel Clark and 100 of his adherents at Clarkston in north Dunklin County on October 26. About 400

Illinois cavalry, infantry, and artillerymen traveled across the Mississippi River from Columbus, Kentucky, shelled Clarkston, then swept through town capturing Colonel Clark and 38 others, as well as 67 horses and mules and 100 rifle-muskets. The Rebel death toll was 30. The Yankees were probably only disappointed that they did not recover the two purloined cannons taken the month before at Bloomfield.[14] It would appear that Clark had remained in the area as an obvious target too long. Perhaps early successes caused him to underestimate the striking power of the large numbers of Federal troops stationed in this region to guard vital shipping on the Mississippi River. H. E. Clark would be exchanged months later and return to southeast Missouri to carry on his war again.

The following day, elements of an unidentified Union militia had three men wounded in a skirmish at Grand Prairie in southwest Dunklin County, probably against some of Clark's men. The Missouri militiamen were probably operating in tandem with the expedition from Columbus, Kentucky.[15] Union army records show the expeditionary force from Columbus fought another skirmish in or near Clarkston on October 28, but few details remain.[16]

Colonel Jeffers Takes Command

Clark's capture did not bring peace to the bootheel region, as his able co-recruiter, Colonel William L. Jeffers, took command of the remainder of Clark's force. Jeffers had already shown himself to be an able opponent to the Union hold on this corner of Missouri during fighting in May and August, and he had been a valued troop leader under Colonel Clark in his September and October actions. About November 6, elements of 12th Cavalry MSM were sent to garrison Jackson in Cape Girardeau County and thereafter began to capture several of Jeffers' recruits throughout the countryside.[17] Also, Federal army reports identified Jeffers as the new Confederate commander of the remnants of Clark's old command at the Chalk Bluffs on the Arkansas side of the St. Francois River at the Dunklin County line.[18] Perhaps they recalled that an earlier Federal expedition had fought Jeffers at the Chalk Bluffs back in May. The Union commander at Cape Girardeau noted that Rebel agents were still obtaining salt and hogs in the bootheel in late November, and even heard that the old nemesis, Colonel M. Jeff Thompson, the "Swamp Fox," had given a speech November 29 at the village of Four Mile in north Dunklin County. Colonel Thompson had just recently returned to his old battleground from serving the Confederacy in other parts of the South.[19] Obviously, partisan warfare was far from over in the bootheel.

Colonel White in the Northern Ozarks

By far, the most guerrilla warfare of southeast Missouri this autumn occurred in south-central Missouri along the Eleven Point, Current, and Black Rivers. These river valleys, running southeast to northwest, were natural infiltration corridors for Rebel guerrillas and recruiters to follow from northeast Arkansas into Missouri.

Between August 30 and September 6, 1862, Major Lothar Lippert led a combined force, mostly of his own 13th Illinois Cavalry, but also including the 24th Missouri Infantry riding in wagons, from their Greenville, Wayne County, base into Ripley County and Arkansas and back again to counter Colonel James D. White and an estimated one thousand Rebels in this region. White was a Georgia-born farmer from near Fredericktown in Madison County, Missouri, and seems to have restricted his role in guerrilla warfare merely to that of behind-the-enemy-lines recruiter. Major Lippert's Yankees skirmished near Ponder's Mill, southwest Ripley County, August 31, with White's pickets, and later found his main camp a few miles inside Arkansas, where they killed and captured many before returning to Greenville.[20]

Several Guerrilla Commands in the Northern Ozarks

About this same time Confederate Colonel William O. Coleman, based at Batesville, Arkansas, sent bands of his irregulars under Captain Joseph A. Spilman—probably a pre-war resident of Texas County—and a Captain Curry into Missouri as far north as Pulaski County. There, near Waynesville, Lieutenant Francis Reichert's patrol of 13th Cavalry MSM on September 8 found and routed Curry's camp, killing two and capturing one. The patrol tracked one escapee about ten miles and, after catching him, forced the bushwhacker to list about 40 area Rebels. The following day, the patrol skirmished with other guerrillas and brought back word that most of Curry's and Spilman's Confederates were in Texas County to the south.[21]

By mid–September Colonel James D. White, supposedly leading about 2,000 Rebels, was reported to be based at or near Birch Tree in southwest Shannon County. A Union patrol from Rolla skirmished in the area with White's pickets, killing two and wounding several.[22]

A few days later the Reverend Tim Reeves's guerrilla command in Ripley County ordered a local doctor and his family to leave the area in retribution for guiding Federal troops through the area earlier.[23] Reeves's band may have been part of Coleman's or White's commands.

At this same time elements of 13th Illinois Cavalry, based at Patterson, drove Colonel David C. Boone's Rebel recruiting command from Reynolds County. The first step of this process took place September 17 when the Yankee cavalry chased about 75 of Boone's men away from their breakfast at Barnesville killing two and wounding some. The same Federals returned September 22, capturing more of these men and torching Barnesville in retaliation for the hospitality shown the Confederates. This was too much for Boone, supposedly from nearby Oregon County, who took the remainder of his command south to Carter County.[24]

Colonel Porter's Command Passes Through

The south-central Missouri counties were quiet for a few days until mid–October, when 250 to 300 of Colonel Joseph C. Porter's Rebels from northeast Missouri crossed the Missouri River and passed through the region heading south for the Confederate army in Arkansas. Colonel Albert Sigel prepared a trap for these travelers with his own 13th Cavalry MSM and elements of 5th Cavalry MSM near California House Inn in Pulaski County. The Federal troops closed the trap October 18, killing 20, wounding about the same number, and capturing three while releasing two men held as prisoners by Porter's men, all at the cost of only one trooper wounded.[25]

Colonel Boone Hard Pressed in Carter County

Area Union authorities finally discovered the presence of Colonel David C. Boone's Rebel command in Carter County about a month after they retreated there from Reynolds County. They sent Lieutenant Colonel Bazel F. Lazear, with a force of 12th Cavalry MSM from their Patterson, Wayne County, garrison to drive the Rebels out. The thickly-forested hills of this region must have favored the attacker to the detriment of the defender, for Lt. Colonel Lazear's troopers surprised Boone's estimated 450 Confederates the evening of October 22, driving them through town and beyond. The Federals kept up the pressure on these Rebels until October 25 near Pike Creek, west Carter County. On that date the troopers found Boone's latest encampment and attacked it from a nearby hill, killing eight and capturing 18. Lazear sent to St. Louis military prisons a total of 40 southern prisoners from this expedition, for a total Union loss of one trooper killed.[26]

Colonel Burbridge Pushed Out of Ripley County

This 12th Cavalry MSM force had little time to celebrate their victory, as they had to ride hard to the south to join another Union expedition in Ripley County against Colonel John Q. Burbridge and over 1,000 Rebel recruits near Pittman's Ferry on the Current River. Ironically, John (Jack) Burbridge, like the Union officer Bazel Lazear mentioned above, was from Pike County in far-away northeastern Missouri, but he was dutifully serving the Confederacy where he was sent. That was his reputation. Colonel M. Jeff Thompson, Missouri's Swamp Fox, once called Jack Burbridge "a thorough soldier" and "always ready for a fight." His brothers William (Bill) and Clinton (Clint) also led southern irregulars in Missouri during the war. Although Jack Burbridge was in Ripley County now, leading irregulars as he had earlier under Jeff Thompson, he also had a hard-won reputation as a regular officer, serving with distinction at Wilson's Creek in August, 1861, where he had suffered a head wound, and at Elkhorn Tavern or Pea Ridge in March of 1862.

Facing Burbridge's southerners in Ripley County was Colonel William Dewey of the 32nd Iowa Infantry, leading his own regiment and companies of the 24th and 25th Missouri Infantry, 1st Cavalry MSM, and other troops, mostly from the Patterson, Wayne County, garrison. The infantrymen were hardly suited to chasing mounted Confederate recruiters and their men through the heavily-wooded and hilly wilderness of Ripley County, but they were close by and much of the Federal cavalry in southeast Missouri was busy dealing with other Rebels. The record does not state, but perhaps the foot soldiers were temporarily mounted or rode in wagons. Dewey's polyglot force did rather well, though, for on October 26, 17 miles north of Pittman's Ferry, they found and chased Colonel Burbridge's early-warning pickets. The next day the Yankees captured a Rebel captain and 13 other pickets seven miles closer to Pittman's Ferry, while Burbridge wisely had his main body retire south of the Current River without offering battle. Colonel Dewey, reinforced with Lazear's force from the Carter County campaign, gamely pursued the southern men several miles into Arkansas, but on October 30 turned back to return to their Missouri bases without having faced the Rebel force in a decisive battle.[27]

The Return of Colonel Boone

Colonel Boone, like Colonel Burbridge, learned to withdraw in the face of an overwhelming Union force and to return quietly after the Yankees futilely searched the woods for a few days and gave up. This particularly made sense for Confederate recruiters leading poorly-armed, poorly-trained neophytes. Indeed, in spite of Lt. Colonel Lazear's flashy efforts in October, some sources showed that Boone's guerrillas had returned to Carter County, camping beside the Current River, by about November 19. This kind of resiliency in regions of strong southern sympathy brought guerrilla units back to these parts of southeast Missouri time after time throughout the war.[28]

December Violence in the St. Francis Hills

The vengeful bushwhacker, Sam Hildebrand, ventured into his home region of the St. Francis Hills repeatedly during the winter of 1862–1863. He killed a Yankee picket or guard in Madison County in early December but retreated south to Stoddard County when a large Federal reaction force came after him. Later, Hildebrand killed a Union informant near Bloomfield, then spent about three weeks with Colonel William L. Jeffers' Rebel recruiting force nearby.[29] In mid–December Federal cavalry arrested 21 southern men in and around Cape Girardeau, Bollinger, and Madison counties including some who might have helped or ridden with Hildebrand in the past.[30]

St. Louis in December 1862

Meanwhile, in the St. Louis area to the north, some phases of guerrilla warfare continued despite the onset of winter. Individual prisoners escaped from the hated Gratiot Street Prison on December 11, 13, and 18.[31] Also on the latter date in nearby St. Louis County, Union authorities offset their embarrassment about recent prison escapes by capturing Rebel Captain Watkins O. Johnson, who had recruited southerners near his home in Audrain County the previous year. Johnson's command had taken part in the Lexington campaign in September, 1861, and fighting in Boone County in December of 1861. Then he had taken his men to the Rebel army through Union lines in March. Evidently, Captain Johnson had returned to

Shooting a Yankee picket. (*Harper's Weekly*, October 5, 1861; courtesy Bob and Mary Younger and Andy Turner)

Missouri to recruit when he was caught.[32] How was he captured? The record does not say, but the Union military in St. Louis had a two-tier system to apprehend disguised Confederates passing through the city. If Rebels managed to pass through a series of careful sentries—who questioned all newcomers and required anyone exiting the city to have a valid pass—they still faced a secret threat. By this time in the war, the Federal military ferreted out the disloyal and the seemingly disloyal with a small army of detectives, informants, and spies. These agents haunted the hotels, taverns, streetcars, boat landings, train station, and the like, not only to eavesdrop on conversations, but also to lure potential Confederates into conversation and trap the unwary. St. Louis had become a city of the suspicious, and a wayfaring Confederate, even in disguise as a peaceable citizen, was hardly equipped to handle it. It seems that the hardest-working of this secret army were men from the rural regions forced to flee to the big city by local southerners who despised their northern sympathies. These men watched the passing crowds carefully to pick out southerners from home and exact a delectable revenge.

President Lincoln, directing his generals in the overall conduct of the war, time and again had to turn away from pressing concerns to extricate senior commanders in Missouri from delicate dilemmas of their own making. One of the more memorable examples of this happened on December 19, when Missouri's Union chief, Major General Samuel R. Curtis, hero of the battle of Pea Ridge, ordered

Union soldiers check passes. (*The Soldier in Our Civil War*, 1890, vol. 1, p. 110; courtesy Terry Harmon)

St. Louis Presbyterian minister Samuel B. McPheeters and his wife banished from Missouri for "active sympathy with the rebellion" and for refusing to pray for U.S. President Abraham Lincoln in church. Lincoln himself put a hold on the order, personally reviewed the McPheeters' file, and overruled the banishment. The president then informed General Curtis that the U.S. military had no business running churches.[33] This was another example in Missouri where the Union military struggled with its role in an internal rebellion not covered by its formal military education. It was also a portent of the future, as the Union military in the coming year would use banishment as a tool to remove from Missouri hundreds of "notorious" southerners, who would discover their constitutional rights had been suspended in order to put down the rebellion.

Union Embarrassment Again in the Bootheel

Union forces from the New Madrid garrison sent out a patrol of 40 foot soldiers of the 32nd Iowa Infantry, December 17 through 21, in an attempt to discover the lair of Rebel Colonel William. L. Jeffers' recruiting command. The Iowans obediently scoured the countryside in New Madrid and Dunklin counties, but the elusive Confederates stayed out of reach, and the patrol found few to shoot at and captured only eight southern men.[34]

Colonel John Scott and his 32nd Iowa Infantry at New Madrid were more embarrassed December 28 when Colonel Scott somehow believed that Rebels were poised to overwhelm the garrison. Colonel Scott led his regiment away to "safety" after destroying some of the fort's artillery and barracks, only to discover he was responding to a false alarm. This regiment would serve well and faithfully in the western theater throughout the rest of the war, but this is one episode they would wish to forget. They had become casualties in the "war of nerves."[35]

More Union Frustration Along the Current River

Yankee forces had been trying all autumn with occasional success to expel persistent Rebel recruiting forces from the northern Ozarks region drained by the Big Piney, Current, and Eleven Point Rivers. They captured Captain Joseph A. Spilman of Colonel William O. Coleman's command in Texas County, December 19.[36] Between December 20 and 24, patrols from the Rolla garrison attempted without success to fight a decisive battle with bushwhackers in the Phelps County area. They killed only two but did manage to capture a shipment of Rebel mail from soldiers in Arkansas to their Missouri families. Union authorities relished finding such mail and turned it over to their local officials in various provost marshal offices to help them ferret out the disloyal and identify particularly "notorious" southerners. Sadly, such letters from separated loved ones became the reason many were cast into prison in Missouri, and became, in effect, "poison pen letters."[37]

Meanwhile, Brigadier General John Wynn Davidson assembled a sizable Union expedition—the Army of Southeast Missouri—to defeat the stubborn, continuous recruiting of Rebel commanders like colonels M. Jeff Thompson, John Burbridge, Colton Greene, William O. Coleman, and others. Davidson was a native Virginian who had early in the war spurned entreaties to join the Confederate high command, which was impressed with his Mexican War and Indian fighting experience. He turned this experience to accolades leading troops in Virginia during the Peninsula Campaign in the summer of 1862, and the Union high command had hopes that his Army of Southeast Missouri could cleanse the northern Ozarks of the pesky Confederate irregulars in the winter of 1862–1863. Unfortunately for northern goals, Davidson's three-month expedition through the Ozarks mud, poor roads, and swollen rivers added a new lesson in futility, as the Confederates, for the most part, ignored the Yankees' misery and failed to oblige them by coming out to fight or even getting close. Davidson's reputation as a great commander became as deflated as the morale of the suffering soldiers who were forced to endure the hardships of winter campaigning in such an inhospitable region. In hindsight, this miserable expedition did serve as a training ground for several thousand heretofore undisciplined western Federal soldiers and prepared them well for the coming two-and-one-half years of campaigning.

Guerrilla warfare did not entirely ignore Davidson's grand failure during the waning days of 1862. On Christmas eve near Van Buren, Carter County, Colonel Colton Green's Confederate irregulars captured a forage train belonging to 11th Wisconsin Infantry, 24th Missouri Infantry, and 33rd Illinois Infantry picking corn in a field. The Rebels got the corn, eight wagons, and 48 U.S. Army mules, plus the weapons, uniforms and accouterments of their captives-valuable indeed to new southern soldiers so far from their own source of supply. Green's men gleefully paroled and released the Yankees to make their way back to their units dressed only in underwear.[38] Perhaps as a result of this affair General Davidson's Federals burned just about every single building in Carter County, perhaps on the assumption that only southerners lived there.[39]

As irregular warfare showed no sign of abating in southeast Missouri, the bat-

The Union army of Southeast Missouri struggled along muddy roads in the northern Ozarks for weeks with nothing to show for its efforts. (Charles C. Coffin, *The Boys of '61*, 1881; courtesy Terry Harmon)

tered year of 1862 drew to a close. The Union hold on the region was as tenuous as it had been when southern recruiters and guerrillas surged into the region in spring, and, in spite of the onset of winter weather, many of them were still around. Northern sympathizers were only safe in larger towns garrisoned by Yankee troops, and those troops were only safe out in the countryside in large enough numbers to dissuade attack by bushwhackers. The brother-against-brother and neighbor-against-neighbor warfare and the resulting house-burning and military confiscation of crops, farm animals, draft animals, wagons, and other private property, had by the close of 1862 resulted in the depopulation of large rural parts of this part of the state. The advent of 1863 did not seem to bring much hope to southeast Missouri.

Eighteen

Fall 1862 in Southwest Missouri

Fall of 1862 still offered good weather for guerrilla warfare in southwest Missouri, and the almost daily tempo of skirmishes slowed only with the advent of cool weather and the withering of good forage for horses. Also, Rebel recruiters returning to the Confederate army in Arkansas, with or without droves of new soldiers, chose southwest Missouri as the "path of least resistance." They rode wide of the well-guarded railroad that terminated at Rolla and appreciated the region's vast prairies for hard riding to outdistance the Federals' generally inferior horses. For the same reasons, many of the bushwhackers also rode through southwest Missouri on their way to winter in warmer climates.

Early September Fighting on the Prairie

The first skirmishes of September 1862 in this part of the state featured Colonel William A. Phillips's 3rd Kansas Indian Home Guard fighting guerrillas near Neosho, Newton County, on September 1, 3, and 5, and along the Spring River, probably in west Jasper County on September 1. These Kansas Indians were mistrusted by most natives of the region for their occasional excesses, and local bushwhackers seemed to enjoy targeting them. No other details of these engagements are known to survive.[1]

For several hours early Sunday morning, September 7, a large expedition of 8th Cavalry MSM and local EMM sweeping along Horse Creek in east Barton County discovered several small bands of partisans and killed 11 altogether as each group took flight when approached. Guerrillas were known to frequent the woods along Horse Creek throughout the war.[2]

A New Rebel Push in the Area: The Newtonia Campaign

By September Major General Thomas C. Hindman, Confederate commander of Arkansas, Missouri, and the Indian Territory, had initialized actions to challenge

Union control over southwest Missouri. As part of this push, Rebel Indian irregulars marched to Newton County, Missouri, from the Indian Territory, September 9, evidently as part of Confederate Colonel Douglas Cooper's command. A portion of 6th Kansas Cavalry out of Fort Scott skirmished with them at Newtonia and drove them back across the state line to Indian Territory at no Union loss and unspecified Rebel losses.[3]

This had been only the opening act of a concerted effort, however. Colonel Jo Shelby's newly-recruited and formed Confederate cavalry brigade attacked a combined force of 3rd Cavalry MSM at or near Newtonia on September 13. Union losses are listed as two killed and thirteen missing, while southern losses were not recorded. One notable mention was made to the effect Colonel Upton Hays, that former guerrilla leader of Jackson County, Missouri, was killed leading his regiment.[4]

About this time, near Mount Vernon in neighboring Lawrence County, a Union spy befriended and then killed a Reverend Turner of Gadfly, northwest Barry County, who bragged too openly about killing several men of northern sympathy in the area. The right of free speech sometimes carried a heavy price in war-torn Missouri.[5] Also near Mount Vernon, September 19, men of 14th Cavalry MSM and local EMM attacked Rebel Captain John Long and 70 others, killing five and wounding several for only one Federal wounded during a running fight on the prairie.[6]

At eight o'clock the next morning near Medoc in northwest Jasper County, noted Confederate Indian commander Colonel Stand Watie, leading several hundred cavalry and accompanied by Thomas R. Livingston's local bushwhackers, attacked a Union Indian combined force of Colonel John Ritchie's 2nd and Colonel William A. Phillip's 3rd Kansas Indian Home Guard. This unique battle was mostly southern Indians fighting against northern Indians, but even Livingston's guerrillas called themselves the "Cherokee Spikes" for some reason. Tragically, the surprised Federal Indians quickly butchered some suspected bushwhackers they held in custody when the fight began, then retreated to protect the large number of Indian women and children present in their camp. The Federal officers rallied the Kansas Indians and led them against the Rebel flank, causing the Confederates to withdraw. Estimated losses from this battle are about 20 killed on each side, not counting the several murdered local residents.[7]

Federals attempted to counterstrike against the aggressive southern units General Hindman was pushing into southwest Missouri, but they were seldom sure who and how many they faced. On September 21, elements of the Union 1st Arkansas Cavalry swept into Cassville, Barry County, and drove off about 100 Rebel irregulars, killing 15 and capturing 19 men, 20 horses, and 15 shotguns. The Federals quickly and prudently withdrew from the town when they learned that Confederate Colonel Charles Carroll's entire 1st Arkansas Cavalry Regiment lurked nearby.[8] Three days later elements of Colonel William R. Judson's 6th Kansas Cavalry skirmished with either Rebel cavalry or guerrillas at Granby, Newton County, but no other details of the fight remain.[9] On Saturday, September 26, a patrol of 1st Iowa Cavalry captured three southern irregulars near Turnback and Sodom's Mills in southwest Dade County.[10]

All this activity was actually the prelude for the September 30 Battle of Newtonia, Newton County, between Union Brigadier General Frederick Salomon, with his 6,500 Kansas and Missouri troops, and Confederate Colonel Douglas H. Cooper, leading about 11,000 southern soldiers. In the battle, the outnumbered Federals fell back after hours of hard fighting, leaving the battlefield and the victory to Cooper, but the Rebels later retired from their tenuous hold on this corner of Missouri. Although this action is not part of guerrilla warfare, it did feature the former bushwhackers in John T. Coffee's, Jo O. Shelby's, and Upton Hays' Missouri regiments.[11]

The Confederate win at Newtonia on September 30 allowed large numbers of Rebels, including some Indians, to remain in the region for several days. In Jasper County a large group of guerrillas, including some Indians, hung a man of northern sympathy and robbed others south of Carthage.[12] Union records hint at an October 3 skirmish near Jollification in northwest Barry County, but omit other details.[13] Sketchy accounts of elements of 1st Iowa Cavalry and 6th Kansas Cavalry skirmishing with Rebel Lieutenant Colonel Michael Woods Buster's cavalry at Granby, Newton County, October 4, imply that area Union forces were willing to contest the brief Confederate toehold in southwest Missouri.[14] The next day parts of 2nd Kansas Cavalry and 3rd Kansas Indian Home Guard skirmished at or near Newtonia.[15] Part of the 1st Iowa Cavalry fought there again on October 7.[16]

Guerrillas in the Osage River Basin

During this same period, guerrillas were active in the Osage River region to the north. In late September, unidentified bushwhackers attacked an ambulance detail of 1st Iowa Cavalry moving wounded or sick troopers near Grand River in Henry or Benton County, but the attack was driven off with minor losses on each side.[17] Starting September 29 a mixed Yankee expedition of 2nd Battalion Cavalry Missouri State Milita from Sedalia and 60th EMM scoured west Henry and north Bates counties for two or three days, killing and capturing several bushwhackers and reclaiming captured government property.[18] A history of Bates County relates how some militiamen of 60th EMM seized horses and killed a man in the north-central part of that county about the time of this patrol.[19] At Cole Camp, northeast Benton County, part of 6th Cavalry MSM skirmished with guerrillas on October 5.[20] Another expedition of 2nd Battalion Cavalry Missouri State Milita and 60th EMM searched Henry, south Cass, and north Bates counties between October 16 and 23. This large patrol found mostly abandoned guerrilla camps and chased several bands of bushwhackers, but killed only three.[21] Either the guerrillas had left the area or had become more proficient at avoiding Union patrols.

Mid-October in Barry County on the Arkansas Line

After a few quiet days in early October, fighting returned to the Missouri counties along the Arkansas line at mid-month. On October 14 the 2nd Kansas cavalry with some Kansas artillerymen had one man killed and two missing in skirmishing at Hazel Bottom in northeast Barry County.[22] That same day in the Cassville area a few miles south, troopers of 7th Missouri Cavalry skirmished several times with mounted Rebels.[23] Two days later elements of 3rd Kansas Battery of Light Artillery fought unidentified foes at Schell's Mill in the southeast corner of McDonald County next to the Barry County line.[24] Whether the southern fighters in these engagements were Confederate regulars or bushwhackers cannot be determined from the brief remaining accounts, but this kind of sporadic warfare was to continue in this corner of Missouri throughout the following year.

Northeast Missouri Rebels Move Through

Starting in late October of 1862, Federal forces in southwest Missouri were alerted to large numbers of guerrillas and Rebel recruits from northeast Missouri who were moving through the region on their way to join the Confederate army to the south. On October 20 Lt. Colonel James Stuart, leading parts of 10th Illinois Cavalry near their station at Marshfield, Webster County, found one such group of migrating southerners. They located and attacked Colonel Caleb Dorsey and his estimated night camp of 300 Rebels, scattering them into the night. The Illinois cavalrymen suffered losses of one killed and one wounded, but they released about 12 Federal soldiers held captive by Dorsey's men. Southern losses were four killed and 27 captured, one of whom was Captain William H. Todd. Prisoner Todd had spent much of the summer recruiting southern men in Howard and Boone counties, and postwar became an attorney in Boone and Saline counties.[25]

Black Troops Strike a Blow

Other southern bands moving south through Bates County provided a tense four-day baptism of fire for one of the first Union black units of the Civil War. On October 26, Captain Henry C. Seaman led 140 men of the newly-formed 1st Kansas Colored Infantry from their Kansas post to south Bates County to investigate reports of guerrilla depredations there. It was not in their plans to intercept the southbound Rebel recruiting command of Colonel Vard Cockrell of Johnson County, who happened along and joined forces with local guerrillas led by Bill Truman and John Handcock, of Osage County. Facing hundreds of southerners, Captain Seaman wisely placed his untested Yankees into a defensive perimeter around a ramshackle farmstead and held off their assaults, including a prairie fire, for three days. When the initial attacks failed against the black troops, Colonel Cockrell wisely withdrew his large, poorly-armed and untrained recruiting command and continued their interrupted journey south before veteran Yankee cavalry could came onto the scene. When the Federals perceived they now faced a Rebel force of the same size as their own, they sent 20 or 30 of the infantrymen to seize a nearby hillock where guerrilla marksmen had held a deadly advantage. This excursion brought on the climax of the siege, when 130 mounted bushwhackers cut off the foot soldiers one-half mile from the main body of northerners. The surrounded black soldiers fought for their very lives, even hand-to-hand, until the main body could rescue them from the deadly bushwhackers. The guerrilla siege broke up after this melee, and the embattled black soldiers returned to their garrison on the Kansas side of the state line. Total Union losses from the four-day fight were eight killed, including a captain, and eleven wounded, but southern losses were estimated to be higher. No Rebel accounts of this action survive, but one has to imagine that these southerners came away with a new respect for the fighting ability of black Yankee troops.[26]

Barton and Jasper Counties in Early November

Both local and traveling Rebels made the Barton and Jasper County area hot during the first few days of November, 1862. William Quantrill and his notorious guerrilla band of about 300—including some from other gangs—rode south a few days late to take part in the fight with the 1st Kansas Colored Infantry in south Bates County, but they brought their distinctive brand of warfare to Lamar, Barton County, on November 5. Near town they met the smaller recruiting command of Colonel Warner Lewis, a former businessman of Cass County, and Quantrill and Lewis planned a concerted assault on the small Union garrison there. Quantrill and his men attacked, beginning at ten at night and for about two hours, without dislodging Captain Martin Breeden's detachment of 8th Cavalry MSM from the brick courthouse. The west-central Missouri bushwhackers lost five or six of their number killed and several wounded, compared to three Federals killed and three mortally wounded, but were furious that Colonel Lewis and his recruits failed to show. They burned about one third of the town to vent their frustration and continued south.[27] A combat patrol of 80 troopers of 3rd Wisconsin cavalry from Fort Scott intercepted Quantrill's band a few miles south and evidently killed one guerrilla.[28]

Tom Livingston's local guerrilla band was also active at this time. Another detachment of 3rd Wisconsin Cavalry rode from Fort Scott on November 7 to southwest Vernon County to stop Livingston's bushwhackers, who were attacking families of northern sympathy there. The cavalry overtook the Rebels near Cow Creek, just over the state line in Kansas, but wounded only one guerrilla in a running fight, although they rescued some captives.[29] A day or so later another detachment of 3rd Wisconsin Cavalry killed four or five of Livingston's men and apprehended four on Spring River near Sherwood in west Jasper County.[30] Sometime this season, part of Livingston's band, led by his brother-in-law, William Parkinson, robbed some war refugees near Preston, north-central Jasper County. These people were attempting to leave the area, their wagons piled high with belongings, but Parkinson took everything, including their wagons and oxen, leaving the poor folks one quilt apiece. Near Nashville, southwest Barton County, Parkinson's gang abducted a man who was never seen again.[31] Also this season, unidentified guerrillas ambushed local Enrolled Missouri Militia near Bowers Mills, east-central Jasper County, killing two, including a lieutenant, and evaded the pursuit.[32]

Incredibly, unidentified bushwhackers attacked Captain Martin Breeden's detachment of 8th Cavalry MSM in the ruins of Lamar again the night of November 10 and fired even more of the remaining buildings. Breeden claimed his antagonists were Quantrill's raiders again, returned to quench their earlier frustration.

Missouri war refugees. (*The Soldier in Our Civil War*, 1890, vol. 1, p. 250; courtesy Terry Harmon)

However, Captain Breeden's claim is not consistent with the postwar memoirs of Quantrill's men or other records of Quantrill's activities. The attackers were probably Livingston's band, known to be in the area at the time.[33]

Colonel Burbridge's Rebels Raid Northern Ozarks

Just a few days after these actions, and miles away to the southeast, Colonel John Q. (Jack) Burbridge led about 375 Rebels, including Colonel Colton Greene's cavalry and a section of artillery, north of the White River into the region drained by the James, Niangua, and Gasconade Rivers. Area Federals heard guerrillas of Burbridge's command were robbing families of northern sympathy in central Ozark County on November 6. Captain Hiram E. Barstow led a mixed force from Marshfield, Webster County, of his own 10th Illinois Cavalry and 2nd Battalion Cavalry MSM and drove in to the Rebel advance on November 7 near Rockbridge in south-central Douglas County. Nine southerners were killed, compared to two troopers dead and two wounded. The large Rebel presence, combined with his scouts' reports of Confederates behind him in two other directions, convinced Captain Barstow to fall back to Big Beaver Creek near Vera Cruz while he sent for help. At this new location, Burbridge besieged the approximately 200 Federals, armed only with revolvers and a two-pounder cannon, for five hours on November 7. Barstow surrendered to the larger force. Colonel Burbridge claimed his Confederates lost only four wounded, but Captain Barstow's Yankees lost four killed and about 150 captured and paroled.[34] Evidently, these same Confederates rode on north to Wright County where they captured and released several local Enrolled Missouri Militia after stripping them of their uniforms.[35]

The Union counter-strike began the next day on November 8. Captain Milton Burch, with 80 men of 2nd Battalion Cavalry MSM from their station at Ozark, Christian County, swept through west Douglas County and south to the hamlet of Dubuque, Arkansas, on the White River, looking for Burbridge's invading Rebels. Most of Burbridge's Confederates were moving in the opposite direction and further to the east, but Burch's Yankees still managed to kill four and capture 25 on November 11 and 12 along the White River, mostly in Taney County.[36]

More Rebels from Northeast Missouri Move Through

Compounding Yankee problems here, groups of northeast Missouri Confederate recruiting commands were also moving south through this part of the state. On November 12 or 13, Captain Charles B. Maus's patrol of 13th Cavalry MSM was sent out from Waynesville, Pulaski County, to watch for these moving bands along the roads. They fired on an unidentified body of Rebels who were attempting to cross the road and chased them over 20 miles, killing six and wounding two.[37] On November 13, Major Thomas O'Halloran, with Camden County Enrolled Missouri Militia routed the Camden County camp of Boone Countian Dr. Julius McGuire and 80 men from north of the Missouri River. The EMM captured only one Rebel that day, but on November 17 caught ten more in Camden County, including some officers.[38]

Between November 17 and 20, patrols of 14th Cavalry MSM skirmished in south Barry County with Rebels, perhaps from the same units Captain Burch's force had encountered in Taney County earlier.[39] Suddenly, on November 24, Burbridge's large Rebel force—which had evidently remained hidden in Wright County after their clash with Captain Barstow's Federals—became active again, attacking a large Union train of 47 wagons moving along the Hartsville-Houston road in east Wright County. Several of the raiders, wearing the EMM uniforms captured earlier, deceived the Yankee escort into thinking they were comrades, then quickly made off with 20 wagons full of supplies. An angry reaction force from Hartville convinced Burbridge to retire south to the White River and the Arkansas line, having imposed losses to his enemies of five or six Federals killed and ten wounded, compared to a similar number of casualties to his own command.[40] If only the north Missouri Rebels infiltrating south through this area had realized that Burbridge's force had been in Wright County, they may have joined them and subsequently reached the Confederate army in Arkansas in safety. Colonel Burbridge's use of captured Federal uniforms for deception was a new tactic in Missouri this season, but it would be used extensively in the future.

Southern horsemen attacking a Union wagon train. (*The Soldier in Our Civil War*, 1890, vol. 2, p. 201; courtesy Terry Harmon)

Colonel Jackman Moves Through and Livingston's Guerrillas Fight On

There was action in other parts of southwest Missouri during November, too. Between November 8 and 15, Tom Livingston's band raided homes of families of northern sympathy again along Dogwood Creek in west Vernon County, killing two men and taking about eight or ten captives. On November 9 elements of 6th Kansas Cavalry skirmished near Drywood with these raiders, but few other details remain.[41] Another sketchy skirmish involved 2nd Kansas Cavalry, November 19, in or near Pineville, McDonald County, without other details.[42] The next day, near Newtonia, a patrol of 7th Cavalry MSM from a garrison in that town tangled with an unidentified Rebel force and lost two troopers captured.[43]

Perhaps the southerners involved may have been part of Colonel Sidney Drake Jackman's 1,000 or so Confederates who rode north into Newton County about November 25. Jackman's command was on its way further north, and dropping off small recruiting teams in their home neighborhoods as they rode along.[44] This body of Rebels attracted Union attention when they rode within ten miles of the Federal garrison at Newtonia between November 24 and 26, so Major George W. Kelly, with over 200 troopers of 4th Cavalry MSM guided by twenty Cedar County EMM, swept the prairie countryside along Horse Creek where Vernon, Barton, and Cedar counties intersect. The Yankees split into small groups to cover more ground, and two of these found Rebels to fight. One such detachment near Lamar killed two guerrillas or recruiters before they dispersed. The other, under Union Captain Joseph Parke, rode down a party of Rebel recruiters under a Captain Thomas, killing two and capturing eight in a running fight that resulted in the death of one of the Yankees. The southern prisoners were mostly from the local area, but one was from Henry County and another from Lafayette County many miles to the north.[45] Meanwhile, Colonel Jackman's main body pushed on north.

The same Captain Parke, now with 130 troopers of 4th Cavalry MSM, on November 30 searched Horse Creek again. In southwest Cedar County they routed the Rebel camp of an officer named Johnson of Osceola, St. Clair County, killing 11, wounding 17, and capturing 89 horses, 20 rifles and shotguns, and the Confederates' camp equipment. Union losses were one trooper slightly wounded and two horses killed.[46] It was painfully obvious that some of these Confederate recruiters did not employ the same careful security that bushwhacker chief Tom Livingston had come to employ for survival. The same day as Johnson's defeat, Union troops at or near Neosho, Newton County, captured Rebel Captain Henderson Jennings and his son—both local men who had returned from the main Confederate forces in Arkansas.[47] The southerners in both these incidents were probably dropped off by Colonel Jackman's band that had moved through earlier.

December Action in the Northern Ozarks

Even in the cool December weather, guerrillas kept Federals busy in the western Ozarks region along the White, Gasconade, and Niangua Rivers. Union troopers of 3rd and 9th Missouri Cavalry fought bushwhackers somewhere near Ozark, Christian County, December 2.[48] Captain Milton Burch led an expedition of his own 14th Cavalry MSM and local EMM along White River between December 9 and 15, looking for guerrillas without much success.[49] On Christmas Eve, Federal troops captured Rebel Captain John A. Basyl of Colonel Myscall Johnson's command in Laclede County, but whether he was recruiting or scouting or just returning home is not clear.[50] Captain Basyl may have been scouting for Brigadier General John Sappington Marmaduke's southwest Missouri raid, which began a few days later on the last day of the year.

December Incidents in the Osage River Region

Meanwhile, miles to the north, guerrilla warfare continued. Local accounts in Benton County assert that unidentified Union troops on December 5 took six area southern men out of the Warsaw jail on the pretense of gathering firewood and shot them down on the banks of the Osage River. Among the victims of this atrocity were two brothers named Gregory—one died and one survived a terrible head wound.[51] About this same time elements of 3rd Wisconsin Cavalry killed eight bushwhackers along the Little Osage and Marais des Cygnes Rivers in south Bates and north Vernon counties. These Federals reported the rest of the guerrillas escaped south to Barton and Jasper counties.[52] On Christmas Eve, Yankee troops executed a returned Rebel soldier because he had been carrying a pistol when found near the Grand River a few days before. He may also have been a recruiter dropped off from Colonel Jackman's band as it moved through days before, as Jackman mentioned in his memoirs leaving off Captain Bill Marchbanks and others to recruit in Bates and Vernon counties nearby.[53]

Hot Actions in Newton and McDonald Counties

The southwest Missouri corner in Newton and McDonald counties was quiet the first two weeks of December 1862, but certainly not the rest of the month. About the middle of December unidentified guerrillas near Neosho attacked a Federal wagon train escorted by members of 3rd Wisconsin Cavalry and either destroyed or captured two wagons and their teams.[54] These may have been the same bushwhackers who skirmished with 3rd Kansas Indian Home Guard also around December 15, but no other details survive.[55] Near Newtonia on December 19, guerrillas shot at a trooper of 8th Cavalry MSM chasing his stray horse, but he escaped and brought back a number of his comrades, who killed one of his assailants and captured four horses and a mule.[56]

Major E. B. Eno led 80 troopers of 8th Cavalry MSM in a sweep of the Sugar Creek Hills in central McDonald County, December 23 through 25. They found and broke up three guerrilla camps—made easier to find with the autumn's dropping of concealing leaves—captured ten men and twelve horses and two wagons, one identified as formerly belonging to 6th Kansas Cavalry. Major Eno complained that his operations were hampered by southern citizens who spread the word of his cavalry's presence to their enemies. The northern sympathizers had nearly all left the countryside in this region long before for the relative safety of the bigger towns.[57] Area guerrillas did seem to covet wagons in these parts, for on Christmas day an unidentified group near Keetsville, Barry County, seized one loaded with a settler's belongings, took it toward this same part of McDonald County, but then abandoned it to a Federal pursuit of 14th Cavalry MSM and escaped.[58]

The day after Christmas marked the demise of brothers Brice and "Crack" Mayfield a few miles to the north. The Mayfields were determined to keep local Union military off balance throughout 1862 in the Vernon County area. Their skill at stealing Yankee horses had made them the bane of the Union troops for many months. The brothers went disguised as northern soldiers to a house on Shoal

Creek near Neosho, perhaps to kill troopers of 6th Kansas Cavalry they heard were spending the night, but the wary Kansans sensed their arrival and shot them both dead as they stepped onto the porch. The death of this stealthy pair was probably rejoiced in Yankee ranks and the remaining northern sympathizers in the area. They were certainly mourned by southerners and by their family members. Indeed, some of the female members of the Mayfield family were already active in supporting the southern cause in the area, and they would continue doing so into the coming year.[59]

On December 28 near Newtonia, guerrillas went to the home of a lady of northern sympathy and took away "her negro girl." Federals of 8th Cavalry MSM failed to catch these bushwhackers, but, not to be outdone, went to a well-known southerner's farm and seized one of the slaves from that place, although the record does not say what they did with the slave. As the violent year of 1862 came to a fitful close in southwest Missouri, one could almost hear these avenging troopers say, "So, THERE!" at this unusual sequel to their frustration. This inappropriate reaction mirrored both the guerrillas' continual freedom of action and a series of awkward Union tactics that typified guerrilla warfare in this part of Missouri throughout 1862.[60]

Nineteen

Fall 1862 in Northeast Missouri

Just as summer 1862 had brought the onslaught of numerous Confederate recruiters and the havoc they created to northeast Missouri, the fall of 1862 brought the departure or demise of many of these officers and their recruits. The summer's rapid tempo of daily events continued into September before it slowed.

Ralph Smith and Other Guerrillas

Major Raphael "Ralph" Smith had departed from Colonel Joseph Porter's larger Rebel command by September 1, and about that date raided the town of Monticello, Lewis County. These southerners were only in town a short time and left rapidly when Major John B. Rogers approached with about 300 men of 11th Cavalry MSM.[1]

On approximately September 2, near Rocheport, west Boone County, unidentified guerrillas robbed two homes of horses, firearms, and a new pair of boots.[2] Evidently, some Confederate recruits were equipping themselves to go off to war. A day or so later Union authorities at Fulton, Callaway County, reported that 70 such Rebel recruits evaded Federal patrols and pickets and successfully crossed the Missouri River near St. Aubert, northern Osage County, probably to begin their long trek to the Confederate forces in Arkansas.[3]

Purcell and Others in the Boone County Area

Guerrilla chief or Rebel recruiter Young A. Purcell of Audrain County still had over 200 men in west-central Callaway County, for a 50-man patrol of 1st Battalion Cavalry MSM from Fulton collided with them there at Prairie Chapel, September 4. The blue-clad cavalrymen fought the southerners for over an hour until their ammunition was expended, then withdrew back to base. The Yankees lost three men missing and presumed captured, but claimed they killed at least seven of the partisans. The persistent Purcell remained in the area.[4]

The following day, September 5, Brigadier General Lewis Merrill, commander of the northeast Missouri district, ordered two guerrillas held as prisoners at

Mexico, Audrain County, executed, but commuted the sentence of a third man to imprisonment due to his brother's service as a captain in the 9th Cavalry MSM.[5] Federals held many captives in area jails who had ridden with Colonels Porter or Poindexter. Over the next few weeks their captors would apply the harshest of penalties, especially to those who had earlier given oaths to the U.S. government and later were captured with firearms in their possession.

Captain Joseph W. Baird led a patrol of 2nd Missouri Cavalry and local 46th Enrolled Missouri Militia from Hudson, Macon County, south September 6 to attack a Rebel camp south of Roanoke in northern Howard County. The Union cavalry killed four irregulars, scattered most of them, inflicting some wounds, and captured three men and a lot of horses and weapons, all at the cost of one man killed—Captain Baird himself.[6]

Union cavalry, probably of 9th Cavalry MSM in Columbia, heard about a Rebel Captain Love and a Lieutenant Bowles who had a camp of about 70 recruits in northwest Boone County. The Federals attacked the camp September 11, killing five and capturing several at no loss to themselves.[7] Purcell's guerrillas or recruits were involved in incidents in Boone County about this same time. They may have been the raiders who robbed a store in Providence of footwear, hats, and gloves. They may have also been the guerrillas ten miles north of Columbia who stole horses from a stage station.[8]

Union Brigadier General Lewis Merrill. (Joseph A. Mudd, *With Porter in North Missouri*, 1909; courtesy Bob and Mary Younger and andy Turner)

Porter and His Subordinates Continue to Raid

There was still guerrilla activity further north, too. Near the Iowa line on September 7, Tice Cain, Bill Dunn, and others led over 70 Rebels in an attack on the EMM post at Lancaster, county seat of Schuyler County. They captured one militiaman but left after his comrades killed two bushwhackers and captured three more, including a captain.[9]

Cain and Dunn had fought under Colonel Joseph C. Porter's banner earlier that summer, and now Porter himself had been quietly building another force. On September 12, leading about 350 Rebels with the assistance of his brother, Jim, Porter re-emerged as a threat, raiding Palmyra, eastern Marion County. The southerners struck early in the morning, delayed interference by seizing the telegraph instruments and cutting the lines, freed approximately 50 comrades from jail, and took firearms from a gunsmith shop. Porter and his leaders attempted to keep the raiders from unnecessary violence and destruction during their stay in Palmyra, but in several incidents they shot a citizen to death, wounded four Union soldiers, and captured and paroled several others, all at their own cost of one guerrilla killed and one wounded. Porter may have taken some satisfaction that one of their captives was Colonel H. S. Lipscomb, former commander of 11th Cavalry MSM and his chief antagonist in the northeast Missouri fights of June 30 and July 1. The Rebels paroled Lipscomb with the rest. The raiders left town with their spoils of war and with two prominent civilians of renowned northern sympathy.[10]

The next day guerrilla chief and former Porter subordinate Ralph Smith, with about 150 men, rejoined Porter. The extra strength didn't prevent their surprise at five that afternoon, September 13, when Brigadier General John McNeil's Union column burst upon their camp near Newark, southeast Knox County. The southerners scattered into the woods. Both sides lost one or two killed, but several Rebels were wounded and 20 were made prisoner. This reverse seemed to stop this latest of Porter's drives in northeast Missouri and henceforth his efforts were more like other area Confederate recruiters, whose main mission this fall seemed to be to infiltrate with their charges back south through Union lines to the Rebel army.[11]

Mid–September in Callaway, Howard, and Boone Counties

Meanwhile, other guerrilla bands were active across the region in mid–September. About this time, some of Alvin Cobb's bushwhackers abducted and hung in north Callaway County a noted local Union scout and guide named Page.[12] On September 14 and 15, a Colonel Thomas L. Crawford, an EMM officer, led a mixed EMM and MSM expedition from Jefferson City on the steamer *Fanny Ogden* to the Rocheport area in west Boone County. These water-borne raiders failed to find guerrillas, but they arrested 27 local residents for harboring bushwhackers and took them back to the Jefferson City jail.[13] Later in the war the Perche Hills around Rocheport became a frequent guerrilla hideout, demonstrating how little Colonel Crawford's expedition accomplished in the long term. It seemed ineffective in the short term, too, for during this same week guerrilla snipers fired on two forage parties of the 9th Cavalry MSM gathering horse feed from the Boone County countryside. No casualties were reported, but one of the details captured two southern men.[14] Evidently, Boone County bushwhackers or Rebel recruits evaded large Yankee forces and struck primarily at smaller targets.

Guerrillas and Rebel Recruiters in Monroe and Ralls Counties

Further to the north in Monroe County unidentified guerrillas skirmished September 16 with elements of 3rd Cavalry MSM, indicating a Rebel presence there, as well.[15] That same day guerrilla chief or Confederate recruiter Washington MacDonald with 80 men in neighboring Ralls County was actively watching from a discreet distance Colonel J.T.K. Hayward's large Union EMM force sweeping the countryside looking for Rebels. "Wash" MacDonald was looking for an opportunity to strike back at his blue-clad enemy, and a juicy target came his way. Colonel Hayward himself, commander of 38th EMM regiment, strayed a little too far from his men and became McDonald's prisoner for a few days until paroled. Meanwhile, elements of Hayward's expedition killed one Rebel that same day near Sidney, northwest Ralls County. The Union force of over 200 EMM continued to scour the farmland and woods looking for their missing colonel and the elusive southerners, until September 18 when their persistence brought them some success. That day at Sandy Creek, east-central Monroe County, the 38th and 53rd Enrolled Missouri Militia found and attacked the combined recruit camp of captains Henry Snider, Ben Ely and Clint Burbridge (all three from Ralls County), Harry Knight of Lincoln County, Braxton Pollard of Florida, Monroe County, a "Barnard" of Adair County, as well as Benjamin F. White and about 120 recruits. The camp outposts gave an effective early alarm, however, and the Yankees killed only two men and captured an almost empty camp. The paroled and embarrassed Colonel Hayward found his way back to his worried soldiers, evidently some time after this fight.[16]

Harsh Union Measures

By mid–September the pace of action in northeast Missouri slowed enough that Federal military authorities at several levels felt free to act, both to punish southern sympathizers for the hundreds of area men who swarmed to Confederate recruiters, and to reassert Union dominance over the remaining inhabitants of this embattled region. In Marion County Yankee officers had burned the homes of at least four southerners who had harbored guerrillas in the summer and fall.[17] Other officials banished six prominent southern sympathizers of Macon County, including the president of McGhee College, to northern Illinois, where the exiled were "...to report by letter, once in three weeks."[18] On September 20, Major John B. Rogers' battalion of 2nd Cavalry MSM near Canton, Lewis County, destroyed Staples Mill on the Fabius River because irregulars used it as a meeting place and had the owners grind meal for them.[19] Lieutenant Cravin Hartman's patrol of 3rd Iowa Cavalry burned Mt. Zion Church near Hallsville, north Boone County, and the buildings of two area farmers for similar reasons and in retaliation for the murder of the Union scout, Mr. Page, in the neighborhood days before.[20]

Missourians of all sympathies seldom noticed such punitive acts outside the neighborhoods where they occurred, but public executions were widely discussed. Brigadier General Lewis Merrill had ten Rebel prisoners executed, September 25, at Macon City, Macon County, for oath violations. These unfortunates had been captured during the campaigning against Confederate Colonels Porter and Poindexter, yet their names were found on previous records for taking oaths not to bear arms against the U.S. government.[21] The next day General Merrill had three more executed in Huntsville, Randolph County, for the same reason of violating the rules of war.[22]

Extreme Southern Acts

Of course, southern irregulars in the region committed harsh acts, too. During the evening hours of both September 18 and 19 in south Boone County, partisans robbed homes of northern sympathizers of horses, overcoats, blankets, as well as a pistol and a watch. When one man resisted, a bushwhacker hit him in the face with a musket.[23] About September 20, Rebels pretending to be EMM abducted a Mr. Perkins near Hunnewell, southeast Shelby County, and he was never seen again. A few days later a southern man confided to an area resident that the guerrillas had hung Perkins, either for being a northern sympathizer or an informant, and buried his body in the Salt River bottom. Searchers could not find the grave.[24]

In mid to late September two spirited young southern maidens of Monroe County conducted recruiting rallies accompanied by Confederate recruiter Captain Clay Price. These two women, 19-year-olds Mildred Elizabeth Powell and Margaret Creath, bedecked themselves in clothing "of rebel colors," wearing braces of pistols and spoke publicly for the southern cause. Union authorities later heard that the girls had done more than speak. One source reported that the pair borrowed or rented a carriage, had a man drive them to Hannibal, bought pistol percussion caps, ammunition, and revolvers, and brought them all back to Monroe County to be hidden for Confederate use. Federal authorities arrested them, then grappled with the problem of what to do with the very spirited and unrepentant lovelies. If they had been men, their fate would not have drawn debate, but Union policymakers seemed unsure how to handle female prisoners at this phase of the war. For a while, both were held in a church; then they were placed on personal parole at Miss Creath's father's home provided they "...abstained from writing and talking treason..."; but eventually they were banished from Missouri—Miss Creath to the Nevada Territory. Postwar, "Maggie" Creath allowed the Missouri chapter of United Daughters of the Confederacy to publish her very colorful and detailed, although one-sided, journal of some of these events. In retrospect, if these ladies had performed such daring acts of defiance to Union authority later in the war, they would have been tried by a military tribunal and committed to prison with hardly any debate.[25]

Late September and Early October Fighting Along the Missouri River

During several days in late September and early October, a number of guerrilla or recruiter bands kept Yankee cavalry occupied in the Missouri River counties of Howard, Boone, and Callaway. On September 22, the day after Iowa cavalry burned Mt. Zion church nearby, Major Charles B. Hunt and some MSM skirmished with irregulars at or near Sturgeon in northern Boone County, but few details remain.[26] Major Frank J. White of 2nd Battalion Cavalry MSM led a combined task force of 13th Cavalry MSM, EMM, and artillery out of their Jefferson City base, by steamboat, to south Boone County on September 23. This force was looking for the partisans who had robbed northern sympathizers here on September 18 and 19, as mentioned earlier. They evidently found one when they apprehended a

William Nevins, who had on his person a mask, as well as a paper earlier issued him by Federals, stating Nevins had taken an oath of allegiance to the U.S. His captors made Nevins name other local bushwhackers, shot him for betrayal of his oath, then burned his house and presumably those of the men he named. Later, Major White's men discovered one of the homes they burned belonged to an actual northern sympathizer and another belonged to a former Rebel who had changed sides and was serving in the militia. Either the vengeful troops were not careful which houses they burned, or Nevins misled them before he died.[27]

About September 22 a patrol of 9th Cavalry MSM near Columbia had more success when they captured four Rebel recruiting officers, including a Major Wills, or Wells, and captains J.D.W. Robinson and Embree, or Emory, carrying "some important correspondence."[28] Another patrol from this regiment, September 25, captured five guerrillas and another on September 26 captured 12 more, in east Howard and northwest Boone County. Guerrillas did not always lose in these encounters, as on the latter date, some along the Missouri River in southeast Chariton County waylaid another patrol of the 9th Cavalry MSM, killing a lieutenant and two others and wounding two more.[29]

Parts of 10th Cavalry MSM, led by Major Richard G. Woodson in Monroe County on September 27 or 28 overwhelmed two bushwhacker or recruit camps, including that of Major Elliott D. Major, capturing 14 Rebels, including Major, as well as horses, weapons, and camp equipment. Missouri-born Major of Monroe County had been in the southern cause in Missouri since the war's beginning, but

Union forces used steamboats to insert troops into suspected guerrilla areas several times during 1862. (*Harper's Weekly*, October 19, 1861; courtesy Bob and Mary Younger and Andy Turner)

he was soon to face a military tribunal and the real possibility of execution.[30] Likewise, a patrol of 4th Cavalry MSM in Callaway County, October 1, found and attacked a recruiting camp of 200, killing eight for a Union loss of five wounded.[31]

Also serving the Union cause in this region this autumn were the troopers of Colonel Arnold Krekel's 1st Battalion Cavalry MSM and Major Frank J. White's 2nd Battalion Cavalry MSM, who could not muster enough troops when organized some months before to qualify as full regiments. Many of the men in these units were German-Americans, and their poor grasp of English, as well as the pro-southern Missouri newspaper propaganda and name-calling directed against them the previous year did not endear them to the local populace. This distrust and dislike seemed to be mutual. A sad outcome of this enmity took place October 4 when Captain Henry Windmuller's patrol of 2nd Battalion Cavalry MSM, from their station at Fulton, Callaway County, arrested William R. Given, his adult son David, and Charles Hill at or near the Given farm seven miles northwest of Fulton on charges they aided a wounded guerrilla. Few details remain, but when unidentified guerrillas ambushed Windmuller's 34-man patrol near the Given place, some of the troopers gunned down the three captives either in fear or rage. No other casualties were reported from this sad incident, but the unit record shows Captain Windmuller resigned his commission on October 7.[32]

The arena of action then seemed to shift west to previously quiet Howard County for a while. The bushwhackers' chief nemesis here for most of the war was the energetic 9th Cavalry MSM. Indeed, a patrol of that regiment, with some EMM, skirmished with 75 irregulars of captains George F. Cameron, who was perhaps from near Brunswick, Chariton County, and John T. Singleton—a former tailor in Columbia—near New Franklin in south county, October 7. In a familiar pattern, the Union troopers surprised the encamped Confederates in a dawn attack, killing three and capturing 25 horses, weapons, clothing, and even love letters, all for the loss of one Yankee horse killed. Captain Singleton must have particularly heaved a sigh of relief in avoiding capture here, as he had escaped the hated Alton, Illinois military prison on March 22 and thus far had avoided recapture.[33] A few days later Union EMM skirmished near the same place, but few details of that fight remain.[34]

Meanwhile, Brigadier General Lewis Merrill reported to his superiors on September 28 that the Perche Hills near Rocheport, as well as Auxvasse Creek in east Callaway County, seemed to be the rendezvous points of literally hundreds of Rebel recruits or guerrillas.[35] Nearly all the Confederate recruits of northeast Missouri were concentrating before cold weather set in to cross the dreaded obstacle of the Missouri River and trek south to join regular Rebel forces in Arkansas. To survive through the gauntlet of Yankee patrols they must pass, these recruiting commands united whenever practicable in order to mass what little firepower and shock action they could muster. To counter this threat in north Boone County, Major Richard G. Woodson led a large portion of 10th Cavalry MSM to the region and pursued a large Rebel band near Centralia on September 29.[36] On this day or the next, Brigadier General Odon Guitar personally led elements of his former regiment, 9th Cavalry MSM, and 2nd Missouri Cavalry from Columbia in a daylight attack on a partisan camp somewhere in Boone County, killing four and capturing five Rebels.[37] On October 2, 80 troopers of 9th Cavalry MSM happened upon Captain George F. Cameron and 75 recruits, 15 miles north of Columbia. At first

Cameron organized his neophytes to defend against the Yankee attack, but the veteran Federals charged repeatedly until the untried Rebel recruits broke and scattered, with the jubilant troopers pursuing some of them several miles. The Union report conservatively claimed they had killed only one partisan with certainty and captured one other along with horses, bedding, weapons, but added gleefully that they had killed Cameron's own horse.[38]

An informant or scout brought word to General Guitar at Columbia, in the middle of the night of October 4, of a camp of 40 or 50 Rebels—Cameron's perhaps—on Cedar Creek, 12 miles southeast of Columbia. As was his nature, Guitar immediately took to the field with the available 60 men of 9th Cavalry MSM, but slyly dismounted them a mile from the camp and assaulted the irregulars just after dawn on foot. The Yankee troopers were almost disappointed to find only seven enemies in camp, but they killed one, captured two and took all seven horses, plus the usual weapons, bedding, and the like.[39]

Excitement to the North

The guerrilla war north of Boone County kept other Federals busy during this period. Union scouts reported about 250 Rebels moving south on September 29 in southwest Shelby County, heading toward Monroe County. General Merrill was particularly alarmed at the portion of this report that claimed the southerners had learned and used his cavalrymen's recognition symbol of wearing white hatbands, and he ordered executions for any irregulars caught so-dressed. The hatband recognition symbol had been initiated because so many of the EMM, actively aiding MSM and other Union cavalry, lacked basic uniforms and served in this period in mostly civilian clothing. Merrill feared guerrillas could use their own white hatbands to deceive and kill Union troops.[40] Soon after, a group of 53 from 29th Enrolled Missouri Militia in Scotland County suffered no reported casualties skirmishing with Bill Dunn's guerrilla band, although they claimed one Rebel killed and another captured, along with 11 horses.[41] Major Jacob Pugh, leading a detachment of 50th EMM from Knox County in west-central Lewis County about October 1, tangled with Captain Gabriel S. Kendrick's band of Confederate recruits, badly wounding one Rebel for no Union loss. Kentucky-born Kendrick lived in Lewis County a number of years before the war.[42] Elements of 3rd Cavalry MSM on October 4 skirmished in Monroe County with guerrillas, but no other details were recorded. These partisans may have been those reported wearing the white hatbands earlier.[43]

Sometimes bushwhackers learned, to their loss, that citizens could fight back. About October 8 or 9, four or five local partisans robbed W. K. Nugent of his horse and some clothes at his home near Paris, Monroe County. The indignant Nugent walked to town that same night and returned with Enrolled Missouri Militiamen of 70th EMM, whom he guided to the home of one of the guerrillas he had recognized. Once there, this impromptu posse arrested two suspects and recovered Nugent's property. This success so encouraged the local EMM that they went out the next night and caught eight more bushwhackers.[44]

Brigadier General Lewis Merrill, on October 10, sentenced captured Rebel recruiter Major Elliott D. Major to death. Merrill had specified the execution was to take place at Mexico, Audrain County, where Major was held. However, Union officials commuted the sentence, October 27, to imprisonment, based largely on the entreaties of large numbers of northern sympathizers from Major's home area in Monroe County. Major Major was later exchanged, and he returned in 1864 to bedevil Union forces in Missouri once again.[45] About this same date near Williamstown, west Lewis County, a large guerrilla band ambushed the advance guard of a 2nd cavalry MSM patrol from Monticello. The Union cavalry counterattacked and routed the Confederates, capturing eight men and ten horses, at a Federal loss of one dead and one wounded lieutenant.[46] The guerrillas may have been Captain Gabriel Hendricks's band, for on October 11 his band of 27 unexpectedly removed themselves from the war by surrendering to Brigadier General John McNeil at nearby Palmyra, Marion County. They also turned in their weapons and 16 horses.[47]

By this time many bands of southern recruits had already been crossing the Missouri River on their long trek south in the autumn, and those who had not yet left the region faced the full attention now of the veteran Federal patrols. One band of 75 recruits must have felt the odds were overwhelming, for they rode into the Union post at Paris, Monroe County, and surrendered in mid–October, even turning in their "arms and contraband property."[48]

The Tempo of Action Finally Slows

The combination of colder weather, southern recruit bands leaving the region, and many former recruits and guerrillas surrendering or being captured finally caused a noticeable reduction in guerrilla actions in northeast Missouri. On October 16, Adair County EMM, perhaps of 50th EMM surprised one band of southerners under a Captain Dennis, killing several, capturing 11, and seizing 20 horses.[49]

Two days later near Uniontown, east Schuyler County, Colonel Samuel M. Wirt led a large mixed EMM force to surround Bill Dunn's camp of about 100 guerrillas. Before the militiamen could close the trap, an accidental gunshot alerted the quarry, and the Confederates bolted. Many of the fearful Rebels stumbled into one group of EMM after another, which groups shot down many disoriented southerners. Dunn and part of his command coolly rode out between the different groups of 29th and 50th EMM wearing the same white hatband recognition symbols ordered for all northeast Missouri EMM. In this case, the white hatbands which were meant to prevent Union militiamen serving without uniforms from being accidentally shot by friendly troops, helped their enemies instead. Dunn's force still bore a heavy toll in casualties, with 11 dead, many wounded, and ten captured by the jubilant militiamen, who reported no losses.[50]

The "Palmyra Massacre"

Also on October 18, 1862, in Palmyra, Marion County, area Union authorities publicly executed ten Confederate prisoners in what has become known even long after the Civil War as the "Palmyra Massacre," cited widely as one of the more notorious examples of depredation by Yankee troops in Missouri. Brigadier General John McNeil and Marion County Provost Marshal W. R. Strachan ordered the execution in retaliation for the murder of Palmyra prominent northern sympathizer Andrew Allsman by Confederate recruiter Colonel Joseph Chrisman Porter's men. Allsman had been abducted during Porter's September 12 raid. It was a sad affair on all sides. Porter and his leaders evidently did not mean to kill Allsman, but after abducting the man, some of his Rebel guards killed the man, either for reasons of their own or thinking that was what their superiors wished. The guards hid the body, which was not discovered for some time, and it is possible that Porter and his staff were ignorant of Allsman's murder. However, McNeil and Strachan were determined to make a horrible example to prevent any other murders of notable northern citizens, so they selected ten prisoners, supposedly at random, to execute as retaliation.

Union Brigadier General John McNeil ordered the execution of Rebel prisoners at Palmyra. (Private collection, courtesy Terry Harmon)

Sadly, some accounts indicate Provost Marshal Strachan replaced some of the condemned with other prisoners after he received sexual favors and other inducements from female relatives of prisoners originally selected. Unlike previous Rebels executed, these unfortunate men were not killed for oath violation or other breaches of rules of warfare; they had not done anything individually to merit such a punishment. One of them, Captain Thomas A. Snider, was a Confederate recruiting officer who had been active in the region. The others were southern men who had been captured as Rebel recruiters or members of Colonel Porter's irregulars, taken prisoner according to conventional rules of war of the period. Many influential people of all loyalties condemned the execution, but to no avail. This act did not seem to garner new respect for the Union cause, just horror that it had been performed. Regrettably, this was not the only such retaliation execution the Federals performed in Missouri during the war.[51]

Execution of the ten Rebels at Palmyra. (Frank H. Sosey, *Robert Devoy: A Tale of the Palmyra Massacre*, 1903; courtesy Bob and Mary Younger and Andy Turner)

Actions in the North

Meanwhile, the strong Union presence and resolve in northeast Missouri continued to shake the confidence of weary southern irregulars. Only the month before, Rebel Captain Washington (Wash) MacDonald had captured 38th EMM's Colonel J.T.K. Hayward in Ralls County and treated him well before paroling and releasing the embarrassed Hayward. Now, in light of the nearby Palmyra executions, MacDonald wondered if he would receive the same civil treatment in the ever-increasing likelihood of his own capture by Union forces. Therefore, about October 24 or 25, the Rebel recruiter sent through intermediaries his query to the Union officers at Hannibal as to what treatment he would receive upon surrender. District chief Brigadier General Lewis Merrill sent a reply to MacDonald that all who surrendered would not be executed, but hinted that as guerrillas such prisoners would not be eligible for exchange like regular Confederate prisoners of war. Wash MacDonald did not surrender this fall and was not captured, but infiltrated back to the Rebel army to the south and returned to recruit in Missouri again in 1864.[52]

On October 31, Lieutenant H. W. Gleason's small squad of Monroe County 70th EMM Regiment located Rebel Captain John S. Williams and ten of his men in a central Monroe County house. Since the militiamen could see the southerners' firearms stacked within view in the house, they brashly rushed into the dwelling and grabbed the weapons, forcing the unarmed Rebels to surrender meekly.[53] Four days later, elements of 6th Cavalry MSM skirmished at or near Huntsville, Randolph County, with some guerrillas, probably local men.[54] Even as late as November 28 a small guerrilla band threatened families of northern sympathy in west Lewis County, taking what they wanted by threat of violence. The following day, elements of 69th EMM came out from LaGrange, searched homes of southerners along the Marion-Lewis County line, recovered stolen property, and arrested five suspects, two of whom admitted wrongdoing.[55] Some of these last incidents seemed to involve not roving gangs of bushwhackers, but southern men who remained at home most of the time and occasionally got together to terrorize their neighbors of northern loyalty.

Fighting Along the Missouri River

During this same period of late October and November, 1862, violence also slowly subsided further south along the Missouri River. A number of Confederate recruiting officers were struggling to get their new soldiers mobilized for the long trek south to Arkansas and the safety of their own lines. In east Callaway County in mid–October, such recruiters as George W. Langston, or Langdon, and James S. Wilson, both of Boone County, and Ohio-born Captain George W. Primrose of Knox County, had united with Captain Young Purcell of Audrain County along the Auxvasse Creek preparatory to starting out. Their combined camp of about 150 men was just too large to escape Federal notice. Major Richard G. Woodson's command of 10th Cavalry MSM found and attacked the camp on October 16, but succeeded only in killing one Rebel and capturing three, as well as shooting off one of Purcell's fingers. The alert southerners followed their tried and true formula of dispersing to rendezvous again later at a pre-arranged site on Cedar Creek.[56]

Major Woodson and his men couldn't be everywhere at once, and they missed their chance to tangle with the ever-elusive Colonel Joseph Chrisman Porter and about 300 of his "reliables." This force was attempting to leave northeast Missouri that same day just a few miles away, near Portland, by crossing that great obstacle, the Missouri River. Porter's irregulars had captured the passing 388-ton, side-wheel steamer *Emilie*—built St. Louis in 1859—and used her to ferry about 170 of the men and their horses to the Osage County side of the river. The owner and captain, Joseph LaBarge, who had named the boat after his daughter, was reluctantly forced to cooperate in order to prevent the southerners from destroying the vessel. A Union lieutenant among the passengers discreetly remained out of sight and avoided capture. Meanwhile, the 1st Battalion Cavalry MSM, led by their unit surgeon, John E. Bruere, came pounding down the road on the Callaway County side, chasing Porter's rear guard and forcing about half of the Rebels to flee upstream along the north bank of the Missouri River. The aggressive doctor, acting for Colonel Arnold Krekel, who had been injured in an earlier fall from his horse, reported later that his troopers killed seven of Porter's men and captured one. The split Rebel unit proceeded into southern Missouri with all available Union troops alerted to their coming.[57]

Rebel Colonel Caleb Perkins managed to cross to the south side of the Missouri River near Rocheport on October 19 with an estimated 400 recruits, just before Colonel Guitar and part of the 9th Cavalry MSM from Columbia rode up. The disappointed Yankees did manage to capture three stragglers and 14 kegs of gunpowder the southerners had hid in a cave nearby.[58] Young Purcell's irregulars finally effected their own difficult crossing of the river, probably in south Boone County, between November 3 and 5, using makeshift rafts. These Rebels were in continual dread that a riverboat would come onto them in midstream and reveal their position to Federal troops. They were particularly upset when several of their horses were marooned on a sand bar for several hours, but they finally finished the tedious process of crossing without suffering harm or alerting local Union troops.[59] Ironically, some of the local Federal troops, Lt. Colonel John F. Williams, and 100 men of 9th Cavalry MSM, were occupied further north in the Rocheport area at about this time tracking down one or two guerrillas at a time, unaware that that Young Pursell's command were easy targets on the Missouri River a few miles away.[60] Williams's large patrol had more success on November 9 when they captured Lt. Colonel Quinton Peacher's small party of Rebel recruiters near Hallsville, north Boone County. Peacher and his small band were unfortunate to ride up from Arkansas into this region at the very time that Union cavalry was so actively combing the countryside looking for Rebel recruits heading the other way. They had already been shot up by another unidentified Union patrol, evidently in Saline County south of the Missouri River, and the wounded among them had probably prevented them from evading Williams's patrol.[61] It was typical of Confederate resolve in this region, however, that recruiters would still be undertaking the hazardous trip through Union army patrols so late in the year, in spite of a season of discouraging reverses in northeast Missouri. On the evening of December 5, a few miles north of Columbia, three guerrillas robbed several homes of mostly cash, but got absolutely nothing from several others. Apparently, the large number of Rebel recruits and guerrillas active in this region this fall had taken nearly everything from some rural families.[62] At the end of December area northern forces even captured two more Rebel recruiting officers in Boone and Howard counties, but complained that the prison escapee and persistent recruiter, John T. Singleton, still eluded their patrols.[63] This measure of southern determination to defy Federal control of northeast Missouri, even in the face of overwhelming numbers and after so many months, was startling evidence that guerrilla violence would continue here for some time.

Twenty

Fall 1862 in Northwest Missouri

The passing of summer in northwest Missouri also saw the passing of most Rebel recruiters and their new men from the area. Many of the bushwhacker bands left with them to take advantage of the increased firepower and thereby ward off the inevitable Yankee cavalry pursuits. As September of 1862 began, some guerrilla groups, particularly Quantrill's, remained to take advantage of the fall fighting weather and assert their defiance to Federal rule over the region. These partisans would give the fatigued Federals no respite.

Quantrill's Olathe, Kansas, Raid

The Union dragnet over "Quantrill Country" (Jackson and Cass counties and western Lafayette and Johnson counties) following Quantrill's mid–August offensive was finished by early September. The weary, frustrated northern troops settled back at their stations with only normal patrols out in the countryside. Since they could not find the partisans in their hidden hideouts, they had no choice but to await the guerrillas' next move. That move came on September 6 when Quantrill led his band to raid Olathe, Kansas, allegedly to avenge the recent execution of one of his band taken prisoner the preceding spring. This raid may also have been to redress the destruction wrought in Jackson County by the Ft. Leavenworth Yankees in late August.

Quantrill's men evidently sought out and killed one or two northern sympathizers or informants on their ride to Olathe. Once there, they effectively surrounded the village to prevent anyone from carrying the alarm. In town the confident raiders captured 125 newly-recruited members of 12th Kansas Infantry. The Rebels killed one infantryman who resisted and paroled the rest later. The eager bushwhackers loaded several wagons with booty, including whole window casements they ripped from buildings. Quantrill proudly displayed to startled villagers the Rebel captain's commission paper given him August 12 by Confederate recruiters. Some of these may have known him before the war. As if to avenge the August 21 Yankee destruction of the Independence *Border Star* newspaper, the guerrillas wrecked the office of the Olathe *Mirror*. Then, on September 7, the whole band, with wagons of booty rode back to Missouri, having killed a total of 11 men during the raid.[1]

More Ineffective Union Countermeasures

Some records show elements of 1st Iowa Cavalry skirmished with bushwhackers along Big Creek in east Cass County, September 9, and possibly these were some of Quantrill's band, dispersed after the Olathe raid.[2] As usual, a large pursuit, or punitive expedition, reacting to the Olathe raid, left Ft. Leavenworth under Lt. Colonel John T. Burris on September 8. This Federal task force foraged along its line of march, burned about 12 homes of suspected guerrillas, and stole or liberated 60 African-Americans, 100 horses, and 100 weapons, but found bushwhackers to fight only in Cass County. On September 10, some cavalry of the expedition chased a few Rebels and recovered three of the stolen Olathe wagons.[3]

Meanwhile, Quantrill took his men to the wooded hills and thick brush of northwest Lafayette County to wait until this latest Ft. Leavenworth expedition got tired of chasing phantoms and went home. Earlier that summer only a few northern sympathizers could be found in this region to form one or two companies of the 71st Enrolled Missouri Militia Regiment. These men seemed so poorly organized, equipped, and led, that the bushwhackers hardly considered them more than a nuisance, but they ignored one great asset of the EMM program—the intimate knowledge of the immediate area that the localized EMM members possessed. It was a great shock to these veteran guerrillas that the amateur local EMM company under a Lieutenant Matt Reid on September 17 or 18, gamely attacked their pickets on the Harvey Gleaves' farm near Wellington. Of course, Quantrill and his subordinate leaders had trained their men through bitter experience to answer any surprise attack with an immediate counterattack of their own. Therefore, the militiamen had the bigger shock when the bushwhackers stole the offensive away from them and counterattacked like a disturbed hive of angry bees. The southerners drove the now-panicked EMM a mile or two back through the village of Wellington to the Sni-A-Bar Creek Bridge, killing at least eight and burning the bridge as a final act of defiance. A search of available records of warfare in this area reveals that never again did this company of the 71st EMM attack Quantrill's band. Considering how poor their chances of success against the bushwhackers were compared to other Union military units that had tried, this is not surprising.[4]

Meanwhile, Quantrill led his band away from the area of the Wellington fight, south through east Jackson County on September 19, in spite of the large numbers of Union troops still there searching for them. The guerrillas skirmished briefly with some Federals near Bone Hill, but kept riding south toward Cass County. Later that same day Captain Daniel H. David and 50 troopers of his own 5th Cavalry MSM and 6th Kansas Cavalry from Burris' task force were amazed to encounter Quantrill and about 150 of his men, five miles north of Pleasant Hill, arrayed in line of battle waiting for them. Captain David accepted the implicit guerrilla invitation to fight and led his Missouri and Kansas cavalrymen in attacking the Rebel line, resulting in one Federal killed and three wounded and two guerrillas killed and several wounded. This was a rare open battle for these bushwhackers, and they seemed to hold their own briefly before they dispersed and scattered. This ten-minute battle seemed to satisfy Lt. Colonel Burris, for on September 22 or 23, he left continued campaigning to Captain David's smaller force and took his expedition back to Kansas, carrying along the seized property and freed blacks.[5]

Assassinations in Johnson County

A day or two before Lt. Colonel Burris' force left the region, an odious form of guerrilla war occurred in Johnson County further to the east. About this time guerrillas had murdered a northern sympathizer named Shaw somewhere in Johnson County.

Perhaps out of revenge, four unidentified Union cavalrymen or militiamen on September 21 rode up to Nathaniel B. Holden's home just outside Warrensburg, called him to the front door and shot him to death, then calmly rode back to town as if they did this every day. Holden, for whom the village of Holden was named, was an influential citizen of this area and had helped to ensure that the Pacific Railroad was built through Johnson County and not through an adjoining county. An investigator assigned by the Union military to ascertain the facts could not obtain the identity of the shooters. However, he did discover that Holden had "...rendered himself very obnoxious to [northern sympathizers] by recommending that they should be shot whilst prisoners at [the siege of] Lexington..." during September of the previous year. Yankee military officials had briefly jailed Holden in July of 1862 evidently for his southern sympathy.[6]

About September 26, four more victims of assassination or murder were discovered a few miles to the north. Someone notified Union authorities in Lexington that the remains of four missing northern spies could be found on the Belles farm in south Lafayette County. Sure enough, the Federals found the bones of the missing men and arrested Mr. Belles for not reporting this to them earlier.[7] It was hard enough for local men to remain out of harm's way in the countryside during the war, and strangers were particularly suspect.

More on Johnson County

Johnson County was somewhat less violent during the fall than it had been in the summer of 1862. A lieutenant and 40 men of the local 40th Enrolled Missouri Militia were sent to southeast Johnson County after a reported guerrilla band. They found them on September 30 on Clear Fork when they rode into an ambush set by 70 bushwhackers. The militiamen aggressively counterattacked, killing four partisans and wounding several with no casualties to themselves.[8] Quantrill's band was last identified several miles west of this area about ten days before and may have been responsible for this skirmish.

About this same time there were depredations by both sides in and around the county. Unknown parties murdered a Mr. Allen for undisclosed reasons.[9] That fall, militia killed old Mr. Raker near Chilhowee, probably because his son, D. M. Raker, had been elected captain of a Rebel company secretly recruited near there in the summer.[10] Independent guerrillas James M. Johnson and John Nichols robbed several families of Union sympathy in east Johnson and west Pettis counties at gunpoint that fall. They had become Missouri's smallest known guerrilla band consisting of two members.[11]

Pre-war Methodist minister Colonel Jeremiah Vard Cockrell returned to his old parish of Johnson County about October 5 and within five days had already recruited 30 men for Confederate service. The reverend was not as famous as his Rebel brother General Francis Cockrell, but he had already proven himself to be a sly and successful recruiter on earlier trips to this region—the last one only a few weeks previous to this. One telling tribute to Vard Cockrell's ability to get around stealthily is that local Yankee authorities did not seem to learn of his presence until about October 13. On that day, miles to the south, a northern patrol in Lawrence County intercepted a rider carrying Cockrell's October 10 letter to Trans-Mississippi Department chief, Major General Thomas C. Hindman. The captured letter detailed Cockrell's plans to return to Arkansas after rendezvousing with his scattered recruiting command and possibly attacking Sedalia and the Pacific Railroad, under construction east of there.[12] Since Rebel recruiting commands had made a shambles out of Federal forces in Independence and Lone Jack in neighboring Jackson County in August, Union authorities took Cockrell's plans very seriously. They dispatched Lt. Colonel Alex M. Woolfolk and 225 troopers of his 1st Cavalry MSM from Lexington to search for the Johnson County preacher, but after four days Woolfolk took his force back to garrison without having caught even a glimpse of the secretive colonel, who never carried out his stated plan.[13]

Southbound Southern Recruits Collide with Union Patrols at Missouri's Center

In the fall of 1862 guerrilla warfare in the central Missouri counties of Pettis, Saline, Cooper, Moniteau, and Cole, south of the Missouri River, had slowed from the frantic summer pace. On September 1, Lieutenant S. E. Hoge led forty local EMM to Moniteau Creek in southeast Cooper or north Moniteau County to investigate reports of horse stealing. Hoge's patrol rode onto thirty Boone and Howard County Rebel recruits who had stopped there to camp on their way south to join the Confederate army. The EMM killed two of the recruits and wounded four or five in a brief firefight after which the Rebels scattered and the northerners captured all their camp equipment, 11 horses, and two mules.[14]

Sometime this same month, guerrillas killed Lieutenant Jacob Bauer of the 43rd Enrolled Missouri Militia at his father's house three miles north of California.[15] Bauer's attackers may have been the survivors of the September 1 fight which took place not far away.

Captain Albert Brackman's patrol of 9th Cavalry MSM, probably from Fayette, Howard County, met violence south of the Missouri River the morning of September 26 near the village of Cambridge in northeast Saline County. There, the small guerrilla band led by John Hawkins fired on them from hiding, killing three of the patrol, including 1st Lieutenant Julius Pinhard, and wounding two more. The bushwhackers also suffered losses of two killed before they could break contact with the Yankees.[16]

On October 6, three unidentified Union soldiers removed a suspected guerrilla named Gentry from the guardhouse at Boonville, Cooper County, on a pretense, and witnesses heard a shot soon after. Over a week later Gentry's decomposed body, showing a bullet wound near the heart, was found in the Missouri River nearby.[17]

On October 12 several guerrillas formerly of James Poindexter's command, now led by Caleb Perkins and Will Todd, rendezvoused at Saline City, northeast Saline County, after the difficult crossing of the Missouri River described earlier. After these southerners heard of a patrol of 71st EMM from Marshall coming to look for them, they set an ambush in the brush, killing one militiaman and wounding six. The battered patrol rode back to the county seat, content to leave the southerners alone for the time being.[18] A patrol of 1st Cavalry MSM skirmished, probably with this same band, near Syracuse, north Morgan County, October 14, but no casualties were mentioned.[19] Perkins's and Todd's passing irregulars may have influenced local southerners to action, for 25 or 30 local southern men robbed Arrow Rock-area families of northern sympathy during the night of October 16, taking horses, guns, bedding, and clothes. Since southern men often took such items by force from northern neighbors preparatory to riding south the join the Rebel army, perhaps these Arrow Rock men were also equipping themselves for such a trip.[20] About October 22, Colonel Henry Neal, with elements of 71st EMM from Lexington, skirmished with undisclosed enemies somewhere in Saline County. It was reported only that Union casualties were two dead and several wounded, but witnesses said the militiamen brought back many horses as trophies.[21] It is possible that the unidentified Rebels were Lt. Colonel Quinton L. Peacher of Boone County and his recruiting team, making their way north to home ground for some late fall recruiting. Peacher's traveling companion on this trip, the secret Rebel mail carrier Captain Absolom C. Grimes, wrote later that their party was engaged in a severe firefight in Saline County about this time. If true, Lt. Colonel Neal's local militia must have been surprised, looking for southbound green recruits, to happen onto Lt. Colonel Peacher's northbound combat veterans. Captain Grimes commented that nearly everyone in the southern group was wounded in some way in that tense skirmish in Saline County. The earlier narrative about northeast Missouri described the later capture of much of Peacher's small command north of the Missouri River.[22]

Other northeast Missouri Rebel recruit bands were not as fortunate infiltrating through Union patrols on the south side of the Missouri River. Captain Julius McGuire led 80 Boone and Howard County Rebels south of the Missouri River to Cooper County in early November. Lt. Colonel A.L. Reaves and Cooper County's 52nd EMM fought with McGuire's southerners between November 12 and 14 at Lone Elm, east of Bell Aire, killing three or four, wounding several, and capturing several. These militiamen or other Union patrols captured several others of the southbound Confederates during the next day or so as the remainder scattered in small groups to evade detection.[23] At about this same time, Union militia in neighboring Saline County shot and killed a James Bower of Monroe County, but no other details were recorded.[24] Perhaps Bower was another Rebel recruit trying to infiltrate south through the Yankee patrols.

Some Guerrilla Warfare North of the Missouri River

Partisan warfare north of the Missouri River also slowly subsided during the fall of 1862. Local northern and southern adherents in east-central Caldwell County held their own private war during September. On September 10 a patrol of the 33rd EMM from Kingston found two local guerrillas in the stable loft of the William Baker farm, including Baker's own son, George. Despite the pleadings of the family, the militiamen led the two men a short distance off and shot them. George Baker's brother, James, struck back the next day, when his shot from ambush killed Captain S.M. Langford of the same EMM regiment. On September 12 vengeful militiamen of three companies of the 33rd EMM killed old William Baker and burned many homes of southerners in the neighborhood.[25]

Having heard of guerrillas in the northeast corner of Carroll County, the Carroll County EMM at Carrollton sent a large force of their own and Grundy County EMM from Chilicothe to investigate. On September 13 the combined force swept through the brush along Grand River there and surprised Captain Logan Ballew, Jim Ryder, and about 75 guerrillas in camp. Shooting from only 75 yards away, the EMM killed at least five bushwhackers, wounded several, and captured nine men and 12 horses, at the loss of one of the Grundy County militiamen killed.[26]

On September 24, Rebel recruiter Colonel Boaz Roberts and guerrilla chieftain Fernando Scott, both of Clay County, waylaid a deputy sheriff out collecting taxes at Barry, southwest Clay County. They released him but kept the deputy's horse, pistol, tax books, and $40.[27]

Back in Caldwell County, violence continued late that same month when local bushwhackers, led partly by George Crews, assaulted the Breckenridge jail in a vain attempt to free comrades, including George's brother, William. George Crews and another of the raiders were killed, and Union authorities arrested Mrs. Crews for helping plan the attempted escape.[28]

Also in late September, guerrilla Lewis Best, with two others, assaulted and killed two Union soldiers on the road eight miles north of Chillicothe, Livingston County. Area northern soldiers were outraged that the bushwhackers had mutilated the victims' bodies.[29] Sometime that fall local EMM in northwest Livingston County, while searching for southerner John Blackburn shot him dead near his home after he tried to evade them.[30]

Also that fall, Kansas jayhawkers returned to raid again in Platte County. It began one evening when Andrew Gutherie, at his home near Weston, shot and wounded a black man he found trying to lead away his horse. The would-be thief escaped into the night, but the next night about 150 Kansas raiders, including many escaped slaves from that neighborhood, robbed Gutherie and some of his neighbors of wagons and stock. Local Union militia caught up to the raiders near the Missouri River, killed four and recovered some of the purloined stock before the remainder crossed over into sanctuary in Kansas.[31]

In spite of setbacks Captain Logan Ballew had remained in the Carroll-Livingston County area, defying Union attempts to stop him. Sometime during October, 1862, Ballew with 16 followers ambushed a company of local EMM near the Rocky Ford of the Grand River in southwest Livingston County, killing one and wounding another. The militia bravely counterattacked, terribly wounding two of the guerrillas and capturing nine others. This latest defeat practically ended Ballew's effectiveness as a recruiter in the region.[32]

By the end of October guerrilla warfare in this region had sputtered into occasional acts of isolated violence. On October 30 in Clinton County a guerrilla hiding by the road sniped at a mounted militiaman passing by and missed. The only significance to this event was that it was later reported in a St. Louis newspaper.[33] On November 5 near Mirabile, southwest Caldwell County, local militia, perhaps of the 33rd EMM, shot down a returned Rebel soldier who ran from his house when they approached. They were sent to investigate why the man had failed to enroll, as required by General Order Number 19 issued in July, and assumed his running from them was a sign of something more sinister. Of course, militia in Caldwell County was already known to be prone to "shoot first and ask questions later."[34]

Quantrill Action in Early October

Meanwhile, terror warfare in "Quantrill country," Jackson, Cass, Lafayette, and Johnson counties, remained hot during October and well into November of 1862. Quantrill united with another area bushwhacker, Richard "Dick" Chiles, to operate with about 130 men against Captain Daniel H. David and his force of 88 troopers of 5th Cavalry MSM in early October. Captain David's Federals were sweeping the countryside of northeast Jackson County near Sibley, and Quantrill wanted to strike at them. Chiles usually operated in the Sibley area, and Quantrill gave him the privilege of controlling the ambush on October 6—a role he usually reserved for himself during 1862. Chiles flubbed the attack by triggering the shooting before the cavalry was within the killing zone of the ambush. The guerrillas were forced to retreat, as their pistols and shotguns lacked the range of the cavalry carbines, and the Union fire began to have a telling effect. Two Federals died and several Rebels were wounded, including Chiles, who died later from a bullet which perforated his lungs. Captain David's force picked up the trail of some of the guerrillas the next day and pursued them toward Independence, where they lost them in the brush.[35]

Another guerrilla band was busy nearby at this same time. The small band of exiled Kansas southerners, led by Bill Reed, still operated in the wooded hills of Lafayette County, whose residents seemed mostly southern in sympathy. Many of these residents were less than enthusiastic in their support of this band, due to it's distinctive "cutthroat" nature, typified by two desperate brothers, Bill and Jim Anderson, who would achieve their own notoriety later in the war. The residents' displeasure with Reed's gang stemmed from being forced to feed them for months and from their propensity for murder and mayhem. Reed's band was probably responsible, during the night of October 1, for taking saddles from one man and terrorizing respected old Colonel Henry C. Chiles in south-central Lafayette County. The raiders took Chiles's watch, boots, two horses, and $80, and forced the old pioneer to accompany them for a distance before releasing him unharmed but shaken. Quantrill and his men were more considerate toward the locals, and the contrast between the way the two gangs deported themselves was glaring.[36]

During the night of October 4, six men, evidently of the same band called southern sympathizer John McFadden out into his yard and shot him dead for reasons never made clear.[37] Perhaps the same gang struck again the following night in southeast Lafayette County where one man was shot, then Henry Perdue was killed nearby in the presence of his son, and a German-American baptism was interrupted and four men killed who had earlier served in the 71st EMM.[38] Evidently, in the same neighborhood, these raiders robbed the stagecoach, taking passengers' valuables and the horses on October 11. The culprits then remained inactive or left the region for several weeks.[39] There is a possibility that some of Quantrill's men performed some of these acts, as some of them showed a propensity for raiding in the German-American community other times during the war, but the sources for this October, 1862, violence do not clearly identify the raiders.

Quantrill's Shawneetown, Kansas, Raid

Quantrill's band raided Kansas again on October 17 and 18, evidently to obtain clothing for their upcoming trip to the south. The band passed Little Santa Fe, southwest Jackson County, the evening of October 17 and just over the state border happened on a Santa Fe Trail freight wagon train camped for the night. The 15 teamsters and soldier escort had carelessly bedded down without posting effective guards, and the raiding bushwhackers quickly killed about half of them before the rest ran off terrified into the dark. Quantrill's men then raided the village of Shawneetown stealing many horses and burning most of the place. The Missourians

The grisly remains of the seven Shawneetown captives that Quantrill's band carried back to Missouri and murdered. (John N. Edwards, *Noted Guerrillas*, 1867; courtesy Bob and Mary Younger and Andy Turner)

killed a couple of residents on the spot and took seven more men back with them to Jackson County on the morning of October 18, where at the Blue River they murdered the unarmed captives. Available accounts of Quantrill exploits, including the memoirs of his men, say little about the Shawneetown raid, perhaps because of its extreme bloodlust.[40] This band thus demonstrated a growing callousness more typical of the nearby band of Kansas exile guerrillas, to the point that it is difficult in the existing historical record to distinguish the acts of the two groups this autumn.

Different Union Countermeasures

The customary and ineffective Union countermeasures did not occur after the Shawneetown raid. This time, no Yankee expedition rode forth from nearby Ft. Leavenworth to redress the latest guerrilla offense. Instead, the Lexington garrison sent company-sized patrols to western Lafayette County between October 22 and 26 looking for the dispersed portions of Quantrill's band reported to be hiding there. One such bushwhacker group of 25 robbed the mail coach, October 22, but patrols of 1st Cavalry MSM could not find the robbers. The troopers even cordoned off and searched the villages of Chapel Hill and Napoleon, but found little.[41]

The Yankee district commander, Brigadier General Benjamin Loan, was a radical Unionist who preached and practiced retribution to all secessionists. Beginning in late October, he ordered widespread arrests of the southerners who allowed or encouraged Quantrill's and the other guerrilla bands. By November 14 Loan crowed to his superiors that he had 250 of these people in jail, that 50 more had been given parole to leave the state within ten days, and that probably 50 more had fled the region rather than face arrest.[42]

Border Fighting in Late October and Early November

During the night of October 29, about 50 partisans of either Quantril's or Reed's band raided the George W. Baker plantation in central Lafayette County and carried off bedding and several black men.[43] Lt. Colonel John T. Burris belatedly brought another Ft. Leavenworth expedition, which roamed around Jackson County between November 1 and 5 without any obvious effect on the bushwhackers. The Federals took back with them a large numbers of southerners' slaves to live free in Kansas, but also took along about 100 horses, and Burris claimed his men killed a few Rebels, too.[44]

Meanwhile, most bushwhackers of this region had answered Quantrill's summons to rendezvous on Big Creek in east Cass County preparatory to a long ride to the south for the winter. Quantrill and some guerrillas of other nearby bands started south on November 2, leaving behind subchief and postwar outlaw Coleman (Cole) Younger to attend to several disabled partisans who were recovering from wounds suffered in recent fighting. Among the 300 or so guerrillas riding south

Quantrill subchief (and postwar outlaw) Cole Younger. (John N. Edwards, *Noted Guerrillas*, 1867; courtesy Bob and Mary Younger and Andy Turner)

were several former members of Benjamin Parker's band, Rebel Captain Charles Harrison, originally from the Colorado Territory, and his 11 local recruits for the Confederate army, and a number of turncoat Union Enrolled Missouri Militiamen from north of the Missouri River. All in all, Quantrill was leading a motley group of irregulars on this particular trip.[45]

Just after setting out, Quantrill's amalgamated group near Harrisonville happened upon Lieutenant W. M. Newby's 72 man escort of 6th Cavalry MSM and thirteen oxen-drawn military supply wagons and their teamsters heading west from Sedalia. Needless to say, the bushwhackers made short work of the wagon train and its escort, capturing Lieutenant Newby and several of his men and killing four soldiers and ten teamsters. Meanwhile, Newby's commander, Colonel Edwin C. Catherwood, learned of the presence of large numbers of guerrillas in the area near where Lieutenant Newby's detail was headed, quickly put together a large force of his own regiment and troopers of 5th Cavalry MSM and rode toward the trouble. Colonel Catherwood's force rode onto the scene of the destroyed wagon train and set off south in pursuit of the guerrilla force. At nine o'clock that night the cavalry crashed into Quantrill's force in southeast Cass County near Dayton killing six guerrillas and wounding several while rescuing Newby and one of his men. The guerrillas moved on south, glad to get away from the large body of angry troopers.[46]

Other November Violence in Northwest Missouri

With the departure of most guerrillas of the region the pace of warfare slowed in November as winter approached. In early November an unidentified body of about 200 Rebel recruits passed through southeast Saline County, taking from farmers of all sympathies horses and other necessities for the long ride south.[47] On November 10 Union Brigadier General Loan and his bodyguard of Captain George Wakerlen's detail of 5th Cavalry MSM, traveling east from Lexington, had an unusual encounter near Waverly, northeast Lafayette County. The general and cavalrymen misinterpreted an uproar and shooting they encountered while passing the John B. Webb plantation as guerrilla action and galloped into the barnyard. In reality, Missouri State Senator William O. Maupin and his son and other locals were fighting with fugitive slaves who were raiding the place. Acting on the wrong assumption, General Loan's bodyguard torched the buildings and a large quantity of hemp and arrested Senator Maupin and the others before they realized that the legislator's party was a posse attempting to protect property. The record gives little about what happened to the fugitive slaves.[48]

Surprisingly, twelve guerrillas claiming to be Quantrill men raided Monticello, Johnson County, Kansas, on November 13. This was probably Cole Younger, leading others of those who remained when the main band had ridden south a few days before. The little band robbed one store and took two horses, so this action seemed to be merely a nuisance raid. Perhaps the light Union pursuit after the Shawneetown raid a few days before emboldened these bushwhackers to try again. Quantrill's "stay-behinders" would remind the Union forces of their presence again and again in this manner throughout the coming winter.[49]

Perhaps the Monticello raid had something to do with a Kansas jayhawker raid into Jackson and west Lafayette counties in late November, a raid that had a novel ending. Beginning November 25 Union troops of 1st and 5th Cavalry MSM responded to frantic pleas and complaints about Kansas troops sacking farmsteads and isolated hamlets. The aroused cavalrymen were able to confront the Kansas raiders the afternoon of November 27. The culprits were Colonel Charles W. Adams and over 200 soldiers of his 12th Kansas Infantry, who invaded Missouri to avenge their comrades killed or captured during the fall Quantrill raids. The Missouri troops sternly escorted the Kansas infantrymen back to the border, although this did not end the depredations. Evidently, some of the Missouri cavalrymen picked up where the jayhawkers left off, shot one citizen who ran when they approached, and hung another farmer from his own barn rafters. Meanwhile, the Kansas and Missouri military and civil leaders had several sharp exchanges about Colonel Adam's little Missouri invasion.[50]

About this time the *Leavenworth Bulletin* newspaper also published an article asserting that Union officers were involved in a large-scale horse-theft ring in west-central Missouri, probably with the base at Leavenworth, Kansas. There were several similar such assertions throughout the war, so it seems that some Kansas military leaders wished to continue their early war habit of jayhawking raids into Missouri, probably more out of the motive of personal greed than restoration of the Union.[51]

Quantrill men Coleman Younger and Harrison Trow, in their postwar memoirs, describe a bevy of small actions they fought against Jackson County area Federals during this time, but Union military records and local newspapers do not corroborate their claims. Their accounts indicate that Quantrill subleader George Todd returned from the South about this time and that he and Younger amiably split the remaining guerrillas into their separate teams for renewed operations. Younger's and Trow's narratives of these small-scale actions against both Kansas and Missouri troops invariably tell of northern casualties with hardly any southern ones. In defense of these bushwhacker memoirs, it is possible that some of these events took place as described and that the embarrassed local Yankee leaders were reluctant to commit it to their records.[52]

Early December Actions

During the evening of December 3, a squad of local 25th Enrolled Missouri Militia near the "Hackle" neighborhood in southeast Buchanan County, arrested in his own home Confederate recruiter Colonel James R. Gibson. Colonel Gibson came quickly out of a special hiding place built into the floor when the militiamen loudly threatened to burn the house if he did not show himself and surrender. Gibson's camp of southern recruits had been attacked and dispersed on August 10, and Union authorities also charged the colonel with setting fire to the railroad bridge near Stewartsville, Southwest DeKalb County, probably during 1861. It is doubtful that James Gibson had remained in hiding in and near his home all those four months since the August attack, but it is possible.[53]

Evidence of a horse-theft ring led by Yankee officers continued to appear in early December. Captain James D. Eads of 1st Cavalry MSM on December 4 accused several Johnson County EMM officers of being ringleaders of the gang, which Captain Eads alleged sold stolen horses at small military garrisons in west-central Missouri.[54]

Just a few miles to the west, the men Quantrill had left behind, along with others who returned from Arkansas, engaged small Union details and patrols in combat almost daily between December 3 and 18, according to guerrilla Harrison Trow's memoirs. By this time another returnee, Albert Cunningham, was leading part of the guerrillas while the others were organized under Coleman Younger and George Todd.[55] Indeed, Union military records of 5th Kansas Cavalry state that a portion of that regiment skirmished with unidentified foes December 6 at Parkersville, northwest Bates County, but give no other details. Confederate recruiter, Captain Bill Marchbanks, was known to operate in Bates and Vernon counties at that time, so possibly he was the 5th Kansas Cavalry's antagonist.[56]

In the Rose Hill neighborhood of southwest Johnson County, guerrillas, probably of the aforementioned groups, on December 9 kidnapped and later murdered Daniel Ramey, possibly because of his kinsman, Captain William K. Ramey, of the local Enrolled Missouri Militia.[57] Unrelated to this but nearby two days later, a patrol of 6th Cavalry MSM in north Henry County captured a war-weary Confederate Colonel A. W. Jones and his black servant. Jones, former a attorney in Independence, seems to have given up on the southern cause and was on his way home when the patrol apprehended him.[58]

Possibly Colonel Jones and his servant had traveled north from Arkansas with accomplished Confederate recruiter Colonel Sidney Drake Jackman and his recruiting command, known to have traveled north toward Saline and Howard counties sometime in mid–December. Colonel Jackman's party dropped small groups of recruiters off along their route north as they approached the home neighborhoods of the men. A patrol of 6th Cavalry MSM sent to northwest Johnson County looking for some of these recruiters captured four of them there on December 23, along with 22 mules. The following day they captured two more.[59]

Even with the departure of most guerrillas of this region to warmer climates for the winter, continued warfare involving the remaining bushwhackers, southern recruiters, and others gave indications that at of the close of 1862 the war was far from over, at least in northwest Missouri.

Afterword

Much of Missouri was devastated by the end of the year 1862. The destruction was not so much physical damage wrought by the few large-scale battles fought on its soil in 1861. There was visible damage in the form of burned and abandoned homesteads and untended cropland in the countryside, as well as town damage from guerrilla raids and from public buildings being converted to stables or barracks for occupying Union soldiers. Notably absent to the discerning eye were signs of a bustling economy, growth, and the hope for a bright business future in the form of new construction and industry. Actually, residents had not lost all hope for progress and growth, but it would seem that the universal agreement among businessmen was to forego expansion a until the cruel war ended.

These were tangible signs that Missouri was part of a nation at war with itself, but the intangible forms of destruction formed a malaise that cast a sense of foreboding across much of the population. Even though Missouri was still counted as a Union state and garrisoned by thousands of northern soldiers, by the end of 1862 all but the simpleminded knew fully that its population was mixed in sentiment and loyalty. Tens of thousands of its residents were away serving in uniform in both armies, and the absence of so many able-bodied men was felt in every community. The larger towns were swollen with war refugees who had fled their rural homes because of violence or threats of violence. Noticeable, too, was the absence of thousands of former residents who had fled the state by the end of 1862 to avoid the violence or military service. Their former homes and farms lay empty and fallow, for the most part, and newcomers to take their place would not readily come until hostilities eased in Missouri.

But there were plenty of signs, across all parts of Missouri, that the end of 1862 did not mark the end of guerrilla warfare and hostilities.

The southeast quarter of Missouri witnessed some of the Confederacy's most successful recruiting in the state throughout 1862, even though Union expeditions limited their success from time to time. Part of this success was due to the frequent presence of Rebel troops in nearby northeast Arkansas. The heavily wooded and hilly nature of much of this part of the state also helped to hide Rebel activities from Union countermeasures. Colonel William O. Coleman's regiment of southern irregulars and others in south-central Missouri repeatedly threatened the Union supply line between Rolla and Springfield and became adept at evading Yankee patrols there. Sam Hildebrand of the St. Francis hills, south of the St. Louis area, began his private war against the Yankees in summer 1862 and would continue past the war's end, with frequent raids into his home region from an Arkansas base. Other guerrilla bands had varied success surviving in southeast Missouri, but a number of them would return in 1863. In fact, all the above southern forces continued beyond 1862, but the Confederacy would never recruit such numbers in this region again.

The large southern population in northeast Missouri produced plenty of southern recruits for daring Confederates like colonels John C. Porter and James A. Poindexter, and their roaming commands were serious threats to Union control of that region during summer and fall of 1862. A number of the guerrilla bands of this region even cast their lot with the larger recruiting commands, providing fewer but more prominent targets for the Yankee military. The intense warfare that resulted seemed to cool southern ardor for recruiting here for the rest of the war, but guerrilla activity would return in the spring of 1863 and continue throughout of the war.

The southwest part of Missouri produced a variety of active southern recruiting commands and bushwhacker bands, particularly during the spring of 1862. However, a combination of large prairie regions that made concealment difficult and Union military determination to control this region eventually squelched much of the southern irregular presence here. However, the southern cause in this region was helped by the presence in nearby northwest Arkansas of Confederate regular military commands, some of whom on occasion surprised Union garrison forces in southwest Missouri. Most guerrilla bands found operating here difficult for anything but short periods, with the exception of former lead miner Colonel Thomas R. Livingston of the Newton County area, who would make his presence felt here for the last time in 1863. The most threatening aspect of guerrilla warfare in southwest Missouri for the Yankee military was the Rebel tendency, which became stronger in 1862, to use this region as a natural avenue to funnel recruiters and guerrillas to and from northwest and northeast Missouri.

The most persistent southern threat to the Union hold on Missouri was in the northwest quarter of the state. Jayhawker punitive raids from Kansas continued here throughout 1861 and into 1862 and fostered fierce anti-northern feeling along the border. Confederate recruiters that dared to ride this far into Union-occupied territory found plenty of recruits that responded to their call. William C. Quantrill, a young opportunist from Ohio and Kansas, gathered southern men to himself and slowly perfected guerrilla tactics that somehow defied continued but inconsistent Union countermeasures in this region. Each clumsy Yankee failure to defeat Quantrill's band in the field only garnered more acclaim to the band, and Quantrill's influence and skills grew at the same time that most other area bushwhacker bands slowly faded from the scene. Along the Kansas-Missouri border in 1863 and for the rest of the war, Quantrill's band would return, with horrible results for northern interests. Publicity about him would encourage other Missouri southern guerrilla bands, which would threaten Union control of the state in the coming year and beyond.

Although Confederate recruiting throughout Yankee-occupied Missouri would never again approach the extent and numbers of 1862, the southern regular military would, in 1863 and beyond push regular cavalry raids into the state to both threaten the Yankee military and encourage southern interests. Meanwhile, southern guerrillas would return in 1863, with perfected tactics and skills to operate far behind enemy lines. The coming year would be another violent one in Missouri.

Notes

ONE

1. *The War of the Rebellion: A Compilation of the Official Record of the Union and Confederate Armies.* Washington, D.C.: Government Printing Office, 1880–1901 vol. 5, 45–6, 507–8 (Hereinafter cited as "*O.R.*" The series' designation is omitted in most references in this work, since they are from series 1, except where stated from series 2). Ewing Cockrell, *History of Johnson County, Missouri.* Topeka: Historical Publishing Company, 1918, 565.

2. "Col. Nugent to Raise Troops in Bates, Jackson, & Cass Counties," *Paris Mercury*, Paris, Monroe County, Missouri, 3 January 1862; *1860 Census of Austin Township*, southern Cass County, Missouri.

3. National Historical Publishing Company, *History of Henry and St. Clair Counties, Missouri.* St. Joseph, Missouri: National Historical Publishing Company, 1883, 503.

4. National Historical Company, *History of Lafayette County, Missouri.* St. Louis: National Historical Company, 1881, 335; "Yesterday by J. L. Ferguson," *Daily Star-Journal,* Warrensburg, Johnson County, 3 September 1976; "The Latest News," *Daily Missouri Democrat*, St. Louis, 6 January 1862.

5. Frank Moore, editor, *The Rebellion Record: A Diary of American Events*, New York: Arno Press, 1977, reprint of 1881–1868 original, vol. 3, 431–2. (This work is cited hereinafter as "Moore, *Rebellion Record.*")

6. Lizzie E. Brannock letter, 13 January 1864, Western Historical Manuscripts Collection, University of Missouri Library, Columbia, Missouri, call number 224, folder 1; Kansas City Historical Company, *The History of Johnson County, Missouri*, Kansas City: Kansas City Historical Company, 1881, 671–2; "Yesterday by J. L. Ferguson," *Daily Star-Journal*, Warrensburg, Johnson County, 28 June 1939; *O.R.*, vol. 8, 46–7; 448–9.

7. Margaret Mendenhall Frazier, editor, *Missouri Ordeal, 1862–1864: Diaries of Willard Hall Mendenhall*, Newhall, California: published by Carl Boyer, III, 1985, 15–19. (Hereinafter cited as "Frazier, *Missouri Ordeal.*")

8. "Gen. Hunter's Last Order," *Daily Missouri Republican*, St. Louis, 4 February 1862.

9. *O.R.*, vol. 8, 829.

10. *O.R.*, vol. 8, 54–6.

11. Joanne Chiles Eakin, *Missouri Prisoners of War From Gratiot Street Prison, St. Louis, Missouri, and Alton Prison, Alton, Illinois, Including Citizens, Confederates, Bushwhackers, and Guerrillas.* Independence, Missouri: published by author, 1995, Barnett, Winsor, and Wood entries. (Hereinafter cited as "Eakin, *Missouri Prisoners of War.*"); *O.R.*, series 2, vol. 1, 168.

12. Richard C. Peterson, James E. McGhee, Kip A. Lindberg, and Keith I. Daleen, *Sterling Price's Lieutenants: A Guide to the Officers and Organization of the Missouri State Guard, 1861–1865.* Shawnee Mission, Kansas: Two Trails Publishing, 1995, 210. (Hereinafter cited as "Peterson, *et al.*, *Price's Lieutenants.*"); George S. Grover, "Civil War in Missouri," *Missouri Historical Review*, vol. 8 (October 1913), 24; George S. Grover, "Major Emory S. Foster," *Missouri Historical Review*, vol. 14 (April-June 1920), 426. (The resourceful Colonel Lewis was exchanged before August 1862, when he returned to this region and resumed active operations for the southern cause in Missouri.)

13. "Refugees, Etc.," *Daily Missouri Democrat*, St. Louis, 23 January 1862.

14. *Ibid.*

15. *Ibid.*

16. *Ibid.*

17. *Ibid.*

18. "From California, Mo," *Daily Missouri Democrat*, St. Louis, 31 January 1862.

19. "Capture of Powder," *Missouri Statesman*, Columbia, Boone County, 31 January 1862.

20. Donald R. Hale, *We Rode With Quantrill*, Clinton, Missouri: The Printery, 1974, 157.

21. Joanne Chiles Eakin and Donald R. Hale, *Branded As Rebels: A List of Bushwhackers, Guerrillas, Partisan Rangers, Confederates, and Southern Sympathizers from Missouri During the War Years*, Independence, Missouri: Wee Print, 1993, 198–9. (Hereinafter cited as "Eakin and Hale, *Branded as Rebels.*")

22. Albert Castel, *William Clarke Quantrill: His Life and Times*, New York: Frederick Fell, Inc., 1962, 67. (Hereinafter cited as "Castel, *Quantrill.*")

23. O. S. Barton, compiler for John McCorkle, *Three Years With Quantrill; A True Story, Told by His Scout John McCorkle*, Armstrong, Missouri: Armstrong Herald Print, 1914, 25–8. (Hereinafter cited as "Barton, *Three Years With Quantrill.*");

Hale, *We Rode With Quantrill*, 155–6; Castel, *Quantrill*, 22–45; William E. Connelley, *Quantrill and the Border Wars*, Cedar Rapids, Iowa: The Torch Press, 1910, 74, 83, 118, 140–180. (Postwar guerrilla memoirs such as McCorkle's and those Hale cited are indispensable to this subject, but as a group they tend to highlight atrocities by northerners while omitting the worst of those committed by southerners. At the time many of these were written, there seemed to be a deliberate effort to glorify the southern lost cause. Connelley, on the other hand, deliberately attacked Missouri guerrillas in the harshest terms, in the same manner as Union officer reports in "*O.R.*" These sources paint southern partisans as brigands, outlaws, and murderers. Castel's 1962 work is one of the first which sought a middle ground—drawing from both types of sources in order to present a balanced, accurate history.)

24. Castel, *Quantrill*, 67, 69; Connelley, *Quantrill and the Border Wars*, 222; Eakin and Hale, *Branded as Rebels*, 152; Hale, *We Rode With Quantrill*, 145–6.

25. Union Historical Publishing Company, *History of Jackson County, Missouri*, Kansas City: Union Historical Publishing Company, 1881, 277; United Daughters of the Confederacy, Missouri Division, *Reminiscences of the Women of Missouri During the Sixties*, Jefferson City, Missouri: Hugh Stephens Printing Company, 1913, 186–7. (Hereinafter cited as "United Daughters of the Confederacy, *Reminiscences*".)

26. *O.R.*, vol. 8, 57; Hale, *We Rode With Quantrill*, 146–7; Castel, *Quantrill*, 67, 69–70; Richard S. Brownlee, *Gray Ghosts of the Confederacy, Guerrilla Warfare in the West 1861–1865*, Baton Rouge: Louisiana State University Press, 1958, 59. (Hereinafter cited as "Brownlee, *Gray Ghosts*." This relatively modern work, by the onetime director of the State Historical Society of Missouri, like Castel's, is a balanced, accurate history that sifted a variety of biased older works.)

27. *O.R.*, vol. 8, 2.

28. "From the Pacific Railroad," *Daily Missouri Democrat*, St. Louis, 13 August 1861; Moore, *The Rebellion Record*, vol. 3, 32–3; Daniel O'Flaherty, *General Jo Shelby: Undefeated Rebel*, Chapel Hill, North Carolina: University of North Carolina Press, 1954, 88–9; Eakin and Hale, *Branded As Rebels*, 390–1; *O.R.*, vol. 8, 424, 429, 438.

29. "Steamer Sunshine," *Daily Missouri Republican*, St. Louis, 19 November 1861; George A. McKee, "Boyhood Impressions of the Lexington, Missouri Area, 1858–1863," *Missouri Historical Review*, vol. 52 (October 1957), 18.

30. Frazier, *Missouri Ordeal*, 19, 23.

31. O'Flaherty, *General Jo Shelby: Undefeated Rebel*, p. 96.

32. Frazier, *Missouri Ordeal*, 24–5.

33. State of Missouri, *Adjutant General's Report of Missouri State Militia For the Year 1865*, Jefferson City: Emory S. Foster, Public Printer, 1866, 122.

34. Coleman Younger, *The Story of Cole Younger by Himself*, Chicago: The Hennebury Company, 1903, p. 17. (The Civil War portion of this famous outlaw's memoir seems mostly true, compared to corroborating accounts of the events he describes.); John P. Burch, *Charles W. Quantrell, A True History of His Guerrilla Warfare on the Missouri and Kansas Border During the Civil War of 1861 to 1865*, Vega, Texas: published by the author, 1923, 37–8. (This work is actually the postwar memoir of Harrison Trow of Quantrill's band, as told to Mr. Burch. Some of the escapades are verified from other accounts, while others are fanciful. Hereinafter cited as Burch, *Quantrell*.)

35. The Ohio Valley Company, *Official Roster of the Soldiers of the State of Ohio in the War of the Rebellion, 1861–1866*, Cincinnati: The Ohio Valley Company, 1889, vol. 11, 108; Brownlee, *Gray Ghosts*, 63; Moore, *The Rebellion Record*, vol. 4, 187–8; Younger, *The Story of Cole Younger By Himself*, 17; Connelley, *Quantrill and the Border Wars*, 223–4; Burch, *Quantrell*, 37; Castel, *Quantrill*, 70.

Two

1. Margaret Louis Fitzgibbons, "Missouri Railroads During the Civil War and Reconstruction," *Missouri Historical Review*, vol. 35 (January 1941), 193; *O.R.*, vol. 8, 463–4; Brownlee, *Gray Ghosts*, 25.

2. Western Historical Company, *History of Boone County, Missouri*, St. Louis: Western Historical Company, 1882, 412–7; National Historical Company, *History of St. Charles, Montgomery, and Warren Counties, Missouri*, St. Louis: National Historical Company, 1885, 35–6; *O.R.*, vol. 8, 43–4, and Series 2, vol. 1, 257; Moore, *The Rebellion Record*, vol. 3, 514–7.

3. Broadfoot Publishing Company, *The Supplement to the Official Records-Series 2- Record of Events-Itineraries of Military Units*, Wilmington, North Carolina: Broadfoot Publishing Company, 1995–1998, vol. 34, 1996, 683, 711–2. (Hereinafter cited as "*Supplement to the O.R.*")

4. Frederick H. Dyer, *A Compendium of the War of the Rebellion*, New York: Thomas Yoseloff, 1959, vol. 2, 800. (Hereinafter cited as "Dyer, *Compendium*.")

5. Goodspeed Publishing Company, *History of Lewis, Clark, Knox, and Scotland Counties, Missouri*, Marceline, Missouri: Goodspeed Publishing Company, 1887, 88–9; *O.R.*, vol. 8, 49–51; "The Battle of Silver Creek," *Daily Missouri Democrat*, St. Louis, 13 January 1862; "From Merrill's Horse," *Daily Missouri Democrat*, St. Louis, 17 January 1862; "More About the Silver Creek Fight," *Daily Missouri Democrat*, St. Louis, 22 January 1862; Moore, *The Rebellion Record*, vol. 4, 25–7; Dr. Charles H. Lothrop, *A History of the First Regiment Iowa Cavalry Veteran Volunteers*, Lyons, Iowa: Beers and Eaton Printers, 1890, 48–55.

6. *O.R.*, series 2, vol. 1, 253–4.

7. *O.R.*, vol. 8, 52; "Battle of Silver Creek," *Missouri Statesman*, Columbia, Boone County, 17 January 1862.

8. R. I. Holcombe, *History of Marion County, Missouri*, St. Louis: E. F. Perkins and Company, 1884, 438.

9. "Rebel Camp Routed in Shelby County," *Missouri Statesman*, Columbia, Boone County, 17 January 1862.
10. Eakin, *Missouri Prisoners of War*, Snedicor entry; "Scouting in Missouri," *Daily Missouri Democrat*, St. Louis, 23 January 1862.
11. Leslie Anders, *The Twenty-First Missouri: From Home Guard to Union Regiment*, Westport, Connecticut: Greenwood Press, 1975, 47.
12. "Secesh Outrages," *Missouri Statesman*, Columbia, Boone County, 31 January 1862.
13. "A Rebel Outrage in Ralls County," *Missouri Statesman*, Columbia, Boone County, 31 January 1862.
14. "From Fulton, Mo," *Daily Missouri Democrat*, St. Louis, 3 February 1862.
15. "Regulations," *Daily Missouri Democrat*, St. Louis, 24 January 1862.
16. *Supplement to the O.R.*, Series 2, vol. 35, 385; Eakin, *Missouri Prisoners of War*, Shacklett entry.
17. North Todd Gentry, manuscript of speech given in 1931, Collection Number 49, Joint Collection, University of Missouri Western Historical Manuscript Collection, Columbia and State Historical Society of Missouri Manuscripts; *O.R.*, series 2, vol. 1, 262.
18. *O.R.*, series 1, vol. 8, 116, 552.
19. Goodspeed Publishing Company, *History of Adair, Sullivan, Putnam, and Schuyler Counties, Missouri*, Chicago: Goodspeed Publishing Company, 1882, 704–5.
20. Private James McCahon of 11th Iowa Infantry Regiment, letter of 14 February 1862, Western Historical Manuscripts Collection, University of Missouri Library, Columbia, Missouri, no call number, one folder labeled "Civil War Documents, 1862–1864."

THREE

1. Betty F. Powell, *History of Mississippi County, Missouri-Beginning Through 1972*, published 1975 by author, 239–40; *O.R.*, vol. 8, 47–8.
2. "Southern Portrait of Jeff Thompson," *Missouri Statesman*, Columbia, Boone County, 24 January 1862.
3. "From Southeast Missouri," *Daily Missouri Democrat*, St. Louis, 14 January 1862.
4. *O.R.*, vol., 52–4.
5. *Supplement to the O.R.*, part 2, vol. 15, 197, 199; *Supplement to the O.R.*, part 2, vol. 19, 250.
6. October 9, 1913, letter in Harvey Wallis Salmon papers, Collection of Missouri Historical Society, St. Louis.
7. Eakin and Hale, *Branded As Rebels*, 294.
8. "From Rolla," *Daily Missouri Democrat*, St. Louis, 24 January 1862.
9. "From Franklin County," *Daily Missouri Republican*, St. Louis, 11 February 1862.
10. "From Rolla," *Daily Missouri Republican*, St. Louis, 1 February 1862.
11. W. H. H. Barker, "My Memories of the Civil War," unpublished manuscript, written Harvey, Indiana, 1926, 31, printed by Camp Pope Bookshop, Iowa City, Iowa; *Supplement to the O.R.*, part 2, vol. 19, 249.

12. *Supplement to the O.R.*, part 2, vol. 35, 225.
13. *O.R.*, vol. 8, 65–7; Goodspeed Publishing Company, *History of Laclede, Camden, Dallas, Webster, Texas, Pulaski, Phelps, and Dent Counties, Missouri*, Chicago: Goodspeed Publishing Company, 1889, 454.
14. *O.R.*, vol. 8, 568–9; *O.R.*, series 2, vol. 1, 267–8.
15. *O.R.*, vol. 8, 72–3; *Supplement to the O.R.*, part 2, vol. 15, 194. (The 1st Indiana Cavalry meekly recorded in their own records that they were "...engaged in action with the enemy..." this date and omitted the embarrassing details.)

FOUR

1. J. B. Johnson, editor, *History of Vernon County, Missouri*, Chicago: C. F. Cooper and Company, 1911, 307–8.
2. *Ibid.*, 282; Carolyn M. Bartels, *The Forgotten Men: Missouri State Guard*, Shawnee Mission, Kansas: Two Trails Publishing Company, 1995, 229–30.
3. J. B. Johnson, *History of Vernon County, Missouri*, 282.
4. *Ibid.*, 306; *History of Vernon County, Missouri*, St. Louis: Brown and Company, 1887, 334.
5. J. B. Johnson, *History of Vernon County, Missouri*, 304; Wiley Britton, *The Civil War on the Border*, New York: G. P. Putnam's Sons, vol. 1, 1891, 185–6; W. S. Burke, *Official Military History of Kansas Regiments (During the War for the Suppression of the Great Rebellion)*, Leavenworth, Kansas: published by author, 1870; reprinted Ottawa, Kansas: Kansas Heritage Press, 1994, 120.
6. "From Jefferson City," *Daily Missouri Democrat*, St. Louis, 20 February 1862; *Supplement to the O.R.*, part 2, vol. 19, 61.
7. "From Rolla," *Daily Missouri Democrat*, St. Louis, 24 January 1862; Peterson, *et al*, *Price's Lieutenants*, 172.
8. *O.R.*, vol. 8, 56–7, 524.
9. *Ibid.*, 58–9.
10. *Ibid.*; Goodspeed Publishing Company, *History of Laclede, Camden, Dallas, Webster, Wright, Texas, Pulaski, Phelps, and Dent Counties, Missouri*, 219–20.
11. *O.R.*, vol. 8, 59.
12. Ward L. Schrantz, *Jasper County, Missouri, in the Civil War*, Carthage, Missouri: The Carthage Press, 1923, 61–3.
13. J. A. Sturges, *Illustrated History of McDonald County, Missouri*, Pineville, Missouri: publisher not identified, 1897, 182, 186–8.
14. *O.R.*, vol. 8, 64–5.
15. *Ibid.*, 74–6; Goodspeed Publishing Company, *History of Newton, Lawrence, Barry, and McDonald Counties, Missouri*, Chicago: Goodspeed Publishing Company, 1888, 638; Senator Emory Melton, "Civil War Days in Barry County," *White River Valley Historical Quarterly*, vol. 5, no. 1, 10.
16. Goodspeed Publishing Company, *History of Newton, Lawrence, Barry, and McDonald Counties, Missouri*, 476–8; Lottie Sedwick Hurley, *His-*

tory of Mt.Vernon and Lawrence County, Missouri, 1831-1931, Mt. Vernon, Missouri: publisher not identified, 1931, chapter 7.
  17. *O.R.*, vol. 8, 75.
  18. Eakin and Hale, *Branded as Rebels*, 298.
  19. Kathleen White Miles, *Bitter Ground. The Civil War in Missouri's Golden Valley*, Clinton, Missouri: The Printery, 1971, 166; Eakin, *Missouri Prisoners of War*, Cross, Dorsey, Price entries; *Supplement to the O.R.*, part 2, vol. 19, 9, 765, 780; and vol. 36, 38.
  20. *Supplement to the O.R.*, part 2, vol. 35, 518, 527, 534, 540.
  21. *Supplement to the O.R.*, part 2, vol. 19, 9, 17, 772, 765.
  22. J. B. Johnson, *History of Vernon County, Missouri*, 281, 296-8; Britton, *The Civil War on the Border*, vol. 1, 183-4; Vernon County Historical Society, *Bushwhacker Musings*, vol. 28, no. 2 (April 1996), 7.

Five

1. *O.R.*, vol. 13, 386-7.
2. *Ibid.*, 457.
3. *O.R.*, vol. 3, 433-4.
4. *O.R.*, vol. 41, part 2, 75-7.
5. Burch, *Quantrell*, 26-7.
6. *O.R.*, vol. 8, 448-9.
7. *Ibid.*, 695-7, 814.
8. *O.R.*, vol. 41, part 2, 704.
9. *O.R.*, vol. 13, 726-8.
10. *Ibid.*, 835.
11. *O.R.*, vol. 41, part 4, 562-3.
12. "From California, Mo.," *Daily Missouri Democrat*, St. Louis, 31 January 1862.
13. *O.R.*, vol. 41, part 1, 307-17.
14. *O.R.*, vol. 22, part 2, 428-9.
15. Burch, *Quantrell*, 26-7.
16. *O.R.*, vol. 53, 907.
17. Daniel Geary, "War Incidents at Kansas City," *Collections of the Kansas State Historical Society*, vol. 11 (1909-1910), 282-91.
18. *Liberty Tribune*, Clay County, 21 June, 1901.
19. Bartels, *The Forgotten Men*, 133.
20. Goodspeed Publishing Company, *History of Newton, Lawrence, Barry, and McDonald Counties, Missouri*, 478.

Six

1. *O.R.*, vol. 8, 611-12.
2. *O.R.*, vol. 13, 200-1.
3. *O.R.*, vol. 41, part 2, 86-9.
4. *Ibid.*, 53.
5. *O.R.*, vol. 22, part 1, 11; vol. 41, part 3, 276.
6. *O.R.*, vol. 3, 13; vol. 48, part 1, 835-6.
7. Hale, *We Rode With Quantrill*, 107.
8. *Ibid.*, 80.
9. Burch, *Quantrell*, 40.
10. *O.R.*, vol. 34, part 4, 221.
11. John Henry Frick, "Recollections of the Civil War," *Missouri Historical Review*, vol. 19 (July 1925), 639.
12. *O.R.*, vol. 8, 424, 429, 438.
13. *O.R.*, vol. 13, 80-2.
14. *Ibid.*, 177-80; Moore, *Rebellion Record*, vol. 5, 563-4; "Skirmishing in Texas County," *Daily Missouri Democrat*, St. Louis, 31 July 1862.
15. Vivian Kirkpatrick McLarty, editor, "The Civil War Letters of Colonel Bazel F. Lazear," *Missouri Historical Review*, vol. 44 (April 1950), 264; *Supplement to the O.R.*, part 2, vol. 8, 131.
16. *O.R.*, vol. 8, 673. (A columbiad was a large siege mortar of that period.)
17. *Ibid.*, 334, 464, 673; vol. 13, 140, 201.
18. "Missouri Items," *Daily Missouri Democrat*, St. Louis, 15 September, 1863.
19. Hamp B. Watts, *The Babe of the Company*, Fayette, Missouri: the Democrat-Leader Press, 1913, 8; Hale, *We Rode With Quantrill*, 148; Brownlee, *Gray Ghosts*, 317-8.
20. "The Robber Bands," *Lexington Weekly Union*, Lafayette County, 7 February, 1863.
21. *O.R.*, vol. 34, part 2, 761.
22. *Ibid.*, 181-2.
23. *O.R.*, vol. 41, part 3, 330.
24. Gregg, "A Little Dab of History Without Embellishment," manuscript written in 1906, Western Historical Manuscripts Collection, University of Missouri Library, Columbia, Missouri, collection number 113, 10.
25. *O.R.*, vol. 22, part 2, 78-82.
26. *O.R.*, vol. 13, 361; vol. 48, part 1, 477, 1117.

Seven

1. *O.R.*, vol. 13, 8.
2. *O.R.*, vol. 8, 378.
3. *O.R.*, vol. 8, 611-12; "General Order," *Daily Journal of Commerce*, Kansas City, 21 March 1862; Brownlee, *Gray Ghosts*, 64.
4. Brownlee, *Gray Ghosts*, 77; "Guerrilla Warfare Recognized by the Rebel War Department," *Daily Missouri Democrat*, St. Louis, 31 July 1862.
5. *O.R.*, vol. 13, 402-3; Brownlee, *Gray Ghosts*, 81.
6. *O.R.*, vol. 8, 641-2.
7. *O.R.*, vol. 8, 663.
8. *O.R.*, vol. 13, 8; Mark M. Boatner III, *The Civil War Dictionary*, New York: David McKay Company, Incorporated, 1988, 726.
9. *O.R.*, vol. 13, 386-9.

Eight

1. Goodspeed Publishing Company, *History of Adair, Sullivan, Putnam, and Schuyler Counties, Missouri*, 708; *Supplement to the O.R.*, part 2, vol. 35, 330-1.
2. Goodspeed Publishing Company, *History of Lewis, Clark, Knox, and Scotland Counties, Missouri*, 686-8; Scotland County Bicentennial Committee and Historical Society, *Scotland County, Missouri: In Retrospect*, Memphis, Missouri: published by the society, 1977, 134; *Supplement to the O.R.* part 2, vol. 35, 702.
3. Goodspeed Publishing Company, *History of Lewis, Clark, Knox, and Scotland Counties, Missouri*, 689-691; Holcombe, *History of Marion County*, 443-4.
4. Peterson et al, *Price's Lieutenants*, 103;

Internet interviews April and May 2002 with Terry Henderson, descendant of Francis Henderson; "From Warren County," *Daily Missouri Democrat*, St. Louis, 31 March 1862.

5. Daughters of Union Veterans of the Civil War, *Missouri: Our Civil War Heritage, 1861–1865*, St. Louis: published by the Julia Dent Grant, Tent #16, 1994, 347; *O.R.*, vol. 8, 330–1, 335, 600; "From Warren County," *Daily Missouri Democrat*, 31 March 1862.

6. Holcombe, *History of Marion County*, 440–1.

7. *Ibid.*, 442–3.

8. "From North Missouri," *Daily Missouri Republican*, St. Louis, 31 March 1862.

9. "Secesh Firing From the Bushes," *Missouri Statesman*, Columbia, Boone County, 21 March 1862.

10. "From Warren County," *Daily Missouri Democrat*, St. Louis, 31 March 1862; National Historical Company, *History of St. Charles, Montgomery, and Warren Counties*, 993; Daughters of Union Veterans of the Civil War, 347.

11. *O.R.*, series 2, vol. 1, 175–6; Leslie Anders, "The Blackwater Incident," *Missouri Historical Review*, vol. 88, no. 4 (July 1994), 418–9; 1860 Census for Brunswick Township, Chariton County, Missouri.

12. "Bushwhackers," *Missouri Statesman*, Columbia, Boone County, 18 April 1862.

13. Eakin, *Missouri Prisoners of War*, entries on Captain Hicks and Lt. Colonel Thoroughman; *Supplement to the O.R.*, part 2, vol. 34, 576; "Sturgeon," *Missouri Statesman*, Columbia, Boone County, 18 April 1862.

14. "Jayhawkers," *Daily Missouri Republican*, St. Louis, 28 April 1862.

15. "More Bushwhacking," *Missouri Statesman*, Columbia, Boone County, 9 May 1862.

16. "Guerrillas in Callaway and Montgomery," *Daily Missouri Democrat*, St. Louis, 9 May 1862; "Sad Affair," *Missouri Telegraph*, Fulton, Callaway County, 9 May 1862.

17. Gentry, Todd, North Collection, file 49, "Some Incidents of the Civil War in Boone County," paper, 8; "Battle of Stonesport," *Missouri Statesman*, Columbia, Boone County, 30 May 1862; Mrs. Ann Hickham, "Civil War Reminiscences," *Daily Tribune*, Columbia, Boone County, 6 May 1914; Eakin, *Missouri Prisoners of War*, entries for D. B. Cunningham and Enoch K. Miller; 1860 Census for Cedar Township, Boone County, Missouri.

18. "Skirmish in Audrain County," *Missouri Telegraph*, Fulton, Callaway County, 14 March 1862; Eakin, *Missouri Prisoners of War*, entries for Daugherty and Murray; Bartels, *The Forgotten Men*, 84.

19. Daughters of Union Veterans, 8.

20. *O.R.*, series 1, vol. 8, 627.

21. "Scouting Party," *Daily Missouri Republican*, St. Louis, 4 April 1862.

22. "Col. Lipscomb Attacked By Guerrillas," *Daily Missouri Republican*, St. Louis, 5 April 1862; Goodspeed Publishing Company, *History of Lewis, Clark, Knox, and Scotland Counties, Missouri*, 89, 689; Holcombe, *History of Marion County*, 442–3.

23. National Historical Company, *History of Carroll County, Missouri*, St. Louis, National Historical Company, 1881, 317–8.

24. Western Historical Company, *History of Boone County*, 420; National Historical Company, *History of Monroe and Shelby Counties, Missouri*, St. Louis: National Historical Company, 1884, 236.

25. "Bushwhacking and Murder Near Mexico, Missouri," *Daily Missouri Democrat*, St. Louis, 22 May 1862.

26. Dyer, *Compendium*, vol. 2, 802.

27. Eakin, *Missouri Prisoners of War*, Whaley entry.

28. "Bushwhacking in Monroe County," *Missouri Telegraph*, Fulton, Callaway County, 6 June 1862.

NINE

1. *Supplement to the O.R.*, part 2, vol. 35, 221.

2. *Supplement to the O.R.*, part 2, vol. 9, 463.; Rose Fulton Cramer, *Wayne County, Missouri*, Cape Girardeau, Missouri: The Ramfire Press, 1972, 150; Dyer, *Compendium*, vol. 2, 804.

3. *O.R.*, vol. 8, 361.

4. *O.R.* vol. 8, 333; Eakin, *Missouri Prisoners of War*, Spilman entry.

5. *O.R.*, vol. 8, 345–6; "From Southwest Missouri," *Daily Missouri Democrat*, St. Louis, 7 April 1862; Clyde Lee Jenkins, *Judge Jenkins' History of Miller County*, Tuscumbia, Missouri: published by author, 1971, 412–3.

6. "From Southwest Missouri," *Daily Missouri Democrat*, St. Louis, 7 April 1862; Eakin, *Missouri Prisoners of War*, Bondurant, Brickery, and West entries.

7. Eakin, *Missouri Prisoners of War*, Carry, Gaines, and Singleton entries.

8. Carl W. Breihan, *Sam Hildebrand, Guerrilla*, Wauwatosa, Wisconsin: Leather Stocking Books, 1984, 11; Henry C. Thompson, *Our Lead Belt Heritage*, publishing place not given, published by author, 1955, 110–1.

9. Moore, *The Rebellion Record*, vol. 3, 402–3; Edison Shrum, *The History of Scott County, Missouri Up to the Year 1880*, Sikeston, Missouri: Scott County Historical Society, 1984, 106.

10. *O.R.*, vol. 8, 347–9.

11. *O.R.*, vol. 8, 362.

12. *O.R.*, vol. 8, 364–5.

13. *O.R.*, vol. 13, 64, 65, 67–8; Robert H. Forister, *History of Stoddard County*, Bloomfield, Missouri: Stoddard County Historical Society, 1971, 20, 29; *Supplement to the O.R.*, part 2, vol. 74, 649–51; Unidentified Union soldier, two letters dated 23 May and 10 June 1862, Columbia, Missouri: Western Historical Manuscripts Collection, University of Missouri Library, Call Number 2008, folder 1.

14. *O.R.*, vol. 13, 336–9; Barker, *My Memories of the Civil War*, 34–41; *Supplement to the O.R.*, part 2, vol. 35, 186, 204, 234; Lewis A. W. Simpson, *Oregon County's Three Flags Via the Horse and*

Buggy, Thayer, Missouri: *The Thayer News*, 1971; "Lieut. Colonel Woods Expedition," *Daily Missouri Democrat*, St. Louis, 25 March 1862.

15. "Civil War Fortress Discovered in Deer Run," *Reynolds County Courier*, 8 May 1997; "Rebel Officers Captured," *Daily Journal of Commerce*, Kansas City, 20 April 1862.

16. Dyer, *Compendium*, vol. 2, 802.

17. *O.R.*, vol. 13, 384–5. (The 1860 census of Oregon County lists several Highfills.)

18. *O.R.*, vol. 13, 391.

19. *O.R.*, vol. 13, 394; "Federal Train Captured," *Daily Journal of Commerce*, Kansas City, 23 May 1862.

20. "Civil War Fortress Discovered in Deer Run," *Reynolds County Courier*, 8 May 1997.

21. *O.R.*, vol. 13, 96.

22. "Prisoners in Rolla," *The Rolla Express*, Phelps County, 31 May 1862.

23. "More Train Burning," *The Rolla Express*, Phelps County, 31 May 1862; *O.R.*, vol. 13, 82, 401.

24. Dyer, *Compendium*, vol. 2, 802.

25. *O.R.*, vol. 13, 96.

TEN

1. *O.R.*, vol. 8, 594.

2. *O.R.*, vol. 8, 187–9; Bessie Janet (Woods) Selleck, *Early Settlers of Douglas County, Missouri*, Berkeley, California: The Professional Press, 1952, 50.

3. Selleck, *Early Settlers of Douglas County*, 50; Goodspeed Publishing Company, *History of Laclede, Camden, Dallas, Webster, Wright, Texas, Pulaski, Phelps, and Dent Counties, Missouri*, 391.

4. *Supplement to the O.R.*, part 2, vol. 35, 774.

5. *O.R.*, vol. 8, 345–6.

6. *O.R.*, vol. 8, 355–6; "From Southwest Missouri," *Daily Missouri Democrat*, St. Louis, 7 April 1862; Clayton Abbott, *Historical Sketches of Cedar County, Missouri*, Stockton, Missouri: published by author, 1968, 93.

7. *O.R.*, series 2, vol. 3, 425; Abbott, *Historical Sketches of Cedar County*, 112–7.

8. *O.R.* series 1, vol. 8, 365–7; vol. 13, 53–7; *History of Vernon County, Missouri*, St. Louis: Brown and Company, 1887, 299, 305; Lothrop, *History of the First Regiment Iowa Cavalry*, 63–7.

9. *Supplement to the O.R.*, part 2, vol. 21, 292; Dyer, *Compendium*, vol. 2, 801.

10. *History of Vernon County, Missouri*, 1887, 336.

11. "Missouri Correspondence," *Daily Missouri Democrat*, St. Louis, 24 June 1862.

12. Dyer, *Compendium*, vol. 2, 802; *Official Roster of the Soldiers of the State of Ohio in the War of the Rebellion, 1861–1866*, Cincinnati: The Ohio Valley Company, 1889, vol. 11, 95; Norton, *Behind Enemy Lines*, 44–6.

13. Pioneer Historical Company, *History of Dade County and Her People*, Greenfield, Missouri: The Pioneer Historical Company, 1917, 113–4.

14. *O.R.*, vol. 8, 343–4; Schrantz, *Jasper County, Missouri in the Civil War*, 64–7.

15. Dyer, *Compendium*, vol. 2, 801.

16. *O.R.*, vol. 8, 363; Goodspeed Publishing Company, *History of Newton, Lawrence, Barry, and McDonald Counties, Missouri*, 309.

17. Dyer, *Compendium*, vol. 2, 801.

18. *Supplement to the O.R.*, part 2, vol. 35, 783.

19. Moore, *The Rebellion Record*, vol. 4, 527.

20. Sturges, *Illustrated History of McDonald County, Missouri*, 177–8.

21. *O.R.*, vol. 13, 61–3; Moore, *The Rebellion Record*, vol. 4, 527–8; Goodspeed Publishing Company, *History of Newton, Lawrence, Barry, and McDonald Counties, Missouri*, 309–310.

22. Dyer, *Compendium*, vol. 2, 801.

23. "The War Trail in Missouri," *Daily Journal of Commerce*, Kansas City, 29 May 1862.

24. *O.R.*, vol. 13, 379–380; Goodspeed Publishing Company, *History of Newton, Lawrence, Barry, and McDonald Counties, Missouri*, 310, 640.

25. Western Historical Company, *History of Greene County, Missouri*, St. Louis: Western Historical Company, 1883, 417.

26. *O.R.*, vol. 13, 89–95, 412; Goodspeed Publishing Company, *History of Newton, Lawrence, Barry, and McDonald Counties, Missouri*, 311–12; John K. Hulston and James W. Goodrich, "John Trousdale Coffee, Lawyer, Politician, Confederate," *Missouri Historical Review*, vol. 77, no. 3 (April 1983), 272–295; Richard L. Norton, editor, *Behind Enemy Lines: The Memoirs and Writings of Brigadier General Sidney Drake Jackman*, Springfield, Missouri: Oak Hills Publishing, 1997, 55–7.

27. *O.R.*, vol. 8, 582, 604.

28. *O.R.*, vol. 8, 600; Norton, *Behind Enemy Lines*, 39–40; Brown and Company, *History of Vernon County, Missouri*, 334; Lothrop, *A History of the First Regiment Iowa Cavalry Veteran Volunteers*, 56.

29. *O.R.*, vol. 8, 341–4, 358, 637, 673, 679; vol. 13, 60–1, 63–4; Dyer, *Compendium*, vol. 2, 801–2; Kathleen White Miles, *Bitter Ground: The Civil War in Missouri's Golden Valley*, Clinton, Missouri: The Printery, 1971, 113, 162–3.

30. *O.R.*, series 2, vol. 1, 279–80.

31. *O.R.*, vol. 8, 274–7, 277–8, 365–7; Goodspeed Publishing Company, *History of Cole, Moniteau, Morgan, Benton, Miller, Maries, and Osage Counties, Missouri*, Chicago: The Goodspeed Publishing Company, 1889, 419, 420.

32. *O.R.*, vol. 8, 365–7.

33. *Ibid*.

34. *The History of Pettis County, Missouri*, 414–5.

35. *O.R.*, vol. 8, 365–7.

36. *Supplement to the O.R.*, part 2, vol. 35, 519, 554.

37. Dyer, *Compendium*, vol. 2, 801.

38. *Supplement to the O.R.*, part 2, vol. 35, 519, 554.

39. Dyer, *Compendium*, vol. 2, 801.

40. Miles, *Bitter Ground*, 113; Dyer, *Compendium*, vol. 2, 802.

41. "Desperate Encounter With The Bushwhackers," *Daily Missouri Democrat*, St. Louis, 22 May 1862.

42. S.L. Tathwell, *The Old Settlers History of Bates County, Missouri*, Amsterdam, Missouri: Tathwell and Maxey, 1897, 40, 100, 201–5.
43. Dyer, *Compendium*, vol. 2, 802.
44. *Ibid.*

Eleven

1. Dyer, *Compendium*, vol. 2, 801; National Historical Company, *History of Caldwell and Livingston Counties, Missouri*, St. Louis: National Historical Company, 1886, 776.
2. *O.R.*, vol. 13, 388–9, 392–3.
3. "The Late Bushwhacking Murder at Cameron," *Missouri Statesman*, Columbia, Boone County, 30 May 1862.
4. *O.R.*, vol. 13, 80; National Historical Company, *History of Caldwell and Livingston Counties*, 784–6; 1860 census of Spring Hill Township, Livingston County, Missouri.
5. "From Howard County," *Daily Missouri Republican*, St. Louis, 21 March 1862.
6. *O.R.*, vol. 8, 331; "From Howard County," *Daily Missouri Republican*, St. Louis, 21 March 1862; "Items of News From the Interior," *Liberty Tribune*, Liberty, Clay County, 4 April 1862; Dyer, *Compendium*, vol. 2 , 801; Missouri Historical Company, *History of Saline County, Missouri*, St. Louis: Missouri Historical Company, 1881, 285–6.
7. *Supplement to the O.R.*, part 2, vol. 19, 18, 40; vol. 35, 435.
8. Missouri Historical Company, *History of Saline County*, 319, 320.
9. Dyer, *Compendium*, vol. 2, 801; Vol. 3, 1325.
10. *O.R.*, vol. 8, 349–50, 637–8.
11. *O.R.*, vol. 8, 356.
12. *O.R.*, vol. 8, 351.
13. James E. Ford, *A History of Moniteau County, Missouri*, California, Missouri: Marvin H. Crawford, 1936, 46.
14. *O.R.*, series 2, vol. 3, 550.
15. Missouri Historical Company, *History of Saline County*, 320.
16. *O.R.*, series 1, vol. 13, 410; "Powder Hid Under A Pulpit," *Daily Missouri Democrat*, St. Louis, 13 June 1862.
17. *Supplement to the O.R.*, part 2, vol. 35, 426.
18. "Battle of Stonesport," *Missouri Statesman*, Columbia, Boone County, 30 May 1862.
19. "From Sedalia," *Daily Missouri Democrat*, St. Louis, 25 March 1862; State of Missouri, *Report of the Committee of the House of Representatives of the Twenty-Second General Assembly of the State of Missouri Appointed to Investigate the Conduct and Management of the Militia*, Jefferson City, Missouri: W. A. Curry, public printer, 1864, 330. (Hereinafter cited as *Report of Committee of Twenty-Second General Assembly to Investigate Conduct of the Militia*.)
20. "From Henry County, "*Daily Missouri Republican*, St. Louis, 1 April 1862.
21. *O.R.*, vol. 8, 344–5, 357–8, 663–4; Vol. 13, 125; "Items of News From the Interior," *Liberty Tribune*, Liberty, Clay County, 4 April 1862; Kansas City Historical Company, *The History of Johnson County*, 642, 678, 689–90; Joanne Chiles Eakin, *The Little Gods: Union Provost Marshals in Missouri, 1861-1865*, vol. 2, Shawnee Mission, Kansas: Two Trails Genealogy Shop, 1996, 43–73; (Hereinafter cited as Eakin, *The Little Gods*, vol. 2).
22. *O.R.*, series 2, vol. 1, 273.
23. *O.R.*, vol. 8, 350–4; Brownlee, *Gray Ghosts*, 66-7.
24. *O.R.*, vol. 8, 356–8; "Skirmish in Johnson County," *Daily Journal of Commerce*, Kansas City, 8 April 1862; "A Smart Brush With the Rebel Banditti Near Warrensburg," *Daily Missouri Democrat*, St. Louis, 7 April 1862; Cockrell, *History of Johnson County*, 1918, 113.
25. *Supplement to the O.R.*, part 2, vol. 35, 456–7.
26. Dyer, *Compendium*, vol. 2, 801.
27. *O.R.*, vol. 13, 58–9.
28. *O.R.*, vol. 8, 335–6; Connelley, *Quantrill and the Border Wars*, 224–8; Brownlee, *Gray Ghosts*, 63; Castel, *Quantrill*, 70–2; "The Rebel Guerrillas Invading Kansas," *Daily Missouri Republican*, St. Louis, 5 April 1862; Albert Castel, "Kansas Jayhawking Raids into Western Missouri in 1861," *Missouri Historical Review*, vol. 54, no. 1 (October 1959), 11; *Supplement to the O.R.*, part 2, vol. 21, 567.
29. *Supplement to the O.R.*, part 2, vol. 34, 636.
30. *O.R.*, vol. 8, 334–5; "From Lafayette County," *Daily Missouri Republican*, St. Louis, 16 March 1862; Frazier, *Missouri Ordeal*, 335–6; 1860 Census of Lafayette County, Missouri, Washington Township, William Greer family. (The identity of the rebel fighters in this action has never been established.)
31. *O.R.*, vol. 8, 614; Burke, *Official Military History of Kansas Regiments*, 122; Burch, *Quantrell*, 41; Connelley, *Quantrill and the Border Wars*, 228–9.
32. *O.R.*, series 2, vol. 1, 271; "Plea For Clemency To Col. Parker," *Daily Journal of Commerce*, Kansas City, 8 April 1862; "Skirmish in Johnson County, " *Daily Journal of Commerce*, Kansas City, 17 April 1862.
33. *O.R.* , series 1, vol. 8, 611–12; Castel, *Quantrill*, 73; Connelley, *Quantrill and the Border Wars*, 237; Brownlee, *Gray Ghosts*, 64.
34. *O.R.*, series 2, vol. 1, 271–3; Brownlee, *Gray Ghosts*, 64; Castel, *Quantrill*, 72–3; Paxton, *Annals of Platte County, Missouri*, 324–5; Edwards, *Noted Guerrillas*, 185; National Historical Company, *History of Clay and Platte Counties*, 223–4; Eakin and Hale, *Branded As Rebels*, 98. (Some of the above sources erroneously credit Quantrill for leading the Liberty raid, but those sources closer to the scene and the event—Paxton's and the *History of Clay and Platte Counties*—clearly name Parker, with Kit Chiles as his second-in-command. Moreover, this was a decisive, satisfying raid for the raiders, and yet Quantrill members mention nothing about it in their detailed memoirs.)
35. *O.R.*.. vol. 8, 346–7; Brownlee, *Gray Ghosts*, 64–8; Barton, *Three Years With Quantrill*, 38–41; Younger, *The Story of Cole Younger By Himself*,

18–20; Castel, *Quantrill*, 73–7; Burch, *Quantrell*, 41–50; Hale, *We Rode With Quantrill*, 129; Gregg, "A Little Dab of History," manuscript, 11–12; "From the Border," *Daily Missouri Democrat*, St. Louis, 28 March 1862; "Execution at Fort Leavenworth of Hoy, One of Quantrill's Guerrillas," *Daily Journal of Commerce*, Kansas City, 31 July 1862; Moore, *The Rebellion Record*, vol. 4, 355–6.

36. [No headline], *Daily Journal of Commerce*, Kansas City, 29 March 1862.

37. *Supplement to the O.R.*, part 2, vol. 34, 438, 637.

38. *O.R.*, vol. 8, 356–8; "A Plea For Clemency to Col. Parker," *Daily Journal of Commerce*, Kansas City, 17 April 1862; "A Plea For Clemency to Col. Parker," *Daily Missouri Democrat*, St. Louis, 12 April 1862; Cockrell, *History of Johnson County*, 1918, 113; Younger, *The Story of Cole Younger By Himself*, 32–4.

39. *O.R.*, vol. 8, 358–9; Brownlee, *Gray Ghosts*, 67–8; Gregg, "A Little Dab of History," manuscript, 52–82; Burch, *Quantrell*, 51–5; Connelley, *Quantrill and the Border Wars*, 248–50.

40. *O.R.*, vol. 13, 57–8; Gregg, "A Little Dab of History," manuscript, 1–2; Castel, *Quantrill*, 79; "A Part of Quantrel's Band Taken," *Daily Journal of Commerce*, Kansas City, 17 April 1862; "From Jackson County," *Daily Missouri Republican*, St. Louis, 24 April 1862.

41. Burch, *Quantrell*, 40.

42. Gregg, "A Little Dab of History," manuscript, 3–2.

43. "The Meeting At Independence," *Daily Journal of Commerce*, Kansas City, 20 April 1862; Brownlee, *Gray Ghosts*, 68.

44. *O.R.*, series 2, vol. 3, 468; Brownlee, *Gray Ghosts*, 68–9.

45. Eakin, *Missouri Prisoners of War*, Cussman & Hart entries; United Daughters of the Confederacy, *Reminiscences*, 202–3.

46. Frazier, *Missouri Ordeal*, 43.

47. *Ibid.*

48. "Three More of Parker's Band Gone Up," *Daily Missouri Democrat*, St. Louis, 21 May 1862.

49. Dyer, *Compendium*, vol. 2, 802; Gregg, "A Little Dab of History," manuscript, 4–2, 4–3.

50. Frazier, *Missouri Ordeal*, 45.

51. *O.R.*, series 1, vol. 13, 66–7.

52. *Ibid.*

53. *Ibid*; Burch, *Quantrell*, 59–61; "Bushwhackers Caught," *Daily Journal of Commerce*, Kansas City, 20 May 1862.

54. Burch, *Quantrell*, 69–72; Gregg, "A Little Dab of History," manuscript, 8–2, 9–2; Younger, *The Story of Cole Younger By Himself*, 22–3; Castel, *Quantrill*, 80; *General History of Macon County, Missouri*, Chicago: Henry Taylor and Company, 1910, 184–5.

55. "Quantrel Unhoused," *Daily Journal of Commerce*, Kansas City, 4 June 1862.

56. Frazier, *Missouri Ordeal*, 450.

57. *O.R.*, vol. 13, 80–2; Edwards, *Noted Guerrillas*, 211; Missouri Historical Company, *History of Saline County*, 289.

Twelve

1. *O.R.*, vol. 13, 506, 518, 534; Castel, *Quantrill*, 87–8; Brownlee, *Gray Ghosts*, 83–4; Frazier, *Missouri Ordeal*, 59; James L. McDonough, "And All for Nothing; Early Experiences of John M. Schofield in Missouri," *Missouri Historical Review*, vol. 64, no. 3 (April 1970), 315; James A. Hamilton, "The Enrolled Missouri Militia: Its Creation and Controversial History," *Missouri Historical Review*, vol. 69, no. 4 (July 1975), 416–9.

Thirteen

1. *O.R.*, vol. 13, 102; Norton, *Behind Enemy Lines*, 48; "News From Fort Scott," *Daily Journal of Commerce*, Kansas City, 15 June 1862.

2. *O.R.*, vol. 13, 119; Goodspeed Publishing Company, *History of Newton, Lawrence, Barry, and McDonald Counties, Missouri*, 640.

3. Joel T. Livingston, *A History of Jasper County, Missouri*, Chicago: The Lewis Publishing Company, 1912, 56–7.

4. *O.R.*, vol. 13, 439–40.

5. *O.R*, vol. 13, 129, 447; Goodspeed Publishing Company, *History of Newton, Lawrence, Barry, and McDonald Counties, Missouri*, 757; Sturges, *Illustrated History of McDonald County, Missouri*, 184–5.

6. *O.R.*, vol. 13, 178–9; Sturges, *Illustrated History of McDonald County, Missouri*, 178–9.

7. Sturges, *Illustrated History of McDonald County, Missouri*, 174–7.

8. *O.R.*, vol. 13, 463.

9. *Supplement to the O.R.*, part 2, vol. 35, 46.

10. *O.R.*, vol. 13, 164–6.

11. *O.R.*, vol. 13, 120.

12. *O.R.*, vol. 13, 127.

13. Joanne Chiles Eakin, *Civil War Union Military Post Returns From Missouri*, Independence, Missouri: Print America, 1995, 87; Eakin, *Missouri Prisoners of War*, Goodlett entry.

14. Dyer, *Compendium*, vol. 2, 802.

15. *Supplement to the O.R.*, part 2, vol. 35, 406.

16. Peterson, *et al.*, *Price's Lieutenants*, 33.

17. "From Sedalia," *Daily Missouri Democrat*, St. Louis, 4 August 1862.

18. *Supplement to the O.R.*, part 2, vol. 35, 777.

19. *Ibid.*

20. Bartels, *The Forgotten Men*, 221; *O.R.*, vol. 13, 165–6; 1860 census of Benton Township, east-central Polk County.

21. *O.R.*, vol. 13, 165–6; Moore, *The Rebellion Record*, vol. 5, 568.

22. *O.R.*, vol. 13, 195–200.

23. *O.R.*, vol. 13,. 222–3.

24. *O.R.*, vol. 13, 234–5.

25. *O.R.*, vol. 13, 531, 537; "Coffee in Greenfield," *Missouri Statesman*, Columbia, Boone County, 15 August 1862; Britton, *Civil War on the Border*, vol. 2, 106–8.

26. Dyer, *Compendium*, vol. 2, 803.

27. *O.R.*, vol. 13, 210–211; Hulston and Goodrich, "John Trousdale Coffee," *Missouri Historical Review*, 279–81; Brown and Company,

History of Vernon County, Missouri, 305–7; Abbott, *Historical Sketches of Cedar County, Missouri*, 83.
28. *O.R.*, vol. 13, 552.
29. *O.R.*, vol. 13, 221–2; Eakin and Hale, *Branded As Rebels*, 301, 437; Brown and Company, *History of Vernon County, Missouri*,. 308–9; J.B. Johnson, *History of Vernon County, Missouri*, 292; Abbott, *Historical Sketches of Cedar County, Missouri*, 85–6.
30. *O.R.*, vol. 13, 224; Goodspeed Publishing Company, *History of Newton, Lawrence, Barry, and McDonald Counties, Missouri*, 314.
31. Eakin, *Missouri Prisoners of War*, Finney entry.
32. *O.R.*, vol. 13, 230; Hulston and Goodrich, "John Trousdale Coffee," *Missouri Historical Review*, 281–2; "Guerrillas Defeated at Stockton," *Daily Missouri Republican*, St. Louis, 14 August 1862; "From Sedalia," *Daily Missouri Democrat*, St. Louis, 14 August 1862.
33. *O.R.*, vol. 13, 200–1; Lothrop, *History of the First Regiment Iowa Cavalry*, 73–5; *Supplement to the O.R.*, part 2, vol. 19, 23–4; Britton, *Civil War on the Border*, vol. 1, 293–4; Miles, *Bitter Ground*, 163–4; "The First Iowa Cavalry," *Daily Missouri Democrat*, St. Louis, 9 August 1862; "News From the Interior," *Liberty Tribune*, Clay County, 15 August 1862.
34. *Supplement to the O.R.*, part 2, vol. 35, 407, 457.
35. Lothrop, *History of the First Regiment Iowa Cavalry*, 75; *Supplement to the O.R.*, part 2, vol. 19, 83.
36. *O.R.*, vol. 13, 586; Britton, *Civil War on the Border*, vol. 1, 340–1.
37. Bartels, *The Forgotten Men*, 253–4.
38. *O.R.*, vol. 13, 591, 593; Castel, *Quantrill*, 95.
39. *O.R.*, vol. 13, 251–3, 591; Britton, *Civil War on the Border*, vol. 1, 341–2; Goodspeed Publishing Company, *History of Newton, Lawrence, Barry, and McDonald Counties, Missouri*, 314.
40. *O.R.*, vol. 13, 257–8; Britton, *Civil War on the Border*, vol. 1, 342; Stephen B. Oates, *Confederate Cavalry West of the River*, Austin, Texas: University of Texas Press, 1961, reprinted 1992, 40–1; Schrantz, *Jasper County, Missouri, in the Civil War*, 72–4; O'Flaherty, *General Jo Shelby: Undefeated Rebel*, 117–8; Livingston, *A History of Jasper County, Missouri*, 56–7; Burke, *Official Military History of the Kansas Regiments*, 76–81; *Supplement to the O.R.*, part 2, vol. 21, 175, 293–4.

Fourteen

1. Goodspeed Publishing Company, *History of Laclede, Camden, Dallas, Webster, Texas, Pulaski, Phelps, and Dent Counties, Missouri*, 454.
2. "Trouble in Crawford County," *Daily Missouri Democrat*, St. Louis, 28 June 1862.
3. Dyer, *Compendium*, vol. 2, 802; Burke, *Official Military History of the Kansas Regiments*, 110.
4. *Supplement to the O.R.*, part 2, vol. 35, 729.
5. Dyer, *Compendium*, vol. 2, 802.
6. *O.R.*, vol. 13, 139–40.
7. *O.R.*, vol. 13, 152.
8. "Guerrillas Surprised," *The Rolla Express*, Phelps County, 26 July 1862; 1860 Census of Texas and Dent Counties, Missouri.
9. (No headline), *The Rolla Express*, Phelps County, 26 July 1862.
10. *O.R.*, vol. 13, 177–80; "Skirmishing in Texas County," *Daily Missouri Democrat*, St. Louis, 31 July 1862; Moore, *Rebellion Record*, vol. 5, 563–4.
11. "Expedition to Hartville," *The Rolla Express*, Phelps County, 9 August 1862.
12. *O.R.*, vol. 13, 459; Breihan, *Sam Hildebrand, Guerrilla*, 17–8; Thompson, *Our Lead Belt Heritage*, 111–2.
13. Thompson, *Our Lead Belt Heritage*, 112.
14. "More Guerrilla Works," *Daily Missouri Democrat*, St. Louis, 17 July 1862; Breihan, *Sam Hildebrand, Guerrilla*, 27–31.
15. *O.R.*, vol. 13, 166–171; Cramer, *Wayne County, Missouri*, 150–2.
16. State of Missouri, *Report of Missouri Adjutant General for the Year 1865*, 726 (for Essroger's correct name and unit); Thompson, *Our Lead Belt Heritage*, 112.
17. Dyer, *Compendium*, vol. 2, 802.
18. Dyer, *Compendium*, vol. 2, 802; "Fight Near Patton, Mo.," *Daily Missouri Democrat*, St. Louis, 29 July 1862.
19. *O.R.*, vol. 13, 181; "Skirmish in Bollinger County," *Daily Missouri Democrat*, St. Louis, 31 July 1862; 1860 Census of Fillmore Township, Bollinger County, Missouri.
20. *Supplement to the O.R.*, part 2, vol. 35, 735.
21. *O.R.*, vol. 13, 542–3; Breihan, *Sam Hildebrand, Guerrilla*, 33–7.
22. (No headline), *Charleston Courier*, Mississippi County, 22 August 1862.
23. *O.R.*, vol. 13, 258–9; McLarty, "The Civil War Letters of Colonel Bazel F. Lazear," *Missouri Historical Review*, 259–69; Bollinger County Bicentennial Committee, *Bollinger County: 1851-1976, A Bicentennial Commemorative*, 100; Ellinghouse, *Old Bollinger: A Collection of Articles From "The Banner Press,"* 45–7.
24. Breihan, *Sam Hildebrand, Guerrilla*, 39–41.
25. *O.R.*, vol. 13, 265; "Doings of the 24th Missouri At Greenville," *Daily Missouri Democrat*, St. Louis, 8 September 1862.
26. Dyer, *Compendium*, vol. 2, 802.
27. Dyer, *Compendium*, vol. 2, 803.
28. *Ibid.*
29. "Trouble in Cape Girardeau County," *Charleston Courier*, Mississippi County, 12 September 1862.
30. Powell, *History of Mississippi County: Beginning Through 1972*, 238.
31. "A Military Affair," *Charleston Courier*, Mississippi County, 22 August 1862; "A Fight on Hogskin," *Charleston Courier*, Mississippi County, 5 September 1862.
32. *O.R.*, vol. 13, 250–1; Forister, *History of Stoddard County*, 21.
33. "More Fighting," *Charleston Courier*, Mississippi County, 22 August 1862; "A Fight on Hogskin," *Charleston Courier*, Mississippi County, 5 September 1862.

34. "Sesech At Smith's Hollow," *The Rolla Express*, Phelps County, 9 August 1862.
35. *O.R.*, vol. 13, 205–6.
36. "Scout in Maries," *The Rolla Express*, Phelps County, 9 August 1862; "Another Fight," *Missouri Statesman*, Columbia, Boone County, 15 August 1862.
37. Dyer, *Compendium*, vol. 2, 803.
38. *O.R.*, vol. 13, 230–1.
39. *O.R.*, vol. 13, 260–1.
40. *O.R.*, vol. 13, 256–7; "Collission," *The Rolla Express*, Phelps County, 30 August 1862.
41. *O.R.*, vol. 13, 256–7; "Attempted Escape of Prisoners of War," *The Rolla Express*, Phelps County, 30 August 1862.
42. *O.R.*, vol. 13, 260–1; series 2, vol. 4, 465–6, 471–2.
43. *O.R.*, vol. 13, 264–5, 605.
44. *O.R.*, series 2, vol. 4, 473.
45. "Escape," *Missouri Statesman*, Columbia, Boone County, 6 June 1862.
46. Eakin, *Missouri Prisoners of War*, Henderson entry.
47. "Escape of Sweeney and Carlin," *Missouri Telegraph*, Fulton, Callaway County, 13 June 1862.
48. "Escaped," *Missouri Statesman*, Columbia, Boone County, 27 June 1862; Bartels, *The Forgotten Men*, 250, 358.
49. "Escape of Thirty-Five Prisoners of War at Alton—Col. Magoffin Among Them," *Daily Missouri Democrat*, St. Louis, 28 July 1862; Eakin, *Missouri Prisoners of War*, numerous entries including two Magoffins, Sweeney, Watson, Davis, McDaniel, Berryhill, Blevins, Dye, two Dyers, Grady, Hood, Jones, Mabie, Martin, Miller, Murrill, Robinson, Newcomb, Page, Peabody, Stephenson, Stores, Tipton, Woodward, and Wood; Eakin and Hale, *Branded As Rebels*, 108; McCorkle, *Three Years With Quantrill*, 107; *The History of Pettis County, Missouri*, 43.
50. *O.R.*, series 2, vol. 5, 113; Hesseltine, "Military Prisons of St. Louis, 1861–1865," *Missouri Historical Review*, 389.
51. Eakin, *Missouri Prisoners of War*, Woodward entry; Eakin and Hale, *Branded As Rebels*, 479.
52. *O.R.*, vol. 13, 232–3; 572; "Camp of Rebels in St. Louis County," *Daily Missouri Democrat*, St. Louis, 15 August 1862; "The Underground Rebels of St. Louis County," *Daily Missouri Democrat*, St. Louis, 1 September 1862; Eakin, *Missouri Prisoners of War*, numerous entries.
53. "The Underground Rebels of St. Louis County," *Daily Missouri Democrat*, St. Louis, 1 September 1862.
54. *O.R.*, vol. 13, 606.
55. Eakin, *Missouri Prisoners of War*, Hickman, McClarny, Moon, and Smith entries.

Fifteen

1. Holcombe, *History of Marion County*, 446.
2. "More Guerrilla Scouts," *Daily Missouri Democrat*, St. Louis, 30 June 1862.
3. Brownlee, *Gray Ghosts*, 82; Goodspeed Publishing Company, *History of Lewis, Clark, Knox, and Scotland Counties, Missouri*, 115.
4. "Bushwhackers at Work," *Missouri Statesman*, Columbia, Boone County, 4 July 1862.
5. *O.R.*, Vol. 13, 136, 463; "From Macon, Mo.," *Daily Missouri Democrat*, St. Louis, 9 July 1862; "Late Fight in Schuyler County," *Daily Missouri Democrat*, St. Louis, 14 July 1862; Goodspeed Publishing Company, *History of Lewis, Clark, Knox, and Scotland Counties, Missouri*, 115–6; Goodspeed Publishing Company, *History of Adair, Sullivan, Putnam, and Schuyler Counties, Missouri*, 708.
6. "From Macon, Mo.," *Daily Missouri Democrat*, St. Louis, 9 July 1862.
7. *O.R.*, vol. 13, 152–3; Goodspeed Publishing Company, *History of Lewis, Clark, Knox, and Scotland Counties, Missouri*, 116.
8. "Bushwhacking in Northeast Missouri," *Daily Missouri Democrat*, St. Louis, 11 July 1862; "From Northeast Missouri," *Daily Missouri Democrat*, St. Louis, 17 July 1862; Goodspeed Publishing Company, *History of Lewis, Clark, Knox, and Scotland Counties, Missouri*, 96.
9. "Bushwhacking in Northeast Missouri," *Daily Missouri Democrat*, St. Louis, 11 July 1862; "From Northeast Missouri," *Daily Missouri Democrat*, St. Louis, 17 July 1862; Goodspeed Publishing Company, *History of Lewis, Clark, Knox, and Scotland Counties, Missouri*, 91.
10. "From Northeast Missouri," *Daily Missouri Democrat*, St. Louis, 17 July 1862; Goodspeed Publishing Company, *History of Lewis, Clark, Knox, and Scotland Counties, Missouri*, 91.
11. Brownlee, *Gray Ghosts*, 82; "From Northeast Missouri," *Daily Missouri Democrat*, St. Louis, 19 July 1862; Goodspeed Publishing Company, *History of Lewis, Clark, Knox, and Scotland Counties, Missouri*, 117; E. M. Violette, *History of Adair County*, Kirksville, Missouri: Denslow Publishing Company, 1911, 95; Joseph A. Mudd, *With Porter in North Missouri: A Chapter in the History of the War Between the States*, Washington, D.C., The National Publishing Company, 1909, 53–75 (Hereinafter called *With Porter in North Missouri*).
12. *O.R.*, vol. 13, 163–4; Moore, *Rebellion Record*, vol. 5, 558; Mudd, *With Porter in North Missouri*, 82–112; Goodspeed Publishing Company, *History of Lewis, Clark, Knox, and Scotland Counties, Missouri*, 118, 519–21; Violette, *History of Adair County*, 95.
13. "Three Rebels Shot," *Missouri Statesman*, Columbia, Boone County, 1 August 1862; Griffin Frost, *Camp and Prison Journal*, Iowa City, Iowa: Camp Pope Bookshop, 1994 reprint of original 1867 edition, 296.
14. "Cowardly and Cold-Blooded Murder," *Missouri Telegraph*, Fulton, Callaway County, 27 June 1862.
15. (Headline not obtained), *Missouri Telegraph*, Fulton, Callaway County, 4 July 1862.
16. William D. Lay and Bob Dyer, "Civil War Incidents in Howard County," *Boone's Lick Heritage*, vol. 5, no. 4 (December 1997), item 25, entitled "August 8, 1862."
17. *Ibid.*; Frederick Way, Jr., *Way's Packet Directory, 1848–1994*, Athens, Ohio: Ohio University Press, 1994, 203.

18. *O.R.*, vol. 13, 172–3; Brownlee, *Gray Ghosts*, 83; Mudd, *With Porter in North Missouri*, 118–134; Goodspeed Publishing Company, *History of Lewis, Clark, Knox, and Scotland Counties, Missouri*, 119; Violette, *History of Adair County*, 95; National Historical Company, *History of Monroe and Shelby Counties, Missouri*, St. Louis: National Historical Company, 1884, 236.

19. Brownlee, *Gray Ghosts*, 86.

20. *O.R.*, vol. 13, 184–9; Violette, *History of Adair County*, 95; Hugh P. Williamson, "The Battle of Moore's Mill," *Missouri Historical Review*, vol. 66, no. 4 (July 1972), 539–544. Moore, *Rebellion Record*, vol. 5, 565–6; Mudd, *With Porter in North Missouri*, 159–197; Goodspeed Publishing Company, *History of Lewis, Clark, Knox, and Scotland Counties, Missouri*, Ibid, 120–1; Western Historical Company, *History of Boone County*, 422; Violette, *History of Adair County*, 95; National Historical Company, *History of Callaway County, Missouri*, St. Louis: National Historical Company, 1884, 391–3.

21. "From Paris, Monroe County," *Missouri Statesman*, Columbia, Boone County, 1 August 1862; Goodspeed Publishing Company, *History of Lewis, Clark, Knox, and Scotland, Counties, Missouri*, 121–2; National Historical Company, *History of Monroe and Shelby Counties, Missouri*, 235.

22. "Fight At Newark, Knox County, Mo.," *Missouri Telegraph*, Fulton, Callaway County, 8 August 1862; Moore, *Rebellion Record*, vol. 5, 567–8; Brownlee, *Gray Ghosts*, 87; Violette, *History of Adair County*, 96; Goodspeed Publishing Company, *History of Lewis, Clark, Knox, and Scotland Counties, Missouri*, 692–8.

23. *O.R.*, vol. 13, 533–4; Violette, *History of Adair County*, 96; Brownlee, *Gray Ghosts*, 87; Anders, *The Twenty-First Missouri*, 94; Goodspeed Publishing Company, *History of Lewis, Clark, Knox, and Scotland Counties, Missouri*, 92–5.

24. *O.R.*, vol. 13, 193–4; National Historical Company, *History of Caldwell and Livingston Counties, Missouri*, 779.

25. Anders, *The Twenty-First Missouri*, 94; Goodspeed Publishing Company, *History of Lewis, Clark, Knox, and Scotland Counties, Missouri*, 388.

26. James E. Moss, editor, "A Missouri Confederate in the Civil War, The Journal of Henry Martyn Cheavens, 1862–1863," *Missouri Historical Review*, vol. 57 (October 1962), 19–20.

27. "Card From Corporal Miles," *Missouri Telegraph*, Fulton, Callaway County, 8 August 1862.

28. *Supplement to the O.R.*, part 2, vol. 35, 420.

29. *O.R.*, vol. 13, 211–219; Brownlee, *Gray Ghosts*, 87–8; "Brilliant Exploit," *Central City and Brunswicker*, Brunswick, Chariton County, 4 September 1862; *General History of Macon County, Missouri*, 181–3; Goodspeed Publishing Company, *History of Lewis, Clark, Knox, and Scotland Counties, Missouri*, 127–132, 522–3; Goodspeed Publishing Company, *History of Adair, Sullivan, Putnam, and Schuyler Counties, Missouri*, 307.

30. *O.R.*, series 2, vol. 4, 886–7; Floyd C. Shoemaker, "The Story of the Civil War in Northwest Missouri," *Missouri Historical Review*, vol. 7, no. 3 (April 1913), 121–2; Goodspeed Publishing Company, *History of Lewis, Clark, Knox, and Scotland Counties, Missouri*, 135–7, 699–700; Violette, *History of Adair County*, 103–4.

31. *O.R.*, series 1, vol. 13, 208, 224; Violette, *History of Adair County*, 106; Goodspeed Publishing Company, *History of Lewis, Clark, Knox, and Scotland Counties, Missouri*, 132; Historical Publishing Company, *History of Daviess and Gentry Counties, Missouri*, Topeka, Kansas: Historical Publishing Company, 1922, 105–7.

32. *O.R.*, vol. 13, 208; Brownlee, *Gray Ghosts*, 88; Goodspeed Publishing Company, *History of Lewis, Clark, Knox, and Scotland Counties, Missouri*, 133; Violette, *History of Adair County*, 106.

33. *O.R.*, vol. 13, 225; Western Historical Company, *History of Boone County*, 422; National Historical Company, *History of Caldwell and Livingston Counties, Missouri*, 779.

34. Moore, *Rebellion Record*, vol. 5, 577–8; Brownlee, *Gray Ghosts*, 90; National Historical Company, *History of Carroll County, Missouri*, 322–4.

35. National Historical Company, *History of Caldwell and Livingston Counties, Missouri*, 781; National Historical Company, *History of Carroll County, Missouri*, 324.

36. S. K. Turner and S. A. Clark, *Twentieth Century History of Carroll County, Missouri*, Indianapolis: B. F. Bowen and Company, 1911, 263.

37. *O.R.*, vol. 13, 224.

38. Moss, "A Missouri Confederate in the Civil War, The Journal of Henry Martyn Cheavens, 1862–1863," 20.

39. *O.R.*, vol. 13, 559, 561; "Portrait of the Guerrilla Cobb," *Liberty Tribune*, Clay County, 29 August 1862.

40. "Excitement in Wellsville," *Daily Missouri Democrat*, St. Louis, 23 August 1862.

41. *O.R.*, vol. 13, 563; Violette, *History of Adair County*, 106; Goodspeed Publishing Company, *History of Lewis, Clark, Knox, and Scotland Counties, Missouri*, 133.

42. Moss, "A Missouri Confederate in the Civil War, the Journal of Henry Martyn Cheavens, 1862–1863," 20; Mudd, *With Porter in North Missouri*, 283–4; Western Historical Company, *History of Boone County, Missouri*, 422; "At Columbia, Mo.," *Daily Missouri Republican*, St. Louis, 14 August 1862; State of Missouri, *Adjutant General's Report of Missouri State Militia For the Year 1865*, 342; Herschel Schooley, *Centennial History of Audrain County*, Mexico, Missouri: McIntyre Publishing company, 1937, 81.

43. Goodspeed Publishing Company, *History of Lewis, Clark, Knox, and Scotland Counties, Missouri*, 137.

44. Goodspeed Publishing Company, *History of Lewis, Clark, Knox, and Scotland Counties, Missouri*, 95–6, 138.

45. *O.R.*, vol. 13, 597; Goodspeed Publishing Company, *History of Lewis, Clark, Knox, and Scotland Counties, Missouri*, 597.

46. *Supplement to the O.R.*, part 2, vol. 35, 698–9.

47. "Shot," *Central City and Brunswicker*, Brunswick, Chariton County, 4 September 1862; Henry Taylor and Company, *Compendium of History and Biography of Linn County, Missouri*, Chicago: Henry Taylor and Company, 1912, 80; National Historical Company, *History of Howard and Chariton Counties, Missouri*, St. Louis: National Historical Company, 1883, 284–5.
48. "Visit From Rebel Soldiers," *Central City and Brunswicker*, Brunswick, Chariton County, 4 September 1862.
49. *Ibid.*
50. "A Brush With Cobb's Band of Guerrillas," *Daily Missouri Democrat*, St. Louis, 21 August 1862.
51. "Pickets Fired Upon," *Missouri Statesman*, Columbia, Boone County, 22 August 1862.
52. "Headquarters, N.E.M. Division, Macon City, Mo., Aug. 19, 1862," *Central City and Brunswicker*, Brunswick, Chariton County, 4 September 1862.
53. "Visit From Rebel Soldiers," *Central City and Brunswicker*, Brunswick, Chariton County, 28 August 1862.
54. "Killed," *Missouri Statesman*, Columbia, Boone County, 29 August 1862; "Killed," *Central City and Brunswicker*, Brunswick, Chariton County, 4 September 1862.
55. "Powder Found," *Central City and Brunswicker*, Brunswick, Chariton County, 28 August 1862.
56. Dyer, *Compendium*, vol. 2, 804.
57. *O.R.*, vol. 13, 606–7; Anders, *The Twenty-First Missouri*, 94; Goodspeed Publishing Company, *History of Lewis, Clark, Knox, and Scotland Counties, Missouri*, 701–3; Scotland County Bicentennial Committee and Historical Society, *Scotland County Missouri in Retrospect*, 134.
58. Dyer, *Compendium*, vol. 2, 804.
59. *O.R.*, vol. 13, 604.
60. *O.R.*, vol. 13, 261; "A Fight At Ashley, Missouri," *Central City and Brunswicker*, Brunswick, Chariton County, 11 September 1862; Mills and Company, *The History of Pike County Missouri*, Des Moines, Iowa: Mills and Company, 1883, 274–6.
61. "Killed," *Central City and Brunswicker*, Brunswick, Chariton County, 4 September 1862; "Killed," *Missouri Statesman*, Columbia, Boone County, 5 September 1862.
62. Dyer, *Compendium*, vol. 2, 804.
63. Goodspeed Publishing Company, *History of Lewis, Clark, Knox, and Scotland Counties, Missouri*, 91–2.
64. National Historical Company, *History of Caldwell and Livingston Counties, Missouri*, 783.

Sixteen

1. *O.R.*, vol. 13, 97–100; Missouri Historical Company, *History of Saline County, Missouri*, 320.
2. *O.R.*, vol. 13, 100–1; "Death of Col. Field," and "Guerrilla Warfare," *Daily Journal of Commerce*, Kansas City, 14 June 1862; "The Death of Col. Field," and "Staying at Home With a Vengeance," *Daily Journal of Commerce*, Kansas City, 15 June 1862.
3. Dyer, *Compendium*, vol. 2, 802.
4. "More Bushwhacking," *Daily Journal of Commerce*, Kansas City, 11 June 1862.
5. *Supplement to the O.R.*, part 2, vol. 35, 386, 457.
6. "Still Another," *Daily Journal of Commerce*, Kansas City, 13 June 1862.
7. "From Johnson County, Mo," *Daily Missouri Democrat*, St. Louis, 13 June 1862.
8. "The Right and the Safe Way," *Daily Missouri Democrat*, St. Louis, 14 June 1862.
9. *O.R.*, vol. 13, 120–2; Gregg, "A Little Dab of History," manuscript, 10–2; Burch, *Quantrell*, 59–61; Brownlee, *Gray Ghosts*, 70.
10. Frazier, *Missouri Ordeal*, 51.
11. *O.R.*, vol. 13, 120–1.
12. "Another Stage Robbed," *Missouri Statesman*, Columbia, Boone County, 27 June 1862.
13. *O.R.*, vol. 13, 120–1; Eakin, *Missouri Prisoners of War*, Henry Johnson entry.
14. *O.R.*, vol. 13, 125, 436, 440; "Robberies—Murder—House Burning, & etc.," *Missouri Statesman*, Columbia, Boone County, 4 July 1862.
15. *O.R.*, vol. 13, 124–5; Edwards, *Noted Guerrillas*, 77.
16. Edwards, *Noted Guerrillas*, 77.
17. *O.R.*, vol. 13, 127–8.
18. "Murder," *Daily Journal of Commerce*, Kansas City, 14 June 1862.
19. Missouri Historical Company, *History of Carroll County, Missouri*, St. Louis: Missouri Historical Company, 1881, 319.
20. "Assassination," *Daily Journal of Commerce*, Kansas City, 2 July 1862.
21. "More Bushwhacking," *Missouri Statesman*, Columbia, Boone County, 11 July 1862.
22. "Trying to Get Out," *Daily Journal of Commerce*, Kansas City, 2 July 1862.
23. *O.R.*, vol. 13, 443; "Hays Party Routed," *Daily Journal of Commerce*, Kansas City, 24 June 1862.
24. *O.R.*, vol. 13, 131–2; Brownlee, *Gray Ghosts*, 71.
25. *O.R.*, vol. 13, 130.
26. *O.R.*, vol. 13, 131–2; "Sent to the Alton Prison," *Daily Missouri Democrat*, St. Louis, 27 July 1863; 1860 census of Carroll Township, Platte County, Missouri.
27. Hale, *We Rode With Quantrill*, 151–2.
28. *O.R.*, vol. 13, 135–6; "From Warrensburg, Mo." *Daily Journal of Commerce*, Kansas City, 4 July 1862; "From Warrensburg, Mo.," *Daily Missouri Democrat*, St. Louis, 2 July 1862.
29. *O.R.*, vol. 13, 140.
30. *Ibid.*, 154–60; *Supplement to the O.R.*, part 2, vol. 21, 290; Gregg, "A Little Dab of History," manuscript, 13; Castel, *Quantrill*, 81; Brownlee, *Gray Ghosts*, 72; Britton, *Border*, vol. 1, 288–9; Lothrop, *History of the First Regiment Iowa Cavalry*, 70.
31. *O.R.*, vol. 13, 154–60; "The Late Fight With Quantrel," *Daily Journal of Commerce*, Kansas City, 16 July 1862; Gregg, "A Little Dab of History," manuscript, 14–22; Hale, *We Rode With Quantrill*, 135; Connelley, *Quantrill and the Border Wars*, 256; Lothrop, *History of the First*

Regiment Iowa Cavalry, 70–3; Castel, *Quantrill*, 81–4; Brownlee, *Gray Ghosts*, 73–7; Britton, *Border*, vol. 1, 288–92. (Captain Miles Kehoe is not to be confused with a similar named officer who served with Custer at the Battle of Little Bighorn in 1876.)

32. "Outlaws Recaptured," *Central City and Brunswicker*, Chariton County, 24 July 1862.

33. "From the Missouri River," *Daily Missouri Democrat*, St. Louis, 22 July 1862; "Bushwhacking in Saline County," *Daily Journal of Commerce*, Kansas City, 24 July 1862.

34. "The Death of Judge Smart," *Daily Journal of Commerce*, Kansas City, 31 July 1862; Frazier, *Missouri Ordeal*, 58; Missouri Historical Company, *History of Saline County, Missouri*, 318.

35. *Supplement to the O.R.*, part 2, vol. 35, 406.

36. (No headline), *Missouri Statesman*, Columbia, Boone County, 22 August 1862; E. J. Melton, *History of Cooper County, Missouri*, 89.

37. "The Murder of Samuel Gaston," *Daily Journal of Commerce*, Kansas City, 24 July 1862; Frazier, *Missouri Ordeal*, 58.

38. "The Robber Band," *Lexington Weekly Union*, Lafayette County, 7 February 1863.

39. Frazier, *Missouri Ordeal*, 58.

40. "Chapel Hill, Mo., July 22, '62," *Daily Journal of Commerce*, Kansas City, 31 July 1862.

41. "Chapel Hill, Mo., July 22, '62," *Daily Journal of Commerce*, Kansas City, 31 July 1862; *O.R.*, vol.13, 173.

42. "Chapel Hill, Mo., July 22, '62," *Daily Journal of Commerce*, Kansas City, 31 July 1862; "From Lexington," *Daily Missouri Democrat*, St. Louis, 31 July 1862; *O.R.*, vol.13, 192.

43. Hale, *We Rode With Quantrill*, 130; Castel, *Quantrill*, 86–7.

44. "Bushwhackers in Westport," *Daily Journal of Commerce*, Kansas City, 31 July 1862; "For the Journal of Commerce," *Daily Journal of Commerce*, Kansas City, 6 August 1862.

45. 1860 Census of Sugartree, Morris, and Hurricane Townships, Carroll County, Missouri.

46. *O.R.*, vol. 13, 190–1; "The Guerrilla War in Missouri," *Daily Missouri Republican*, St. Louis, 4 August 1862; Missouri Historical Company, *History of Carroll County, Missouri*, 320–1.

47. *O.R.*, vol. 13, 190–1, 527; "Steamer *War Eagle* Fired Into," *Daily Journal of Commerce*, Kansas City, 1 August 1862; "The Guerrilla War in Missouri," *Daily Missouri Republican*, St. Louis, 4 August 1862; "Another Outrage," *Liberty Tribune*, Clay County, 1 August 1862; Frazier, *Missouri Ordeal*, 61; Frederick Way, Jr., *Way's Packet Directory, 1848-1994*, Athens, Ohio: Ohio University Press, 1994, 480.

48. *O.R.*, vol. 13, 190–1; Missouri Historical Company, *History of Carroll County, Missouri*, 320–1.

49. *O.R.*, vol. 13, 190–1; "The Guerrilla War in Missouri," *Daily Missouri Republican*, St. Louis, 4 August 1862; Missouri Historical Company, *History of Carroll County, Missouri*, 320; National Historical Company, *History of Caldwell and Livingston Counties, Missouri*, 771.

50. *O.R.*, vol. 13, 194–5; "Rebels Routed in Carroll County," *Missouri Statesman*, Columbia, Boone County, 15 August 1862; National Historical Company, *History of Caldwell and Livingston Counties, Missouri*, 777–8; Missouri Historical Company, *History of Carroll County, Missouri*, 320–1.

51. "News From the Interior," *Liberty Tribune*, Clay County, 15 August 1862; "News From the Interior," *Daily Journal of Commerce*, Kansas City, 9 August 1862; "Well Done! " *The Rolla Express*, Phelps County, 9 August 1862; Frazier, *Missouri Ordeal*, 61. (As a possible explanation why the *War Eagle* raiders were found on both sides of the Missouri River afterwards, perhaps Austin's command collaborated with that of Edwards and they later parted company.)

52. *O.R.*, vol.13, 193.

53. *O.R.*, vol.13, 192.

54. "Yesterday by J. L. Ferguson," *Daily Star-Journal*, Warrensburg, Johnson County, 18 March 1933.

55. Historical Publishing Company, *History of Cooper County, Missouri*, Topeka, Kansas: Historical Publishing Company, 1919, 205.

56. *Supplement to the O.R.*, Part 2, vol. 35, 375; vol. 38, 215; Miles, *Bitter Ground*, 111–2.

57. "From Grundy County, Mo.," *Daily Missouri Democrat*, St. Louis, 9 August 1862.

58. *O.R.*, vol. 13, 207–8; Historical Publishing Company, *History of Daviess and Gentry Counties, Missouri*, 105–7.

59. *O.R.*, vol. 13, 219–20.

60. "Expedition to the 'Hackle,'" *Daily Missouri Democrat*, St. Louis, 15 August 1862; "Important Arrest," *Daily Journal of Commerce*, Kansas City, 10 December 1862; *Report of the Missouri Adjutant General for the Year 1865*, 476.

61. National Historical Company, *History of Clay and Platte Counties, Missouri*, 703.

62. Dyer, *Compendium*, vol. 2, 804; "Fight With Guerrillas in Platte County," *Daily Missouri Democrat*, St. Louis, 28 August 1862; National Historical Company, *History of Clay and Platte Counties, Missouri*, 703–4.

63. National Historical Company, *History of Caldwell and Livingston Counties, Missouri*, 786–8.

64. *Ibid.*, 780; William Ray Denslow, *Centennial History of Grundy County, Missouri*, Trenton, Missouri: published by author, 1939, 264–5.

65. *O.R.*, vol. 13, 618–9; *Central City and Brunswicker*, Chariton County, 4 September 1862; National Historical Company, *History of Clay and Platte Counties, Missouri*, 232.

66. "Killed," *Central City and Brunswicker*, Chariton County, 4 September 1862; National Historical Company, *History of Caldwell and Livingston Counties, Missouri*, 784.

67. (No headline), *Central City and Brunswicker*, Chariton County, 4 September 1862.

68. *Ibid.*

69. *O.R.*, vol.13, 547.

70. *O.R.*, vol. 13, 225–30; Brownlee, *Gray Ghosts*, 92–7; Castel, *Quantrill*, 88–92; Burch, *Quantrell*, 77–84; Younger, *The Story of Cole Younger by Himself*, 23–5; Barton, *Three Years With Quantrill*, 29–33; Gregg, "A Little Dab of

History," manuscript, 22–3; Britton, *Border*, vol. 1, 313–325; Hale, *We Rode With Quantrill*, 129–30; Moore, *Rebellion Record*, vol. 5, 576–7; Union Historical Publishing Company, *History of Jackson County, Missouri*, 278–30.

71. "Quantrill's General Orders," *Daily Missouri Democrat*, St. Louis, 19 August 1862; Gregg, "A Little Dab of History, manuscript, 23; Barton, *Three Years With Quantrill*, 33; Younger, *The Story of Cole Younger By Himself*, 24–6; Castel, *Quantrill*, 92.

72. *O.R.*, vol. 13, 231–2.

73. *O.R.*, vol. 13, 581–2, 979; O'Flaherty, *General Jo Shelby: Undefeated Rebel*, 116; Edwards, *Shelby and His Men*, 56–69; Oates, *Confederate Cavalry West of the River*, 39–40.

74. *O.R.*, vol. 13, 235–9; Britton, *Border*, vol. 1, 326–335; Brownlee, *Gray Ghosts*, 98–100; Moore, *Rebellion Record*, vol. 5, 581–2; Castel, *Quantrill*, 93–4; Younger, *The Story of Cole Younger By Himself*, 26–30; Burch, *Quantrell*, 85–95; Gregg, "A Little Dab of History," manuscript, 24–5; Hulston and Goodrich, "John Trousdale Coffee," 282–4; Leslie Anders, "Fighting the Ghosts at Lone Jack," *Missouri Historical Review*, vol. 79, no. 3 (April 1985), 332–356; Union Historical Publishing Company, *History of Jackson County, Missouri*, 281–8. (The most authoritative accounts of this battle can be found in Dr. Anders' journal article and Britton's book, both cited above.)

75. "Affairs at Lexington," *Daily Missouri Democrat*, St. Louis, 27 August 1862.

76. "The Hemp Burning at Lexington," *Daily Missouri Democrat*, St. Louis, 21 August 1862; Frazier, *Missouri Ordeal*, 64–5.

77. "Affairs at Lexington," *Daily Missouri Democrat*, St. Louis, 27 August 1862; "The Robber Band," *Lexington Weekly Union*, Lafayette County, 7 February 1863; "Lafayette County Board Proceedings, 1862," Western Historical Manuscripts Collection, Columbia, Missouri: University of Missouri Library, call number 1145, vol. 1.

78. Britton, *Border*, vol. 1, 345–6; Brownlee, *Gray Ghosts*, 100–1.

79. *O.R.*, vol. 13, 253–6; Britton, *Border*, vol. 1, 345–6; Castel, *Quantrill*, 95.

80. "A Warrensburg Family During the Civil War," *Missouri Historical Review*, vol. 38 (July 1934), 454.

81. Gregg, "A Little Dab of History," manuscript, 26–8; Brownlee, *Gray Ghosts*, 101; Castel, *Quantrill*, 95–6; Barton, *Three Years With Quantrill*, 34–5; *Report of the Missouri Adjutant General for the Year 1865*, 524; *Supplement to the O.R.*, part 2, vol. 34, p. 639. (Dr. Ander's journal article lists Levi S. Copeland among the dead of the 2nd Battalion Cavalry MSM from the Battle of Lone Jack August 16, 1862, with the rank of Private, but Copeland's own unit records list him as associated with the Lone Jack fight as a 1st lieutenant with the notation "made prisoner by the enemy." First Lieutenant Copeland had been a member of Lt. Colonel Andrew G. Nugent's home guard of the Cass-Bates County area in the bitter border fighting there at the start of the war. Nugent's unit was mustered in during spring of 1862 as the 2nd Battalion Cavalry MSM, and its members were held in contempt by many area southerners for the unit's part in the bitter border warfare. Quantrill's men, many from the same area in which Nugent's unit operated, would be very aware of this Yankee unit's reputation and possibly knew Copeland as well. Of course, this is not to presume 1st Lieutenant Copeland's guilt in the deeds charged him by Quantrill's men.)

Seventeen

1. Dyer, *Compendium*, vol. 2, 804.

2. *O.R.*, vol. 13, 270; "Successful Skirmish," *Daily Missouri Democrat*, St. Louis, 15 September 1862.

3. Breihan, *Guerrilla*, 43–6.

4. *O.R.*, vol. 13, 673.

5. "Missouri Items," *Central City and Brunswicker*, Chariton County, 16 October 1862; Jenkins, *Judge Jenkins' History of Miller County*, 452–3; Richard Antweiler, "The Scourge of Central Missouri," *Missouri Life*, vol. 9, no. 6 (November 1981), 43–6.

6. "Secesh Mail Captured," *Missouri Statesman*, Columbia, Boone County, 26 September 1862; Eakin, *Missouri Prisoners of War*, Grimes entry.

7. "Slave Catching at Hermann," *Daily Missouri Democrat*, St. Louis, 29 November 1862.

8. Moore, *Rebellion Record*, vol. 6, 249–50; "Guerrilla Raid in Crawford County," *Daily Missouri Democrat*, St. Louis, 18 December 1862.

9. *O.R.*, vol. 13, 268; vol. 22, part 2, 1079; "From Southwest Missouri," *Daily Missouri Republican*, St. Louis, 22 September 1862; Forister, *History of Stoddard County*, 21; McLarty, "The Civil War Letters of Colonel Bazel F. Lazear," *Missouri Historical Review*, 264.

10. *Supplement to the O.R.*, part 2, vol. 37, 308.

11. *O.R.*, vol. 13, 715.

12. *O.R.*, vol. 13, 749; "Guerrillas on the River," *Daily Missouri Democrat*, St. Louis, 22 October 1862; "Cairo, Oct. 20," *Charleston Courier*, Mississippi County, 24 October 1862.

13. *O.R.*, vol. 13, 749; "Latest War News," *Charleston Courier*, Mississippi County, 24 October 1862.

14. *O.R.*, vol. 13, 338; vol. 22 Part 2, 1079; *Supplement to the O.R.*, part 2, vol. 12, 782.

15. Dyer, *Compendium*, vol. 2, 805.

16. Dyer, *Compendium*, vol. 2, 805.

17. *Supplement to the O.R.*, part 2, vol. 35, 739.

18. "From Patterson, Wayne Co., Mo.," *Daily Missouri Democrat*, St. Louis, 25 November 1862.

19. *O.R.*, vol. 22, part 1, 814–5.

20. *O.R.*, vol. 13, 265; "Doings of the 24th Missouri at Greenville," *Daily Missouri Democrat*, St. Louis, 8 September 1862; Shrum, *The History of Scott County*, 106; Jerry Ponder, *A History of the 15th Missouri Cavalry Regiment, C.S.A.*, Doniphan, Missouri: Ponder Books, 1994, 8; 1860 Census of Castor Township, Madison County, Missouri, White family.

21. *O.R.*, vol. 13, 264–5; series 2, vol. 4, 556–7.
22. *O.R.*, series 1, vol. 13, 641–2.
23. "Ironton," *Daily Missouri Democrat*, St. Louis, 1 October 1862.
24. *Supplement to the O.R.*, part 2, vol. 35, 738–9; "Civil War fortress Discovered in Deer Run," *Reynolds County Courier*, Ellington (formerly Barnesville), Reynolds County, 8 May 1997; Frederick Behlendorf, *The History of the Thirteenth Illinois Cavalry Regiment Volunteers, U.S. Army from September 1861 to September 1865*, Grand Rapids, Michigan: publisher and page number not obtained, 1888. Author's note: That the 13th Illinois Cavalry burned Barnesville, Reynolds County, is beyond dispute since Major Behlendorf wrote in the regimental history of the 13th Illinois Cavalry that his united burned the place.
25. *O.R.*, vol. 13, 321.
26. *O.R.*, vol. 13, 337–8; "From Patterson, Missouri," *Daily Missouri Democrat*, St. Louis, 5 November 1862; Gene Oakley, *The History of Carter County*, Van Buren, Missouri: J.G. Publishing Company, 1970, 22–3.
27. *O.R.*, vol. 13, 271, 340, 774; "From Patterson, Missouri," *Daily Missouri Democrat*, St. Louis, 5 November 1862; Oakley, *The History of Carter County*, 22–3; Moore, *Rebellion Record*, vol. 6, 58–60.
28. "From Patterson, Wayne Co., Mo.," *Daily Missouri Democrat*, St. Louis, 25 November 1862.
29. "From Fredericktown," *Daily Missouri Republican*, St. Louis, 5 December 1862; Breihan, *Sam Hildebrand, Guerrilla*, 50–2.
30. "Captured Guerrillas From Cape Girardeau," *Daily Missouri Democrat*, St. Louis, 16 December 1862.
31. Eakin, *Missouri Prisoners of War*, Bell, Cook, and McLaughlin entries.
32. Bartels, *The Forgotten Men*, 189; Eakin, *Missouri Prisoners of War*, Johnson entry; Schooley, *Centennial History of Audrain County*, 80.
33. *O.R.*, vol. 22, part 1, 877–8; Milan James Kedro, "The Civil War's Effect Upon an Urban Church: The St. Louis Presbytery Under Martial Law," *The Bulletin of Missouri Historical Society*, vol. 27, no. 3 (April 1871), 181–3.
34. *O.R.*, vol. 22, part 1, 163–4.
35. *O.R.*, vol. 22, part 1, 173–7, 882; John Scott, *Story of the Thirty Second Iowa Infantry Volunteers*, Nevad, Iowa: published by the author, 1896, 81 and following.
36. Eakin, *Missouri Prisoners of War*, Spelman entry.
37. "Pilot Knob," *Daily Missouri Democrat*, St. Louis, 27 December 1862.
38. *O.R.*, vol. 22, part 1, 873–4, 890; General Isaac H. Elliott, *History of the Thirty-Third Regiment Illinois Veteran Volunteer Infantry*, Gibson City, Illinois: published by regimental association, 1902, 32; *Supplement to the O.R.* part 2, vol. 10, 480; vol. 37, 324, 327, 328, 349; vol. 38, 172–3; John F. Bradbury, Jr., "'This War Is Managed Might Strange': The Army of Southeastern Missouri, 1862–1863," *Missouri Historical Review*, vol. 89, no. 1 (November 1994), 36; Mark Mayo Boatner III, *The Civil War Dictionary*, New York: David McKay Co., Inc., 1959, 223.
39. Jerry Ponder, *The Civil War in Ripley County, Missouri*, Doniphan, Missouri: The Prospect-News, 1992, 8.

Eighteen

1. Dyer, *Compendium*, vol. 2, 804.
2. *O.R.*, vol. 13, 623–4.
3. *Supplement to the O.R.*, Part 2, vol. 21, 294.
4. Dyer, *Compendium*, vol. 2, 804.
5. *O. R.*, vol. 13, 655.
6. *O.R.*, vol. 13, 272; Goodspeed Publishing Company, *History of Newton, Lawrence, Barry, and McDonald Counties, Missouri*, 474.
7. *O. R.*, vol. 13, 277; Schrantz, *Jasper County, Missouri in the Civil War*, 836; Livingston, *A History of Jasper County, Missouri*, 57.
8. "Fight At Cassville," *Daily Missouri Republican*, St. Louis, 29 September 1862; Edwin C. Bearss, "The Army of the Frontier's First Campaign; The Confederates Win At Newtonia," *Missouri Historical Review*, vol. 69 (April 1966), 284.
9. Dyer, *Compendium*, vol. 2, 804.
10. Lothrop, *History of the First Regiment Iowa Cavalry*, 80.
11. *O.R.*, vol. 13, 287–303; Schrantz, *Jasper County, Missouri in the Civil War*, 89–92; Britton, *Civil War on the Border*, vol. 1, 347–363; Bearss, "The Army of the Frontier's First Campaign," *Missouri Historical Review*, 283–319; Dyer, *Compendium*, vol. 2, 804; Goodspeed Publishing Company, *History of Newton, Lawrence, Barry, and McDonald Counties, Missouri*, 316–8.
12. Schrantz, *Jasper County, Missouri in the Civil War*, 108–9.
13. Dyer, *Compendium*, vol. 2, 804.
14. *Ibid.*; Goodspeed Publishing Company, *History of Newton, Lawrence, Barry, and McDonald Counties, Missouri*, 318–9.
15. Dyer, *Compendium*, vol. 2, 804; Goodspeed Publishing Company, *History of Newton, Lawrence, Barry, and McDonald Counties, Missouri*, 319.
16. Dyer, *Compendium*, vol. 2, 804.
17. Lothrop, *History of the First Regiment Iowa Cavalry*, 80.
18. "From Henry County, Mo.," *Daily Missouri Democrat*, St. Louis, 28 October 1862.
19. Tathwell, *The Old Settlers History of Bates County, Missouri*, 153–4.
20. Dyer, *Compendium*, vol. 2, 804.
21. "From Henry County, Mo.," *Daily Missouri Democrat*, St. Louis, 28 October 1862.
22. Dyer, *Compendium*, vol. 2, 805.
23. Goodspeed Publishing Company, *History of Newton, Lawrence, Barry, and McDonald Counties, Missouri*, 644.
24. Dyer, *Compendium*, vol. 2, 805.
25. *O.R.*, vol. 13, 323–4; Cummins, *Jim Cummins' Book*, 43–4; "Fight with Three Hundred Guerrillas Near Marshfield," *Daily Missouri Democrat*, St. Louis, 1 November 1862; Goodspeed Publishing Company, *History of Laclede,*

Camden, Dallas, Webster, Wright, Texas, Pulaski, Phelps, and Dent Counties, Missouri, 220–1.
   26. *O.R.*, vol. 53, 455–8; Moore, *The Rebellion Record*, vol. 6, 52–5; Lorenzo J. Greene, Gary R. Kremer, Anthony F. Holland, *Missouri's Black Heritage: The Sable Arm*, St. Louis: Forum Press, 1980, 67.
   27. *O.R.*, vol. 13, 348; Schrantz, *Jasper County, Missouri in the Civil War*, 101–2; Castel, *Quantrill*, 99–100; Brownlee, *Gray Ghosts*, 106; Edwards, *Noted Guerrillas*, 132; Barton, *Three Years With Quantrill*, 43–4; Burch, *Quantrell*, 103; Gregg manuscript, 41–2.
   28. *O.R.*, vol. 13, 352; Schrantz, *Jasper County, Missouri in the Civil War*, 102.
   29. *O.R.*, vol. 13, 352–3; Schrantz, *Jasper County, Missouri in the Civil War*, 102–6.
   30. *O.R.*, vol. 13, 353.
   31. Schrantz, *Jasper County, Missouri in the Civil War*, 106–8.
   32. Schrantz, *Jasper County, Missouri in the Civil War*, 101.
   33. *O.R.*, vol. 13, 353.
   34. *O.R.*, vol. 13, 354–6; *Supplement to the O.R.*, part 2, vol. 3, 780–1.
   35. Goodspeed Publishing Company, *History of Laclede, Camden, Dallas, Webster, Wright, Texas, Pulaski, Phelps, and Dent Counties, Missouri*, 394.
   36. *O.R.*, vol. 13, 356–8; "From Ozark, Mo.," *Daily Missouri Democrat*, St. Louis, 21 November 1862.
   37. Wilhelm and Augustus Seyffert, Notebook of activities of Company E, 13th Cavalry MSM, while stationed at Waynesville, Missouri, October 1862–September 1864, Columbia, Missouri: Western Historical Manuscripts Collection, University of Missouri Library, call number C2888, vol. 2.
   38. "From Linn Creek," *Daily Missouri Democrat*, St. Louis, 25 November 1862; "From Camden County," *Daily Missouri Republican*, St. Louis, 23 November 1862.
   39. *O.R.*, vol. 13, 356–8.
   40. "A Federal Supply Train Attacked," *Daily Missouri Democrat*, St. Louis, 29 November and 3 December 1862; "Train Burned," *The Rolla Express*, Phelps County, 29 November 1862; Columbus Bryan, Private, 33rd EMM, letter dated 4 December 1862, Columbia, Missouri: Western Historical Manuscripts Collection, University of Missouri Library, call number C209, folder 1; Goodspeed Publishing Company, *History of Laclede, Camden, Dallas, Webster, Wright, Texas, Pulaski, Phelps, and Dent Counties, Missouri*, 393–4.
   41. "From Fort Scott," *Daily Missouri Democrat*, St. Louis, 24 November 1862; Dyer, *Compendium*, vol. 2, 805.
   42. Dyer, *Compendium*, vol. 2, 805.
   43. *Supplement to the O.R.*, part 2, vol. 35, 408.
   44. *O.R.*, vol. 22, part 1, 37; Norton, *Behind Enemy Lines*, 143–5.
   45. *O.R.*, vol. 22, part 1, 37; Schrantz, *Jasper County, Missouri in the Civil War*, 110; "From Southwest Missouri," *Daily Missouri Republican*, St. Louis, 2 December 1862; "Affair on Horse Creek," *Daily Missouri Republican*, St. Louis, 5 December 1862.

   46. "From Springfield, Mo.," *Daily Missouri Democrat*, St. Louis, 10 December 1862; "Southwest Missouri," *Daily Journal of Commerce*, Kansas City, 14 December 1862.
   47. *Supplement to the O.R.*, part 2, vol. 35, 408.
   48. Dyer, *Compendium*, vol. 2, 804.
   49. *O.R.*, vol. 22, part 1, 159–61; Moore, *The Rebellion Record*, vol. 6, 250–1.
   50. "Prison Reports For August 1st and 2nd," *Daily Missouri Republican*, St. Louis, 4 August 1863.
   51. Miles, *Bitter Ground*, 167–8.
   52. *O.R.*, vol. 22, part 1, 837–8.
   53. "Civil War Years in Bates County," Pamphlet written for third Butler re-enactment (author not stated), Butler, Bates County, 1; National Historical Company, *The History of Cass and Bates County, Missouri*, 858; Norton, *Behind Enemy Lines*, 145.
   54. *O.R.*, vol. 22, part 1, 837.
   55. Dyer, *Compendium*, vol. 2, 805.
   56. *Supplement to the O.R.*, part 2, vol. 35, 329.
   57. *O.R.*, vol. 22, part 1, 166.
   58. *Supplement to the O.R.*, part 2, vol. 35, 776.
   59. Johnson, *History of Vernon County, Missouri*, 309; Brown and Company, *History of Vernon County, Missouri*, 336–7.
   60. *O.R.*, vol. 22, part 1, 166.

Nineteen

   1. Goodspeed Publishing Company, *History of Lewis, Clark, Knox, and Scotland Counties, Missouri*, 91–2.
   2. "Missouri Items," *Daily Missouri Republican*, St. Louis, 15 September 1862.
   3. *O.R.*, vol. 13, 266.
   4. *O.R.*, vol. 13, 265–6.
   5. *O.R.*, vol. 13, 611–12; Schooley, *Centennial History of Audrain County, Missouri*, 81.
   6. *O.R.*, vol. 266; "Capt. Baird Killed," *Missouri Statesman*, Columbia, Boone County, 12 September 1862; "Missouri Items," *Daily Missouri Republican*, St. Louis, 15 September 1862.
   7. "A Guerrilla Camp Routed," *Missouri Statesman*, Columbia, Boone County, 19 September 1862; " Killed and Wounded," *Missouri Statesman*, Columbia, Boone County, 26 September 1862.
   8. "More Rebel Robberies," *Missouri Statesman*, Columbia, Boone County, 12 September 1862; "Missouri Items," *Daily Missouri Republican*, St. Louis, 15 September 1862.
   9. *O.R.*, vol. 13, 266; Goodspeed Publishing Company, *History of Adair, Sullivan, Putnam, and Schuyler Counties, Missouri*, 710–1.
   10. *O.R.*, vol. 13, 625–6; Mudd, *With Porter in North Missouri*, 408–414; Brownlee, *Gray Ghosts*, 88; Anders, *The Twenty-First Missouri*, 94; Goodspeed Publishing Company, *History of Lewis, Clark, Knox, and Scotland Counties, Missouri*, 138–9; Violette, *History of Adair County*, 106; Henry Taylor and Company, *General History of Macon County, Missouri*, 181–3.
   11. *O.R.*, vol. 13, 269–70; Anders, *The Twenty-First Missouri*, 94; Violette, *History of Adair*

County, 106–7; "Porter Routed Again by McNeil," *Daily Missouri Democrat*, St. Louis, 22 September 1862; Goodspeed Publishing Company, *History of Lewis, Clark, Knox, and Scotland Counties, Missouri*, 139–42.

12. "Outrageous Conduct of Federal Troops," *Central City and Brunswicker*, Chariton County, 2 October 1862; National Historical Company, *History of St. Charles, Montgomery, and Warren Counties, Missouri*, 638.

13. "News From Rocheport," *Missouri Statesman*, Columbia, Boone County, 19 September 1862; "Expedition to Rocheport," *Daily Missouri Republican*, St. Louis, 22 September 1862.

14. "Prisoners Captured," *Missouri Statesman*, Columbia, Boone County, 19 September 1862; "More Robberies and Bushwhacking," *Central City and Brunswicker*, Chariton County, 2 October 1862.

15. Dyer, *Compendium*, vol. 2, 804.

16. *O.R.*, vol. 13, 270–2; "Col. Hayward and the Bushwhackers," *Daily Missouri Republican*, St. Louis, 22 September 1862; Goldena Roland Howard, *Ralls County, Missouri*, Marceline, Missouri: Walsworth Publishing Company, 1980, 107–8.

17. "Rebel Houses Burned," *Central City and Brunswicker*, Chariton County, 2 October 1862.

18. "Banished," *Central City and Brunswicker*, Chariton County, 2 October 1862.

19. (No headline), *Central City and Brunswicker*, Chariton County, 2 October 1862; Goodspeed Publishing Company, *History of Lewis, Clark, Knox, and Scotland Counties, Missouri*, 91.

20. "Outrageous Conduct of Federal Troops," *Central City and Brunswicker*, Chariton County, 2 October 1862; Moss, "A Missouri Confederate in the Civil War," *Missouri Historical Review*, 23; Western Historical Company, *History of Boone County, Missouri*, 424.

21. *O.R.*, vol. 13, 660–1; Brownlee, *Gray Ghosts*, 88; National Historical Company, *History of Randolph and Macon Counties, Missouri*, St. Louis: National Historical Company, 1884, 855–60; Mills and Company, *The History of Pike County, Missouri*, 283–4.

22. *O.R.*, series 2, vol. 4, 549–50.

23. "More Robberies and Bushwhacking," *Central City and Brunswicker*, Chariton County, 2 October 1862.

24. "Union Man Murdered," *Central City and Brunswicker*, Chariton County, 2 October 1862.

25. *O.R.*, series 2, vol. 5, 78; Missouri Division, United Daughters of the Confederacy, *Reminiscences*, 149–183.

26. Dyer, *Compendium*, vol. 2, 804.

27. *O.R.*, vol. 13, 281–2; "Another Burning Affair," *Central City and Brunswicker*, Chariton County, 23 October 1862.

28. *O.R.*, vol. 13, 681–2.

29. *O.R.*, vol. 13, 283–4.

30. *O.R.*, vol. 13, 682; "Skirmish With Guerrillas in Monroe County, " *Daily Missouri Democrat*, St. Louis, 30 September 1862; "From Hudson, Missouri," *Daily Missouri Republican*, St. Louis, 30 September 1862.

31. *Supplement to the O.R.*, part 2, vol. 35, 92.

32. National Historical Company, *History of Callaway County, Missouri*, 395; *Supplement to the O.R.*, part 2, vol. 34, 471; State of Missouri, *The Report of the Missouri Adjutant General For the Year 1865*, 522.

33. *O.R.*, vol. 13, 314.

34. Dyer, *Compendium*, vol. 2, 805.

35. *O.R.*, vol. 13, 681–2; *Supplement to the O.R.*, part 2, vol. 35, 596; Eakin, *Missouri Prisoners of War*, Singleton entry.

36. *O.R.*, vol. 13, 681–2.

37. *O.R.*, vol. 13, 689.

38. *O.R.*, vol. 13, 308.

39. *O.R.*, vol. 13, 311–2; "Gen. Guitar routs another Rebel Band," *Missouri Statesman*, Columbia, Boone County, 10 October 1862.

40. *O.R.*, vol. 13, 689.

41. *O.R.*, vol. 13, 307–8.

42. Goodspeed Publishing Company, *History of Lewis, Clark, Knox, and Scotland Counties, Missouri*, 704.

43. Dyer, *Compendium*, vol. 2, 804.

44. "From Monroe County," *Daily Missouri Republican*, St. Louis, 17 October 1862.

45. *O.R.*, series 2, vol. 4, 604, 657.

46. *O.R.*, vol. 13, 315–6.

47. *Ibid.*; Goodspeed Publishing Company, *History of Lewis, Clark, Knox, and Scotland Counties, Missouri*, 704.

48. *O.R.*, vol. 13, 754.

49. "Routing of Guerrillas in Callaway and Adair Counties," *Daily Missouri Democrat*, St. Louis, 22 October 1862; "A Guerrilla Band Defeated," *Daily Missouri Republican*, St. Louis, 22 October 1862.

50. *O.R.*, vol. 13, 908–910; "From Knox County," *Daily Missouri Democrat*, St. Louis, 1 November 1862; Goodspeed Publishing Company, *History of Adair, Sullivan, Putnam, and Schuyler Counties, Missouri*, 711–12; Scotland County Bicentennial Committee and Historical Society, *Scotland County, Missouri: In Retrospect*, 134.

51. *O.R.*, vol. 22, part 1, 816–9; Brownlee, *Gray Ghosts*, 89–90; Moore, *Rebellion Record*, vol. 6, 27–9; Holcombe, *History of Marion County, Missouri*, 489–97; Violette, *History of Adair County, Missouri*, 106.

52. *O.R.*, vol. 13, 749–50; series 2, vol. 4, 646.

53. *O.R.*, series 1, vol. 13, 781.

54. Dyer, *Compendium*, vol. 2, 805.

55. "From Lewis County," *Daily Missouri Republican*, St. Louis, 8 December 1862.

56. *O.R.*, vol. 13, 318; Moss, "A Missouri Confederate in the Civil War," *Missouri Historical Review*, 21–2; "Routing of Guerrillas in Callaway and Adair Counties," *Daily Missouri Democrat*, St. Louis, 22 October 1862; "A Guerrilla Band Defeated," *Daily Missouri Republican*, St. Louis, 22 October 1862.

57. *O.R.*, vol. 13, 319; Brownlee, *Gray Ghosts*, 88; "Good News From Lexington," *Daily Missouri Democrat*, St. Louis, 18 October 1862; "Later, " *Daily Missouri Republican*, St. Louis, 19 October 1862; Goodspeed Publishing Company,

History of Lewis, Clark, Knox, and Scotland Counties, Missouri, 147; Hiram Martin Chittenden, *History of Early Steamboat Navigation on the Missouri River: Life and Adventures of Joseph LaBarge*, vol. 2, New York: Francis P. Harper, 1903, 258–9; Frederick Way, Jr., *Way's Packet Directory 1848–1994*, Athens, Ohio: Ohio University Press, 1994, 148.

58. "Rebels Crossing the River," *Missouri Statesman*, Columbia, Boone County, 31 October 1862.

59. Moss, "A Missouri Confederate in the Civil War," *Missouri Historical Review*, 23–4.

60. *O.R.*, vol. 13, 346–7.

61. *Ibid.*; "Captures," *Daily Missouri Republican*, St. Louis, 24 November 1862; James Bradley, *The Confederate Mail Carrier*, Mexico, Missouri: published by author, 1894, 83–4.

62. "Thieves and Robbers," *Missouri Statesman*, Columbia, Boone County, 12 December 1862.

63. *O.R.*, series 2, vol. 5, 166; Eakin, *Missouri Prisoners of War*, Johnson, Loury, Payton entries; Bartels, *The Forgotten Men*, 286.

Twenty

1. *O.R.*, Vol. 13, 803; Connelley, *Quantrill and the Border Wars*, 270–3; Brownlee, *Gray Ghosts*, 101–2; Burch, *Quantrell*, 91–2; Castel, *Quantrill*, 96–7; Gregg manuscript, 29–31; Younger, *The Story of Cole Younger By Himself*, 34–5, 40; Hale, *We Rode With Quantrill*, 46–9; Hale, *They Called Him Bloody Bill*, 7.

2. Dyer, *Compendium*, Vol. 2, 804.

3. *O.R.*, vol. 13, 267–8; Connelley, *Quantrill and the Border Wars*, 273; Brownlee, *Gray Ghosts*, 101–2; Edwards, *Noted Guerrillas*, 120–1; Castel, *Quantrill*, 97; Gregg manuscript, 33.

4. Gregg manuscript, 31–2; Frazier, *Missouri Ordeal*, 72–3; Harry R. Voigt, *Concordia, Missouri: A Centennial History*, Concordia: Centennial Committee, 1960, 26; William Young, *Young's History of Lafayette County, Missouri*, Indianapolis: B. F. Brown and Company, 1910, 119–20.

5. "R. R. Spedden to B. G. Loan," 10 October 1862, H. R. Gamble Papers, St. Louis: Missouri Historical Society.

6. *Ibid.*; Kansas City Historical Company, *The History of Johnson County, Missouri*, 411; "From Warrensburg, Mo.," *Daily Journal of Commerce*, Kansas City, 4 July 1862; Fellman, *Inside War*, 118, 288; "From Warrensburg, Mo.," *Daily Missouri Democrat*, St. Louis, 2 July 1862.

7. Frazier, *Missouri Ordeal*, 76.

8. *O.R.*, vol. 13, 307.

9. "R. R. Spedden to B. G. Loan," 10 October 1862, H. R. Gamble Papers.

10. Cockrell, *History of Johnson County, Missouri*, 112; Kansas City Historical Company, *The History of Johnson County, Missouri*, 864.

11. State of Missouri, *Report of the Committee of the Twenty-Second General Assembly to Investigate the Conduct and Management of the Militia*, 342–4.

12. *O.R.*, vol. 13, 732.

13. *O.R.*, vol. 13, 744; "Good News From Lexington," *Daily Missouri Democrat*, St. Louis, 18 October 1862; Frazier, *Missouri Ordeal*, 80–1.

14. "Skirmish at Bull Run, Near Tipton, Mo.—Guerrillas Completely Routed," *Daily Missouri Democrat*, St. Louis, 8 September 1862.

15. Ford, *A History of Moniteau County, Missouri*, 45.

16. *O.R.*, vol. 13, 283–4; "Murder of Lieut. Pinkard and Others By the Bushwhackers," *Daily Missouri Democrat*, St. Louis, 4 October 1862; *Supplement to the O.R.*, part 2, vol. 35, 604–5; Dyer, *Compendium*, vol. 2, 804.

17. (No headline), *Central City and Brunswicker*, Chariton County, 23 October 1862.

18. *O.R.*, vol. 13, 316–7; Frazier, *Missouri Ordeal*, 80; Jim Cummins, *Jim Cummins' Book*, Denver: Reed Publishing Company, 1903, 42.

19. Dyer, *Compendium*, vol. 2, 805.

20. Nicholas P. Hardeman, "Bushwhacker Activity on the Missouri Border: Letters to Dr. Glen O. Hardeman," *Missouri Historical Review*, vol. 58, no. 3 (April 1964), 269–70.

21. Frazier, *Missouri Ordeal*, 82.

22. Bradley, *The Confederate Mail Carrier*, 81–4.

23. Moss, "A Missouri Confederate in the Civil War," 24; "Fight in Cooper—Capt. Purcell and His Band Routed," *Daily Missouri Democrat*, St. Louis, 24 November 1862; "Missouri Items," *Daily Missouri Republican*, St. Louis, 24 November 1862; National Historical Company, *History of Howard and Cooper Counties, Missouri*, St. Louis: National Historical Company, 1883, 769–70.

24. "Tobacco," *Daily Missouri Republican*, St. Louis, 24 November 1862.

25. National Historical Company, *History of Caldwell and Livingston Counties, Missouri*, 188–90.

26. "From North Missouri," *Daily Missouri Democrat*, St. Louis, 22 September 1862; *Supplement to the O.R.*, part 1, vol. 3, 56–7.

27. National Historical Company, *History of Clay and Platte Counties, Missouri*, 232.

28. "Two Men Shot," *Daily Missouri Republican*, St. Louis, 5 October 1862; "Two Shot," *Missouri Statesman*, Columbia, Boone County, 10 October 1862; National Historical Company, *History of Caldwell and Livingston Counties, Missouri*, 796–7; National Historical Company, *History of Daviess and Gentry Counties, Missouri*, 121. (In 1866 two local men murdered William Crews at a church function to prevent him from taking revenge for his brother's wartime death. Evidently, his killers escaped legal punishment for this act.)

29. Walter Williams, editor, *A History of Northwest Missouri*, Chicago: The Lewis Publishing Company, 1915, vol. 1, 564–5.

30. National Historical Company, *History of Caldwell and Livingston Counties, Missouri*, 784.

31. National Historical Company, *History of Clay and Platte Counties, Missouri*, 704.

32. Missouri Historical Company, *History of Carroll County, Missouri*, 326–7.

33. (Headline not obtained), *Daily Missouri Democrat*, St. Louis, 4 November 1862.
34. National Historical Company, *History of Caldwell and Livingston Counties, Missouri*, 216–7.
35. O.R., vol. 13, 312–4; Castel, *Quantrill*, 97–8; Connelley, *Quantrill and the Border Wars*, 273–4; Brownlee, *Gray Ghosts*, 102–3.
36. "From Jefferson City," *Daily Missouri Republican*, St. Louis, 19 October 1862; Frazier, *Missouri Ordeal*, 78.
37. "The Robber Band," *Lexington Weekly Union*, Lafayette County, 7 February 1863; Frazier, *Missouri Ordeal*, 78–9.
38. "From Jefferson City," *Daily Missouri Republican*, St. Louis, 19 October 1862; Frazier, *Missouri Ordeal*, 79; Voigt, *Concordia, Missouri: A Centennial History*, 22–3, 26, 28–33; Robert W. Frizzell, "Killed By Rebels: A Civil War Massacre and It's Aftermath," *Missouri Historical Review*, vol. 61, no. 4 (July 1977), 380–1.
39. "From Jefferson City," *Daily Missouri Republican*, St. Louis, 19 October 1862.
40. O.R., vol. 13, 747; "Guerrilla Raid Into Kansas," *Daily Missouri Democrat*, St. Louis, 20 October 1862; "Kansas Again Invaded!," *Daily Missouri Republican*, St. Louis, 23 October 1862; Castel, *Quantrill*, 98; Connelley, *Quantrill and the Border Wars*, 274–5; Burch, *Quantrell*, 91; Brownlee, *Gray Ghosts*, 103; Gregg manuscript, 36–7.
41. O.R., vol. 13, 339; *Supplement to the O.R.*, part 2, vol. 35, 130.
42. O.R., vol. 13, 791–2; Frazier, *Missouri Ordeal*, 88–9.
43. Frazier, *Missouri Ordeal*, 84.
44. O.R., vol. 13, 345–6, 779.
45. Castel, *Quantrill*, 99; Younger, *The Story of Cole Younger By Himself*, 32–4; Barton, *Three Years With Quantrill*, 42; Edwards, *Noted Guerrillas*, 133, 188; Gregg manuscript, 35.
46. O.R., vol. 13, 347–8; Castel, *Quantrill*, 99; Connelley, *Quantrill and the Border Wars*, 275–6; Brownlee, *Gray Ghosts*, 105; Burch, *Quantrell*, 97–8; Barton, *Three Years With Quantrill*, 42–3; Gregg manuscript, 38–40; "Catherwood After Quantrill," *Daily Missouri Democrat*, St. Louis, 11 November 1862.
47. Unidentified writer, letter dated 14 November 1862, from central Missouri, Columbia, Missouri: Western Historical Manuscripts Collection, Call Number 1835, Folder 1. (The writer identifies the neighbors who were robbed by the Rebels as Fountain Roberts and a Captain Durrett, both families living in Arrow Rock Township, southeast Saline County, according to the 1860 census.)
48. O.R., vol. 13, 791–2; Frazier, *Missouri Ordeal*, 87; State of Missouri, *Report of the Committee of the Twenty-Second General Assembly to Investigate the Conduct and Management of the Militia*, 76–7.
49. "Another Raid in Kansas," *Daily Missouri Republican*, St. Louis, 20 November 1862; Burch, *Quantrell*, 105–7; Younger, *The Story of Cole Younger By Himself*, 35.
50. O.R., vol. 13, 721–2, 796–802; vol. 22, Part 1, 39–41, 808, 821–6, 841–51; Castel, *Quantrill*, 108; Brownlee, *Gray Ghosts*, 108–9; Frazier, *Missouri Ordeal*, 90–1; Hale, *We Rode With Quantrill*, 147.
51. "Bands of Outlaws in Kansas," *The Rolla Express*, Phelps County, 29 November 1862, quoting an earlier edition of *The Leavenworth Bulletin*.
52. Burch, *Quantrell*, 105–7; Younger, *The Story of Cole Younger By Himself*, 35–6.
53. "Important Arrest," *Daily Journal of Commerce*, Kansas City, 10 December 1862.
54. State of Missouri, *Report of the Committee of the Twenty-Second General Assembly to Investigate the Conduct and Management of the Militia*, 361. (This Captain Eads is not to be confused with James B. Eads, builder of ironclads in St. Louis.)
55. Burch, *Quantrell*, 107–8.
56. Dyer, *Compendium*, vol. 2, 805; Norton, *Behind Enemy Lines*, 145.
57. Kansas City Historical Company, *The History of Johnson County, Missouri*, 581; "Another Rebel Colonel Bagged—A Rule That Works Both Ways," *Daily Missouri Democrat*, St. Louis, 18 December 1862.
58. "A Rebel Colonel Surrenders Himself," *Daily Missouri Republican*, St. Louis, 14 December 1862; "Another Rebel Colonel Bagged—A Rule That Works both Ways," *Daily Missouri Democrat*, St. Louis, 18 December 1862.
59. *Supplement to the O.R.*, part 2, vol. 35, 262.

Bibliography

This bibliography is divided into several sections: Manuscripts, Missouri Civil War Newspapers, Missouri Post–Civil War Newspapers, Periodical Articles, U.S. Government Publications, Missouri Government Publications, Military Unit Histories and Memoirs, County and Local Histories, and Books

Manuscripts

Barker, W. H. H. "My Memories of the Civil War." Unpublished manuscript written in Harvey, Indiana, 1926. Iowa City, Iowa: Camp Pope Bookshop.

"Civil War Years in Bates County." Pamphlet for third Butler re-enactment. Butler, Missouri: publisher not stated. Year of publication not given. 1–17.

Collection of Missouri Historical Society. St. Louis.
- Harvey Wallis Salmon Papers. Letter dated 9 October 1913.
- H.R. Gamble Letters. Letter dated 10 October 1862 "R. R. Spedden to B. G. Loan."

Mayes, Jack F. "The Civil War in Iron County." Pamphlet. Publisher and year not given. 1–9.

Western Historical Manuscripts Collection. University of Missouri Library. Columbia, Missouri.
- Benton, Richard Higgins. Typed copy of memoirs dated 1912. Collection number 995.
- Brannock, Lizzie E. Letter dated 13 January 1864. Collection number 224.
- Bryan, Private Columbus of 33rd EMM. Letter dated 4 December 1862. Collection number 209.
- "Elvira Ascenith Weir Scott Diary, 1860–1887." Collection number 1053, folders 3 through 7.
- Gentry, North. Todd papers. "Some Incidents of the Civil War in Boone County." Text of speech given 14 October 1931. Collection number 49.
- Gregg, William E. "A Little Dab of History Without Embellishment." Manuscript written 1906. Collection number 113.
- "Lafayette County Board Proceedings, 1862." Notebook. Collection number 1145.
- McCahon, Private James, of 11th Iowa Infantry Regiment. Letter dated 14 February 1862. Folder labeled, "Civil War Documents 1862–1864."
- Seyffert. Wilhelm, and Augustus Seyffert. Notebook of activities of Company E, 13th Cavalry MSM, while stationed at Waynesville, Missouri October 1862–September 1864. Collection number 2888.
- Unidentified Union soldier. Two letters dated 23 May and 10 June 1862. Collection number 2008.
- Unidentified writer. Letter dated 14 November 1862 from central Missouri. Collection number 1835.

Missouri Civil War Newspapers

Central City and Brunswicker. Brunswick, Chariton County, weekly, 1862.
Charleston Courier. Mississippi County, weekly, 1862.
Daily Journal of Commerce. Kansas City, 1862.
Daily Missouri Democrat. St. Louis, 1862.
Daily Missouri Republican. St. Louis, 1862.
Lexington Weekly Union. Lafayette County, 1862 and 1863.
Liberty Tribune. Clay County, weekly, 1862.
Missouri Statesman. Columbia, Boone County, weekly, 1862.
Missouri Telegraph. Fulton, Callaway County, weekly, 1862.
The Rolla Express. Phelps County, weekly, 1862.

Missouri Post–Civil War Newspapers

Columbia Daily Tribune. Boone County, 1914.
Liberty Tribune. Clay County, 1901.
Reynolds County Courier, 1997.
Warrensburg Daily Star-Journal, 1933, 1939, 1976.

Periodical Articles

Anders, Leslie. "Fighting the Ghosts at Lone Jack." *Missouri Historical Review* 79, no. 3 (April 1985): 332–356.

———. "The Blackwater Incident." *Missouri Historical Review* 88, no. 4 (July 1994): 416–429.

Antweiler, Richard. "The Scourge of Central Missouri." *Missouri Life* 9, no. 6 (November 1981): 43–46.

Bearss, Edwin C. "The Army of the Frontier's First Campaign: The Confederates Win at Newtonia." *Missouri Historical Review* 60, no. 3 (April 1966): 283–319.

Bradbury, John F., Jr. "'This War is Managed Mighty Strange:' The Army of Southeastern Missouri, 1862–1863." *Missouri Historical Review* 89, no. 1 (November 1994): 28–47.

Canan, Howard V. "Milton Burch: Anti-Guerrilla Fighter." *Missouri Historical Review* 59, no. 2 (January 1965): 223–242.

Castel, Albert. "Kansas Jayhawking Raids into Western Missouri in 1861," *Missouri Historical Review* 54, no. 1 (October 1959): 1–11.

Cheatham, Gary L. "Desperate Characters: The Development and Impact of the Confederate Guerrillas in Kansas." *Kansas History* 14, no. 3 (autumn 1991): 144–161.

———. "Divided Loyalties in Civil War Kansas." *Kansas History* 11, no. 2 (summer 1988): 93–107.

Doerschuk, Albert N. "Extracts From War-Time Letters, 1861–1864." *Missouri Historical Review* 23, no. 1 (October 1928): 99–110.

Fannin, William. "Defenders of the Border: Missouri's Union Military Organizations in the Civil War." *Pioneer Times* 6, no. 3 (July 1982): 187–206.

Fitzsimmons, Margaret Louis. "Missouri Railroads During the Civil War and Reconstruction." *Missouri Historical Review* 35, no. 2 (January 1941): 188–206.

Frick, John Henry. "Recollections of the Civil War." *Missouri Historical Review* 19, vol. 4 (July 1925): 630–654.

Frizzell, Roebert W. "'Killed By Rebels:' A Civil War Massacre and Its Aftermath." *Missouri Historical Review* 71, no. 4 (July 1977): 369–395.

Geary, Daniel. "War Incidents at Kansas City." *Collections of the Kansas State Historical Society* 11 (1909–1910): 282–291.

Grover, George S. "Civil War in Missouri." *Missouri Historical Review* 8, no. 1 (October 1913): 1–28.

———. "Major Emory S. Foster." *Missouri Historical Review* 14, no. 3 (April 1920): 425–432.

Hamilton, James A. "The Enrolled Missouri Militia: Its Creation and Controversial History." *Missouri Historical Review* 69, no. 4 (July 1975): 413–432.

"Hamilton R. Gamble." Famous Personages of the Civil War in Missouri Series. *Missouri Historical Review* 56, no. 1 (October 1961): back cover.

Hardeman, Nicholas P. "Bushwhacker Activity on the Missouri Border: Letters to Dr. Glen O. Hardeman." *Missouri Historical Review* 58, no. 3 (April 1964): 265–277.

Herklotz, Hildegarde Rose. "Jayhawkers in Missouri, 1856–1863." *Missouri Historical Review* 17, no. 3 (April 1923): 266–284; 17, no. 4 (July 1923): 505–513; 18, no. 1 (October 1923): 64–101.

Hesseltine, W. B. "Military Prisons of St. Louis, 1861–1865." *Missouri Historical Review* 23, No. 3 (April 1929): 380–399.

Hulston, John K., and James W. Goodrich. "John Trousdale Coffee: Lawyer, Politician, Confederate." *Missouri Historical Review* 77, no. 3 (April 1983): 272–295.

Kedro, Milan James. "The Civil War's Effect Upon An Urban Church: The St. Louis Presbytery Under Martial Law." *The Bulletin of Missouri Historical Society* 27, no. 3 (April 1971): 173–193.

Lay, William D., and Bob Dyer. "Civil War Incidents in Howard County." *Boone's Lick Heritage* 5, no. 4 (December 1977).

Lewis, Warner. "Civil War Reminiscences." *Missouri Historical Review* 2, no. 3 (April 1908): 221–232.

Mahnkey, Douglas. "Alf Bolin's Buried Treasure." *White River Valley Historical Quarterly* 5, no. 6: 1–4.

McDonough, James L. "And All For Nothing: Early Experiences of John M. Schofield in Missouri." *Missouri Historical Review* 64, no. 3 (April 1970): 306–321.

McKee, George A. "Boyhood Impressions of the Lexington, Missouri Area, 1858–1863." *Missouri Historical Review* 52, no. 1 (October 1957): 16–24.

McLarty, Vivian Kirkpatrick, ed. "The Civil War Letters of Colonel Bazel F. Lazear." *Missouri Historical Review* 44, no. 3 (April 1950): 254–273; 44, no. 4 (July 1950): 387–401; 45, no. 1 (October 1950): 47–63.

Melton, Senator Emory. "Civil War Days in Barry County." *White River Valley Historical Quarterly* 5, no. 1: 8–11.

Moss, James E., ed. "A Missouri Confederate in the Civil War: The Journal of Henry Martyn Cheavens, 1862–1863." *Missouri Historical Review* 57, no. 1 (October 1962): 16–52.

"Odon Guitar." Famous Personages of the Civil War in Missouri Series. *Missouri Historical Review* 58, no. 1 (October 1963): back cover.

Palmer, Henry E. "The Black-Flag Character of War on the Border." *Transactions of the Kansas State Historical Society* 9 (1905–1906): 455–466.

"Quantrill and His Famous Command." *Confederate Veteran* 18 (June 1910): 278–279.

Rotts, Karen. "Missouri's 'Little General,' Odon Guitar, Faced Political As Well As Military Adversaries In His Tumultuous Career." *America's Civil War* 10, no. 3 (July 1997): 8–16.

"Samuel Ryan Curtis." Famous Personages of the Civil War in Missouri Series. *Missouri Historical Review* 57, no. 2 (January 1963): back cover.

Swindler, William F. "The Southern Press in Missouri, 1861–1864." *Missouri Historical Review* 35, no. 3 (April 1941): 394–400.

Thompson, Dorothy Brown. "A Young Girl in the Missouri Border War," *Missouri Historical Review* 58, no. 1 (October 1963): 55–69.

Vernon County Historical Society. *Bushwhacker Musings* 28, no. 2 (April 1996): 7.

"A Warrensburg Family During the Civil War." *Missouri Historical Review* 38, no. 4 (July 1934): 452–458.

Williamson, Hugh P. "The Battle of Moore's Mill," *Missouri Historical Review* 66, no. 4 (July 1972): 539–548.

U.S. Government Publications

U.S. Bureau of the Census. *Eighth Census of the United States, 1860: Population*. Washington, D. C.: Government Printing Office, 1864.

U.S. Department of War, Adjutant General's Office. *Official Army Register of the Volunteer Force of the United States Army for the Years 1861–'65*. Washington, D. C.: Adjutant General's Office, 1861–1865.

U.S. Department of War. *The War of the Rebellion: A Compilation of the Official Records of Union and Confederate Armies*. 128 volumes. Washington, D. C.: Government Printing Office, 1880–1901.

Missouri Government Publications

State of Missouri. *Annual Report of the Adjutant General of Missouri For the Year 1863*. St. Louis: Public Printer, 1864.

State of Missouri. *Annual Report of the Adjutant General of Missouri For the Year 1864*. Jefferson City, Missouri: W. A. Curry, Public Printer, 1865.

State of Missouri. *Annual Report of the Adjutant General of Missouri For the Year 1865*. Jefferson City, Missouri: Emory S. Foster, Public Printer, 1866.

State of Missouri. *Report of the Committee of the House of Representatives of the Twenty-Second General Assembly of the State of Missouri Appointed to Investigate the Conduct And Management of the Militia*. Jefferson City, Missouri: W. A. Curry, Public Printer, 1864.

Military Unit Histories and Memoirs

Anders, Leslie. *The Twenty-First Missouri: From Home Guard to Union Regiment*. Westport, Connecticut: Greenwood Press, 1975.

Barton, O. S. *Three Years With Quantrill: A True Story told by His Scout John McCorkle*. Armstrong, Missouri: *Armstrong Herald* Print. 1914. Reprinted Norman, Oklahoma: University of Oklahoma Press, 1992.

Bradley, James. *The Confederate Mail Carrier*. Mexico, Missouri: published by author,. 1894.

Breihan, Carl W. *Sam Hildebrand, Guerrilla*. Wauwatosa, Wisconsin: Leather Stocking Books, 1984.

Broadfoot Publishing Company. *Supplement to the Official Records of the Union and Confederate Armies*. About 100 volumes. Wilmington, North Carolina: Broadfoot Publishing Company, 1994–2002.

Burch, John P. *Charles W. Quantrell, A True History of His Guerrilla Warfare on the Missouri And Kansas Border During the Civil War of 1861 to 1865*. Vega, Texas: published by author, 1923.

Burke, W. S. *Official History of Kansas Regiments (During the War for the Suppression of the Great Rebellion)*. Leavenworth, Kansas: W. S. Burke, 1870. Reprinted Ottawa, Kansas: Kansas Heritage Press, 1994.

Crute, Joseph H., Jr. *Units of the Confederate States Army*. Midlothian, Virginia: Derwent Books, 1987.

Cummins, Jim. *Jim Cummins' Book*. Denver: Reed Publishing Company, 1903. Reprinted Provo, Utah: Triton Press, 1988.

Elliott, General Isaac H. *History of the Thirty-Third Regiment Illinois Veteran Volunteer Infantry*. Gibson City, Illinois: published by regimental association, 1902.

Frazier, Margaret Mendenhall, ed. *Missouri Ordeal, 1862–1864: Diaries of Willard Hall Mendenhall*. Newhall, California: Carl Boyer, III, 1985.

Frost, Griffin. *Camp and Prison Journal*. Quincy, Illinois: *Quincy Herald* Book and Job Office,. 1867. Reprinted Iowa City, Iowa: Camp Pope Bookshop, 1994.

Hale, Donald R. *We Rode With Quantrill*. Clinton, Missouri: The Printery, 1974.

Lothrop, Dr. Charles H. *A History of the First Regiment Iowa Cavalry Veteran Volunteers*. Lyons, Iowa: Beers and Eaton, Printers, 1890.

Missouri Division, United Daughters of the Confederacy. *Reminiscences of the Women of Missouri During the Sixties*. Jefferson City, Missouri: Hugh Stephens Printing Company, 1913.

Mudd, Joseph A. *With Porter in North Missouri: A Chapter in the History of the War Between the States*. Washington, D. C.: The National Publishing Company, 1909.

Reprinted Iowa City, Iowa: Camp Pope Bookshop, 1992.
Norton, Richard L., compiler and editor. *Behind Enemy Lines: The Memoirs and Writings of Brigadier General Sidney Drake Jackman.* Springfield, Missouri: Oak Hills Publishing, 1997.
The Ohio Valley Company. *Official Roster of the Soldiers of the State of Ohio in the War of the Rebellion, 1861–1866.* 11 volumes. Cincinnati: The Ohio Valley Company, 1889.
Ozarks Genealogical Society. *Confederate Organizations, Officers and Posts, 1861–1865: Missouri Units.* Springfield, Missouri: Ozarks Genealogical Society, 1988.
Peterson, Richard C., James E. McGhee, Kip A. Lindberg, and Keith I. Daleen. *Sterling Price's Lieutenants: A Guide to the Officers and Organization of the Missouri State Guard, 1861–1865.* Shawnee Mission, Kansas: Two Trails Publishing, 1995.
Ponder, Jerry. *A History of the 15th Missouri Cavalry Regiment, C. S. A.* Doniphan, Missouri: Ponder Books, 1994.
Quaife, Milo M., ed. *Absalom Grimes, Confederate Mail Runner.* New Haven, Connecticut: Yale University Press, 1926.
Scott, John. *Story of the Thirty-Second Iowa Infantry Volunteers.* Nevada, Iowa: published by author, 1896.
Sifakis, Stewart. *Compendium of the Confederate Armies. Kentucky, Maryland, Missouri, The Confederate Units and the Indian Units.* New York: Facts on File, 1995.
Starr, Stephen Z. *Jennison's Jayhawkers: A Civil War Cavalry Regiment and Its Commander.* Baton Rouge: Louisiana State University Press, 1973.
Watts, Hamp B. *The Babe of the Company.* Fayette, Missouri: The *Democrat-Leader* Press, 1913.
Younger, Coleman. *The Story of Cole Younger by Himself.* Chicago: The Hennebury Company, 1903.

County and Local Histories

Abbott, Clayton. *Historical Sketches of Cedar County, Missouri.* Stockton, Missouri: published by author, 1968.
Abbott, Clayton and Lewis B. Hoff, *Missouri History in Cedar County.* Greenfield, Missouri: Vedette Publishing Company, 1971.
Bartels, Carolyn. *Clay County, Missouri, The Civil War Years.* Vol. 1. Shawnee Mission, Kansas: Two Trails Publishing Company, 1993.
Block, William Neil. *Shades of Gray: Confederate Soldiers and Veterans of Randolph County, Missouri.* Shawnee Mission, Kansas: Two Trails Publishing Company, 1996.
_____, and Merrill M. Brockman, *Records of Confederate Soldiers, POWS, & Southern Partisans From Howard County, Missouri During the War Between the States 1861–1865*, 1995.
Bollinger County Bicentennial Committee. *Bollinger County: 1851–1976, A Bicentennial Commemorative.* Marceline, Missouri: Walsworth Publishing Company, 1977.
Bradbury, John F. *Phelps County in the Civil War.* Rolla, Missouri: published by author, 1997.
Brown and Company. *History of Vernon County, Missouri.* St. Louis: Brown and Company, 1887.
Cedar County Historical Society. *Cedar County, Missouri: History and Families.* Paducah, Kentucky: Turner Publishing Company, 1998.
Clay County Archives and Historical Library. *Missouri Pioneers of Clay County.* Bowling Green, Missouri: Info Tech Publications, 1992.
Cockrell, Ewing. *History of Johnson County, Missouri.* Topeka: Historical Publishing Company, 1918.
Cooper, Martha. *The Civil War and Nodaway County, Missouri.* Signal Mountain, Tennessee: Mountain Press, 1989.
Cramer, Rose Fulton. *Wayne County, Missouri.* Cape Girardeau, Missouri: The Ramfire Press, 1972.
Denslow, William Ray. *Centennial History of Grundy County, Missouri.* Trenton, Missouri: published by author, 1939.
Ellinghouse, Cletis R., ed. *Old Bollinger: A Collection of Articles From "The Banner Press."* Publisher and place of publication not given. 6 volumes, 1975.
Farthing, C. M. *Chronicles of the Civil War in Monroe County.* Independence, Missouri: Two Trails Publishing Company, 1997.
Ford, James E. *A History of Moniteau County, Missouri.* California, Missouri: Marvin H. Crawford, 1936.
Forister, Robert H. *History of Stoddard County.* Bloomfield, Missouri: Stoddard County Historical Society, 1971.
Goodspeed Publishing Company. *History of Adair, Sullivan, Putnam, and Schuyler Counties, Missouri.* Chicago: The Goodspeed Publishing Company, 1902.
_____. *History of Andrew and DeKalb Counties, Missouri.* Chicago: The Goodspeed Publishing Company, 1888.
_____. *History of Cole, Moniteau, Morgan, Benton, Miller, Maries, and Osage Counties, Missouri.* Chicago: The Goodspeed Publishing Company, 1889.
_____. *History of Franklin, Jefferson, Washington, Crawford, and Gasconade Counties, Missouri.* Chicago: The Goodspeed Publishing Company, 1888.
_____. *History of Hickory, Polk, Cedar, Dade, and Barton Counties, Missouri.* Chicago: The Goodspeed Publishing Company, 1889.

———. *History of Laclede, Camden, Dallas, Webster, Wright, Texas, Pulaski, Phelps, and Dent Counties, Missouri*. Chicago: The Goodspeed Publishing Company, 1889.

———. *History of Lewis, Clark, Knox, and Scotland Counties, Missouri*. Chicago: The Goodspeed Publishing Company, 1887.

———. *History of Lincoln County, Missouri*. Chicago: The Goodspeed Publishing Company, 1888.

———. *History of Newton, Lawrence, Barry, and McDonald Counties, Missouri*. Chicago: The Goodspeed Publishing Company, 1888.

Historical Publishing Company. *History of Cooper County, Missouri*. Topeka, Kansas: Historical Publishing Company, 1919.

———. *History of Daviess and Gentry Counties, Missouri*. Topeka, Kansas: Historical Publishing Company, 1922.

History of Pettis County, Missouri. Publisher and place of publication not given, 1882. Reprinted Clinton, Missouri: The Printery, 1974.

Holcombe, R. I. *History of Marion County, Missouri*. St. Louis: E. F. Perkins, 1884.

Howard, Goldena Roland. *Ralls County, Missouri*. Marceline, Missouri: Walsworth Publishing Company, 1980.

Hurley, Lottie Sedwick. *History of Mt. Vernon and Lawrence County, Missouri, 1831–1931*. Mt. Vernon, Missouri: publisher not identified, 1931.

Iron County Historical Society. *Past and Present: A History of Iron County, Missouri, 1857–1994*. vol. 1. Marceline, Missouri: Heritage House Publishing, 1995.

Jenkins, Clyde Lee. *Judge Jenkins' History of Miller County*. Tuscumbia, Missouri: published by author, 1971.

Johnson, J. B. *History of Vernon County, Missouri*. Chicago: C. F. Cooper and Company, 1911.

Kansas City Historical Company. *The History of Johnson County, Missouri*. Kansas City, Missouri: Kansas City Historical Company, 1881.

Kuhn, Kate Ray. *A History of Marion County*. Hannibal, Missouri: Western Printing and Lithographing Company, 1963.

Lang, Delta. *Along Old Gravois: A History of Northwest Jefferson County*. St. Louis: Beaumont Graphics, Limited, 1983.

Livingston, Joel T. *A History of Jasper County, Missouri*. Chicago: The Lewis Publishing Company, 1912.

McGhee, James E., and James R. Mayo, *Stoddard Grays: Confederate Soldiers of Stoddard County, Missouri 1861–1865*. Shawnee Mission, Kansas: Two Trails Publishing Company, 1995.

Melton, E. J. *History of Cooper County, Missouri*. Columbia, Missouri: E. W. Stephens Publishing Company, 1937.

Miles, Kathleen White. *Bitter Ground. The Civil War in Missouri's Golden Valley*. Clinton, Missouri: The Printery, 1971.

Mills and Company. *The History of Pike County, Missouri*. Des Moines: Mills and Company, 1883.

Missouri Historical Company. *History of Carroll County, Missouri*. St. Louis: Missouri Historical Company, 1881.

———. *History of Lafayette County, Missouri*. St. Louis: Missouri Historical Company, 1881.

———. *History of Ray County, Missouri*. St. Louis: Missouri Historical Company, 1881.

———. *History of Saline County, Missouri*. St. Louis: Missouri Historical Company, 1881.

Napton, William Barclay. *Past and Present of Saline County, Missouri*. Chicago: B. F. Brown and Company, 1910.

National Historical Company. *The History of Bas and Bates Counties, Missouri*. St. Louis: National Historical Company, 1883.

———. *History of Callaway County, Missouri*. St. Louis: National Historical Company, 1884.

———. *History of Carroll County, Missouri*. St. Louis: National Historical Company, 1881.

———. *History of Caldwell and Livingston Counties, Missouri*. St. Joseph, Missouri: National Historical Company, 1886.

———. *History of Clay and Platte Counties, Missouri*. St. Louis: National Historical Company, 1885.

———. *History of Howard and Cooper Counties, Missouri*. St. Louis: National Historical Company, 1883.

———. *History of Monroe and Shelby Counties, Missouri*. St. Louis: National Historical Company, 1884.

———. *History of Randolph and Macon Counties, Missouri*. St. Louis: National Historical Company, 1884.

———. *History of St. Charles, Montgomery, and Warren Counties, Missouri*. St. Louis: Paul V. Cochran Company, 1885.

National Historical Publishing Company. *History of Henry and St. Clair Counties, Missouri*. St. Joseph, Missouri: National Historical Publishing Company, 1883.

Oakley, Gene. *The History of Carter County*. Van Buren, Missouri: J-G Publishing Company, 1970.

Paxton, William M. *Annals of Platte County, Missouri*. Kansas City, Missouri: Hudson-Kimberly Publishing Company, 1897.

Pioneer Historical Company. *History of Dade County and Her People*. Greenfield, Missouri: The Pioneer Historical Company, 1917.

Ponder, Jerry. *The Civil War in Ripley County, Missouri*. Doniphan, Missouri: *The Prospect-News*, 1992.

Powell, Betty F. *History of Mississippi County: Beginning Through 1972*. Place of publication not given: published by author, 1975.

Schooley, Herschel. *Centennial History of Audrain County.* Mexico, Missouri: McIntyre Publishing Company, 1937.

Schrantz, Ward L. *Jasper County, Missouri, in the Civil War.* Carthage, Missouri: The Carthage Press, 1923.

Scotland County Bicentennial Committee and Historical Society. *Scotland County, Missouri In Retrospect.* Memphis, Missouri: Scotland County Bicentennial Committee and Historical Society, 1977.

Selleck, Bessie Janet (Woods). *Early Settlers of Douglas County, Missouri.* Berkeley, California: The Professional Press, 1952.

Shrum, Edison. *The History of Scott County, Missouri Up to the Year 1880.* Sikeston, Missouri: Scott County Historical Society, 1984.

Simpson, Lewis A. W. *Oregon County's Three Flags Via the Horse & Buggy.* Thayer, Missouri: The Thayer News, 1971.

Smith, Geraldine Sanders. *Civil War Soldiers of Madison County, Missouri (and Surrounding Counties).* St. Louis: published by author, 1997.

_____. *Civil War Times in Madison County, Missouri and Surrounding Counties.* St. Louis: published by author, 1999.

Smyth-Davis, Mary F. *History of Dunklin County, Missouri.* St. Louis: Nixon-Jones Printing Company, 1896.

Sturges, J. A. *Illustrated History of McDonald County, Missouri.* Pineville, Missouri: publisher not given, 1897.

Tathwell, S. L. *The Old Settlers History of Bates County, Missouri.* Amsterdam, Missouri: Tathwell and Maxey, 1897.

Taylor, Henry and Company. *Compendium of History and Biography of Linn County, Missouri.* Chicago: Henry Taylor and Company, 1912.

_____. *General History of Macon County, Missouri.* Chicago: Henry Taylor and Company, 1910.

Thompson, Henry C. *Our Lead Belt Heritage.* Place of publication not given: published by author, 1955.

Turner, S. K., and S. A. Clark. *Twentieth Century History of Carroll County, Missouri.* Indianapolis: B. F. Bowen and Company, 1911.

Union Historical Company. *The History of Jackson County, Missouri.* Kansas City, Missouri: Union Historical Company, 1881.

Vienna Centennial Committee. *Maries County, Missouri, 1855–1955.* Vienna, Missouri: Vienna Centennial Committee, 1955.

Violette, E. M. *History of Adair County.* Kirksville, Missouri: Denslow History Company, 1911.

Voigt, Harry R. *Concordia, Missouri: A Centennial History.* Concordia, Missouri: Centennial Committee, 1960.

Western Historical Company. *History of Boone County.* St. Louis: Western Historical Company, 1882.

_____. *History of Greene County, Missouri.* St. Louis: Western Historical Company, 1883.

Wilcox, Pearl. *Jackson County Pioneers.* Independence, Missouri: published by author, 1975.

Winter, William C. *The Civil War in St. Louis: A Guided Tour.* St. Louis: Missouri Historical Society Press, 1994.

Woodson, W. H. *History of Clay County, Missouri.* Topeka, Kansas: Historical Publishing Company, 1920.

Young, William. *Young's History of Lafayette County, Mo.* Indianapolis: B. F. Brown and Company, 1910.

Books

Bartels, Carolyn. *The Civil War in Missouri Day by Day 1861 to 1865.* Shawnee Mission, Kansas: Two Trails Publishing, 1992.

_____. *The Forgotten Men: Missouri State Guard.* Shawnee Mission, Kansas: Two Trails Publishing Company, 1995.

_____, transcriber. *Missouri Confederate Deaths Union Prisons and Hospitals.* Shawnee Mission, Kansas: Two Trails Publishing, 1996.

Behlendorf, Frederick. *The History of the Thirteenth Illinois Cavalry Regiment Volunteers, U.S. Army from September 1861 to September 1865.* Grand Rapids, MI: 1888.

Boatner, Mark M. III. *The Civil War Dictionary, Revised Edition.* New York: David McKay Company, Incorporated, 1988.

Britton, Wiley. *The Civil War on the Border.* 2 volumes. New York: G. P. Putnam's Sons, 1890–1891.

Brownlee, Richard S. *Gray Ghosts of the Confederacy, Guerrilla Warfare in the West 1861–1865.* Baton Rouge: Louisiana State University Press, 1958.

Castel, Albert. *William Clarke Quantrill: His Life and Times.* New York: Frederick Fell, Incorporated, 1962.

Chittenden, Hiram Martin. *History of Early Steamboat Navigation on the Missouri River: Life And Adventures of Joseph Labarge.* Volume 2. New York: Francis P. Harper, 1903.

Connelley, William Elsey. *Quantrill and the Border Wars.* Cedar Rapids, Iowa: The Torch Press. 1910. Reprinted Ottawa, Kansas: Kansas Heritage Press, 1992.

Cornish, Dudley Taylor. *The Sable Arm: Negro Troops in the Union Army, 1861–1865.* New York: Longmans, Green and Company, 1956.

Daughters of Union Veterans of the Civil War, 1861–1865. *Missouri: Our Civil War Heritage.* St. Louis: Julia Dent Grant Tent, no. 16 of Daughters of Union Veterans of the Civil War, 1861–1865, 1994.

Dyer, Frederick H. *A Compendium of the War*

of the Rebellion. 3 volumes. New York: Sangamore Press, Incorporated, 1959.

Eakin, Joanne Chiles. *Civil War Union Military Post Returns From Missouri*. Independence, Missouri: Print America, 1995.

———. *The Little Gods: Union Provost Marshals in Missouri, 1861–1865*. Volume 1. Independence, Missouri: published by author, 1996.

———. *The Little Gods: Union Provost Marshals in Missouri, 1861–1865*. Volume 2. Shawnee Mission, Kansas: Two Trails Genealogy Shop, 1996.

———. *Missouri Prisoners of War From Gratiot Street Prison, St. Louis, MO and Alton Prison, Illinois Including Citizens, Confederates, Bushwhackers, and Guerrillas*. Independence, Missouri: published by author, 1995.

Eakin, Joanne Chiles, and Donald R. Hale, *Branded As Rebels*. Independence, Missouri: Wee Print, 1993.

Edwards, John N. *Noted Guerrillas, or the Warfare of the Border*. St. Louis: H. W. Brand and Company, 1877.

———. *Shelby and His Men: or The War in the West*. Cincinnati: Miama Printing and Publishing Company, 1867.

Fellman, Michael. *Inside War: The Guerrilla Conflict in Missouri During the American Civil War*. New York: Oxford University Press, 1989.

Gibson, Charles Dana, and E. Kay Gibson. *Dictionary of Transports and Combatant Vessels, Steam and Sail, Employed by the Union Army, 1861–1868*. The Army's Navy Series. Camden, Maine: Ensign Press, 1995.

Goodrich, Thomas. *Black Flag: Guerrilla Warfare on the Western Border, 1861–1865*. Bloomington, Indiana: Indiana University Press, 1995.

Greene, Lorenzo J., Gary R. Kremer, and Anthony F. Holland, *Missouri's Black Heritage, The Sable Arm*. St. Louis: Forum Press, 1980.

Hale, Donald R. *They Called Him Bloody Bill*. Clinton, Missouri: The Printery, 1975.

Hodges, Miss Nadine, and Mrs. Howard W. Woodruff, compilers. *Genealogical Notes From the 'Liberty Tribune,' 1858–1868*. Volume 2. Liberty, Missouri: published by compilers, 1975.

Ingenthron, Elmo. *Borderland Rebellion: A History of the Civil War on the Missouri-Arkansas Border*. Ozark Regional History Series, book 3. Branson, Missouri: The Ozarks Mountaineer, 1980.

Ingmire, Frances and Carolyn Ericson. *Confederate POW's: Soldiers and Sailors Who Died in Federal Prisons and Military Hospitals in the North*. St. Louis: Ingmire Publications, 1984.

The Kingdom of Callaway Historical Society. *The 133rd Anniversary of 'The Battle of Moore's Mill,' July 15 and 16, 1995*. Fulton, Missouri: The Kingdom of Callaway Historical Society, 1995.

McKee, Ivan N. *Lost Family—Lost Cause*. Freeman, South Dakota: Pine Hill Press, 1978.

Miles, Kathleen White. *Bitter Ground. The Civil War in Missouri's Golden Valley*. Clinton, Missouri: The Printery, 1971.

Monaghan, Jay. *Civil War on the Western Border 1854–1865*. New York: Crown Publishers. 1955.

Moore, Frank, ed. *The Rebellion Record: A Diary of American Events, with Documents, Narratives, Illustrative Incidents, Poetry, etc.* 12 volumes. New York: G. P. Putnam. 1861–1868; D. VanNostrand, 1862–1871. Reprinted New York: Arno Press, 1977.

Oates, Stephen B. *Confederate Cavalry West of the River*. Austin, Texas: University of Texas Press, 1961. Reprinted by same, 1992.

O'Flaherty, Daniel. *General Jo Shelby: Undefeated Rebel*. Chapel Hill, North Carolina: University of North Carolina Press, 1954.

Shoemaker, Floyd C., ed. *Missouri—Day by Day*. 2 volumes. Columbia, Missouri: State Historical Society of Missouri, 1943.

Way, Frederick, Jr. *Way's Packet Directory, 1848–1994*. Athens, Ohio: Ohio University Press, 1994.

Webb, W. L. *Battles and Biographies of Missourians, or the Civil War Period of Our State*. Kansas City, Missouri: Hudson-Kimberly Publishing Company, 1903.

Williams, Walter, ed. *A History of Northwest Missouri*. 3 volumes. Chicago: The Lewis Publishing Company, 1915.

Index

Numbers in *bold italics* indicate photographs.

Abolitionists 40
Adair County, Missouri 136, 137, 141, 189
Adams, Col. Charles W. (Northern) 209
Adams, 1st Lt. James A. (Northern) 66
Alexandria, Clark County, Missouri 135
Allen (civilian) 201
Allen, Capt. (Southern) 135, 139
Allsman, Andrew (civilian) 195
Alton, Illinois military prison 71, 126–28, 192
American Revolution *see* Revolution, American
Anders, Dr. Leslie 4, 228
Anderson, Editor C. P. (civilian) 88
Anderson, Jim (Southern) 93, 151, 205
Anderson, William T. "Bloody Bill" (Southern) 39, 49, 54, 55, 57, 93, 151, 205
Andrae, Capt. Henry (Southern) 74–75
Anthony, Lt. Col. Daniel R. (Northern) 7–9
Anthony, Susan B. (civilian) 7
Arkansas, state of 29, 58, 69, 71, 72, 73, 76, 77, 79, 97, 100, 110, 113, 114, 116, 117, 119, 120, 122, 124, 127, 134, 142, 143, 146, 157, 162, 164, 165, 166, 167, 168, 169, 173, 175, 177, 181, 186, 192, 197, 198, 202, 210, 211, 212
Arkansas troops: 1st Arkansas Cavalry Regiment 176
Army of Southeast Missouri (Northern) 173–74
"Army" revolvers, caliber 44, 54
Arrow Rock, Saline County, Missouri 88, 203

Arrow Rock Township, Saline County, Missouri 233
Artillery employed against Southern irregulars 29, 72–3, 81, 88, 90, 102, 111, 113, 119, 134, 136, 137, 138, 159, 161, 162, 166, 172, 190
Ashley, Pike County, Missouri 142
Assessment (financial) of Southerners 104
Atchison, Kansas 10
Aubrey, Kansas 91, 93, 96
Audrain County, Missouri 17, 66, 68, 134, 170, 186, 187, 194, 197
Austin, Capt. Bob (Southern) 150–51, 152–54, 227
Austin, Cass County, Missouri 93
Austrian carbines 77; *see also* Carbines
Auxvasse Creek, Callaway County, Missouri 134, 192, 197
Avery, Capt. George S. (Northern) 125
Aylward, Dr. William (civilian) 132

"Backwash" of the war *see* Missouri as a "backwash" of the war
Baird, Capt. Joseph W. (Northern) 187
Baker, George W. (civilian) 207
Baker, William, and George, and James (Southern) 204
Baker, Willis (Southern) 131
Ballew, Capt. Logan H. (Southern) 153, 204–5
Ballinger, Capt. John (Northern) 148
Balls Ford, on Sni-A-Bar Creek, Jackson County, Missouri 98

Banishment *see* Countermeasures against guerrillas
Banzhaf, Maj. Charles (Northern) 149
Barker, Elias (civilian) 161
Barnard, Capt. (Southern) 189
Barnes, Charles (Southern) 124, 165
Barnes, Lt. T. H. (Northern) 66
Barnesville (present-day Ellington) Reynolds County, Missouri 168
Barnum, P. T. (circus) 84
Barry County, Missouri 36, 37, 81, 107, 176, 177–78, 181, 184
Barstow, Col. Hiram E. (Northern) 111, 180
Barton County, Missouri 79, 80, 115, 175, 179, 183, 184
Bass, Deputy Provost Marshal Tolbird 70; *see also* Provost marshals in Missouri
Basyl, Capt. John A. (Southern) 183
Bates County, Missouri 7, 34, 82, 85, 109, 114, 150, 160, 177, 178–79, 184, 210, 228
Batesville, Arkansas 168
Baton Rouge, Louisiana 64
Bauer, Lt. Jacob (Northern) 202
Bear Creek, Boone County, Missouri 65
Beck, Moses (Southern) 142
Bell Aire, Cooper County, Missouri 203
Belles (civilian) 201
Benton County, Missouri 37, 84, 85, 177, 183
Best, Lewis (Southern) 204
Big Beaver Creek, Douglas County, Missouri 180
Big Creek, Cass County, Missouri 97, 150, 200, 207

243

Big Creek, Lincoln County, Missouri 64
Big Creek, Wayne County, Missouri 69
Big Piney River, Missouri 117, 173
Biggers, Maj. Thomas B. (Northern) 153
Bill of Rights, *see* Countermeasures against guerrillas
Birch Tree, Shannon County, Missouri 168
Black, Capt. Thomas C. (Northern) 124
Black Creek, Shelby County, Missouri 67
Black flag 44
Black people: abducted 207; as disguise 27, 127; as informants 10, 89, 143; with jayhawkers 204; liberated from slavery 156, 200–1, 209; mistreatment of 10, 161, 185; recruiting of 41
Black River, Missouri 164, 167
Blackburn, John (civilian) 204
Blackwater River, Missouri 91, 149
"Bleeding Kansas" 7, 34, 44, 52
Bloomfield, Stoddard County 25, 52, 72, 120, 166, 167, 170
Blue (*or* Big Blue) River, Missouri 144, 207
Blunt, Andy (Southern) 44, 98–9
Bob's Creek, Lincoln County, Missouri 64
Bolen, Alf (Southern) 110
Bolin, Capt. Nathan (Southern) 71
Bolivar, Polk County, Missouri 84, 113
Bollinger County, Missouri 25, 72, 121, 122, 170
Bond, Melville (civilian) 148
Bone Hill, Jackson County, Missouri 200
Bonne Femme Creek, Boone County, Missouri 66
Boone, Col. David C. (Southern) 168, 169, 170
Boone, Capt. Hampton L. (Southern) 27, 126
Boone, Col. John C. (Southern) 128
Boone County, Missouri 10, 15, 17, 19, 23, 65–6, 88, 89, 126, 130, 133, 135, 139, 141, 142, 170, 178, 181, 186, 187, 188, 189, 190, 191, 197, 198, 202, 203
Boonville, Cooper County, Missouri 102, 117, 136, 151, 203
"Bootheel" 23, 30, 123, 166, 167
Border Star (newspaper) Independence, Jackson County, Missouri 162, 199
Bower, James (civilian?) 203
Bowers Mills, Jasper County, Missouri 179
Bowles, Capt. Dick (Southern) 72
Bowles, Lieutenant (Southern) 187
Boyd, Col. Sempronius H. (Northern) 124
Brackman, Capt. Albert (Northern) 202
Breckenridge, Caldwell County, Missouri 204
Breckinridge, Capt. James (Northern) 148
Bredett, Maj. Eliphalet (Northern) 102, 149
Breeden, Capt. Martin (Northern) 82, 179–80
"Bridgeburners" 15, 16, 17
Brinker, John (Southern) 90–1, 146, 147
Brinker, Mattie (civilian) 147
Brisco, John (Southern) 65
Brisco, Dr. Warner (civilian) 65
Britts, Capt. John H. (Southern) 7
Brown, Capt. Ed (Southern) 88
Brown, Col. Egbert B. (Northern) 99, 119
Brown, Capt. John (Southern) 139
Bruere, Surg. John E. (Northern) 197
Brunswick, Chariton County, Missouri 65, 192
Buchanan County, Missouri 10, 148, 149, 155, 210
Buel, Lt. Col. James T. (Northern) 145, 157–58
Buffalo Creek, McDonald County, Missouri 81, 109
Burbridge, Clinton (Southern) 142, 169, 189
Burbridge, John Q. "Jack" (Southern) 142, 169–70, 173, 180–81
Burbridge, William (Southern) 142, 169
Burch, Capt. Milton (Northern) 110, 181, 183
Burris (Southern) 90
Burris, Lt. Col. John T. (Northern) 155, 158, 161, 200–1, 207
Buster, Col. Michael Woods (Southern) 177
Butler, Bates County, Missouri 85, 150
Butler County, Missouri 69, 114, 119

Cain, Tice (Southern) 130, 187
Caldwell, Maj. Henry C. (Northern) 68, *133*–34
Caldwell County, Missouri 204, 205
Calhoun, Henry County, Missouri 90, 110
California House Inn, Pulaski County, Missouri 125, 169
California, Moniteau County, Missouri 88, 202
California Weekly News (newspaper) California, Moniteau County, Missouri 88
Call, Capt. James (Northern) 119
Call, Lt. Joseph H. (Northern) 63
Callaway County, Missouri 17, 19, 21, 66, 133, 135–36, 138, 139, 140, 141, 186, 188, 190, 192, 197
Cambridge, Saline County, Missouri 202
Camden County, Missouri 34, 76, 181
Cameron, Capt. George F. (Southern) 192–93
Cameron, Clinton County, Missouri 87
Camp Jackson seizure 41
Campbell, J. C. (Southern) 77
Canada, nation of 44
Canton, Lewis County, Missouri 135, 189
Cape Girardeau, Cape Girardeau County, Missouri 31, 72, 116, 121, 122, 123, 167, 170
Caples, the Rev. William Goff (Southern) 65
Caps, percussion 101, 133, 144, 190
Carbines 37, *38*, 52, *53*, 77, 98, 150, 205 *see* Austrian carbines
Carlin (Southern) 126
Carlin, Col. W. P. (Northern) 69
Carroll, Col. Charles (Southern) 176
Carroll County, Missouri 148, 150–54, 204

Carrollton, Carroll County, Missouri 153, 204
Carter County, Missouri 69, 74, 124, 168, 169, 170, 173
Carthage, Jasper County, Missouri 80, 81, 177
Carver, Robert Granville (Northern) 17
Cason, Capt. James (Southern) 140
Cass County, Missouri 7–9, 91, 93, 94, 97, 100, 101, 144, 145, 150, 154, 162, 177, 179, 199, 200, 205, 207, 208, 228
Cassville, Barry County, Missouri 37, 107, 176
Castleman, Col. Abraham (Southern) 124
Catherwood, Col. Edwin C. (Northern) 208
Cavalry, value of in guerrilla warfare 31, 48, 60, 81
Cedar County, Missouri 77, 113, 183
Cedar Creek, Boone County, Missouri 135, 193, 197
Centralia, Boone County, Missouri 192
Chalk Bluffs, St. Francis River, Missouri 72, 167
Chapel Hill, Lafayette County, Missouri 207
Chariton County, Missouri 21, 65, 135, 138, 141, 191, 192
Chariton River, Missouri 135, 138, 141
Charleston, Mississippi County, Missouri 23, 123
"Cherokee Spikes" 37, 176
Cherry Grove, Schuyler County, Missouri 130
Chicago, Illinois 93
Chiles, Christopher Lillard "Kit," Sr. (Southern) 96, 97, 147, 148, 157–58, 221
Chiles, Col. Henry C. (civilian) 205
Chiles, Richard "Dick" (Southern) 205
Chillicothe, Livingston County, Missouri 86, 156, 204
Chilton family (civilians) 125
Chilton, State Sen. Joshua "King of Shannon County" (civilian) 125
Christian County, Missouri 110–11, 125, 181, 183
Civil law enforcement 66, 70, 165, 209
Civil rights, suspension of 40
Civil War in Johnson County, Missouri 4

Clark, Col. Henry E. (Southern) 52, 166–67
Clark, Jesse P. (civilian) 156
Clark, Samuel (civilian) 97
Clark County, Missouri 131, 135
Clarkston, Dunklin County, Missouri 166, 167
Clay County, Missouri 44, 86, 96, 112, 156, 204
Clayton, Lt. Col. Powell (Northern) 80
Clear Fork, Johnson County, Missouri 201
Clendenning, Maj. Robert M. (Northern) 30
Clifford, Col. Charles H. (Southern) 110
Clinton County, Missouri 86–7, 150, 157, 205
Clinton, Henry County, Missouri 110, 114
Clopper, Maj. John Y. (Northern) *132*
Cloud, Col. William F. (Northern) 107, 115
Cobb, Alvin (Southern) 134, 139, 140, 141, 142, 188
Cochran, Capt. J. Franklin (Northern) 145
Cockrell, Gen. Francis Marion (Southern) 9, 160, 202
Cockrell, Col. Jeremiah Vardaman (Southern) 9, 10, 114–15, 160–61, 178, 202
Coffee, Col. John Trousdale (Southern) 37, 43, 81, 82, 107, 111, 113, 114–15, 160–61, 177
Cole Camp, Benton County, Missouri 177
Cole County, Missouri 34, 87, 89, 124–25, 165, 202
Coleman, Col. William O. (Southern) 23, 29, 52, 70, 73–5, 116–19, 124, 168, 173, 211
Colorado Territory 44, 208
Colt's revolving rifle 52, *80*, 81
Columbia, Boone County, Missouri 17, 19, 65, 134, 139, 141, 142, 187, 191, 192, 193, 198
Columbus, Johnson County, Missouri 9, 152, 160
Columbus, Kentucky 23, 167
Commerce, Scott County, Missouri 166
Compton's Ferry, Livingston County, Missouri 138, 153–54
Conscription into Southern service 43, 72; *see also* Draft

Continental (vessel) 166
Coon Creek, Barton County, Missouri 115
Cooper, Charles (Southern) 86, 87
Cooper, Col. Douglas H. (Southern) 81, 176–77
Cooper County, Missouri 66, 87, 88, 117, 136, 150, 154, 202, 203
Copeland, 1st Lt. Levi S. (Northern) 162, 228
Council Grove, Morris County, Kansas 93
Countermeasures against guerrillas 11, *172*; banishment 172, 189, 190, 207; burn out homes of enemies 173, 189, 191, 200, 204, 210; capture Rebels at social gatherings 11, 25, 29, 149 *see also* Dance; chain of posts across prairie 107; control rivers, roads, railroads 19, 41; control Southern expression in newspapers 41, 88; defending Missouri with Missourians 60, 102–6, 159; discretion of Union troops in the field 80; employ informants, spies, and detectives 171; enrollment of all men into militia 41, 102–6 *see also* Orders, Northern; escort Northern sympathizers to safety 81, 106; execute guerrillas 46, 60, 95, 99, 136, 189 *see also* Prisoners, execution of; force Southerners to carry mail 145; hide in the brush to catch guerrillas 149; impotent countermeasures 40–1, 83–4, 90, 99, 102–6, 136, 149, 158–59, 161–62, 190, 200–1, 212; intimidation of Southern preachers 65, 171–72; keep Kansas troops out of Missouri 99, 209; military tribunals 46, 151, 156, 190; Napoleonic severity against partisans 15, 46; revenge-taking 189, 194–6; sentry system with passes 171; shoot those who run 109, 205, 209; suspend Bill of Rights 40, 65, 157 *see also* Bill of Rights; use disguises 81; *see also* Provost marshals in Missouri
Cow Creek, Kansas 179
Cow Creek, Saline County, Missouri 87

Cowherd or Cowert farm, Jackson County, Missouri 162
Cowskin Prairie, McDonald County, Missouri 81, 107
Crabtree, "General" (Southern) 124–25, 165
Cravensville, Daviess County, Missouri 155
Crawford, Col. Thomas (Northern) 188
Crawford County, Missouri 29, 117, 165
Creath, Margaret (Southern) 190
Crews, George and Mrs. and William (Southern) 204, 232
Crooked Creek, Bollinger County, Missouri 122
Cross Timbers, Hickory County, Missouri 110
Cunningham, Albert (Southern) 210
Cunningham, the Rev. David B. (Southern) 66
Cunningham, Robert (civilian) 141
Current River, Missouri 69, 167, 170, 173
Curry, Captain (Southern) 168
Curtis, Maj. Gen. Samuel R. (Northern) 171–72
Cycle of violence 63, 67–8

Dade County, Missouri 37, 79, 81, 107, 111, 114, 160, 176
Daily Missouri Democrat (newspaper) St. Louis, Missouri 43
Dallas, Bollinger County, Missouri 25, 122
Dallas County, Missouri 34, 76, 109, 110
Dances 11, 25, 29, 149
Daniel E. Miller (vessel) 73
Daniels, Col. Edward (Northern) 72
Daugherty, Lt. Col. Joseph H. (Southern) 66
Daughters of the Confederacy *see* United Daughters of the Confederacy
Davenport, Mrs. (civilian) 147
David, Capt. Daniel H. (Northern) 153, 200, 205
Davidson, Brig. Gen. John Wynn (Northern) 173–74
Daviess County, Missouri 155
Davis, Ambrose (Southern) 87
Davis, Asa (Southern) 87
Davis, Dr. (Southern) 155
Davis, Pres. Jefferson (Southern), authorizing partisan rangers 60

Dayton, Cass County, Missouri 7, 10, 208
Deepwater, Henry County, Missouri 85
Dees (Southern) 121
Deitzler, Col. George W. (Northern) 9
DeKalb, Buchanan County, Missouri 148
Democrat (newspaper) Carrollton, Carroll County, Missouri 153
Dennis, Captain (Southern) 194
Dent County, Missouri 29, 73, 117, 124
Dewey, Col. William (Northern) 169–70
DeWitt, Carroll County, Missouri 153
Dexter, Stoddard County, Missouri 122
Diamond Grove, Newton County, Missouri 80
Disguises: to escape detection 56, 65, 68, 83, 101, 112–13; to escape from captivity 27, 126, 127; to fool victims 190, 191, 193; to spy 81, 157; to travel long distances 101, 171
"Dixie" (song) 141
Dogwood Creek, Vernon County, Missouri 182
Doniphan, Butler County, Missouri 69
Dorsey, Col. Caleb (Southern) 15, 17, 52, 64, 178
Doubleday, Col. Charles (Northern) 107
Douglas County, Missouri 76, 119, 180, 181
Dover, Lafayette County, Missouri 102
Draft 41, 44, 104; *see also* Conscription into Southern forces
Drake, Maj. William C. (Northern) 29
Draper, Capt. Daniel M. (Northern) 66
"Drumhead court martial" *see* Prisoners, execution of
Drywood Creek, battle of 32
Drywood, Vernon County, Missouri 182
Dubuque, Arkansas 181
"Ducates" (Southern) 149
Ducates, Frank (Southern) 149
Dunklin County, Missouri 73, 123, 166, 167, 172
Dunn, Bill (Southern) 15–6, 17, 21, 63, 130, 131–32, 187, 193, 194

Dunn, Capt. Robert E. (Southern) 64–5
Durrett, Captain (civilian) 233

Eads, James B. (civilian) 233
Eads, Capt. James D. (Northern) 210
Early warning networks 57, 149, 160, 184
Edina, Knox County, Missouri 63
Edwards, Capt. William B. "Squirrel Tail" (Southern) 102, 154, 227
Eleven Point River, Missouri 167, 173
Elkhorn Tavern, battle of *see* Pea Ridge
Elliott, Col. Benjamin F. (Southern) 7–9, 10
Ellis, Abraham (civilian) 91
Ely, Capt. Ben (Southern) 189
Embree (or Emory), Captain (Southern) 191
Emerson, Marion County, Missouri 65, 68
Emilie (vessel) 197
Eminence, Shannon County, Missouri 117
Englehart, Capt. Joseph (Southern) 87
Eno, Maj. E. B. (Northern) 184
Eppstein, Lt. Col. Joseph A. (Northern) 117, 118
Essroger, Capt. Bernard (Northern) 121, 223
Ewing, Brig. Gen. Thomas, Jr. (Northern) 44
Ewing, Capt. William (Northern) 63, 141, 142

Fabius River, Missouri 139, 189
Fairmont, Clark County, Missouri 131
Fanny Ogden (vessel) 188
Fayette, Howard County, Missouri 202
Fields, Colonel (civilian) 143
Fisk, Brig. Gen. Clinton D. (Northern) 57
Flag 80, 117, 139, 166; *see also* Black flag
Flenty, Capt. William (Northern) 72
Florida, Monroe County, Missouri 67, 68, 133–34, 189
Foliage for concealment 59, 94, 164, 184
Forsyth, Taney County, Missouri 110
Fort Leavenworth, Kansas 9, 86, 112, 155, 159, 161, 162, 199, 200–1, 207

Index

Fort Scott, Kansas 32, 51, 79, 109, 111, 112, 115, 176, 179
Foster, Maj. Emory S. (Northern) 10, 90, 97, 147, 160–61
Foster, Col. John D. (Northern) 21
Four Mile, Dunklin County, Missouri 123, 167
Fowler (Southern) 123
Fowler, Captain (Southern) 140
Fox Creek, Douglas County, Missouri 76
Frankfort, Saline County, Missouri 150–51
Franklin County, Missouri 29, 117
Frazier, Julian (Southern) 77
Fredericktown, Madison County, Missouri 121, 122, 168
Freedom Township, Lafayette County, Missouri 161
Fulton, Callaway County, Missouri 21, 134, 136, 140, 141, 186, 192

Gadfly, Newton County, Missouri 109, 176
Gallup, Maj. Henry A. (Northern) 117
Gamble, Prov. Gov. Hamilton R. (Northern) 103, 135
Garrison Creek, Lafayette County, Missouri 9
Gasconade County, Missouri 117, 141, 165
Gasconade River, Missouri 76, 110, 180, 183
Gaston, Samuel (civilian) 151
Gatewood, Capt. James M. (Southern) 32, 37–8
Gayoso, Pemiscot County, Missouri 122
General orders *see* Orders
Gentry (Southern) 203
Georgia, state of 168
German-American people: generally favoring Northern side 161, 165; murder of 206; as Union soldiers 41, 67, 87, 101, 192
Gibson, Capt. James R. (Southern) 155, 210
Given, David and William R. (civilians) 192
Gleason, Lt. H. W. (Northern) 196
Gleaves, Harvey (civilian) 200
Glover, Col. John M. (Northern) 63
Goodlett, Col. Michael C. (Southern) 109

Granby, Newton County, Missouri 176, 177
Grand Pass, Saline County, Missouri 52
Grand Prairie, Dunklin County, Missouri 167
Grand River: northwest Missouri 138, 156, 204; southwest Missouri 107; west-central Missouri 114, 177
Gratiot Street Prison, St. Louis, Missouri 27, 126, 127–28, 170
Gray, Francis O. (Southern) 45
Gray, Col. John B. (Northern) 128
Greene, Col. Colton (Southern) 173, 180–81
Greene County, Arkansas 120
Greene County, Missouri 76
Greenfield, Dade County, Missouri 79, 111
Greenton, Lafayette County, Missouri 151
Greenville, Wayne County, Missouri 121, 123, 124, 164, 166, 168
Greer, William (civilian) 93
Gregg, Lt. William (Southern) 57, 100, 158, 162
Gregory brothers (civilians) 184
Grimes, Capt. Absolom (Southern) 165, 203
Grundy County, Missouri 154, 156, 204
Guitar, Col. Odon (Northern) 66, *67*, 89, *134*, 138, 192, 193, 198
Gunpowder, hidden 10, 21, 89, 90, 101, 114, 141, 146, 198
Gutherie, Andrew (civilian) 204

The "Hackle," Buchanan and Platte Counties, Missouri 155, 210
Hainesville, Clinton County, Missouri 157
Halleck, Maj. Gen. Henry W. 9–10, 15, *16*, *47*, 61, *95*; "guerrilla forfeits his life" order 60; Northern disgust for Kansas incursions 9, 41; order keeping Missouri troops out of Kansas 10; "shoot on sight" order 15, 46
Haller, Bill (Southern) 93, 158
Hallsville, Boone County, Missouri 15, 189, 198
Handcock, John (Southern) 178–179

Hannibal, Marion County, Missouri 101, 190, 196
Harmon, Mark (Northern) 36
Harris, D. (civilian) 9
Harrison, Col. Charles (Southern) 44, 93, 208
Harrisonville, Cass County, Missouri 93, 97, 100, 150, 154, 208
Hartman, Lt. Cravin (Northern) 189
Hartville, Wright County, Missouri 76, 181
Hatbands, white 193, 194
Hawk, Capt. Foster R. (Northern) 102
Hawkins, John (Southern) 202–3
Hayes (Southern) 123
Hays, Col. Upton (Southern) 11, 109, 111, 146, 147, 148, 149–50, 152, 157–58, 176–77
Hayward, Col. J. T. K. (Northern) 189, 196
Hazel Bottom, Barry County, Missouri 177
H. D. Bacon (vessel) 133
Henderson, Capt. Francis G. (Southern) *64*, 65
Hendricks, Capt. Gabriel (Southern) 194
Henry, County, Missouri 37, 82, 85, 90, 109, 110, 149–50, 177, 183, 210
Hermann, Gasconade County, Missouri 141, 165
Heusack, Lt. John (Northern) 124–26
Hickerson, Capt. Silas (Southern) 66
Hicklin's Branch, Livingston County, Missouri 156
Hickory County, Missouri 37, 84
Hicks, Capt. Absolom (Southern) 65
Highfill, Captain (Southern) 73, 220
Hildebrand, Henry (civilian) 121
Hildebrand, Sam (Southern) 70–*71*, 119–*120*, 122, 164, 166, 170, 212
Hill, Charles (civilian) 192
Hill, Woot (Southern) *57*
Hindman, Maj. Gen. Thomas C. (Southern) 43, 175, 176, 202
Hoge, Lt. S. E. (Northern) 202
Hogskin Ridge, Mississippi River, Missouri 123
Holden, Nathaniel B. (civilian) 201

Holden, Johnson County, Missouri 10, 151, 201
Holmes, Maj. Gen. Theophilus (Southern) 42
Holt County, Missouri 99
Holtzclaw, Capt. Clifton D. (Southern) 49
Hornersville, Dunklin County, Missouri 73
Horse Creek, southwest Missouri 79, 111, 175, 183
Horse-theft ring 209, 210
Hostages 123; *see also* Prisoners
Houston, Texas County, Missouri 29, 73, 181
Houts, Capt. Thomas W. (Northern) 90, 136
Houx, Matthias "Matt" (Southern) 89–91, 154
Howard County, Missouri 16, 34, 65, 126, 133, 136, 141, 160, 178, 190, 191, 192, 198, 202, 203, 210
Howell County, Missouri 29, 73, 74, 119
Hoy, Perry (Southern) 162
Hubbard, Capt. Henry (Northern) 96
Hubbard, Maj. James M. (Northern) 80–1, 113
Hubble Creek, Cape Girardeau County 72
Hudson, Macon County, Missouri 187
Hughes, Col. John T. (Southern) 157–58
Humansville, Polk County, Missouri 77
Hume, Capt. George H. (Southern) 118
Hunnewell, Shelby County, Missouri 16, 17, 132, 190
Hunt, Maj. Charles B. (Northern) 190
Hunter, Maj. Gen. David (Northern) 9–10; *see also* Orders
Hunter, Col. DeWitt Clinton (Southern) 160–61
Hunting shirts 55, 57
Huntsville, Randolph County, Missouri 189, 197
Huston, Col. Daniel, Jr. (Northern) 145, 161
Hutchinson (Southern) 10
Huzza Creek, Crawford County, Missouri 165
Hyde, Capt. Henry (Northern) 166

Iberia, Miller County, Missouri 124
Ice (Southern) 123
Illinois, state of 160, 189
Illinois troops: 166–67; 2nd Illinois Cavalry Regiment 123; 3rd Illinois Cavalry Regiment 74; 5th Illinois Cavalry Regiment 69; 7th Illinois Cavalry Regiment 25, 30, 72; 10th Illinois Cavalry Regiment 75, 119, 178, 180; 13th Illinois Cavalry Regiment 73, 74, 122, 123, 168; 17th Illinois Infantry Regiment 25, 30; 21st Illinois Infantry Regiment 69; 33rd Illinois Infantry Regiment 173; 37th Illinois Infantry Regiment 107, 111
Independence-Harrisonville Road, Jackson County, Missouri 100, 145
Independence, Jackson County, Missouri 13, 14, 93, 98, 99, 109, 144, 145, 148, 152, 157–158, 160, 162, 199, 202, 205, 210
Indian fighting experience 173
Indian Territories or Nations 79, 80, 175–76
Indian troops: Northern 175, 176, 177; Southern 80, 81, 176
Indiana troops 82, 160–61; 1st Indiana Cavalry Regiment 25, 30–1, 75, 217; 26th Indiana Infantry Regiment 84
Infantry use in guerrilla warfare 31, 48, 81, 82, 84
Inman's Hollow, Dent County, Missouri 117
Iowa, state of 63, 130, 135, 142
Iowa troops: 67, 73, 82; 1st Iowa Cavalry Regiment 16–7, 34, 37, 46, 52, 66, 77, 80, 82, 84, 85, 88, 90, 91, 93, 109, 110, 113, 114, 150, 176, 177, 200; 3rd Iowa Cavalry Regiment 17, 19, 29, 36, 52, 68, 73, 133–4, 141, 189, 190
"Iron Brigade" 114
Iron County, Missouri 25, 120, 164, 165
Ironclads 233
Ironton, Iron County, Missouri 116, 120, 121
Isbell, Capt. William (Southern) 81

Jackman, Col. Sidney Drake (Southern) 34, 79, 83, 89–91, 107, 112, 113–14, 160–61, 183, 184, 210
Jackson, Gov. Claiborne Fox (Southern) 109
Jackson, Cape Girardeau County, Missouri 123, 167
Jackson County, Missouri 11, 13, 86, 91–3, 95, 96–7, 99, 100, 101, 109, 114, 144, 145, 146, 147, 148–49, 151, 152, 157–58, 162, 176, 199, 200, 202, 205, 206, 207, 209
Jail breaks *see* Prison breaks
James, Frank (Southern) 45, 48
James River, Missouri 180
Jasper County, Missouri 36, 37, 45, 80, 82, 107, 114, 175, 176, 177, 179, 184
Jayhawkers 1, 7–10, 11, 39, 41, 91, 99, 156, 204, 209, 212
Jeffers, Col. William (Southern) 72, 121, 122, 167, 170, 172
Jefferson City, Cole County, Missouri 21, 34, 66, 88, 89, 110, 188, 190
Jefferson County, Missouri 120, 128
"Jeffries" *see* Jeffers, Col. William
Jennings, Capt. Henderson (Southern) 183
Jennison, Dr. Charles R. (Northern) 9, 41
John H. Dickey (vessel) 166
Johnson, Captain (Southern) 146
Johnson, Captain (of Osceola, St. Clair County, Missouri) 183
Johnson, Capt. Henry or Harry (Southern) 146
Johnson, James M. (Southern) 202
Johnson, Maj. Myscall (Southern) 125, 183
Johnson, Capt. Watkins O. (Southern) 170
Johnson County, Missouri 7–9, 10, 82, 89–91, 93, 97, 109, 112, 114, 127, 144, 149, 150, 151, 152, 154, 157, 160, 162, 178, 199, 201, 202, 205, 210
Johnstown, Bates County, Missouri 114
Jollification, Newton County, Missouri 109, 177
Jones, Col. A. W. (Southern) 210
Jones, Capt. G. Byron (Southern) 155
Jones Creek, Jasper County, Missouri 36
Judson, Col. William R. (Northern) 176

Kaiser, Capt. John B. (Northern) 87, 99

Index

Kansas, state of 77, 86, 91, 146, 156, 199–200, 204, 206–7, 212
Kansas City, Jackson County, MO 89, 97, 101, 112, 143, 144, 151, 152, 155, 156, 157, 158, 159, 162
Kansas exile guerrilla band (led by Bill Reed) 93, 94, 151, 161, 205, 207
Kansas troops 1, 209; 1st Kansas Colored Infantry Regiment 178–79; 1st Kansas Infantry Regiment 9, 13; 2nd Kansas Cavalry Regiment 96, 115, 177, 182; 2nd Kansas Indian Home Guard Regiment 176; 3rd Kansas Battery of Light Artillery 178; 3rd Kansas Indian Home Guard Regiment 175, 176, 177, 184; 5th Kansas Cavalry Regiment 79, 80, 81, 117, 210; 5th Kansas Infantry Regiment 91; 6th Kansas Cavalry Regiment 34, 37–8, 79, 80, 93–4, 101, 110, 115, 148, 149, 162, 176–77, 182, 184, 185, 200; 7th Kansas Cavalry Regiment 7–9; 8th Kansas Infantry Regiment 91, 162; 9th Kansas Cavalry Regiment 7, 52; 10th Kansas Cavalry Regiment 107; 12th Kansas Infantry Regiment 199, 209;order forbidding them to enter Missouri 9
Keetsville, Barry County, Missouri 184
Kehoe, Capt. Miles (Northern) 150, 227
Kelly, Maj. George W. (Northern) 183
Kendrick, Capt. Gabriel S. (Southern) 193
Kentucky, state of order forbidding them to enter Missouri 9, 15, 23, 34, 86, 87, 88, 130, 139, 142, 149, 153, 160, 167, 193
Keytesville, Chariton County, Missouri 49, 135
Kingston, Caldwell County, Missouri 204
Kingsville, Johnson County, Missouri 9
Kirk, Capt. Joe (Southern) 87, 155–56
Kirksville, Adair County, Missouri 136–37
Kitchens, Col. Solomon (Southern) 72
Knight, Capt. Harry (Southern) 189
Knox County, Missouri 19, 63, 130–31, 135, 136, 141, 188, 193, 197
Krekel, Col. Arnold (Northern) 66, 192, 197

LaBarge, Capt. Joseph (civilian) 197
Laclede, Linn County, Missouri 140
Laclede County, Missouri 34, 76, 183
Lacy, Lt. Alexander H. (Northern) 125
Lafayette County, Missouri 7–9, 10, 13, 51, 57, 91–3, 94, 95, 100, 101, 102, 112, 113, 114, 144, 145, 146, 151, 152, 154, 157, 158, 159, 160, 161, 183, 199, 200, 201, 205, 206, 207, 208, 209
LaGrange, Lewis County 197
Lair, Capt. Wesley (Northern) 135
Lamar, Barton County, Missouri 179, 183
LaMine Bridge, Cooper County, Missouri 154
Lancaster, Schuyler County, Missouri 21, 63, 187
Lane, United States Senator James (Northern) 41
Langford, Capt. S. M. (Northern) 204
Langston or Langdon, Capt. George W. (Southern) 197
Lawrence, Kansas raid 47, 85
Lawrence County, Missouri 36, 37, 77, 80, 81, 82, 176, 202
Lawther, Col. Robert (Southern) 110, 111, 125–26
Lazear, Maj. Bazel F. (Northern) 122, 169
Leavenworth Bulletin (newspaper) Leavenworth, Kansas 209
Leavenworth, Kansas 209
Lebanon, Laclede County, Missouri 34
Leeper, Capt. William T. (Northern) 30–1, 57, 121
Leesville, Henry County, Missouri 37, 83
Lewis, Lt. Reese J. (Northern) 37–8
Lewis, Col. Warner F. (Southern) 10, 179, 215
Lewis County, Missouri 129, 130, 131, 139, 142, 186, 189, 193, 194, 197
Lexington, Lafayette County, Missouri 9, 13, 14, 89, 93, 100, 101, 145, 151, 159, 201, 202, 203, 207, 208
Lexington, Missouri siege of September 1861 13, 170, 201
Liberty, Clay County, Missouri 44, 86, 96, 97, 156, 221; seizure of United States arsenal at Liberty in 1861 96
Lick Creek, Ralls County, Missouri 17
Licking, Texas County, Missouri 73, 74
Lincoln, Pres. Abraham (Northern) 88, 171–72
Lincoln County, Missouri 17, 64, 65, 189
Linn County, Missouri 140, 154
Linn Creek, Camden County, Missouri 34
Lippert, Maj. Lothar (Northern) 122, 123, 167–68
Lipscomb, Col. H. L. (Northern) 130, 188
Little Blue (vessel) 148, 149
Little Blue River, Jackson County, Missouri 96, 97, 100, 144, 152, 162
"Little Dixie" 15, 129
Little Drywood Creek, Vernon County, Missouri 37–8
Little Osage River, Missouri 184
Little Piney Creek, Texas County, Missouri 117, 124
Little River, Missouri 72, 73, 166
Little Santa Fe, Jackson County, Missouri 96, 148, 206
Littleby, Audrain County, Missouri 68
Livingston, Capt. Thomas R. (Southern) 37, 45, 79, 107, 112, 115, 176, 179–80, 182, 183, 212
Livingston County, Missouri 86, 138, 148, 150, 153–54, 155–56, 157, 204
Lloyd, Capt. Louis (Southern) 99
Loan, Brig. Gen. Benjamin F. (Northern) 138, 207, 208–9
Lofton, Capt. Thomas (Southern) 110
Lone Elm, Cooper County, Missouri 203
Lone Jack, Jackson County, Missouri 101, 114, 149, 159–61

Index

Lone Jack battle, August 1862 159–61, 202, 228
Long, Capt. John (Southern) 176
Long, Capt. William A. (Northern) 100
Longacre family (civilian) 162
Louisiana, state of 64
Louisville, Kentucky 143
Love, Captain (Southern) 187
Loving (Southern) 64
Lowe, Jordan (civilian) 148
Lowe, Lt. Sandy (Northern) 147
"Lowe place," Jackson County, Missouri 98–9
Lynch's Slave Market *see* Myrtle Street Prison, St. Louis, Missouri
Lyon, Maj. Gen. Nathaniel (Northern) 41, 61

MacDonald, Washington "Wash" (Southern) 188, 196
Macon City, Macon County, Missouri 189
Macon County, Missouri 137, 187, 189
Madison County, Missouri 121, 164, 168, 170
Magi (vessel) 17
Magoffin, Maj. Beriah (Southern) 127
Magoffin, Col. Ebenezer (Southern) 10, 127
Mail, secret Southern 71, 124, 165, 173, 191, 192, 202, 203
Main, Dr. George W. (civilian) 151
Major, Maj. Elliott D. (Southern) 191, 194
Mammoth Spring, Oregon County, Missouri 73
Manasseth Gap, Jackson County, Missouri 13; *see also* Independence-Harrisonville Road
Marais des Cygnes River, Missouri 85, 184
Marchbanks, Capt. William "Bill" (Southern) 32, 56, 82, 184, 210
Maries County, Missouri 70, 73, 117, 124, 125
Marion, Gen. Francis "Swamp Fox" (American Revolution) 41, 60
Marion County, Missouri 17, 64–5, 68, 130, 139, 187–8, 189, 190, 194, 195, 197
Marmaduke, Brig. Gen. John Sappington (Southern) 183

Marshall, Maj. George C. (Northern) 10
Marshall, Saline County, Missouri 87, 203
Marshfield, Webster County, Missouri 34, 178, 180
Marthasville, Warren County, Missouri 65
Martin, Brice (Northern) 36
Martin, David (Southern) 156
Maryland, state of 11
Maupin, State Sen. William D. (civilian) 209
Maus, Capt. Charles B. (Northern) 181
Mayfield, Brice and Crawford "Crack" (Southern) 32, 37, 79, 184–85
McCarthy's Branch, Vernon County, Missouri 79
McClanihan, Capt. Perry D. (Northern) 63
McClurg, Lt. Col. Joseph W. (Northern) 77
McConnell, Captain (Southern) 141
McCullough (Southern) 79
McCullough, Col. Frisby H. (Southern) 136, *137*
McDaniel, Giles (Southern) 27
McDonald County, Missouri 36, 81, 107–8, 114, 178, 184
McDowell (vessel) 140
McDowell's Medical College *see* Gratiot Street Prison
McFadden, Capt. James W. (Northern) 65
McFadden, John (civilian) 206
McGhee College, Macon County, Missouri 189
McGuire, Capt. Julius (Southern) 135, 139, 181, 203
McKee, Maj. David (Northern) 67, 146
McNeil, Col. John (Northern) 136, 137, 188, 194, *195*
McNeill, Capt. John Hanson (Southern) 126
McPheeters, the Rev. Samuel B. (civilian) 171–72
Medicine Creek, Livingston County, Missouri 86
Medoc, Jasper County, Missouri 176
Memphis, Scotland County, Missouri 131–32
Memphis, Tennessee 166
Merrick, Capt. John L. (Southern) 152–4
Merrill, Brig. Gen. Lewis (Northern) 139, 141, 186, *187*, 189, 192, 193, 194, 196

Merriman, Capt. Clark S. (Northern) 9
Messick, Maj. John L. (Northern) 9
Methodist Episcopal (South) Church 65, 125, 202
Mexican War (1846–1848) veterans 72, 122, 160, 173
Mexico, Audrain County, Missouri 17, 66, 68, 187, 194
Miami, Saline County, Missouri 87, 143, 151
Miami Creek, Bates County, Missouri 85
Middle Fabius River, Missouri 132
Milford, Johnson County, Missouri, battle of (December 1861) 127
Miller County, Missouri 34, 70, 76, 124, 125
Millport, Knox County, Missouri 141
Millville, St. Charles County, Missouri 64
Mingo Swamp, Stoddard County, Missouri 30–1
Mirabile, Caldwell County, Missouri 205
Mirick, Lt. John S. (Northern) 155
Mirror (newspaper) Olathe, Kansas 199
Mississippi, state of 165
Mississippi County, Missouri 23, 123
Mississippi River, Missouri 23, 65, 166, 167
Missouri as a "backwash" of the war 4, 42, 51, 55, 103
Missouri Central Railroad 29
Missouri River, Missouri 10, *19*, 21, 52, 65–6, 70, 86, 87, 88, 89, 96, 102, 117, 133, 136, 139, 140, 141, 146, 147, 148, 150, 151, 152, 153, 154, 155, 156, 157, 162, 165, 168, 186, 190, 191, 192, 194, 197, 198, 202, 203, 204, 208
Missouri troops: 1st Battalion Cavalry Missouri State Militia 64, 66, 186, 192, 197; 1st Cavalry Regiment Missouri State Militia 87, 135, 137, 142, 148, 150, 153, 155, 169–70, 202, 203, 207, 209, 210; 1st Infantry Regiment Missouri State Militia 128; 1st Missouri Cavalry Regiment 10, 34, 81, 96, 97, 98–9, 100, 113, 143, 149, 150; 1st Missouri Light Artillery Regiment 37, 52, 90, 111; 1st

Regiment United State Reserve Corps 121; 2nd Battalion Cavalry Missouri State Militia 97, 145, 151, 152, 157–58, 162, 177, 180–81, 190, 192, 228; 2nd Cavalry Regiment Missouri State Militia 130, 189, 194; 2nd Missouri Cavalry Regiment (Merrill's Horse) 10, 17, 21, 51, 63, 65, 132, 138, 140, 141, 177, 187, 192; 2nd Missouri Light Artillery Regiment 122; 3rd Cavalry Regiment Missouri State Militia 65, 72, 121, 141, 156, 157, 176, 188, 193; 3rd Missouri Cavalry Regiment 16, 17, 63, 117, 119, 124, 125; 4th Cavalry Regiment Missouri State Militia 113, 141, 183, 192; 4th Missouri Cavalry Regiment 76, 84, 124; 5th Cavalry Regiment Missouri State Militia 10, 153, 155, 164, 169, 200, 205, 208, 209; 6th Cavalry Regiment Missouri State Militia 86–7, 96, 154, 157, 176, 177, 197, 208, 210; 6th Missouri Cavalry Regiment 29, 36, 73, 80, 112, 114, 119; 6th Missouri Infantry Regiment 88; 7th Cavalry Regiment Missouri State Militia 10, 67, 87, 88, 89, 90, 91, 110, 114, 136, 138, 147, 148, 151, 154, 160, 183; 7th Missouri Cavalry Regiment 100, 102, 143, 144, 145, 147, 148, 149, 150, 151, 152, 154, 157–58, 178; 7th Missouri Infantry Regiment 13, 14, 30–1, 100; 8th Cavalry Regiment Missouri State Militia 71, 77, 110, 175, 179–80, 184, 185; 9th Cavalry Regiment Missouri State Militia 47, 66, 68, 89, 134, 135, 187, 188, 191, 192, 193, 198, 202; 10th Cavalry Regiment Missouri State Militia 191, 192, 197; 10th Missouri Cavalry Regiment 77; 10th Missouri Infantry Regiment 16; 11th Cavalry Regiment Missouri State Militia 63, 67, 129, 130, 132, 135, 140, 142, 186; 12th Cavalry Regiment Missouri State Militia 25, 30–1, 121, 122, 167, 168, 169; 13th Cavalry Regiment Missouri State Militia 117, 118, 125, 126, 138, 168, 169, 181, 190; 14th Cavalry Regiment Missouri State Militia 77, 82, 107, 109, 110–11, 125, 176, 183, 184; 22nd Missouri Infantry Regiment 21; 24th Missouri Infantry Regiment 73, 75, 122, 124, 166, 168, 169–70, 173; 25th Enrolled Missouri Militia Regiment 210; 25th Missouri Infantry Regiment 169–70; 27th Missouri Mounted Infantry Regiment 10, 89; 29th Enrolled Missouri Militia Regiment 193, 194; 33rd Enrolled Missouri Militia Regiment 204, 205; 38th Enrolled Missouri Militia Regiment 189, 196; 40th Enrolled Missouri Militia Regiment 201; 43rd Enrolled Missouri Militia Regiment 202; 46th Enrolled Missouri Militia Regiment 187; 50th Enrolled Missouri Militia Regiment 193, 194; 52nd Enrolled Missouri Militia Regiment 203; 53rd Enrolled Missouri Militia Regiment 189; 60th Enrolled Missouri Militia Regiment 177; 69th Enrolled Missouri Militia Regiment 197; 70th Enrolled Missouri Militia Regiment 193, 196; 71st Enrolled Missouri Militia Regiment 200, 203, 206; Boonville Battalion Cavalry Missouri State Militia (Eppstein's) 87, 88, 98, 99–100, 101 see also 13th Cavalry Regiment Missouri State Militia; Camden County Enrolled Missouri Militia unit 181; Carroll County Enrolled Missouri Militia unit 204; Cass County Home Guard unit 7; Cedar County Enrolled Missouri Militia unit 183; Enrolled Missouri Militia program (EMM) 41, 103–5, 112, 125, 135, 136, 141, 142, 153, 154, 155, 156, 163, 164, 165, 166, 175, 176, 179, 183, 187, 188, 190, 192, 193, 200, 202, 204, 208, 210; Eppstein's Boonville Battalion Cavalry Missouri State Militia see Boonville Battalion Cavalry Missouri State Militia; Grundy County Enrolled Missouri Militia unit 204; Hawkins' Independent Company 69; home guards program 97, 103–4; McClurg's Battalion Cavalry Missouri State Militia 71, 77–9, 84, 85 see also 8th Cavalry Regiment Missouri State Militia; Missouri State Guard (MSG) 10, 21, 37, 41, 43, 64, 89, 93, 95, 110, 114, 141, 146, 153, 166; Missouri State Militia program (MSM) 60, 61, 72, 99, 103, 104, 163, 164; Phelps' Regiment Missouri Infantry 77

Missouri University, Columbia, Boone County, Missouri 19

Monegaw Springs, St. Clair County, Missouri 85

Moniteau County, Missouri 10, 83, 87, 88, 89, 146, 202

Moniteau Creek, Cooper and Moniteau Counties, Missouri 202

Monroe County, Missouri 16, 17, 67, 68, 126, 133–34, 135, 139, 140, 189, 190, 191, 193, 194, 196, 203

Montevallo, Vernon County, Missouri 77–9, 111, 112

Montgomery, Maj. Samuel (Northern) 112

Montgomery County, Missouri 134, 139, 140, 142, 165

Monticello, Johnson County, Kansas 209

Monticello, Lewis County, Missouri 131, 142, 186, 194

Montreal, Texas County, Missouri 77

Mooney, Joe Heall (Southern) 118

Moore, Col. David (Northern) 17

Moore's Mill, Callaway County, Missouri 134, 139

Morgan County, Missouri 49, 70, 83–4, 114, 154, 203

Morris County, Kansas 161

Morristown, Cass County, Missouri 7

Moselle, Franklin County, Missouri 29

Moss, Col. Charles E. (Northern) 77–9, 84

Mount Vernon, Lawrence County, Missouri 36, 37, 82, 176

Mt. Zion Church, Boone County, Missouri 15, 189, 190

Mountain Grove Seminary, Texas County, Missouri 77

Mountain Store, Texas County, Missouri 119
Murphy, Capt. George (Northern) 154
Murray, Lt. Col. John F. (Southern) 66
Murrell, Lt. Col. R. K. (Southern) 127
Myrtle Street Prison, St. Louis, Missouri 27, 126

Napoleon, Lafayette County, Missouri 207
Napoleon's severity against partisans 15, 46
Nash, Lt. George W. (Northern) 98, 100, 143
Nashville, Barton County, Missouri 179
"Navy" revolvers, caliber .36 54
Neal, Col. Henry (Northern) 203
Neosho, Newton County, Missouri 81, 82, 107, 108, 112, 114, 175, 183, 184, 185
Nettleton, Lt. A. Bayard (Northern) 14
Nevada territory 190
Nevada, Vernon County, Missouri 34
Nevins, William (Southern) 190–91
New Bloomfield, Callaway County, Missouri 19, 135–36
New Franklin, Howard County, Missouri 192
New Madrid, New Madrid County, Missouri 31, 51, 72, 116, 122, 166, 172
New York, state of 45
Newark, Knox County, Missouri 130–31, 135, 188
Newby, 1st Lt. William M. (Northern) 86–7, 208
Newspapers 3, 19, 23, 29, 41, 65, 81, 88, 93, 95, 97, 101, 105, 120, 122, 130, 143, 145, 151, 152, 153, 162, 165, 192, 199, 205, 209
Newton County, Missouri 36, 37, 45, 80, 81, 82, 107, 108, 109, 111, 112, 113, 114, 175–77, 183, 184, 212
Newtonia, battle of (30 September 1862) Newton County, Missouri 176–77
Newtonia, Newton County, Missouri 111, 113, 176–77, 182, 184, 185
Niangua River, Missouri 34, 76, 110, 180, 183

Nicaragua, William Walker expedition in 1855 126
Nichols, John (Southern) 202
"No quarter" see Prisoners
North Carolina, state of 15, 110
North Missouri Railroad 16; see also Railroads
Novelty, Knox County, Missouri 19
Nugent, Col. Andrew G. (Northern) 7, 228
Nugent, W. K. (civilian) 193

Oaths 19, 61, 64, 79, 84, 111, 131, 137, 140, 155, 157, 187, 189, 191, 195
O'Halloran, Maj. Thomas (Northern) 181
Ohio, state of 11, 44, 65, 121, 142, 166, 197, 212
Ohio troops 16–7; 2nd Ohio Cavalry Regiment 14, 79, 81, 107, 108, 109
Olathe, Kansas 199–200
Oliver, Capt. William S. (Northern) 13, 14
Orders: General Order Number 2, 13 March 1862, by Halleck mandating death to Guerrillas captured under arms 46, 60, 95; General Order Number 18, 29 May 1862, by Schofield mandating recruiters and guerrillas executed on the spot 60–2; General Order Number 19, July 1862, by Schofield ordering all men into Enrolled Missouri Militia 41, 103, 129, 134–35, 142, 143, 152, 153, 154 157, 158, 205; Halleck's 22 December 1861, order to "shoot on sight" to protect railroads 15, 63; Halleck's 24 January 1862 order to control all river traffic 19, 41; Halleck's order forbidding Missouri troops from entering Kansas 10; Hindman's 17 June 1862 partisan ranger order 43, 136, 158; Hunter's order forbidding Kansas troops from entering Missouri 9; Jefferson Davis' 21 April 1862 partisan ranger order 60, 136, 158; local commander's order for 7th Missouri Cavalry Regiment to execute guerrillas on the spot 145; local commander's order for Enrolled Missouri Militia to wear white hatbands 141; local commander's short-lived order to hang Southerners in revenge for murders of Northerners 30; Missouri Provost Marshal General forbids the Rev. Caples from preaching 65; Quantrill's August 1862 three general orders 158
Oregon County, Missouri 73, 74, 124, 168
Osage County, Missouri 117, 125, 178, 186, 197
Osage River, Missouri 34, 82, 84, 109, 113, 114, 157, 177
Osceola, St. Clair County, Missouri 183
Ousley, Capt. William (Southern) 135
Owen, Maj. John L. (Southern) 129
Ozark, Christian County, Missouri 110–11, 181, 183
Ozark County, Missouri 180
Ozark region, Missouri 29, 34, 73, 76, 116, 117, 173, 183

Pacific Railroad 10, 88, 201, 202; see also Railroads
Page (Northern) 188, 189
Palmyra, Marion County, Missouri 17, 64, 130, 187–88, 194–96
"Palmyra Massacre" 194–*196*
Panther Creek, Macon County, Missouri 137
Paris, Monroe County, Missouri 16, 68, 135, 140, 193, 194
Parke, Capt. Joseph (Northern) 183
Parker, Col. Benjamin F. (Southern) 14, 44, 56, 90–1, 93, 94–5, 95–6, 97, 147, 148, 221; his band after his capture 97, 100, 208; his capture 91, 97
Parkersville, Bates County, Missouri 210
Parkinson, William (Southern) 179
Parkville, Platte County, Missouri 155
Parole see Prisoners
Partisan rangers 42, 43, 60, 136, 158
Patterson, Captain (Southern) 121
Patterson, Wayne County, Missouri 69, 122, 168, 169
Patton, Jefferson (Southern) 155

Pea Ridge, Arkansas battle (March 1862) 76, 127, 169, 171
Peabody, Capt. Albert P. (Northern) 98
Peacher, Lt. Col. Quinton (Southern) 198, 203
Pemiscot County, Missouri 122, 166
Pendleton, Warren County, Missouri 65
Penick, Col. William R. (Northern) 155, 157
Peninsula Campaign, Virginia (March through July 1862) 173
Pennsylvania, state of 158
Penny, Capt. Sylvester (Southern) 134
Perche Hills, Boone County, Missouri 15, 133, 188, 192
Percussion caps *see* Caps, percussion
Perdue, Henry (civilian) 206
Perkins (civilian) 190
Perkins, Col. Caleb (Southern) 15, 197, 203
Pettis County, Missouri 10, 37, 82, 87, 88, 91, 143, 154, 157, 202
Petty, Capt. W. F. (Southern) 126
Phelan, Col. William G. (Southern) 72
Phelps County, Missouri 29, 73, 74, 118, 124, 173
Phillips, Col. William A. (Northern) 175, 176
Pike County, Missouri 17, 52, 122, 141, 169
Pike Creek, Carter County, Missouri 169
Pilot Grove, Cooper County, Missouri 151
Pilot Grove, Jasper County, Missouri 107
Pilot Knob, Iron County, Missouri 31
Pineville, McDonald County, Missouri 37, 107–8, 182
Pinhard, Lt. Julius (Northern) 202
Pink Hill, Jackson County, Missouri 100, 145
Piper, Lt. A. S. (Northern) 140
Pisgah, Cooper County, Missouri 88
Pistols 54, 82–3, 98, 101, 135, 150, 184, 190, 204, 205; *see also* Revolvers
Pitman's Ferry, Ripley County, Missouri 69, 170

Platte City, Platte County, Missouri 86, 155
Platte County, Missouri 10, 86, 149, 155, 157, 159, 162, 204
Platte River, Missouri 155
Platte Valley (vessel) 166
Plattsburg, Clinton County, Missouri 86, 87
Pleasant Hill, Cass County, Missouri 97, 145, 150, 151, 154, 162, 200
Poindexter, Col. John A. (Southern) 16–7, 68, 129, 135, 136, 137–38, 139, 142, 153, 154, 187, 189, 203, 212
Polk County, Missouri 77, 84, 109, 113
Pollard, Capt. Braxton (Southern) 189
Pomeroy, Maj. James (Northern) 96
Pomme de Terre River, Missouri 34, 84
Ponder's Mill, Ripley County, Missouri 122, 168
Pope, Brig. Gen. John (Northern) 39
Porter, Capt. James W. "Jim" (Southern) 130–*131*, 187–88
Porter, Col. Joseph Chrisman (Southern) 43, 49, 129, 130, 131–32, 133–35, 136–37, 138, 139–40, 141, 142, 168–69, 186, 187–88, 189, 195, 197, 212
Portland, Callaway County, Missouri 19, 140, 141, 197; posse of citizens 86, 110
Post Oak Creek, Johnson County, Missouri 90
Pottenger (Southern) 123
Powell, Mildred Elizabeth (Southern) 190
Prairie Chapel, Callaway County, Missouri 186
Prairie fighting 81
Pratt, Ezekial (civilian) 131
Presbyterian Church 172
Preston, Jasper County, Missouri 179
Price, Capt. Clay (Southern) 190
Price, Brig. Gen. Edwin "Stump" (Southern) 37
Price, Maj. Gen. Sterling (Southern) 7, 32, 34, 37, 41, 43, 44, 76
Primrose, Capt. George W. (Southern) 197
Prison breaks 19, 25–7, 126–28
Prisoners: escaping 19, 25–7, 126–*27*; exchange of 46, 97, 196, 215; execution of 60–2,
96, 97, 98, 106, 112, 136, 137, 140, 145, 187, 189, 196, 199, 201; guerrillas not taken prisoner 46, 60, 95, 97, 106, 112; mistreatment of 9, 30, 98; murder of 125–26, 132, 158, 161, 176, 192, 206–7; paroling of 10, 13, 17, 37, 88, 96, 130, 135, 158, 173, 188, 196, 199; release of 107, 132; "revolving door" aspects of captures and escapes/releases 71
Providence, Boone County, Missouri 187
Provost marshal system in Missouri 41, 70, 128, 156, 173, 195
Pugh, Maj. Jacob (Northern) 193
Pulaski County, Missouri 29, 73, 74, 117, 119, 124, 125, 168, 169, 181
Pulliam, George (Southern) 126
Purcell, Capt. Young A. (Southern) 68, 134, 139, 186, 197, 198
Purington, Maj. George A. (Northern) 81
Purse, Capt. William H. (Northern) 142
Putnam County, Missouri 142

Quantrill, Capt. William Clarke (Southern) *11*, 39, 44, 48, 86, 94, 99, 100, 101, 117, 144, 145, 146, 148, 149, 151, 152, 162, 200–1, 205, 206, 207–8, 209, 210, 212, 221; Aubrey, Kansas raid 91–3; background 11, 44, 91, 94, 95; "Balls Ford fight" 98; beginning guerrilla campaign 11–3; Big Creek fight 149–50; "Clark House fight" 97–8; commitment to "no quarter" 95; general orders 158; his band in Lone Jack battle 160–61; his band sworn into Confederate service 158; his band's descent to Arkansas in autumn 179–80; Independence battle (August 1862) 157–58; "Lowe House fight" 98–9; Manasseth Gap ambushes 13, 48, 100; Olathe, Kansas raid 199–200; sanctuaries and popular support 56–7; Shawneetown, Kansas raid 206–7; tactics 14, 50, 54, 97, 98, 99, 100; "Tate House

fight" 96–7; trip to obtain pistol percussion caps 101; two Independence raids (February 1862) 14; uniforms 55; weapons 54, 96, 98; Wellington fight 200
Quincy, Hickory County, Missouri 84

Rafter, Capt. Bill (Southern) 83
Railroads 10, 15, 16, 17, 29, 47, 63, 104, 106, 155, 175, 201, 210; *see also* Missouri Central Railroad, North Missouri Railroad, and Pacific Railroad
Raker (civilian) 201
Raker, Capt. D. M. (Southern) 201–2
Ralls County, Missouri 17, 140, 188, 189, 196
Ramey, Daniel (civilian) 210
Ramey, Capt. William K. (Northern) 210
Randlett, 2nd Lt. Reuben A. (Northern) 91, 95
Randolph County, Missouri 16, 68, 129, 135, 136, 137–38, 142, 189, 197
Ransom, Maj. Wyllis C. (Northern) 148
Rawalt, Maj. Jonas (Northern) 72
Ray County, Missouri 112, 153
Reaves, Lt. Col. A. L. (Northern) 203
Reed, Bill, (Southern) 93, 151, 161, 205, 207; *see also* Kansas exile guerrilla band
Reedsville, Callaway County, Missouri 141
Reeves, Col. Tim (Southern) 43, 120–21, 168
Reichert, Lt. Francis (Northern) 168
Reid, John W. (civilian) 152
Reid, Lt. Matt (Northern) 200
Renegades 1, 11
Revolution, American 41, 42–3, 60
Revolvers 52–3, *54*, 55, 96, 100, 113, 190; *see also* Pistols
Reynolds County, Missouri 25, 73, 74, 117, 121, 124, 168, 169
Richmond, Ray County, Missouri 153
Riggs, Ewell (civilian) 37
Ripley County, Missouri 69, 119, 122, 168, 169
Ritchie, Col. John (Northern) 176
River traffic 13, 17, 19, 41, 43, 47, 64, 96, 106, 166, 188, 190, 198
Roanoke, Howard County, Missouri 16, 187
Roan's Tanyard, battle of *see* Silver Creek
Roberts, Col. Boaz (Southern) 204
Roberts, Fountain (civilian) 233
Robinson, Capt. J. D. W. (Southern) 191
Rocheport, Boone County, Missouri 133, 186, 188, 192, 197, 198
Rock Prairie, Dade County, Missouri 79
Rockbridge, Douglas County, Missouri 180
Rocky Bluff, Platte County, Missouri 155
Rocky Ford, Livingston County, Missouri 204
Rogers, Maj. John B. (Northern) 186, 189
Rolla, Phelps County, Missouri 23, 29, 45, 51, 73, 74, 75, 116, 124, 125, 168, 173, 175, 212
Rolla-Springfield wagon road 27–9, 73–4, 118, 125
Rose Hill, Johnson County, Missouri 7, 210
Rowena (vessel) 94–5, 97, 148
Rucker, James (Southern) 133
Rules of war 189, 195
Rushville, Buchanan County, Missouri 155
Russell, Maj. Frank (Southern) 107
Rutledge, McDonald County, Missouri 36
Ryder, Jim (Southern) 204

Sabers 52, 83
Sac River, Missouri 77
St. Aubert, Osage County, Missouri 19, 133, 186
St. Charles County, Missouri 64, 127
St. Clair County, Missouri 34, 82, 85, 109, 110, 113, 114, 183
Ste Genevieve County, Missouri 122
Ste. Genevieve Plaindealer (newspaper) Ste Genevieve County 122
St. Francis Hills, Missouri 170
St. Francis River, Missouri 72
St. Francois County, Missouri 25, 71, 119–20, 121, 164
St. Francois Mountains, Missouri 70, 119
St. Joseph, Buchanan County, Missouri 23, 89, 126, 148, 155
St. Louis, Missouri 10, 19, 25–9, 43, 46, 61, 66, 68, 71, 85, 93, 95, 119, 120, 126–28, 133, 140, 145, 153, 162, 165, 169, 170, 171, 172, 197, 212
St. Louis County, Missouri 128, 170
Salem, Arkansas 73
Salem, Dent County, Missouri 29, 117, 124, 125
Saline City, Saline County, Missouri 203
Saline County, Missouri 27, 52, 54, 87–8, 89, 102, 114, 143, 146, 150, 151, 153, 154, 198, 202, 208, 210, 233
Salomon, Brig. Gen. Frederick (Northern) 176
Salt River, Missouri 132, 190
Sand Hill, Scotland County, Missouri 63
Sandy Creek, Monroe County, Missouri 189
Santa Fe Trail 206
Sappington family (Southern) 128
Sarcoxie, Jasper County, Missouri 82
Sartain, Calvin (Southern) 126, 140
Savage revolvers *121*; *see also* Pistols and revolvers
Schell's Mill, McDonald County, Missouri 178
Schofield, Maj. Gen. John M. (Northern) 39, 52, *61*–2, 103, 128
Schuyler County, Missouri 17, 21, 63, 130, 187, 194
Scotland, nation of 151
Scotland County, Missouri 16, 17, 19, 63, 132, 141, 193
Scott (Southern) 7
Scott, Capt. Ferdinando (Southern) 44, 204
Scott, Col. John (Northern) 172
Scott, Col. Walter (Southern) 126
Scott County, Missouri 25, 166
Seaman, Capt. Henry C. (Northern) 178
Searcy (outlaw) 11
Sedalia, Pettis County, Missouri 10, 82, 88, 89, 143, 154, 157, 202, 208
Selby, Capt. Charles (Southern) 135, 139
Sexual assault *see* Women, violence and improprieties against

Shacklett, Maj. Benjamin W. (Southern) 19
Shanghai, Johnson County, Missouri 10
Shanklin, Lt. Col. John H. (Northern) 156
Shannon County, Missouri 116–17, 125, 165, 168
Sharps breech-loading firearms 37–38, 52; *see also* Carbines
Shaw (civilian) 201
Shawneetown, Kansas 206–7, 209
Shelby, Col. Joseph Orville (Southern) 13, 43, 51–2, 113, 114, 115, 160–61, 176–77
Shelby County, Missouri 16, 17, 67, 88, 132, 140, 146, 189, 193
Sherwood, Jasper County, Missouri 179
Shoal Creek, Livingston County, Missouri 148
Shoal Creek, Newton County, Missouri 184–85
Shotguns 52, 98, 205
Sibley, Jackson County, Missouri 148, 205
Sidney, Ralls County, Missouri 189
Sieges 96, 98, 130–31, 135, 178
Sigel, Col. Albert (Northern) 126, 169
Sikeston, Scott County, Missouri 72
Silver Creek, Randolph County, Missouri 16–7, 137, 138
Singleton, Capt. John T. (Southern) 192, 198
"Sink Hole Woods," west of Jefferson City, Missouri 88
Sinking Creek, Shannon County, Missouri 124
Sleighs 17
Smart, Judge Robert G. (civilian) 151
Smith, Henry (Southern) 124
Smith, Capt. Raphael "Ralph" (Southern) 131, 142, 186, 188
Snapp's Mill, Taney County, Missouri 110
Snedicor, Capt. James P. (Southern) 17
Snelling, Benjamin L. (Southern) 10, 146, 147
Sni-A-Bar Creek, Jackson and Lafayette Counties, Missouri 98, 200
Sni Hills or Sniabar Hills, Jackson and Lafayette Counties, Missouri 94
Snider, Capt. Henry (Southern) 189

Snider, Capt. Thomas A. (Southern) 195
Sodom's Mills, Dade County, Missouri 176
South Carolina, state of 41
Spencer, Columbus (civilian) 148
Spilman, Capt. Joseph A. (Southern) 70, 168, 173
Spring Creek, Dent County, Missouri 117
Spring Hill, Livingston County, Missouri 87, 148, 156
Spring River, Missouri 80, 175, 179
Springfield, Greene County, Missouri 27–9, 32, 34, 36, 51, 112, 212
Stacy, Tom (Southern) 16, 17, 67–8, 131–32
Stagecoaches 145, 206, 207
Staples Mill, Lewis County, Missouri 189
Stevenson, Col. John D. (Northern) 13
Stewartsville, DeKalb County, Missouri 210
Stockton, Macon County, Missouri 137
Stoddard County, Missouri 25, 30, 52, 72, 120, 122, 123, 166, 170
Stonesport, Boone County, Missouri 66, 89
Stony Point, Jackson County, Missouri 97
Strachan, Provost Marshal W. R. (Northern) 195; *see also* Provost marshal system in Missouri
Stringtown, Cole County, Missouri 34
Stuart, Lt. Col. James (Northern) 178
Sturgeon, Boone County, Missouri 65, 190
Sugar Creek, Henry County, Missouri 150
Sugar Creek Hills, McDonald County, Missouri 184
Sullivan County, Missouri 130
Sunshine (vessel) 13
Swain (jayhawker) 156
"Swamp Fox" *see* Thompson, Col. Meriwether Jeff
"Swamp Rats" of the "Bootheel" 23, 71, 72, 123, 142
Swink, Capt. George M. (Southern) 34
Swinney, Capt. Robert W. (Southern) 126, 127

Switzler's Mills, Chariton County, Missouri 138
Sword cane 85
Syracuse, Morgan County, Missouri 88, 110, 154, 203

Taberville, St. Clair County, Missouri 109, 110, 113, 114
Tactics, of guerrillas 14, 48–51, 54, 97, 98, 99, 100, 132, 150, 151
Tallaifarro, Capt. James T. (Northern) 75
Taney County, Missouri 110–11, 125, 181
Tate, David (civilian) 96–7, 162
Taylor, Judge (Southern) 123
Taylor, Capt. William Henry (Southern) 34, 37, 38, 79
Telegraph 106, 119, 187
Tennessee, state of 15, 32, 110, 165
Texas, state of 79; Confederate cavalry from 36–7; as a guerrilla winter refuge 58
Texas County, Missouri 29, 52, 70, 73, 74, 77, 116, 117, 118, 168, 173
Thomas, Captain (Southern) 183
Thomasville, Oregon County, Missouri 74, 75
Thompson, Col. Gideon W. (Southern) 157–58
Thompson, Capt. Joe (Southern) 135
Thompson, Matthew (Southern) 126
Thompson, Col. Meriwether Jeff "Swamp Fox" (Southern) 23, *25*, 43, 71, 72, 123, 142, 167, 169, 173
Thrailkill, Capt. John (Southern) 56
Thurman, Capt. William *see* Truman, Capt. William
Thurston, Capt. Henry "Long" (Southern) 84
Tipton, Moniteau County, Missouri 83, 89
Todd, George (Southern) 44, 48, 49, 101, 145, 150, *152*, 158, 209, 210
Todd, Capt. William H. (Southern) 178, 203
Tompkins, Lt. Ambrose R. (Southern) 66
Torrence, Maj. W. M. G. (Northern) 16–7
Totten, Brig. Gen. James (Northern) 61, 99
Tracy, Col. John Charles (Southern) 150–51

Trans-Mississippi Department (Confederate) 42, 43, 202
Tribunals *see* Countermeasures against guerrillas
Trow, Harrison (Southern) 39, 44, 50, 149, 209, 210
Troy, Lincoln County, Missouri 64
Truman, Capt. William (Southern) 85, 178–79
Tucker, James (Southern) 100
Turn Back Creek, Dade and Lawrence Counties, Missouri 81
Turnback, Dade County, Missouri 176
Turner, the Reverend (Southern) 176
Tuscumbia, Miller County, Missouri 70

Uniforms 4, 55–56; guerrillas wearing Union uniforms 56, 151–52, 181; lack of 112
Union, Franklin County, Missouri 29
Union Mills, Platte County, Missouri 155
Uniontown, Schuyler County, Missouri 194
United Daughters of the Confederacy 190
United States troops: 1st United States Infantry Regiment 162
Utica, Livingston County, Missouri 138

Van Buren, Carter County, Missouri 124, 173
Vasser Hill, Scotland County, Missouri 132, 133
Vera Cruz, Douglas County, Missouri 76, 180
Vernon County, Missouri 32–4, 37–8, 77–9, 109, 112, 114, 160, 179, 182, 183, 184, 210
Versailles, Morgan County, Missouri 49, 83–4
Vigilantes 11
Virginia, state of 7, 15, 66, 87, 126, 173

Wadesburg, Cass County, Missouri 149
Wakerlen, Capt. George (Northern) 208
Walker, Andy (Southern) 11
Walkersville, Shelby County, Missouri 67
Walnut Creek, Adair County, Missouri 137
War Eagle (vessel) 153, 154, 277

War of 1812 161
Warren, Col. Fitz-Henry (Northern) 46, 85, 114, *115*
Warren, Dr. (Southern) 10, 90
Warren County, Missouri 65
Warrensburg, Johnson County, Missouri 9, 10, 90, 91, 97, 145, 146, 147, 150, 151, 160, 162, 201
Warsaw, Benton County, Missouri 37, 84, 85, 89, 184
Washington County, Missouri 120, 121, 124, 164
Washington University, St. Louis, Missouri 61
Watie, Col. Stand (Southern) 80, 176
Watkins, Joseph (Southern) 17
Watson, Capt. James B. (Southern) 17, 21
Waverly, Lafayette County, Missouri 13, 102, 113, 154, 208
Wayman's Mill, Phelps County, Missouri 125
Wayne County, Missouri 25, 45, 57, 69, 121, 122, 123, 124, 164, 166, 168, 169
Waynesville, Pulaski County, Missouri 74, 75, 117, 124, 168, 181
Webb, John B. (civilian) 208–9
Webster County, Missouri 34, 76, 178
Wellington, Lafayette County, Missouri 200
West Ely, Marion County, Missouri 17
West Plains, Howell County, Missouri 29, 74, 75
West Point, Bates County, Missouri 7
West Point, United States Military Academy 46
West Prairie, New Madrid County, Missouri 122
Weston, Platte County, Missouri 204
Westport, Jackson County, Missouri 11, 93, 146, 148, 152
Whaley, Capt. John Calvin (Southern) 68
White, Capt. Benjamin F. (Southern) 189
White, Maj. Frank J. (Northern) 190–91, 192
White, Col. James (Southern) 122, 168
White Cloud (vessel) 140
White River, Missouri 80, 110–11, 180–81, 183

Wilber, Maj. John C. (Northern) 111
Williams, Col. John F. (Northern) 47, 198
Williams, Capt. John S. (Southern) 196
Williamsburg, Callaway County, Missouri 66
Williamstown, Lewis County, Missouri 131, 194
Wills or Wells, Major (Southern) 191
Wilson, Capt. James S. (Southern) 197
Wilson's Creek battle (10 August 1861) 9, 13, 32, 169
Windmuller, Capt. Henry (Northern) 192
Wirt, Col. Samuel M. (Northern) 194
Wisconsin troops: 1st Wisconsin Cavalry Regiment 72–3, 122, 123, 166; 2nd Wisconsin Cavalry Regiment 89, 107; 3rd Wisconsin Cavalry Regiment 111, 115, 162, 179, 184; 9th Wisconsin Infantry Regiment 81; 11th Wisconsin Infantry Regiment 173
Wiseman, Joseph (civilian) 129
Women, violence and improprieties against: by Northerners 13–4, 147, 195; by Southerners 90, 129–30, 147
Wood, Maj. J. C. (Southern) 127
Wood, Lt. Col. Samuel N. (Northern) 29, 73
Woodsmall, Capt. Henry (Southern) 155, 162
Woodson, Maj. Richard G. (Northern) 191, 192, 197
Woodson, Capt. Tom (Southern) 88
Woodward, Charles E. (Southern) 127–28
Woolfolk, Lt. Col. Alexander M. (Northern) 87, 135, 137, 202
Wright, Col. Clark (Northern) 80, 114
Wright County, Missouri 76, 77, 119, 181

Yeager, Dick (Southern) 152
Yellow Creek, Chariton County, Missouri 138
Yocum (Southern) 109
Younger, Coleman "Cole" (Southern) 207, *208*, 209, 210

www.ingramcontent.com/pod-product-compliance
Lightning Source LLC
Chambersburg PA
CBHW081158230426
43666CB00016B/2856